iOS App Development

PORTABLE GENIUS

Richard Wentk

iOS App Development Portable Genius

Published by
John Wiley & Sons, Inc.
10475 Crosspoint Blvd.
Indianapolis, IN 46256
www.wiley.com

Published simultaneously in Canada

ISBN: 978-1-118-32989-4

Manufactured in the United States of America

10 9 8 7 6 5 4 3 2 1

For general information on our other products and services or to obtain technical support, please contact our Customer Care Department within the U.S. at (877) 762-2974, outside the U.S. at (317) 572-3993 or fax (317) 572-4002.

John Wiley & Sons, Inc. also publishes its books in a variety of electronic formats and by print-on-demand. Some content that appears in standard print versions of this book may not be available in other formats. For more information about Wiley products, visit us at www.wiley.com.

Library of Congress Control Number is available from the Publisher.

About the Author

Richard Wentk covers Apple products and developments for *Macworld* and *MacFormat* magazines and also writes about technology, creativity, and business strategy for titles such as *Computer Arts* and *Computer Music*. As a trainer and a professional Apple developer, he has more than 15 years of experience making complicated technology simple for experts and beginners alike. He lives online but also has a home in Wiltshire, England. For details of apps and other book projects, visit www.zettaboom.com.

Credits

Acquisitions Editor
Aaron Black

Project Editor
Martin V. Minner

Technical Editor
Brad Miller

Copy Editor
Gwenette Gaddis

Editorial Director
Robyn Siesky

Business Manager
Amy Knies

Senior Marketing Manager
Sandy Smith

Vice President and Executive Group Publisher
Richard Swadley

Vice President and Executive Publisher
Barry Pruett

Project Coordinator
Katie Crocker

Graphics and Production Specialists
Joyce Haughey
Andrea Hornberger

Proofreading and Indexing
BIM Indexing & Proofreading Services
Potomac Indexing, LLC

For Annette.

"The best way to predict the future is to invent it"—Alan Kay

Acknowledgments

Although this book has my name on the cover, all books are a team effort. I'd like to thank acquisitions editor Aaron Black for getting the project started and project editor Martin V. Minner for support and good humor. Sincere thanks are also due to the rest of the team at Wiley for their hard work behind the scenes, especially copy editor Gwenette Gaddis and technical editor Brad Miller.

Personal gratitude to Annette, Hilary, Alexa, Michael, and the ET Tribe for keeping me informed, educated, entertained, and—not infrequently—fed.

iOS software development is also a team effort. The days of the solo developer working in isolation are long gone. There are too many indirect contributors to this book to list them all, but my sincere gratitude goes to all of them for sharing their time and skills so freely.

Finally, thanks as ever to Team HGA for making it all possible.

Contents

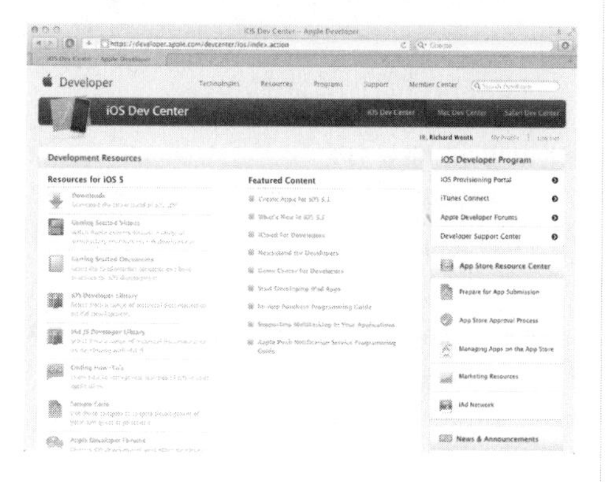

Developer
iOS Dev Center
Development Resources
Resources for iOS 5
Featured Content
iOS Developer Program
iOS Provisioning Portal
iTunes Connect
Apple Developer Forums
Developer Support Center
App Store Resource Center
News & Announcements

chapter 2

How Do I Get Started with Xcode? 24

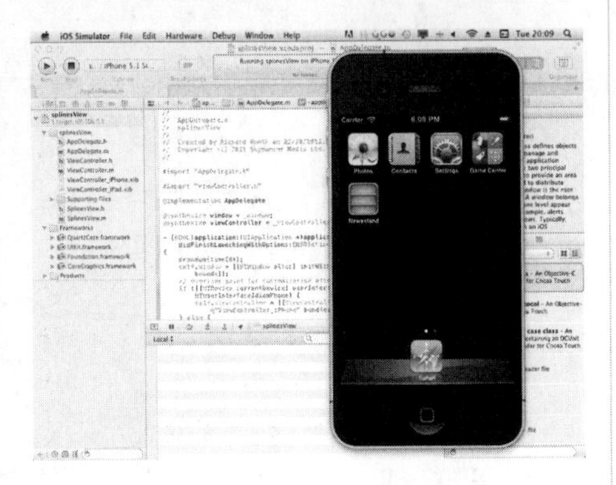

chapter 3

How Do I Build and Run an Application? 56

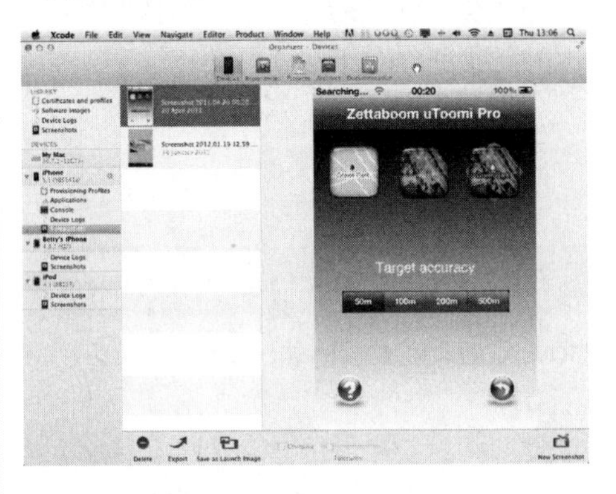

chapter 4

What Are Applications Made Of? 86

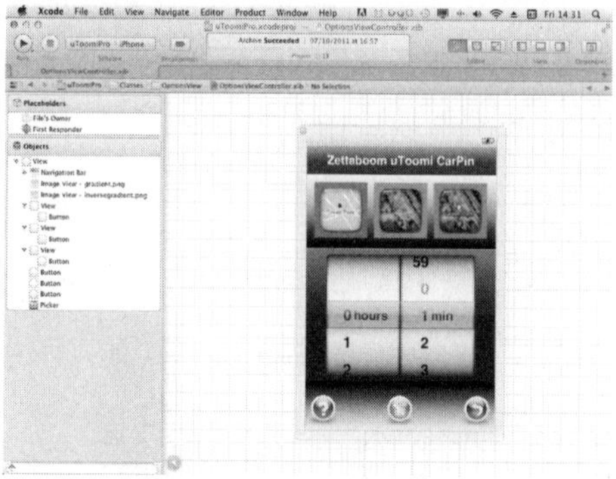

chapter 5

How Do I Create Code? 114

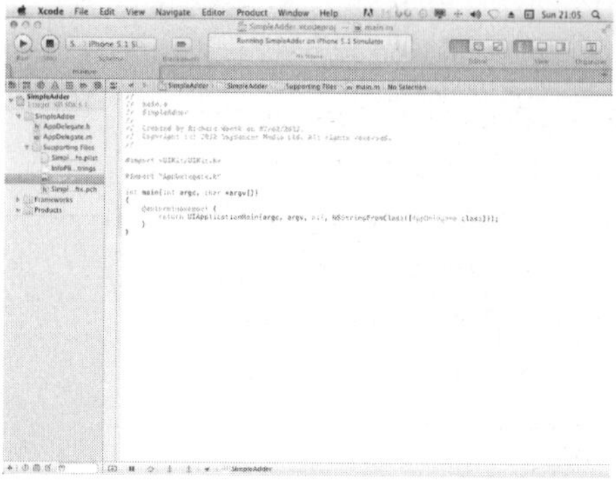

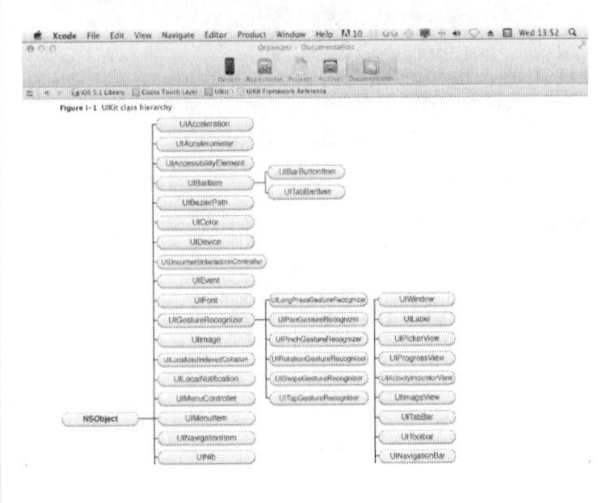

chapter 7

How Can I Use Objects to Manage Data and Schedule Events? 180

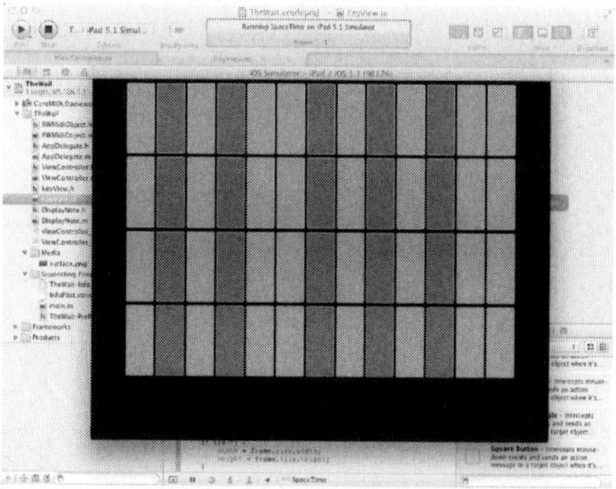

chapter 8

How Do I Handle Input from the User? 206

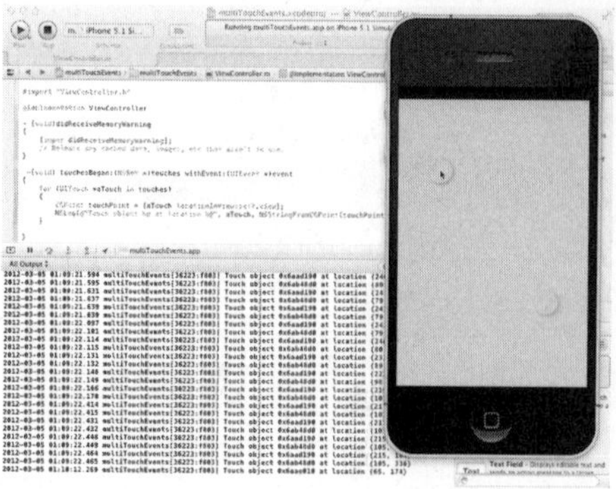

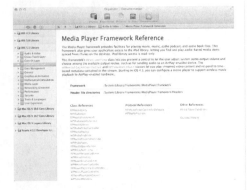

chapter 12

How Do I Test and Fix My App? 340

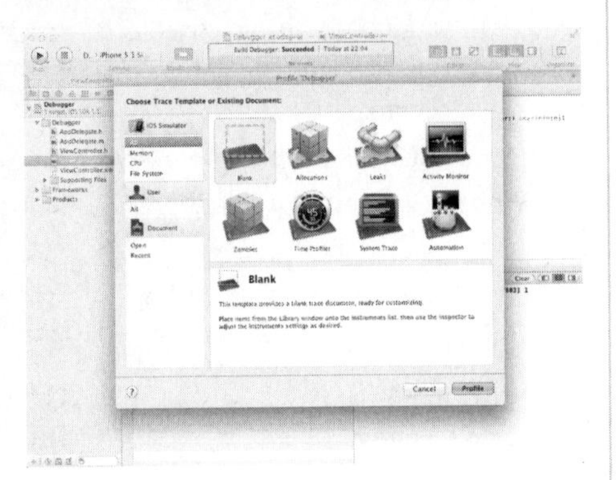

chapter 13

How Do I Distribute Apps for Sale and Testing? 362

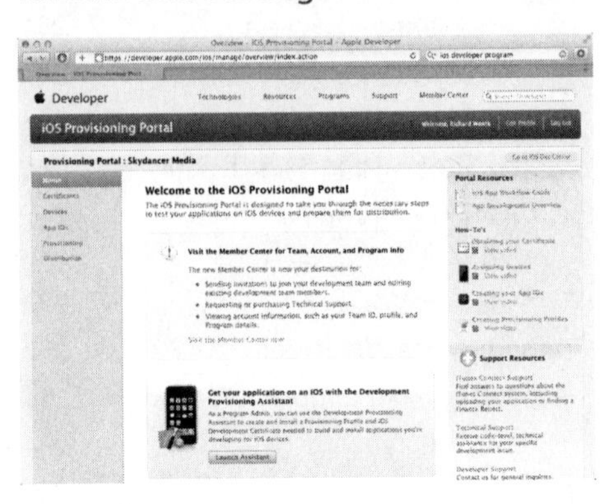

Introduction

Why develop your own apps? Because you can! Almost anyone with a Mac can get started making his own apps, as many people with little or no experience have already found out for themselves.

The benefits are obvious. Instead of relying on third-party apps in the App Store, you can create the apps you want using your own ideas and designs. For example, you can:

- **Create custom apps for friends and family.** For example, you may want to share information or send messages privately.
- **Create applications for your business.** If you travel, you can create an app that collects data onsite and sends it back to your main office.
- **Experiment with creative ideas for music, video, photography, and design.**
- **Explore and invent new games.**

The challenges are obvious too. As a beginner, getting started with app development is easy. But mastering the skills you need for more complex apps will take you longer.

This book gives you a good grounding in the basic features of iOS, but a detailed introduction to every feature would need an entire shelf of books. Fortunately, learning how to learn is a key developer skill. This book explains how to get the information you need from the two main sources of help—the official Apple documentation and the online forums and blogs, where you'll find a truly vast collection of worked examples and informal professional support.

After a couple of finished apps, you may even find that you can improve your chances in the job market. Professional developers are highly sought after and can be very well paid. Although some developers have years of programming experience, others are hired on the basis of a couple of successful submissions to the App Store.

Most of all, app development can be satisfying and enjoyable. After you've tried it, you'll be hooked—and you'll soon be able to use your new skills for fun, entertainment, and profit.

How Can I Start Developing for iOS?

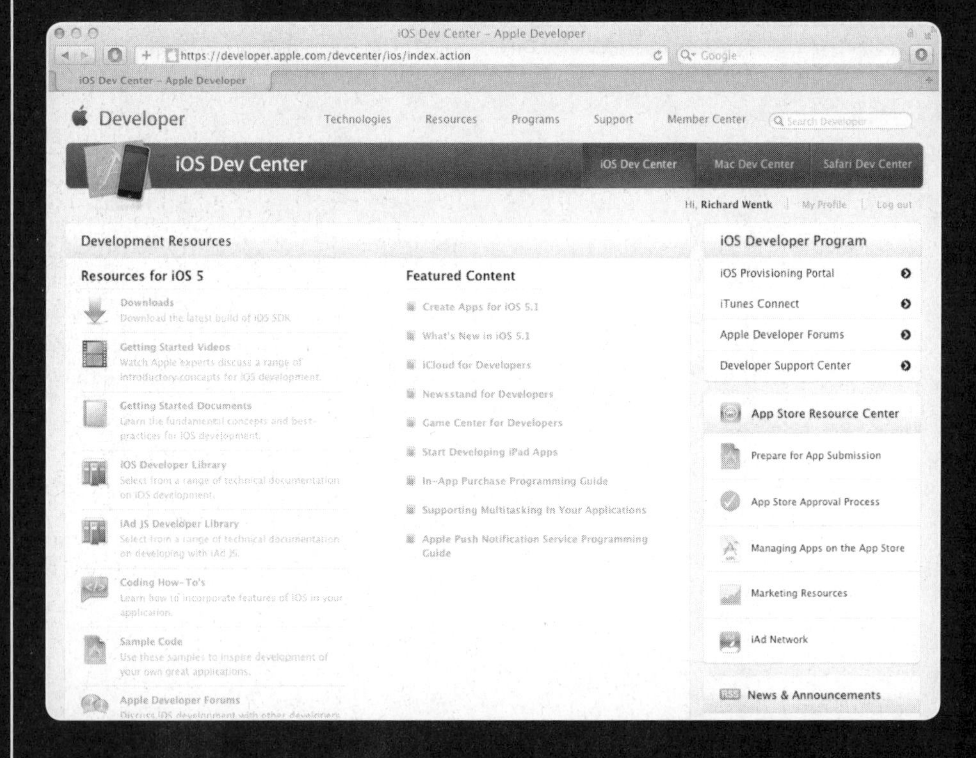

App development relies on a single unified development tool called Xcode. Xcode is free for the curious, but experienced and dedicated developers can get advanced information about updates to iOS by paying a small annual fee to enroll in Apple's iOS Developer Program. This chapter explains how to install Xcode, how to enroll as a developer, why you need lots of bandwidth for downloads, and why sometimes you'll have more than one version of Xcode installed at the same time.

Getting Started with App Development

iOS development doesn't have to be expensive. In fact, you need only two tools to develop iOS apps:

- **A recent Mac.** Although you can use any recent Mac, some models and specifications are more productive than others. You can find more details later in this chapter.
- **A copy of Xcode.** Xcode, shown in Figure 1.1, is Apple's app development toolkit. It has much in common with a standard Mac application, but it has some unusual extra features you'll learn about later in this book. Xcode is available free from the Mac App Store.

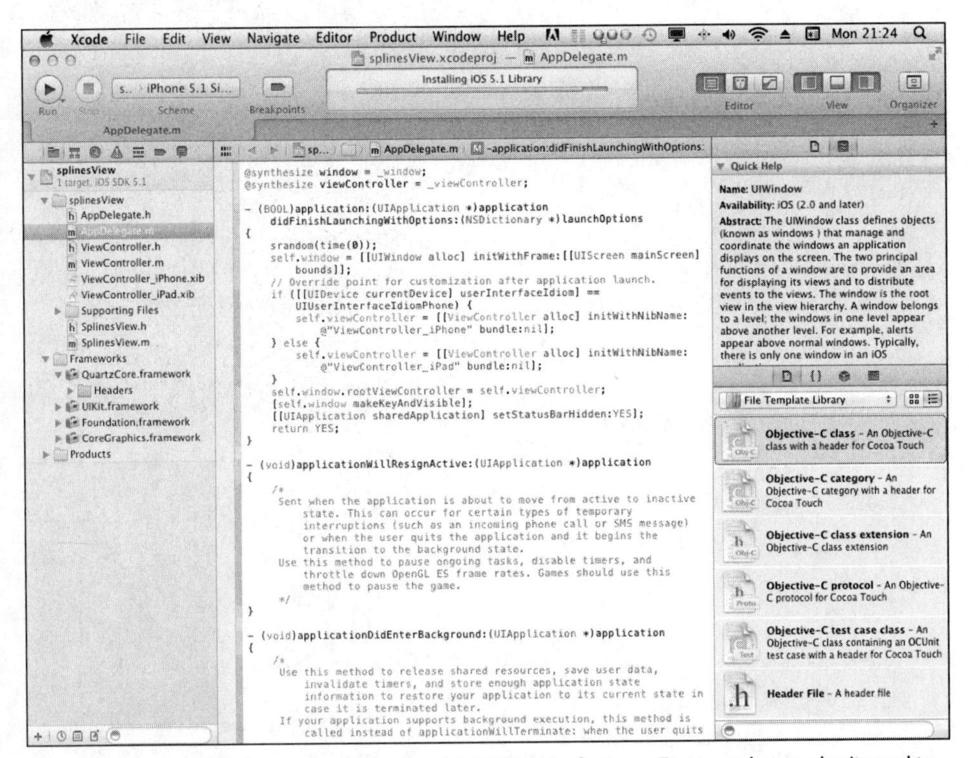

1.1 Xcode is a big, complex, powerful application with many features. Fortunately, you don't need to master everything it does to develop apps successfully.

Two further assets are optional, but very useful:

- **An iOS device.** You might expect this to be essential, but it isn't. Xcode includes the *Simulator*—a tool that can run and test iOS apps in an OS X mockup of either an iPhone, shown in Figure 1.2, or an iPad.
- **Membership in the iOS Development Program.** This program for dedicated developers costs $99 a year.

1.2 The Simulator built into Xcode can run iOS software, but its features are limited, and it isn't a substitute for testing apps on real devices.

Although membership in the iOS Development Program is optional, it offers important benefits:

- **Pre-release (beta) versions of iOS.** Apple often makes the latest versions of iOS available to developers before they're released to the public. This option also gives developers time to make new apps ready for sale as soon as the new version of iOS is released to the public or to modify existing apps to fix possible incompatibilities.
- **The latest versions of Xcode.** Similarly, Apple makes new versions of Xcode available to developers before they're released to the public.
- **Live device testing.** Only members of the iOS Development Program can test their apps on real devices. The Xcode Simulator is adequate for basic testing, but it has significant limitations, so this is an essential option for dedicated developers.
- **Access to help and support information.** This includes developer forums, and developer support videos, some of which are taken from the WWDC (World Wide Developer Conference) of the previous year.
- **Access to the App Store.** Only members of the iOS Development Program can sell apps through the App Store.

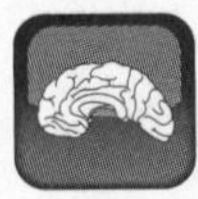
Genius

Xcode can be used to develop both iOS and OS X applications. OS X developers have a separate paid-for program that gives access to the OS X App Store. But because you don't need special hardware to test OS X apps, you can create and test OS X apps with Xcode before you sign up as an OS X developer.

Choosing a Mac

Although you can use any recent Mac for iOS development, not all Macs are equally productive. If you are developing for fun or curiosity, this may not matter to you, but it's useful to understand the benefits and limitations of each possible choice.

Choosing a processor

Processor speed affects development times, but speed isn't as critical as it is for high-performance applications such as gaming and video editing. Most iOS apps are small and simple, and Xcode doesn't take long to convert your raw instructions—known as *source code*—into a working application.

Note

In Xcode, this process is called *building an application.*

Currently, Xcode runs on OS X Lion, so at a minimum your Mac must have a Core 2 Duo series processor with 64-bit addressing and two cores. An i-Series processor may give better performance, depending on clock speed and number of cores. But using more cores won't make a huge difference to your productivity, especially when starting out. There's no need to invest in an expensive multi-core MacPro, at least not until you're earning enough from your apps to justify spending your development budget on one.

Note

Older versions of Xcode that work under Snow Leopard can be found online. If your Mac can't run OS X Lion, you can experiment with these, but you won't be able to use them to submit apps to the App Store.

Selecting memory

Xcode is a large application. If you're dedicating a Mac to development, it will run comfortably in 4GB. But if you plan to have multiple windows open in Safari or some other web browser (a good way to read Xcode's help files and documentation), you can easily run out of space with 4GB, as shown in Figure 1.3. A more realistic minimum is 8GB.

If you have too little memory, your Mac will stall for a minute or two every time you switch applications. If you plan to run Xcode, a browser, Mail, and perhaps some other applications simultaneously, you can avoid these distracting waits by expanding your Mac's RAM to 8GB.

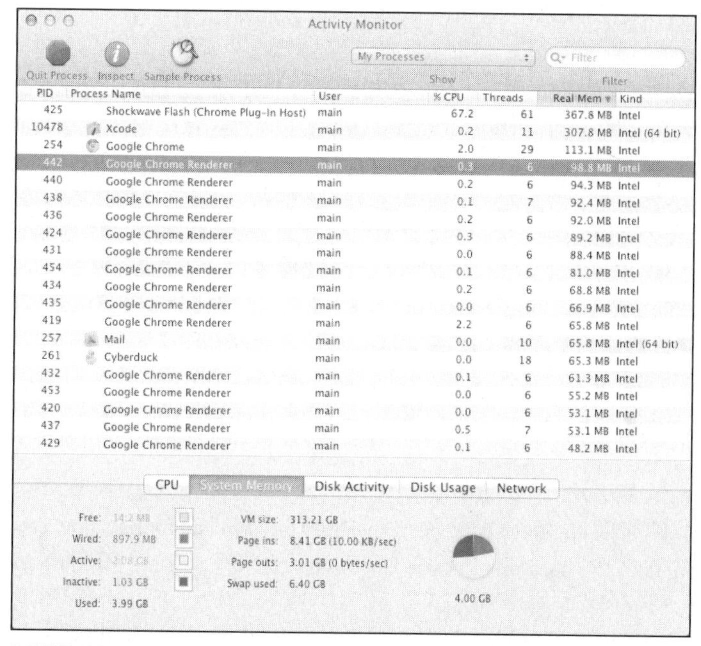

1.3 This Mac is running Xcode and the Chrome web browser. It has just 14.2MB of free RAM, guaranteeing a long wait when swapping between applications.

Genius

You can check how much memory applications are using, and how much memory is free, by running the Activity Monitor utility in /Applications/Utilities.

Selecting a monitor

Monitor size has a direct and immediate influence on productivity in Xcode. The larger your monitor, the more windows you can have open simultaneously, and the less time you'll waste opening, closing, moving, and scrolling between various windows and panes.

When you use Xcode, you'll spend more time editing, searching the web, and typing than you will building. You may also need to run supporting software, including sound, image, and perhaps video editing tools, at the same time as Xcode.

When starting out, expect to spend lots of time searching and reading the Xcode documentation. The more information you can view at once, the more easily you can make sense of what you're learning.

So in practice, you'll be significantly more productive with a large monitor—even a relatively cheap, non-Apple monitor—than with a small one.

Another option is to use multiple affordable 22-inch or 24-inch monitors simultaneously. Two monitors will be more productive than one, and if you can resurrect an old PC or Mac to use as a documentation browser, three or more monitors will help you work even more efficiently.

Selecting other peripherals

Printing out code—the instructions that make up an app—is often seen as an old-fashioned memory aid. But it can be surprisingly helpful, because it can be difficult to hold the entire structure of an app in (human) memory at the same time.

The other essential peripheral is a backup device. Any external hard drive will do for backups. You can simply copy project folders to the hard drive as you go, or you can rely on Time Machine to automate backups for you.

You can also speed up development significantly by using an SSD (Solid State Drive)—a very fast hard drive with no moving parts. Many Mac models support SSD as an option. It's often possible to add an SSD to an existing Mac, although the cost is high compared to a standard hard drive, drive capacities are usually lower, and the upgrade can be physically difficult.

Caution

Code backups are *not optional.* If you have apps for sale, losing the source code for them can be a disaster.

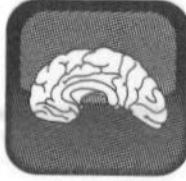

Genius

Experienced developers keep their code online in a *repository*—a web site that stores code safely and manages versions. Optionally, you can set up a repository to share your code with other developers so they can contribute to your projects. There's more information about this in Chapter 13.

Selecting a form factor

The physical size and configuration of your Mac has a direct influence on how easily and quickly you master app development. Although portable development is tempting, a permanent workstation is always more productive.

Running Xcode on a laptop

You can run Xcode on a laptop, including the MacBook Air models shown in Figure 1.4. This can seem an appealing option, but the small screen and relatively slow processor will slow down development. Most developers find they're most productive in a quiet environment or one with customizable music and sound. Coffee shops and other public locations aren't ideal. However, a MacBook Air or MacBook Pro can be useful to demonstrate app development in business meetings.

1.4 Portable development with a laptop can seem attractive, but it's rarely as productive as working in a fixed location with a bank of large monitors.

Running Xcode on an iMac

An iMac, shown in Figure 1.5 is a good choice for development. It's relatively affordable, easy to work with, includes a monitor, and can be expanded with further displays. You'll find large-screen iMacs particularly productive. Make sure you use a model with at least 4GB of memory, but consider expanding it to 8GB if you can, especially if the iMac is your family's main computer and it's used regularly for other tasks.

1.5 An iMac can be an ideal development machine.

Running Xcode on a Mac Pro

As the name suggests, Apple's Mac Pro line is aimed at professional Mac users. There's no reason *not* to use a Mac Pro, shown in Figure 1.6, if you have access to one. But keep in mind the memory and processor requirements of Xcode and the fact that monitor size has more influence on development speed than raw processor power. It's likely you'll waste most of the power of a Mac Pro unless you pair it with two or more large monitors.

1.6 A Mac Pro is a good choice for professional developers with large budgets, but it's excessive for beginners.

Running Xcode on a Mac Mini

The Mac Mini, shown in Figure 1.7, is a small and convenient solution for small office and home use. Mac Mini models aren't outstandingly powerful, but they're small enough to be unobtrusive, and they can easily be paired with two monitors. Most models have 2GB or 4GB of RAM; consider expanding this for dedicated development.

1.7 A Mac Mini is ideal for light and medium performance applications, but may struggle as a professional web server for e-commerce.

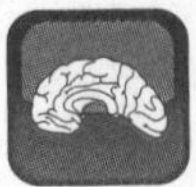

Genius

It's well known among developers that the cheapest way to expand a Mac's memory is to use third-party memory products. They're significantly cheaper than Apple's own memory, but offer identical performance. If you want to do the job yourself, Apple's support web pages include detailed specifications and instructions. For example, http://support.apple.com/kb/ht1423 includes information about expanding the memory of an iMac.

Joining the iOS Developer Program

Enrollment is optional for casual developers who are experimenting with iOS, but essential for more dedicated developers who want to test apps on real iOS devices and also want access to the App Store.

Understanding enrollment options

There are two enrollment options. The $99 annual fee is the same for both, but they have different benefits:

- **Individual.** For this option, you need an existing Apple ID, although it can be useful to create a new one even if you already have one, because there are occasional incompatibilities between developer and public Apple IDs. Individual enrollment is usually completed within 48 hours. Personal ID is confirmed via your credit card details.
- **Company.** Enrolling as a company is more complex. In addition to an Apple ID, you'll also be asked to provide proof of incorporation, with a valid address. The company name must be legally registered: Trade names aren't allowed. Business enrollment can take up to two weeks, although it's usually completed more quickly.

Individual developers have simplified access to the *provisioning* process used to manage test devices. As an individual, you work as a team of one and all possible team roles are available to you.

This is a benefit when getting started, but may become a limitation if your apps become very successful and you try to hire other developers to help you.

Support for team development is available only for company enrollment. A designated team leader can add or remove team members. He or she can also limit access to test devices and control which members are allowed to upload finished apps to the App Store.

Each option has legal and financial implications as well. If you enroll as an individual, Apple pays you as an individual. This may affect your tax status. Some countries, especially the U.S., withhold a percentage of the earnings of foreign developers unless they apply for them to be released. This process can take between three months and a year to complete.

If you enroll as a company, you are taxed as a company, which is usually simpler and more direct.

To summarize, if you already have a company, the extra wait at the start of the development process is a relatively small price to pay for the extra team options and the simpler financial processing.

If you don't have a company or you have no need for team development, individual enrollment is a simpler option. It may cause issues later if your apps become very successful, but few app developers reach the stage where team development becomes necessary.

Enrolling in the iOS Developer Program

For individuals, enrollment isn't a complicated process. To begin, open a web browser and navigate to https://developer.apple.com/programs/ios, shown in Figure 1.8.

1.8 The iOS Developer Program sign-up page.

Click the Enroll Now button, and work your way through the questions. You'll be asked for your Apple ID, name, address, e-mail, nationality, and other basic information. Once enrollment is complete and you pay the enrollment fee, you'll receive confirmation within 24 hours— although the confirmation e-mail usually arrives more quickly. You can then access the Developer Program features.

For companies, the process is similar, but you'll be asked to confirm details of incorporation, usually by faxing a copy of your documents to Apple's HQ in Cupertino. Company applications are checked manually, so the process takes longer. You may also be contacted by an Apple representative with some basic questions. Once enrollment is complete, you can access the Program features, but your account is set up with the extra team management features that aren't offered to individuals.

Note

Apple offers a separate Enterprise Program for large corporations that want to develop apps in-house and distribute them internally. Details are outside the scope of this book, but you can find the latest information at http://developer.apple.com/programs/ios/enterprise.

Will apps make me rich?

Realistically, it's unlikely that app sales will make you rich. iOS apps continue to be more successful than apps for any other platform, including Android. But the iOS app store is heavily saturated, and many users already have more apps than they want or need.

App sales are heavily concentrated among a small number of super-sellers, who can be extremely successful. A slightly larger number of app developers make four or five figures a year, especially if they combine app sales with ad revenue captured from Apple's iAD program. But many sellers are lucky to break even.

A successful app has four ingredients: a genuinely original idea or a popular existing idea; aggressive marketing, which may include a sizeable marketing budget; impressive graphic design; and a certain amount of luck. If you can adapt your apps for novel markets—for example, relatively few apps are written for the Chinese market—you can increase your chances of financial success.

However, at the time of writing, app developer skills are very much in demand among employers. While you may not be able to make a fortune selling your apps directly, you'll certainly be able to increase your employability. Some developer compensation packages are very generous, so it's well worth investigating this career option.

Downloading and Installing Xcode

The App Store and Developer Program versions of Xcode are different—sometimes significantly different—and they're installed in different ways. Before you get started with downloading and installation, let's look at a critical element of Xcode, the SDK (Software Development Kit).

Caution

Xcode is a continual work in progress. The versions of iOS it supports change with almost every release, but Apple also varies key features without notice, and delivery and installation options also change. The information that follows is valid for the public release of Xcode 4.3 for iOS 5.1. Don't be surprised if some of the details have changed again by the time you read this.

Understanding SDKs and betas

Xcode has two main components. The current toolset includes the tools you use to edit, build, test, and distribute apps. Xcode is a fairly mature application now, so these tools change relatively slowly.

As iOS develops, new features are added and old features become obsolete. The other component in Xcode is called the SDK (Software Development Kit), and it manages this information.

Internally, the SDK is a collection of files and supporting documentation that defines all the features in a single version of iOS. Whenever iOS is updated, Apple releases a new version of Xcode with an updated SDK.

This seems simple, but there are complications. Basically, Xcode is always available in two versions:

- **The public version in the App Store includes the SDK for the most recent public version of iOS.**
- **The Developer Program version usually includes the SDK for the *next* version of iOS.** This version is a work in progress. It includes provisional features that may change before the final release.

A critical fact is that the Developer Program version goes through multiple updates. Each update is called a beta or preview, and is available for a period that can vary between a week and a month. When a new beta version is released, it replaces the previous preview, which becomes obsolete.

Just before a final public release, Apple announces a special version called a Release Candidate (RC) version. Unlike earlier previews, the RC version can usually be used to submit apps with the new features to the App Store. Occasionally, the RC version goes through one or two further updates to fix last-minute issues. More typically, it's released "as is" after a couple of weeks. This gives developers a chance to submit compatible apps to the App Store and gives Apple time to review them.

Table 1.1 summarizes the process.

Table 1.1 Xcode and SDK versions

Xcode Release	Availability	SDK	App Store Submissions?
Public	App Store and Developer Portal	Current public version of iOS	Yes
Early Preview	Developer Portal only	Preview of next version of iOS	No
Release Candidate	Developer Portal only	Advanced preview—imminent public release	Usually yes

Caution

It would make sense for Apple to make each SDK update downloadable as a separate small file that could be installed in Xcode. Unfortunately, Apple doesn't do this. Whenever the SDK is updated, you have to download a complete new version of Xcode.

Note

Occasionally, Apple makes major changes to Xcode to update its editors and build tools. The last time this happened (in 2011), Xcode went through its own set of beta preview versions. Instead of an RC version, Apple eventually released a version called a GM (Gold Master) Seed. This process may happen again during the lifetime of this book.

Installing Xcode from the App Store

To install the current public version of Xcode from the Mac App Store, follow these steps:

1. **Launch the App Store application on your Mac.**
2. **Type** Xcode **into the search box at the top right, as shown in Figure 1.9.**
3. **Click the Free button.**
4. **Wait while the App Store downloads an extremely large file.**

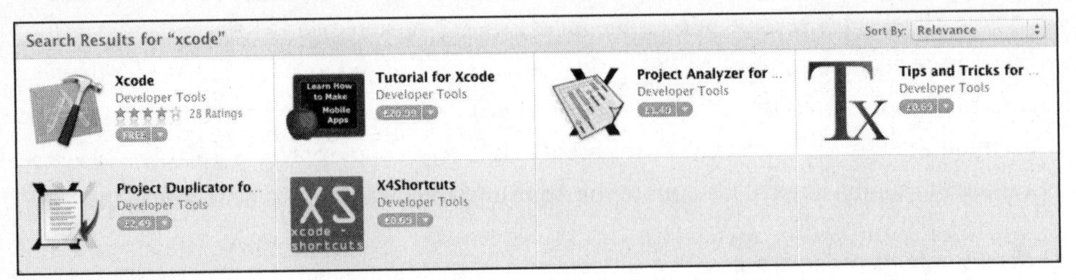

1.9 You can get Xcode for free in the Mac App Store, but beware of the download size!

5. **After the download completes, the App Store installs Xcode in /Applications, as shown in Figure 1.10.**

Caution

Xcode is currently 3.4GB. This is a big, big download, and if you don't have fast broadband, you'll probably need to leave it running overnight. If you don't have broadband at all, you won't be able to download it directly. If you have a laptop, it can be worth visiting a local WiFi hotspot with good connectivity, such as an Internet café, and downloading Xcode there. (Not all café owners appreciate very large downloads, so it's polite to check that this is okay before you start!)

6. **Double-click Xcode to launch it.** For convenience, you can also drag the application icon to your Dock.

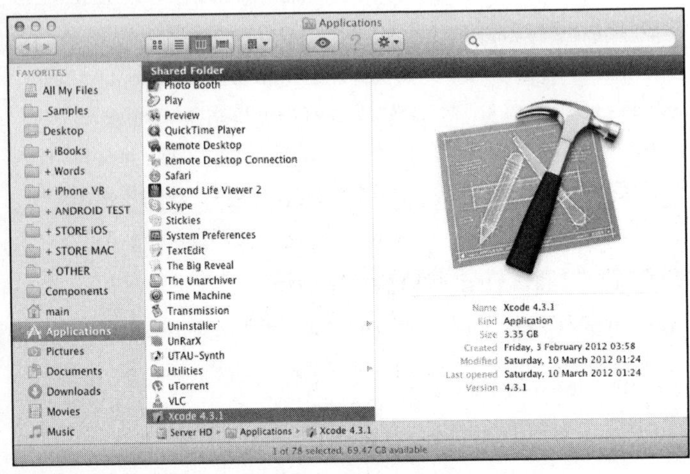

1.10 The App Store downloads a separate installer and copies it into /Applications.

Installing Xcode from a developer download

Many developers find the App Store process inconvenient. From version 4.3, Apple rolled the complete Xcode package into a single, giant application that includes Xcode itself and assorted other tools you'll meet briefly later in this book.

The giant application is bundled into a single .dmg file. Installation is much simpler than it was: You simply mount the .dmg file in Finder and drag a single Xcode application file to a folder of your choice.

It's not yet clear if Apple is reserving this new installation method for developers or if future public App Store versions will work the same way. Whatever the outcome, the following steps summarize this alternative installation process:

Caution

You must be enrolled in the iOS Developer Program to access the web pages and files shown in this section.

1. **Open a web browser, and navigate to the iOS Dev Center landing page at https://developer.apple.com/devcenter/ios.**
2. **Click the Log in button near the top of the page, and enter your Apple ID and password.**
3. **When a beta (developer preview) version is available, it appears as a link or button to the right of the main public version; click the button to access the beta area, shown in Figure 1.11.**
4. **Scroll down to the Downloads links.** You can also click the Downloads link near the top left.
5. **Click the Xcode and iOS download link to begin downloading Xcode.** Depending on your browser and your individual preferences, you may choose to download the file to a specific location. Otherwise, the file will be copied to /Downloads on your Mac.
6. **Wait...** until the download completes.
7. **Create a new folder on the root of your system disk.** The name doesn't matter, but "iOS Beta" is a good choice.
8. **Navigate to the downloaded .dmg file in Finder.**

Note

While you can install this version manually into /Applications, it's better to keep it in a different custom folder. You also may want to rename to avoid confusion with the current public version, especially if you also move it to the Dock.

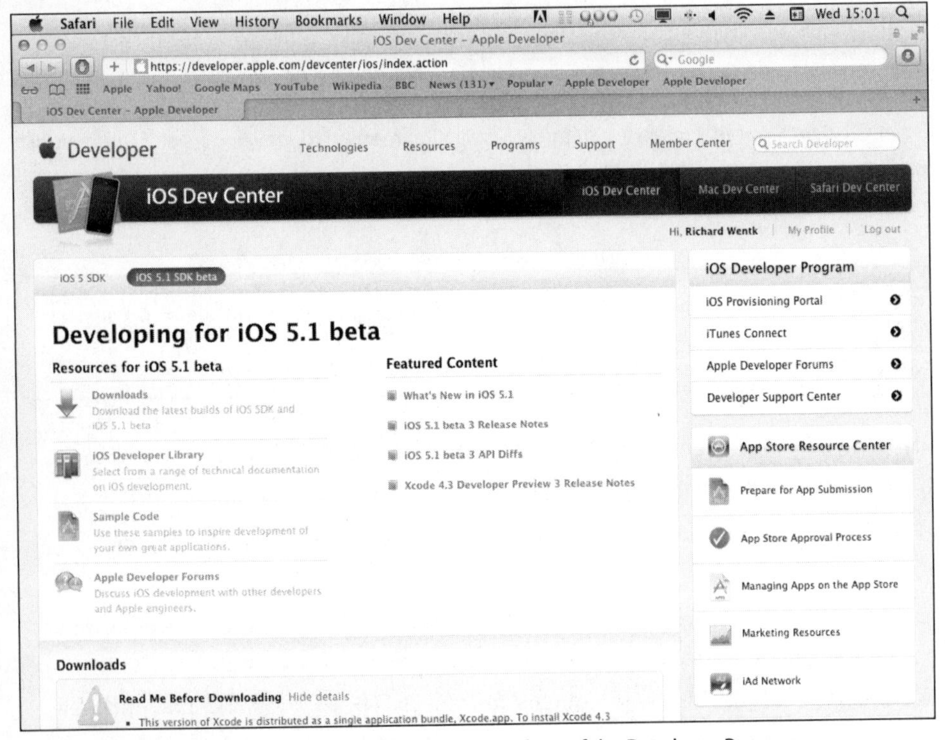

1.11 The iOS beta/preview area is available only to members of the Developer Program.

9. **Double-click the .dmg file.** The contents should appear in a new window. You'll see the .dmg file appear under the Devices list at the left of Finder.
10. **Drag the Xcode file from the new window to the folder you created in Step 7, as shown in Figure 1.12.**
11. **Double-click the Xcode file to launch it.** You can also drag its icon to the Dock for convenience.

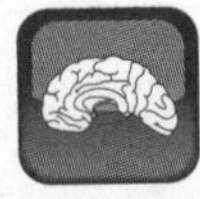

Genius

If you enroll as a developer, you'll often have two versions of Xcode in the Dock at the same time—the public version, used for current app development, and a beta/preview. You can rename the application files by hand to tell them apart. For example, you can rename the preview version to Xcode Beta.

Caution In addition to the /Developer and /Beta folders, you should also create one or more project folders for your apps. *Do not* save apps inside the Xcode folders; they can be deleted without notice when you install an update.

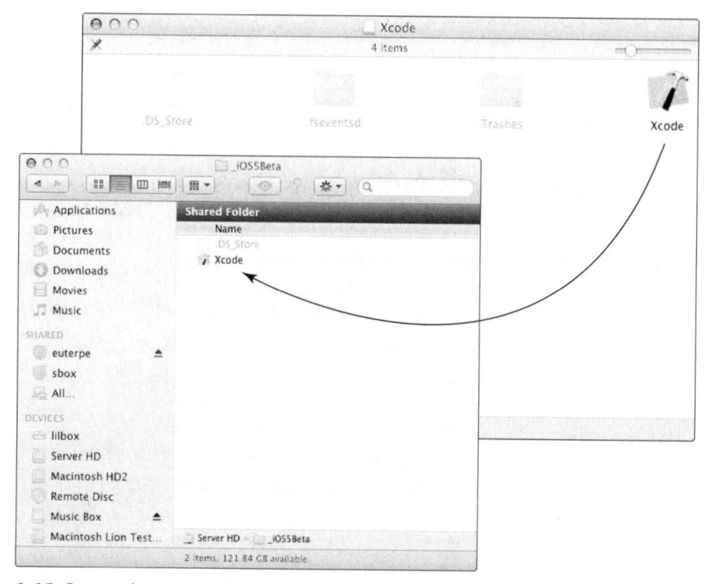

1.12 Currently, you can install the developer version of Xcode by dragging it to a folder of your choice.

Understanding other installation requirements

There's more to know about the preview process—and more files to download. In addition to the most recent version of Xcode with the newest SDK, you must also download the following:

- **A firmware update file for each of your test devices.** This file updates the device to run the latest preview/beta version of iOS.
- **Xcode's internal documentation files.** This process is described later in this chapter.
- **Optionally, a new version of iTunes.** Apple is moving to on-air updates of iOS devices, which means that iTunes is no longer required for iOS updates. However, this option isn't always available, so you may still need to download a special beta/preview version of iTunes before you can update the firmware in your devices.

Note

Developer versions of iTunes download and install like any other .dmg packaged application: Double-click the .dmg file to mount it, and then double-click the installer. One critical difference is that preview versions of iTunes usually include a built-in expiration date. After a preview expires, you can download the most recent version of iTunes from www.apple.com/itunes.

Note

Firmware is the name given to a device's internal software. Firmware is usually stored in a special memory that isn't dependent on battery power, so it isn't lost if the device loses all power. Technically, you *flash* firmware when you update it.

It should be obvious from this list that updating your development tools to the most recent SDK can mean lots of downloading. The total bandwidth for a new beta/preview SDK with Xcode, firmware for a single device, and associated documentation can total more than 5GB. If you have multiple test devices and need to update to a preview of iTunes, this can climb toward 7GB.

Updates can happen weekly. It's not obligatory to download every preview/beta; you can usually skip some of the earlier betas, but expect to download at least 15-20GB a month.

Caution

Some broadband ISP contracts limit the amount of data you can download each month. If your broadband supplier implements a bandwidth cap, consider switching to a supplier that doesn't limit you in this way.

Updating devices

Firmware is supplied either as a .dmg file or as an .ipsw file. (To find the .ipsw file inside a .dmg file, double-click it to open it.)

To update a device to the latest preview version of iOS with iTunes, follow these steps:

1. **Connect your device to your Mac using a cable, and launch iTunes.** (Although iTunes offers backup over WiFi and to iCloud, cable connections are more reliable.)
2. **Select the device from the list at the left.**
3. **Click the option labeled Back up to this computer in the Backup pane.** Optionally, you can also set a password.

4. **Click the Sync button at the bottom right.** Wait for the backup to complete.
5. **Hold down the option button on your Mac's keyboard, and click Restore.**
6. **Navigate to the .ipsw file you downloaded, select it, and click Open, as shown in Figure 1.13.** If the .ipsw file was packed inside a .dmg file, select the .dmg file from the list of Devices at the left, and then select the .ipsw file.

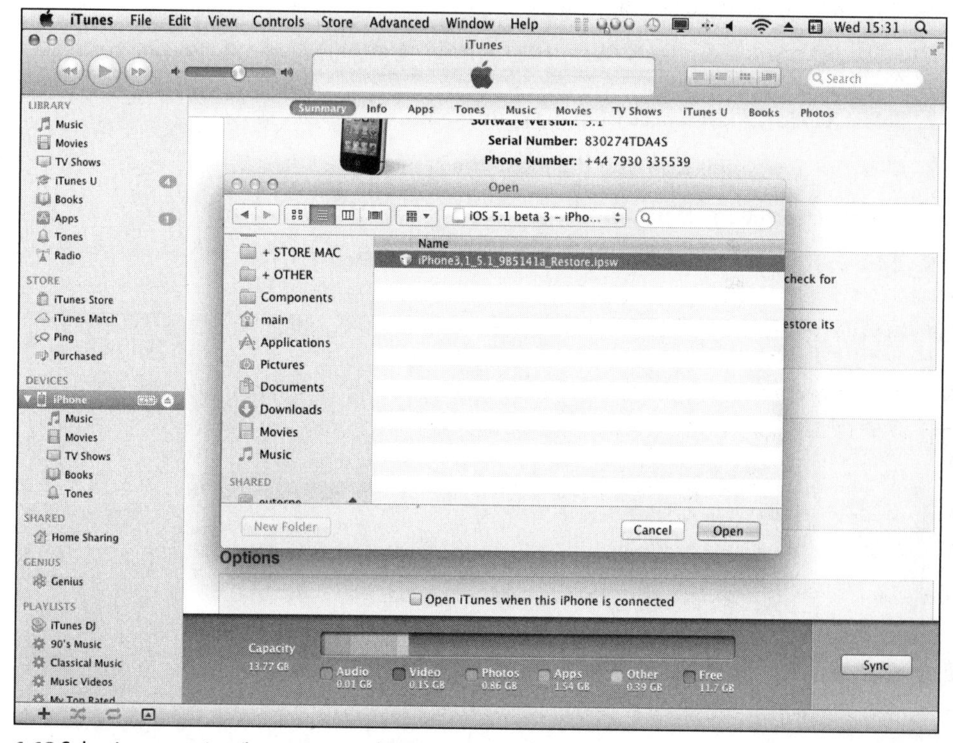

1.13 Selecting a preview/beta version of iOS in iTunes to install it.

7. **Wait while iTunes flashes the new version of iOS to your device.** This can take 10-15 minutes.
8. **The Set Up Your (iOS Device) page appears automatically in iTunes.** Select your most recent backup from the menu on this page, and click Continue.
9. **Wait while iTunes restores your apps, data, and settings.** This can take another 15-20 minutes.
10. **Your device can now be used for testing with the latest developer version of Xcode.**

If you have multiple devices—for example, more than one iPhone, an iPhone and an iPad, an iPhone and an iPod Touch—you must update all devices you want to use for testing with the new version of iOS.

Installing documentation

Although Xcode is a huge download, it doesn't include all the documentation and help files you need. To install these files, follow these steps:

1. **Launch Xcode.**
2. **Select Xcode ⇨ Preferences from the main menu.**
3. **Click the Downloads icon near the top of the pane.**
4. **Click the Documentation tab.**
5. **Click the Check and Install Now button, as shown in Figure 1.14.**

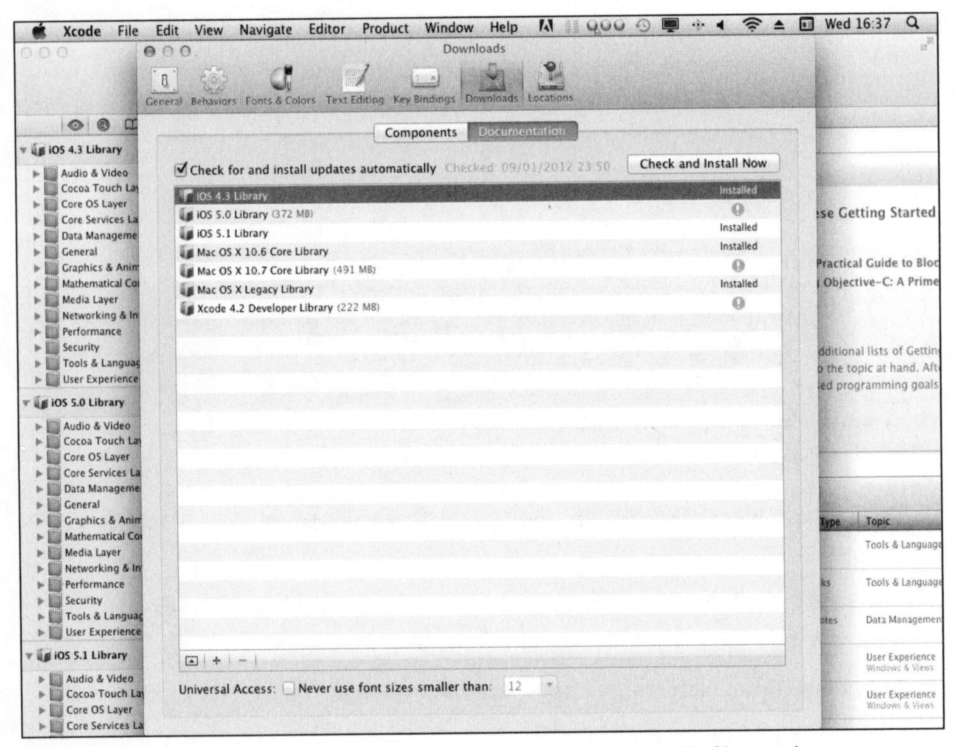

1.14 Reviewing the installed documentation. You don't need every possible file, just the more recent ones.

Each file is 300-400MB. You don't need to install every file; for example, you don't need the OS X 10.6 Core Library if you're developing iOS apps. But you do need the files for the current version of iOS and the Xcode Developer Library for help with Xcode itself.

Note

If you check the check box labeled Check for and install updates automatically at the top left of this page, Xcode downloads all the documentation it needs as soon as it can. However, the download process isn't bullet-proof, so you should always check manually that files have downloaded correctly.

Now that you've learned about the Developer Program, SDKs, and Xcode, you're ready to start exploring Xcode's developer-friendly features in more detail.

How Do I Get Started with Xcode?

1 2 3 4 5 6 7 8 9 10 11 12 13

Xcode is a powerful package with many features. You don't need to master it all to get started, but you do need to have a basic understanding of its most obvious features. In addition to getting started with Xcode, you also need to start learning about iOS and the technical details of app design. You can find help for all these topics in Apple's official documentation and in supporting unofficial documentation that can be yours for the price of a web search.

Understanding Xcode

Xcode is a tool for converting code—text instructions—into an app that can run on an iOS device.

Apps are built from more than one kind of data. In addition to the raw binary instructions that run on the processor, apps also include sound files, graphic files that define screens, backgrounds, buttons or game tokens, font files, and other supporting information.

When you build an app, Xcode combines these elements into a single file, called the *product*. Most of the build process is automatic.

You have three jobs as a developer:

- **Creating code.** Code is kept in a collection of text files. The instructions you create define how the app responds to events and circumstances, such as a finger tap, a finger drag, an incoming message or notification, an out-of-memory error, and so on. Xcode includes a *code editor* to help you write code.
- **Creating a look and feel.** Xcode includes a design tool called *Interface Builder,* shown in Figure 2.1, that manages the look and feel of the app. You can use it to place buttons and switches, control the order in which screens appear to the user, and define the graphics the user sees.
- **Managing files.** You'll often have to create files using an outside editor; for example, you may want to create a background screen in Adobe Photoshop. Xcode includes a file manager called the *Navigator* that tells Xcode which supporting files you want to include in your app.

Writing good code can be difficult, so Xcode includes many further features to help you:

- **A debugger.** This tool helps you eliminate mistakes ("bugs"). You can literally step through your code line by line to confirm that each line is working as you think it should.
- **A complete documentation library.** Every feature in iOS is documented in detail. There are also pre-written code examples, introductory orientation essays with live links to further help, introductory tutorials, and video descriptions of key elements.
- **A small library of app templates, code snippets, and standard graphics.** In fact, there's more than one library. You can use this feature to include buttons, sliders, and other standard iOS features in your app and to add boilerplate code to manage them.

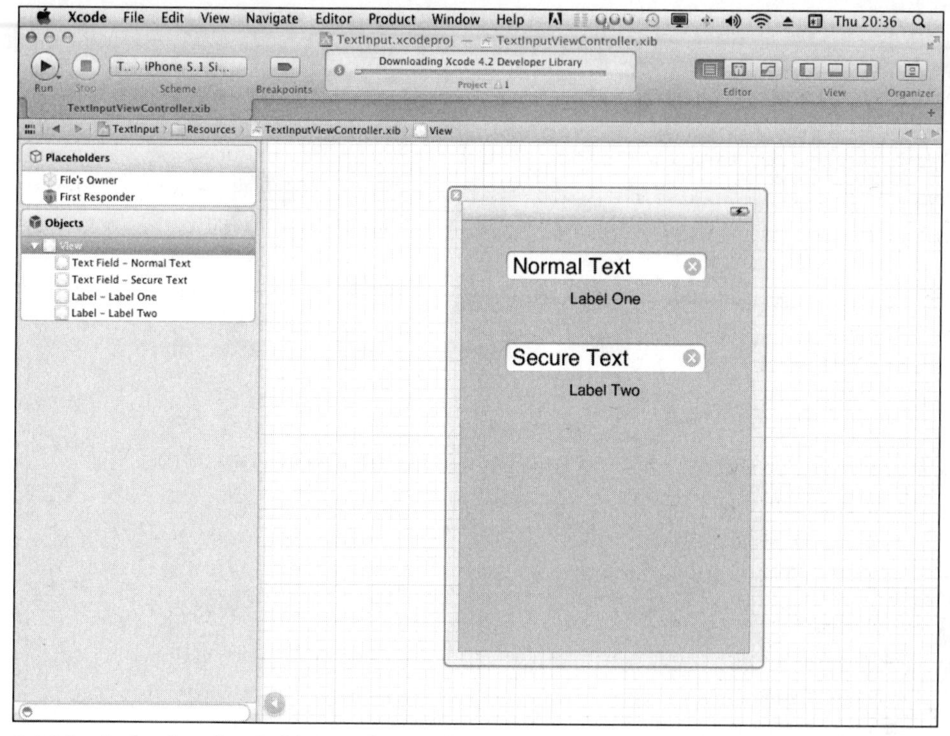

2.1 A first look at Interface Builder, Xcode's graphical app design tool. The Navigator area is at the left of the screen.

- **Live testing.** These include the Simulator mentioned in Chapter 1. A further set of tools, called *Instruments*, is shown in Figure 2.2. Instruments can check the memory usage and performance of an app, in detail, while it's running. Xcode can also be set up to work with a collection of specific iOS devices, and you can collect crash and memory information from these devices, even after testing is complete.

You can see that Xcode has many features. But it doesn't have many windows. The interface has been condensed, so you'll spend most of your time working in one main window that can be set to display up to four panes.

An optional further floating window is used to display supporting information, including Xcode's documentation. You also can occasionally open a preferences window to set up various Xcode options.

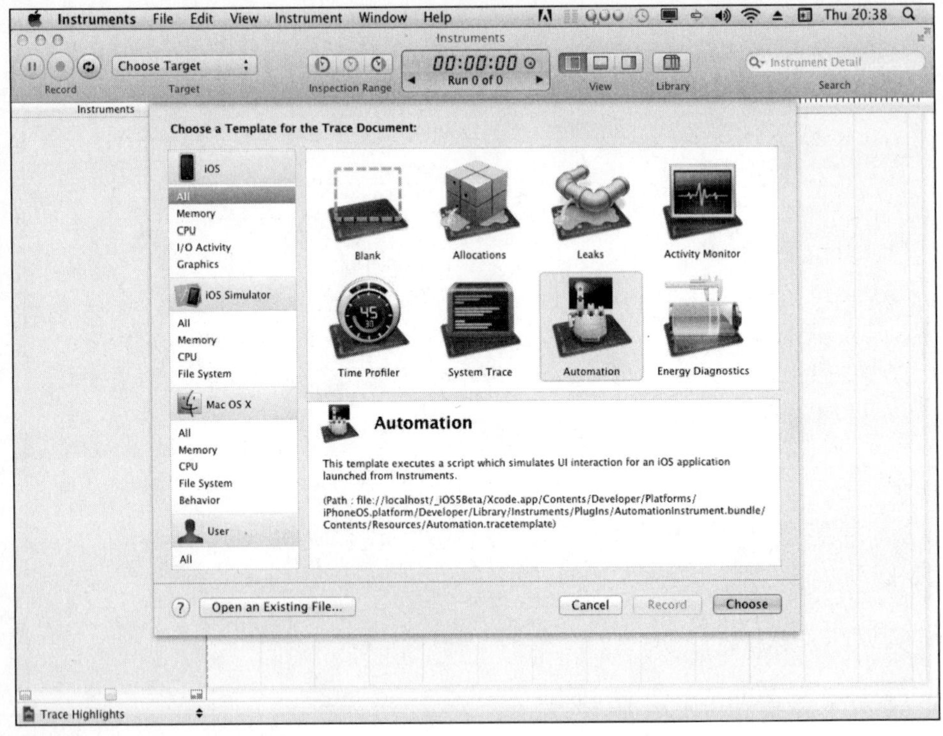

2.2 Introducing Instruments, Xcode's performance and resource testing tool.

Caution

Xcode is *not* a consumer product. It's important to understand that as a developer, you're expected to solve problems using your own initiative. Critical features in Xcode—which can include installation and delivery options—change regularly. Often you have no more than a few terse notes and perhaps some online discussion to help you. For better or worse, this self-sufficiency is part of developer culture. If you're used to working with more streamlined and stable consumer products, it can leave you with some culture shock.

Introducing Xcode's User Interface

When you launch Xcode for the first time, you see the Welcome to Xcode window shown in Figure 2.3. With the four options here, you can do the following:

- **Create a new Xcode project.** Clicking this button takes you to Xcode's project templates, which are described in Chapter 3.

- **Connect to a repository.** You can use this feature to access a web repository to download, upload, or share code, as discussed in Chapter 13. If you're new to Xcode, you can ignore this option for now.
- **Learn about using Xcode.** This option opens a new window with a documentation viewer. If this is your first view of Xcode, it can be worth reviewing this introductory information, although most of it is covered more comprehensively—and perhaps accessibly—in this book.
- **Go to Apple's developer portal.** This opens your web browser and loads the main developer page at http://developer.apple/com. You can't change this link, and the iOS Dev Center pages at http://developer.apple.com/devcenter/ios are more useful. So you won't be using this option much.

2.3 Welcome to Xcode. Experienced developers often bypass this window.

Note

Although it's down to personal taste, many developers deselect the Show this window when Xcode launches check box near the bottom left of the pane. Although the Recents list of projects at the right can be useful, both the recent files and the other features in this window here can be accessed just as quickly from the main menu in Xcode.

Introducing the main Xcode window

Xcode's main window, shown in Figure 2.4, has six main elements. You can use the buttons at the top right of the toolbar at the top of the screen to control which elements are visible.

Note

A user interface (UI) defines the windows, panes, menus, and other features a user can access to work with an application. As a developer, you'll spend lots of time defining the UI of your apps. A good UI is easy to understand, with a clear relationship between obvious features and useful tasks. The relationship between a UI and the features of an app is called the User Experience, often abbreviated to UX.

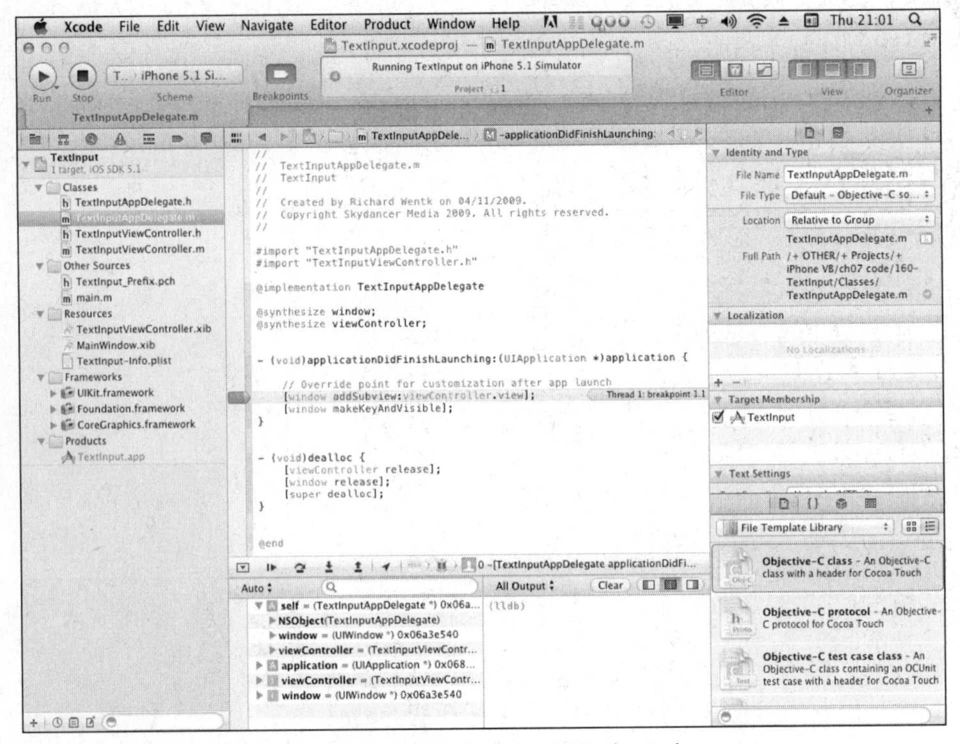

2.4 You'll spend most of your development time in the main Xcode window.

The elements are described in detail later in this chapter. But let's start with a quick overview.

- **The main toolbar.** This includes the buttons that control Xcode's critical features.
- **A tabbed file area.** This small area under the toolbar works like the tab feature in most web browsers. You can have multiple files open at the same time, and you can switch between them by clicking them.

- **The Navigator.** This area at the left of the window is a combined file selector and status/information area. You can select what it does by clicking the icons above it. Typically you use the Navigator to select files as you edit. Occasionally, you'll use one of its other features, introduced later in this chapter.
- **The Editor.** This area in the middle of the window displays code and other information you can change. Although it looks like a simple text editor, it has powerful code-editing features.
- **The Utility Area.** The area at the right of the window displays supporting information, including quick help reminders, pre-written code snippets, and details about selected files that don't fit elsewhere. Like the Navigator, you can select different features by clicking the icons that appear above it.
- **The Debugger.** This area slides up from the bottom of the screen into the Editor area. It displays information and status messages that tell you what your app is doing while you debug it.

One further feature, called the Organizer, is shown in Figure 2.5. The Organizer is a grab-bag of features and options that don't fit anywhere else. Like the other features, it's described in detail later in this chapter. A critical point to remember is that the Organizer includes access to the iOS documentation.

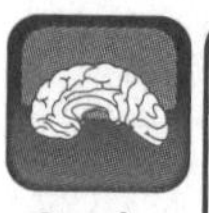

Genius

You can drag the vertical dividing lines between the areas to resize them.

Viewing and hiding UI features

If your monitor is large enough, you can have every element of the Xcode UI, including the Organizer, visible at the same time. This is the most efficient working option, because nothing is hidden and you don't have to waste time hiding and revealing the different areas.

Smaller monitors don't give you enough space for this, so you must learn how to view and hide the different features as you work.

Xcode's designers have made this a simple process, although there are a few minor gotchas that can trip you up, and some of the features are tied to other features in ways that may not be obvious.

The buttons that control the areas are at the top right of the toolbar. Look at them now, and you'll see there are two groups of three, with one extra button for the Organizer.

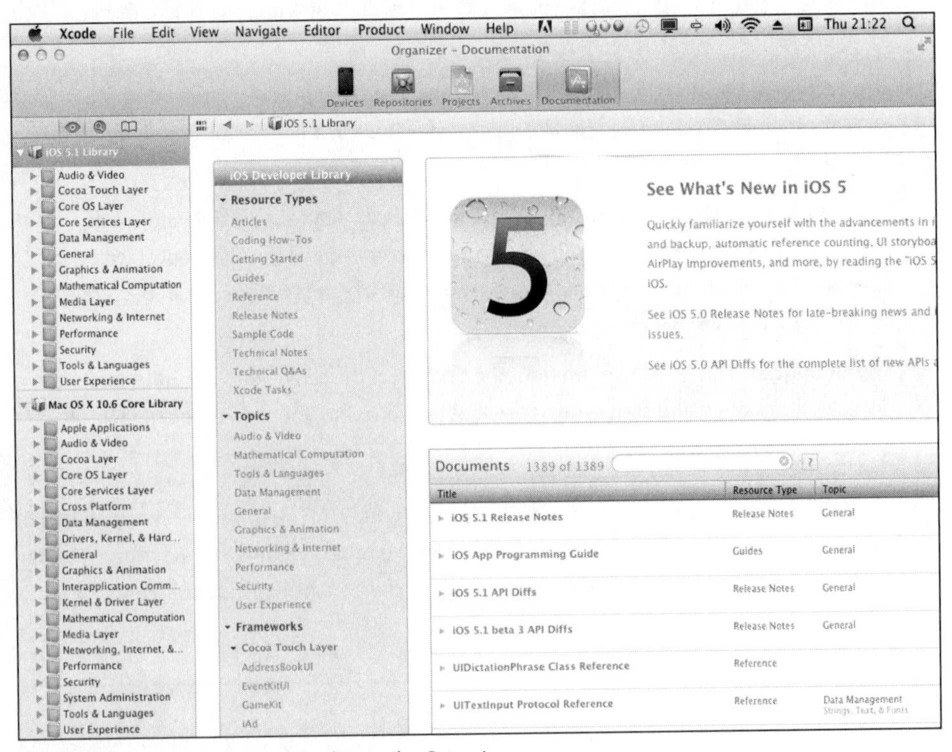

2.5 The Documentation viewer built into the Organizer.

Using the View buttons

The three View buttons are the easiest to understand. From left to right, you can use them to:

- **Hide and show the Navigator area**
- **Hide and show the Debugger**
- **Hide and show the Utility area**

Take some time to experiment with these buttons now. Figure 2.6 shows the Xcode window with all three areas hidden. Note that the Editor area is always visible; you can't hide it. But you can use the buttons to maximize its size, as shown in the figure. This can be useful if you need an extra wide view of your code—or if you're using the dual-pane Assistant feature, introduced later.

Caution The Debugger window is unusual because it appears automatically when you test an app. This isn't always a good thing; often, it's just plain distracting. The setting that controls this option is buried in the Preferences. For details, see Chapter 12.

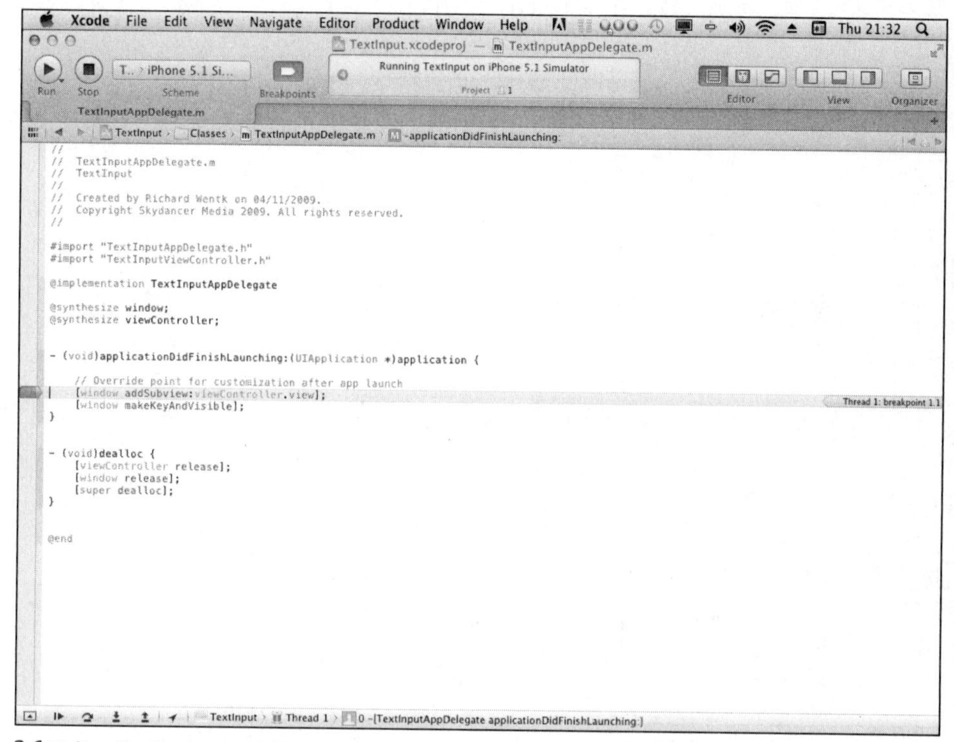

2.6 Hiding the Navigator, Utility, and Debugger areas to maximize the Editor.

Using the Editor buttons

You may want to maximize the width of the Editor area because it can be split to show two files simultaneously. The Editor buttons select the optional second file on the right, as follows:

- **The Standard Editor.** This displays a single Editor window, showing a single file.
- **The Assistant Editor.** This shows two files side by side, as shown in Figure 2.7. Xcode selects the file in the right pane automatically, based on the relationship you select by clicking the Counterparts menu above the right editor area.
- **The Version Editor.** Xcode compares two versions of the same file and highlights the changes between them.

Understanding the Assistant Editor

The Assistant Editor is a very powerful tool. When you select a file for the left area, Xcode automatically displays a related file in the right area. This can be very convenient, and it saves manual selection and file switching.

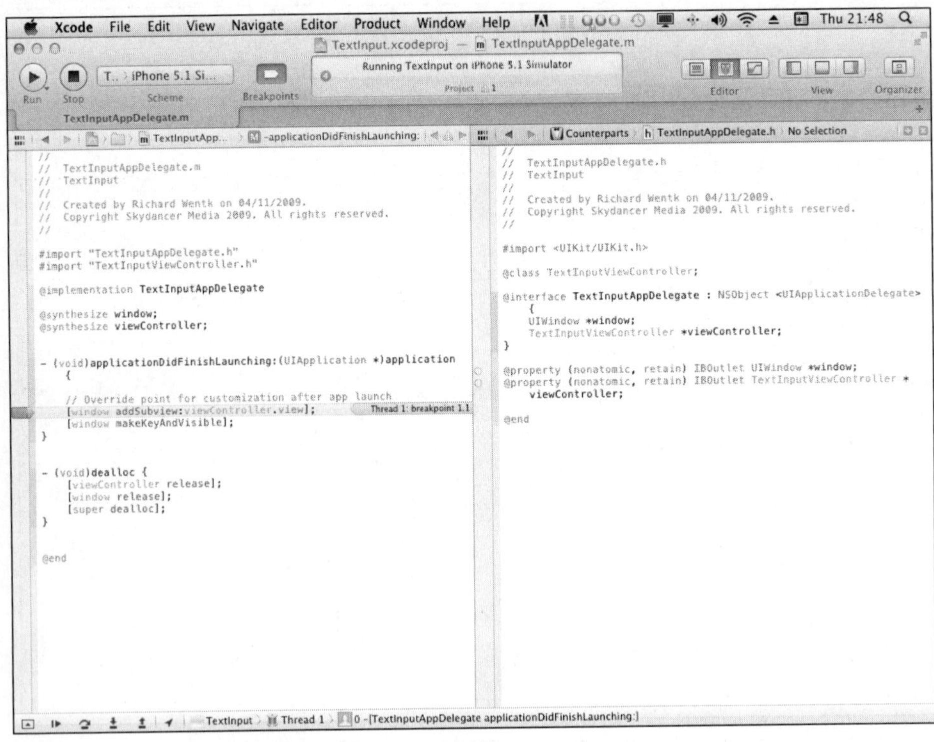

2.7 Using the Assistant Editor to show two related files.

Selection is controlled by clicking the Counterparts icon above the Assistant Editor window, as shown in Figure 2.8. If you're new to app development, you probably won't know what the words in this menu mean. If you have experience in other object-oriented programming environments, you should be able to make an educated guess.

The details don't matter for now. You'll understand the most important options as you work through this book, while other options are obscure—even for experienced developers.

You can come back to this feature later. For now, leave the default selection unchanged.

We'll look at this feature again when we explore objects and classes in Chapter 6.

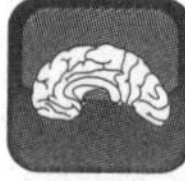

Genius

If you select View ➪ Assistant Editor in the main Xcode menu, you'll see menu options to change the position of the assistant area. We'll use the standard assistant-on-right layout throughout this book, but you may want to experiment with the layouts.

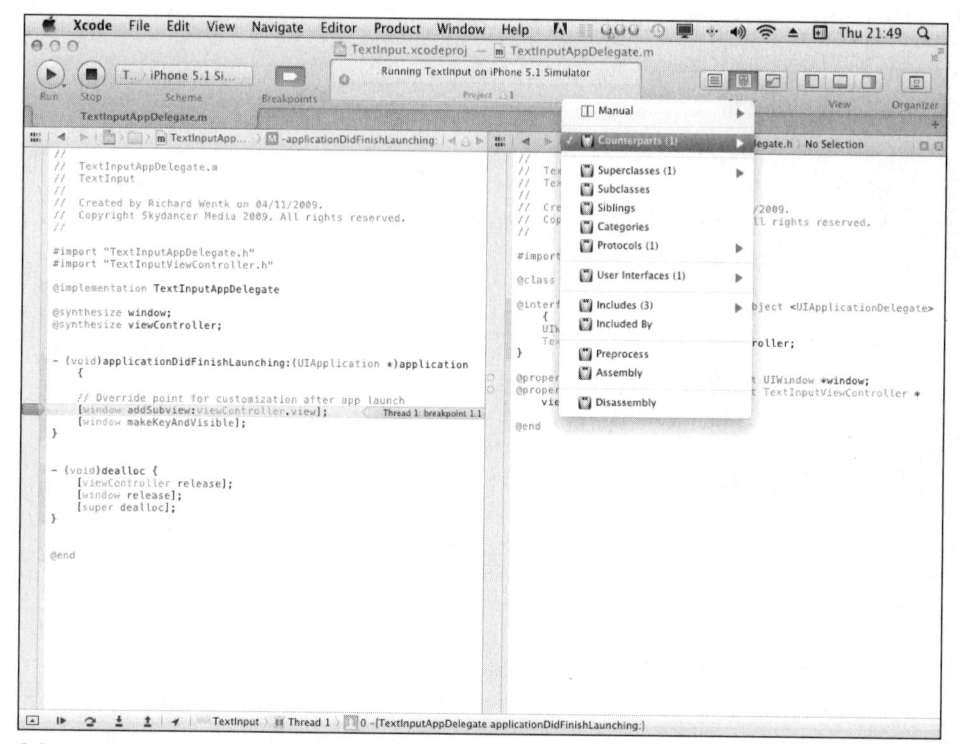

2.8 Selecting the relationship between the file in the left editor pane and the file selected automatically in the right.

Understanding the Version Editor

The Version Editor is an advanced feature. Basically, Xcode includes powerful version management and *source control* features. You can save versions of projects as you go, and you can split projects into different versions—for example, to allow different developers to work on different features before combining their work again.

This feature can be a powerful tool, but you need to know more about both editing and coding before you can make the best use of it.

Using the Organizer

Clicking the Organizer icon at the far right opens the Organizer window, shown in Figure 2.9.

The Organizer window is independent and free-floating. If your monitor is large enough, you can move it to one side. If you have multiple monitors, you can move it to a side monitor to keep it out of the way.

Note that you can have only the one Organizer window open at a time. Although it has multiple features, you can't view them simultaneously. You can switch between them by clicking the icons at the top of the window.

Note

The fact that you can view only a single documentation file at a time is particularly unhelpful during development. Fortunately, there's a workaround, which is described later in this chapter.

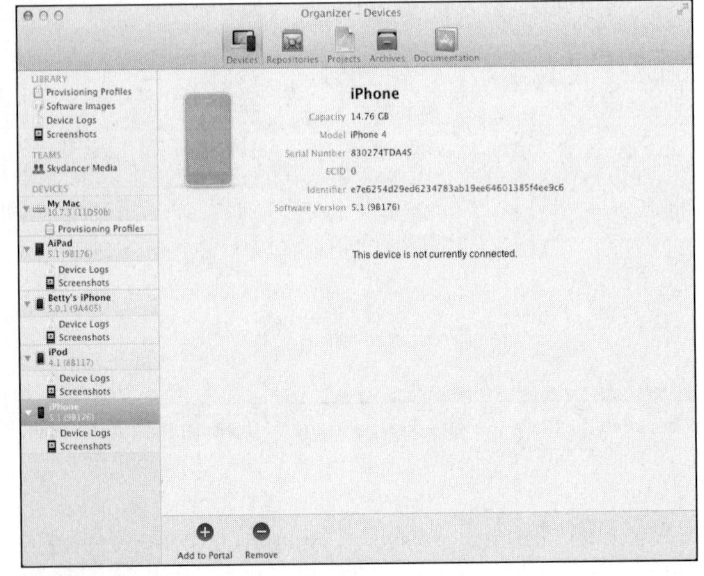

2.9 Viewing the Organizer's floating window.

Using the other toolbar features

The main Xcode toolbar has five more features. These features are easy to understand, and you'll use them all regularly as you code:

- **Run button.** This button builds your project to create an app and then attempts to run the app. There's more about it in Chapter 3.
- **Stop button.** This button stops the build/run process, or at least it tries to stop the process. Depending on the context, it doesn't always succeed.
- **Scheme menu.** Use this menu to select whether to test a build on an attached device, a simulated iPhone, or a simulated iPad.
- **Breakpoints.** This button is set automatically when you use the Debugger tool. You can use it to enable and disable *breakpoints*—pauses you can insert into your code that give you a chance to check what your app is doing. For details see Chapter 12.
- **Status pane.** This glassy-looking mini-window reports what Xcode is doing. It also reports current errors.

Introducing the Navigator area

The icons above the navigator area are somewhat cryptic. Some are useful only while debugging. Here's a short summary of each option. The first three items are used for editing:

- **Project navigator (file icon).** Click this icon to show the files included in a project.
- **Symbol navigator (one large and two small blocks).** Click this icon to show the symbols used in the project. See Chapter 5 for more information symbols, classes, and objects.
- **Search navigator (magnifying glass).** Use this option to perform find or replace operations on words and expressions in the files in your project.

The next four items are used while testing and debugging:

- **Issue navigator (warning triangle).** Click this icon to list errors in the project after a build fails. Errors can include mistakes in the code and in the project settings.
- **Debug navigator (two thin lines around a thicker dashed line).** This advanced option shows multiple *threads*. iOS can do many things simultaneously—as can your apps, with suitable code. This is called *multi-threading*. This feature can select one thread for debugging.

- **Breakpoint navigator (breakpoint arrow).** This option shows all the current breakpoints inserted into the project. You can use it to enable, disable, and delete breakpoints. (This is quicker than looking through every file in the project by hand.)
- **Log navigator (speech balloon).** Whenever you build or debug a project, Xcode creates a log file. This navigator shows all log files created for the current project.

Using the Project navigator

You'll spend most of your time using the Project navigator. Clicking a file in this navigator loads it into the Editor area.

Note

This auto-loading is one of Xcode's sleeker features. You don't need to use File ➪ Open to load files into the Editor; you can simply click them in the navigator. You don't need to save them either. All modified files are saved automatically before you build a project.

The Project navigator has some hidden subtleties. Because it's such a critical part of Xcode, it's vital that you understand how it works. If you don't, you can destroy a saved project by accident, with no way to get it back.

You need to remember these three key points:

- **The Project navigator is not a Finder window.** Although the window looks like a view of files and folders on disk, the "folders" that appear here are called groups; they don't exist on disk. They appear in the navigator because it's convenient to group related files together, but the groupings are a tool for convenient display—and nothing more.
- **Files in a project can be anywhere on disk.** It's possible, but unusual, to keep every file in a project in a single folder on disk. More typically, a project includes a core collection of files in one folder, plus other files kept in other locations. This makes it easy to reuse important files in multiple projects without having to copy them.

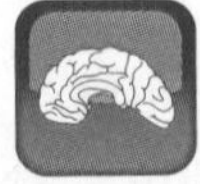

Genius

You can find files on disk by selecting them in the Project navigator and then showing the Identity pane in the Utility window. (Select the first icon.) Xcode uses the information here to show the full or relative path to a file. Most files use a "relative to Group" path, which makes it possible to copy a project folder without destroying the relationships between files. If Xcode loses a file, click the tiny icon under the menu arrows to open a Finder window and find it again.

- **You must use the Project navigator to access build settings.** Clicking the project name at the top of this area opens a special editor window for these settings; you'll read more about them later in this chapter.

Listing and grouping project files

Figure 2.10 shows a typical Project navigator display. When you create a new project of your own in Chapter 3, you'll see a similar list of files and folders.

However, you must remember a critical point about this display. Although it looks like a view of folders and files on disk, *it isn't.* In fact, the navigator displays the files included in your project. The files can be anywhere on disk.

The icons that look like folders aren't folders at all; they're *groups,* and they don't actually exist on disk. Groups are files you choose to group together in the navigator for your convenience. You can arrange the files and groups in the navigator as you want. Adding and removing groups doesn't change the organization of the files you see in Finder, as shown in Figure 2.11.

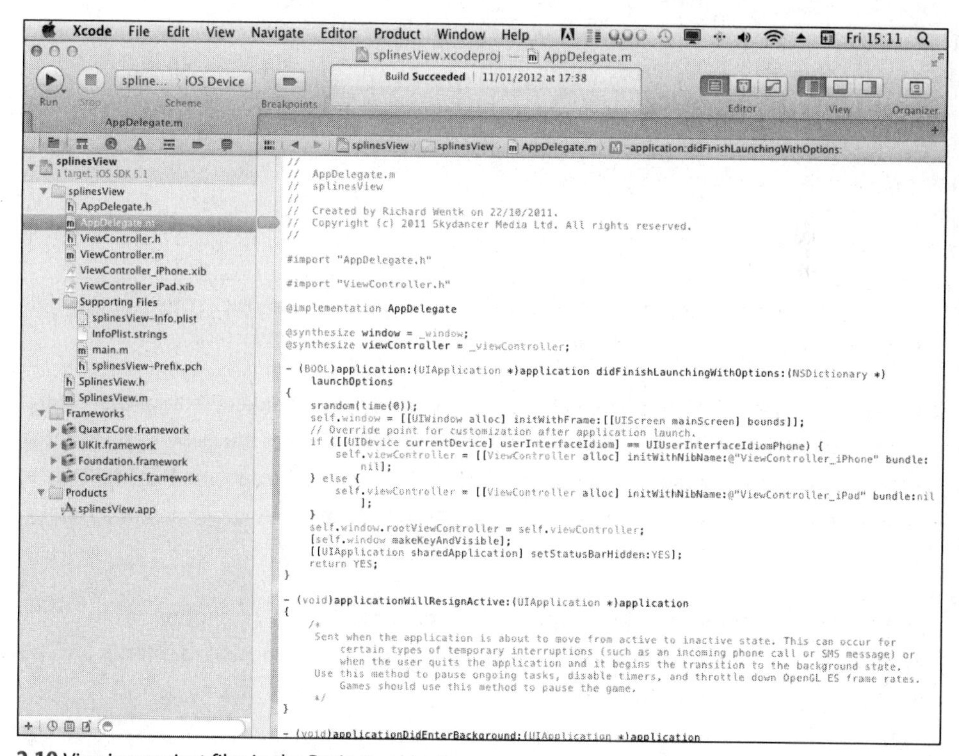

2.10 Viewing project files in the Project navigator.

Viewing build settings

When you click the light blue icon/bar that includes the project name at the top of the Project navigator, you see the area shown in Figure 2.12.

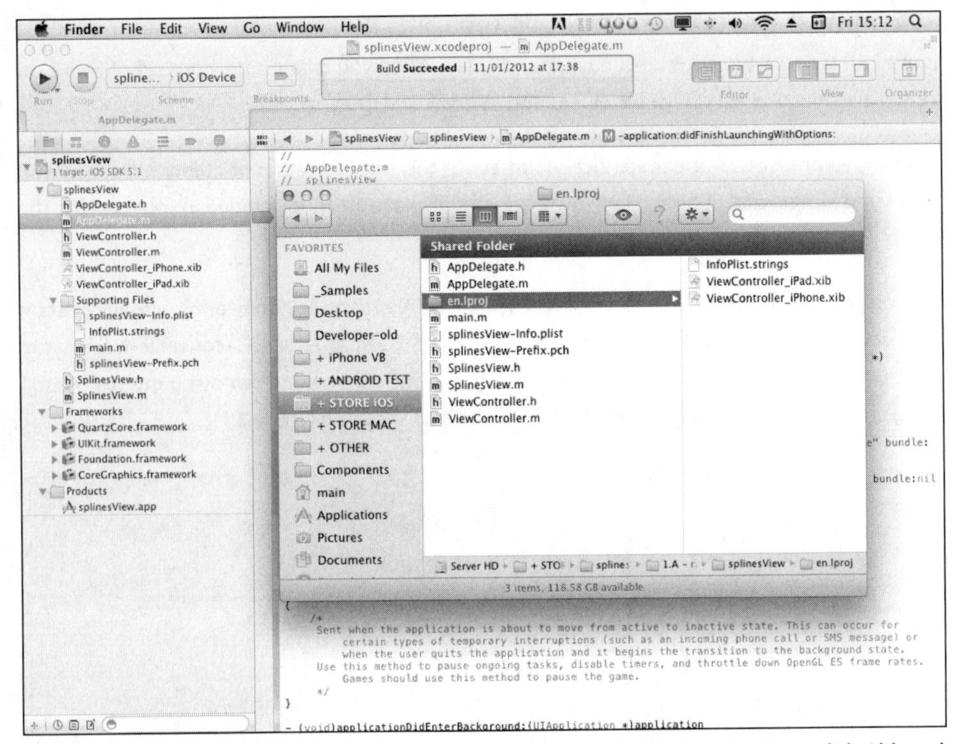

2.11 Viewing the same files in Finder. The organization shown in Xcode doesn't exist on disk. Although Xcode does keep most files in a single folder on disk, some files may be in other locations.

You can use these pages to access *build settings*—basic and advanced project settings that control how Xcode converts code into an app. Only a few of the hundred or so settings here are essential; for example, you must use the build settings to define the name of the app and the image (icon) file that appears when it's installed on an iOS device. These essential settings are described later in this book.

Other settings are useful, but optional. Advanced developers use these settings to customize the steps Xcode uses as it builds an app and to control which files are included. Most settings are very optional indeed, and you can ignore them.

Caution

Clicking the project name is the only way to access these settings. This option isn't clearly labeled, and it's easy to miss it if you don't know about it. It's a good idea to view and hide the build settings a few times so you'll remember this feature when you need it.

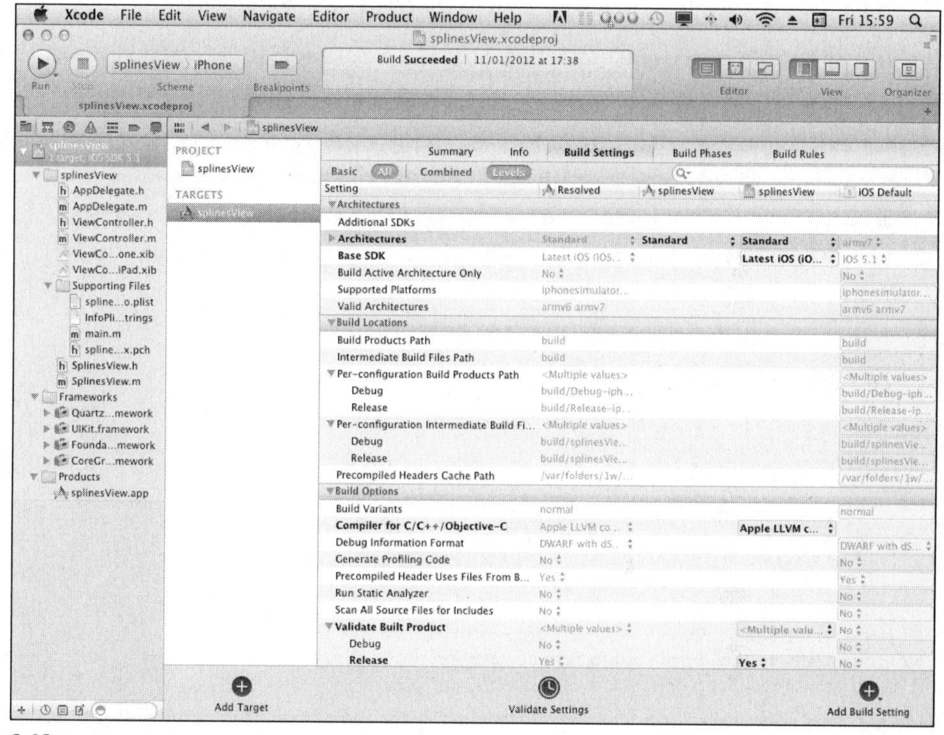

2.12 Viewing project build settings.

Caution

Don't experiment with the build settings until you know more about what they do. You can't damage your Mac, but you can damage a project and keep it from building successfully.

Introducing the Editor area

The Editor area, shown in Figure 2.13, includes basic text-editing features, but it offers much more:

- **Color highlighting.** Different elements in the code are automatically displayed with different colors. For example, keywords appear in pink, code you enter is in black, comments are in green, and so on.

- **Auto-completion.** Xcode does its best to guess your intentions as you type. Much of the time, you can type a few letters, hit the Tab or Return key, and Xcode will complete your typing for you. Where there's more than one auto-completion option, you can use the up/down arrow keys to select between them.
- **Error flagging and correction.** Xcode checks your code as you type. Errors are marked almost immediately. Some basic errors can be corrected automatically.
- **Automatic indentation and bracketing.** Xcode automatically indents code as you type. There's also an automated bracket ("delimiter") highlighting and auto-insertion feature.
- **Automatic editor selection.** Most code files contain text and appear in the text editor. Files with the .xib extension are created and edited in Interface Builder, Xcode's graphic UI design tool, which was introduced briefly in Chapter 1. When you click a file with an .xib extension—known as a *nib file*—Xcode loads it into Interface Builder automatically.

```
{
    srandom(time(0));
    self.window = [[UIWindow alloc] initWithFrame:[[UIScreen mainScreen] bounds]];
    self.window
                                   customization after application launch.
                                   Device] userInterfaceIdiom] == UIUserInterfaceIdiomPhone) {
        self.viewController = [[ViewController alloc] initWithNibName:@"ViewController_iPhone" bundle:nil
            ];
    } else {
        self.viewController = [[ViewController alloc] initWithNibName:@"ViewController_iPad" bundle:nil];
    }
    self.window.rootViewController = self.viewController;
    [self.window makeKeyAndVisible];
    [[UIApplication sharedApplication] setStatusBarHidden:YES];
    return YES;
}

- (void)applicationWillResignActive:(UIApplication *)application
{
    /*
     Sent when the application is about to move from active to inactive state. This can occur for certain
         types of temporary interruptions (such as an incoming phone call or SMS message) or when the
         user quits the application and it begins the transition to the background state.
     Use this method to pause ongoing tasks, disable timers, and throttle down OpenGL ES frame rates.
         Games should use this method to pause the game.
     */
}
```

2.13 Xcode's editor, showing a floating auto-completion suggestion box.

Caution

Interface Builder is a large add-on to Xcode. Files with the .xib extension may take a minute or two to load after you click them.

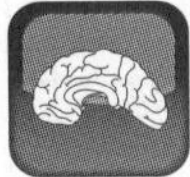

Genius

The Editor ➪ Structure option in the main Xcode menu includes some useful editing time-savers. Re-indent tidies up a selected block of code after editing. You can also comment or uncomment entire blocks by selecting them and typing ⌘/. Advanced developers can use the related Editor ➪ Code Folding menu option to move blocks of code between files, but a full description is outside the scope of this book.

Introducing iOS and the Apple Documentation

At first sight, the iOS documentation appears to be an intimidating jumble of documents. If you're new to app development, the introductory page shown in Figure 2.14 includes an impressive collection of words you won't have encountered before. You may feel that it's not obvious where to start or how to find what you need to know.

Before looking at the documentation in detail, let's look at iOS from a developer's point of view. As a developer, you can think of iOS as a kit of ready-made parts that you can include in your apps. It's up to you to select the parts to use and to "wire" them together with code so they exchange information with each other and with iOS itself.

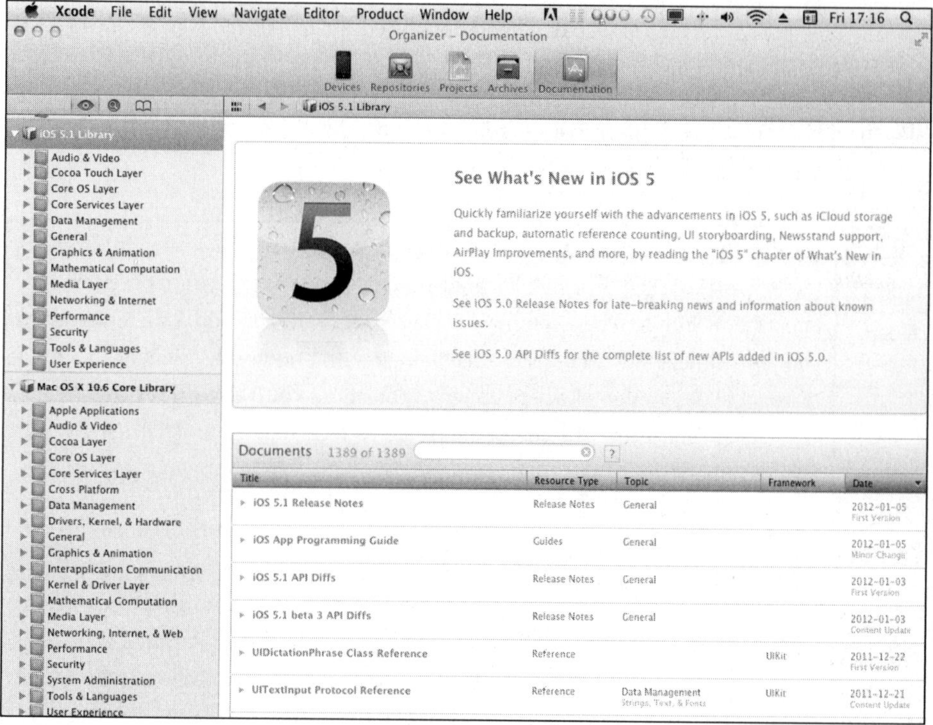

2.14 Apple's documentation includes all the details developers need to create iOS apps.

A few of the standard parts are obligatory. One obligatory part contains the app itself, and it must be included before other parts work.

A slightly larger number of parts aren't obligatory, but they're used in almost every app. For example, most apps include a part called a *view controller* that manages the visible elements in the app and responds to user actions. Many apps also include *arrays* and *dictionaries* that organize information used by the app.

Most parts are optional. For example, iOS includes a complete kit of parts for displaying and using maps. If your app doesn't use a map, you don't need these parts. You can ignore them, and if you never add a map to an app, you need never learn about them. Similarly optional app elements include sound support, video support, advanced text effects, advanced graphic effects, animations—and hundreds of other features.

Apple can't know in advance which parts developers want to use, so *the documentation includes details for all of them.* It also includes selected example projects that demonstrate how to use certain parts. These basic elements are supported with summaries, notes, and introductory essays. These documents are intended to help beginners get started and to help more experienced developers avoid pitfalls and common mistakes.

Using the documentation effectively is a key skill in its own right. Before you look at it in detail, it's useful to understand how it's organized.

Note

Technically, parts are called *classes* and *objects.* A class is a specification that defines the information that a part holds and how it behaves when your app exchanges information with it. When you use the class specification to add a working part to your app, it becomes an object. (This definition isn't rigorously scientific, but it's a reasonable description of what happens in practice.) You'll also come across *protocols,* which define how objects communicate with each other, and *functions,* which are convenient prewritten code snippets that you can drop into your app to solve common problems.

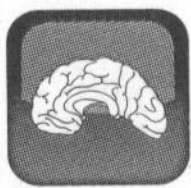

Genius

Note that you can customize existing parts to modify them and extend. You can also create new parts to your own design. Most apps include at least a handful of customized parts. Technically, customization is called *subclassing*. There's more about classes, objects, and customization in Chapter 6.

Understanding Resource Types

The documentation launches with an entry point for browsing, with a brief introduction at the top of the page; this is usually a graphic, and it usually includes some links. A sortable and searchable list of documents appears under this area.

A key entry point for the Documentation is the list of Resource Types at the top left of this starting window, shown in Figure 2.15. Although there are ten document types here (another one or two are posted by Apple regularly but don't appear here), there are really only four kinds of information:

- **Release notes and API diffs.** These documents summarize the most recent changes to iOS. Release notes describe the changes, and API (Application Programming Interface) diffs summarize the classes (parts) that have been changed, added, or removed. When a new version of iOS is announced, you can read these notes for a list of important changes.
- **General technical help.** This is a slightly chaotic collection of Articles, Technical Notes, Coding How-Tos, Guides, Technical Q&As, Getting Started, and Xcode Tasks. These documents are written summaries of key information. Some have supporting illustrations. They vary from short introductions to very detailed notes about specific issues.
- **Sample code.** These documents are working sample projects. They include all the code and files you need to load them into Xcode, build them, and run them. You can read the code, edit it, and experiment with it.
- **Reference.** You'll spend most of your time reading reference documents. The references include detailed class specifications that list the features of a class. Use this information to discover what a class does and how to use it.

Caution

The quality of the general technical help is extremely variable. Some documents are genuinely helpful. Many are terse, even those labeled as Getting Started documents. Quite a few are so terse that they leave out critical information, or they are written in a style that makes them difficult to understand until you've mastered the content. As you'll see later in this chapter, the most productive way to learn app development is to combine the documentation with help from other sources.

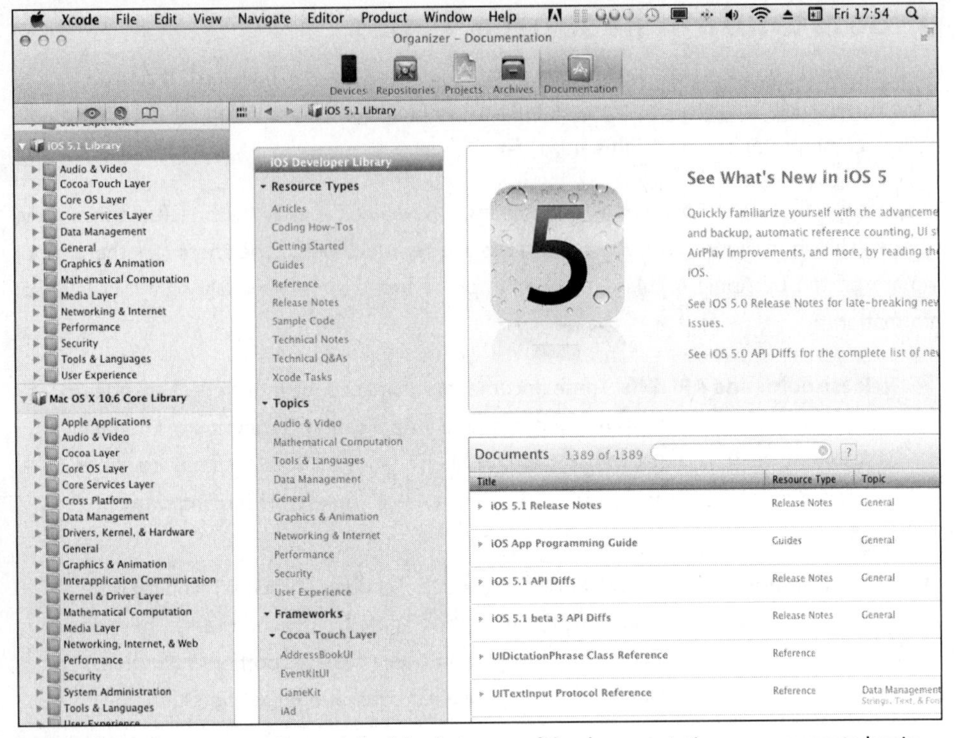

2.15 The Resource Types at the top left of the first page of the documentation are one way to begin exploring it.

Understanding Topics

The Topics headers filter the documents in the library, so you can select them by broad topic areas and hide the documents that aren't relevant to a topic.

Topics include the standard selection of resource types. For example, the Audio and Video topic shown in Figure 2.16 includes a Coding How-To, a Getting Started, a selection of Guides, and so on.

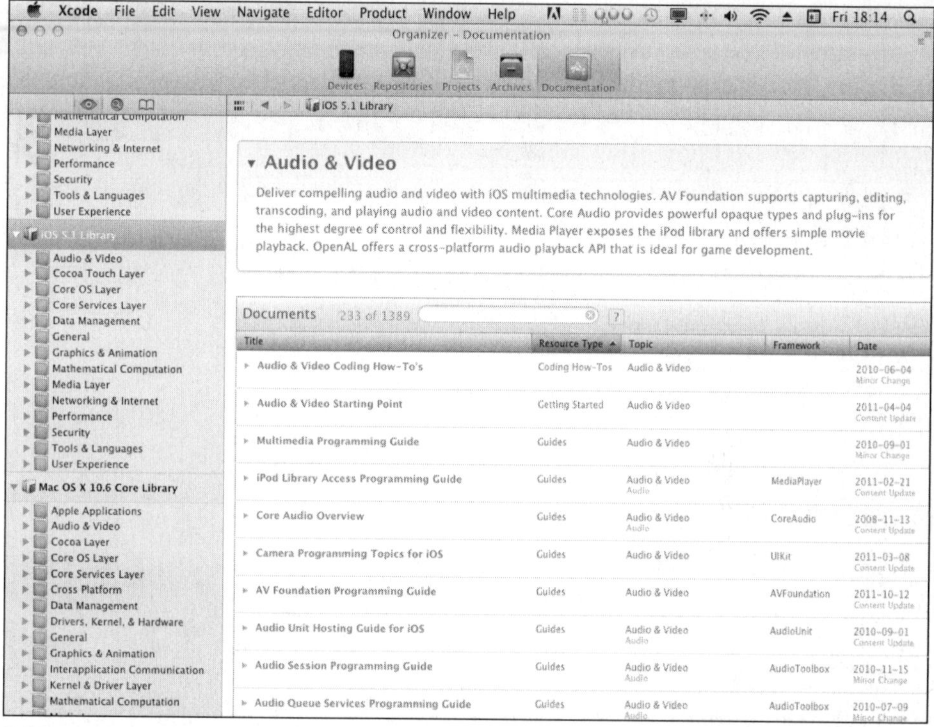

2.16 Selecting the Audio & Video topic filters the list of documents so that only relevant documents are shown.

Understanding frameworks and layers

Beginners often begin looking at the documentation by trying to understand layers. Unfortunately, layers are one of the more confusing and least consistent elements in iOS. It's better to ignore them and concentrate instead on *frameworks.*

Where classes are individual parts that do a single specific job, frameworks are collections of related classes. For example, the UIKit framework shown in Figure 2.17 is one of the largest frameworks in iOS. It includes all the parts and features you need to create and manage your app's user interface, including buttons and sliders, image display classes, printer support, gesture recognizers, and hundreds of others options.

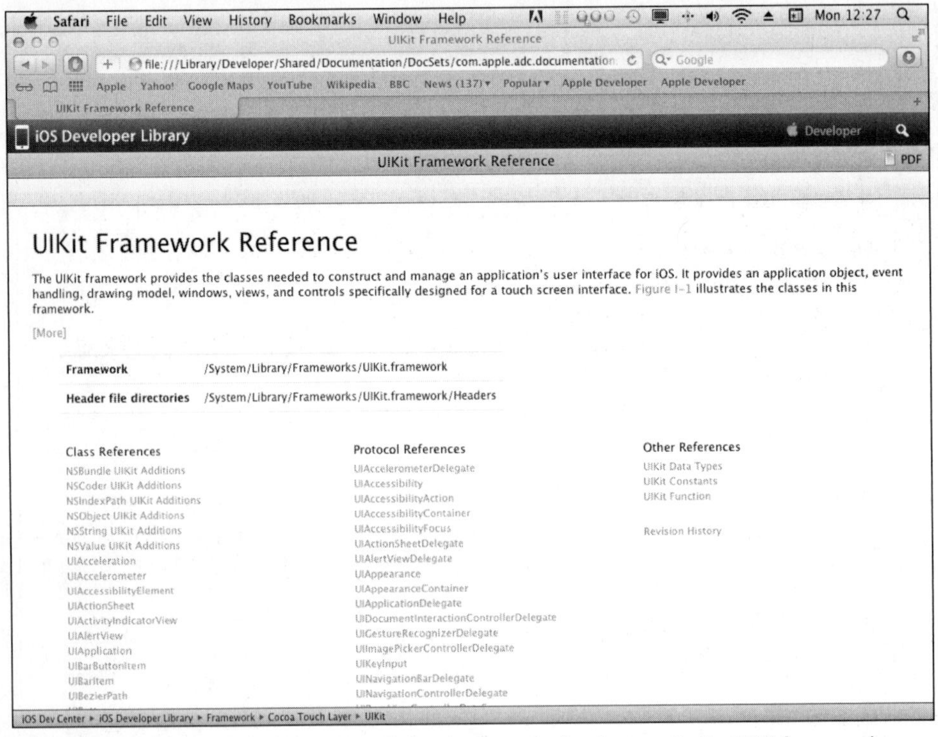

2.17 The UIKit Reference document lists all the classes and other features in the UIKit framework.

Note

Technically, frameworks are collections of related classes, and layers are collections of related frameworks. This seems to make sense, until you discover that the number and organization of the layers in iOS is described differently in different parts of the documentation.

Caution

One of the most challenging parts of learning iOS is realizing that words don't always mean what you expect them to. You'll discover categories, protocols, classes, frameworks, delegates, and others. The technical meanings of these words aren't closely related to their plain-English meanings. When you meet a new word, *forget the English meaning* and spend some time understanding what it means in the context of iOS.

You must remember these critical points when dealing with frameworks:

- **Three frameworks are included in every app by default.** They're listed in Table 2.1. You should read the relevant framework reference to explore the features.
- **You must add other frameworks to your project by hand before you can use the classes in them.** There's more about this in Chapters 6 and 7.
- **Audio, video, and graphics features are spread across multiple frameworks.** You might expect them to be bundled together, but they're not. This is because...
- **...there's more than one way to add audio, video, and graphics features to your app.** You can usually choose a simple framework with limited options or a more challenging framework with powerful features. For some applications, you'll choose both; when you're working with graphics, you get even more options.
- **You *must* look at the Framework Reference document before using a framework.** This is the only way to find recent additions to the framework and to see which functions and other supporting features are available.

Table 2.1 Default Frameworks in iOS

Framework	Used for...
UIKit	Creating the user interface. Manages visible objects such as buttons, sliders, and tables. Also manages touch events, gesture recognition, printing, and accelerometer features, among many others.
Foundation	A grab-bag of miscellaneous classes and functions that manage objects, network connections, and other essential low-level features. (Don't confuse Foundation with the Core Foundation framework. They're not identical.)
CoreGraphics	Many low-level graphics features, including support for paths, colors, and basic geometry. You'll usually need to add other graphics frameworks for more advanced effects, including animations and game support.

Caution

If you don't check the reference document for a framework reference, you *will* miss critical features. At best, this leads to confusion; for example, you won't be able to understand how related sample code works. At worst, you can waste lots of time reinventing features that already exist.

Using the documentation browser

Understanding the documentation browser is a key way to cut through the apparent clutter. You can use the browser to highlight certain types of information by clicking the gray bar above the "links" to select different views of the documentation, as follows:

- **Title.** Click this header to display an unordered alphabetical list. You'll find this is one of the least useful options.
- **Resource Type.** Click this to sort by resource type, as shown in Figure 2.18. This option is particularly useful for finding sample code and class references.
- **Topic.** Click this to sort by topic. Note that some files aren't tagged with a topic and that the list of topics matches the list at the left of the Organizer, but it isn't the same as the list of topics at the left of the main browser window.

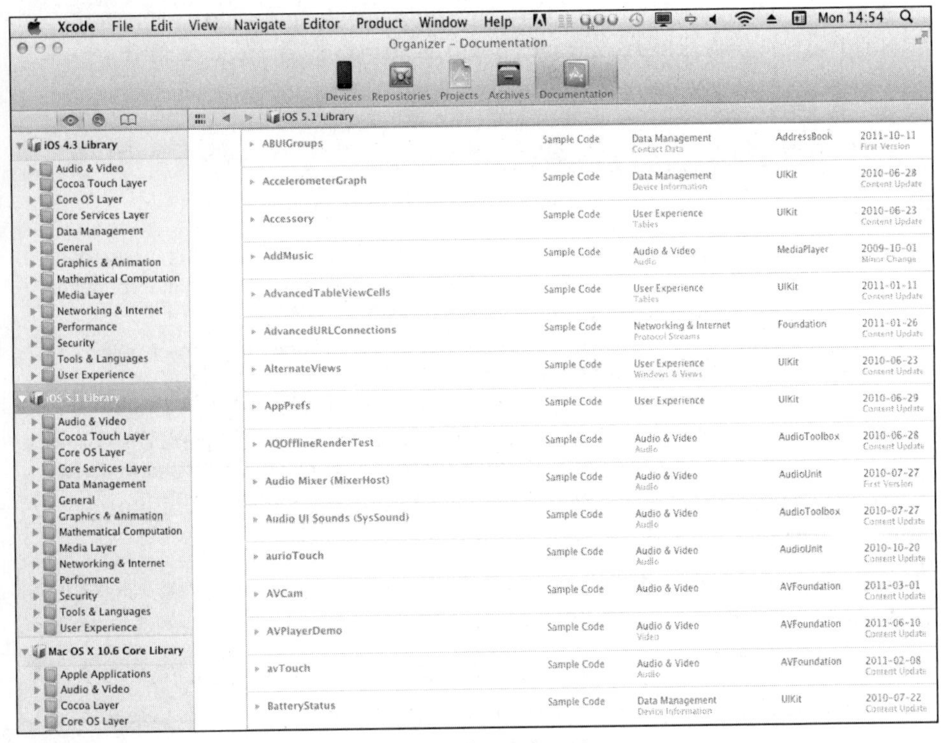

2.18 Sorting by resource type to select and view all sample projects.

- **Framework.** Click to sort the Framework column into an alphabetical list. Use this option to find documents about a specific framework.
- **Date.** Click to sort by date. Click again to alternate between the most recent and the oldest date. Use this option to show the most recent updates to iOS and the most recent documents that describe them.

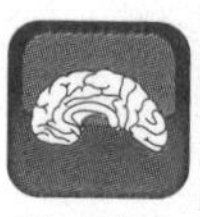

Genius

If you sort by resource type and need to resort alphabetically, click the Title header and click the Resource Type header again.

Accessing the documentation

Now that you've been introduced to the contents of the documentation, you can begin to use it. You can access the documentation in three ways:

- **Click the Documentation icon in the Organizer.**
- **Click the iOS Developer Library link on the main iOS Dev Center page.**
- **Run a web search.**

Each choice offers different options.

Accessing documentation in the Organizer

There are four advantages to viewing documentation within Xcode itself:

- **You can view and search the documentation for all related operating systems.** This is both a benefit and a danger. *Be careful to select the correct version of iOS.* And don't read the documentation for OS X; the two operating systems share some classes, but otherwise they have little in common. You can't use OS X-only classes in iOS.
- **You can view an extended list of topics.** The topic lists at the left of the Organizer view include an extra few topics not shown in the standard browser view.
- **You can use built-in search tools to look through the entire documentation.** Click the magnifying glass icon to open the search feature, shown in Figure 2.19. You can view extended search options by clicking the tiny black triangle in the search box. Use this option to eliminate older versions of iOS from your searches.
- **You can create your own bookmarks.** Click the bookmark icon to create a bookmark. (Note that bookmarks have a habit of disappearing when you uninstall or update Xcode.)

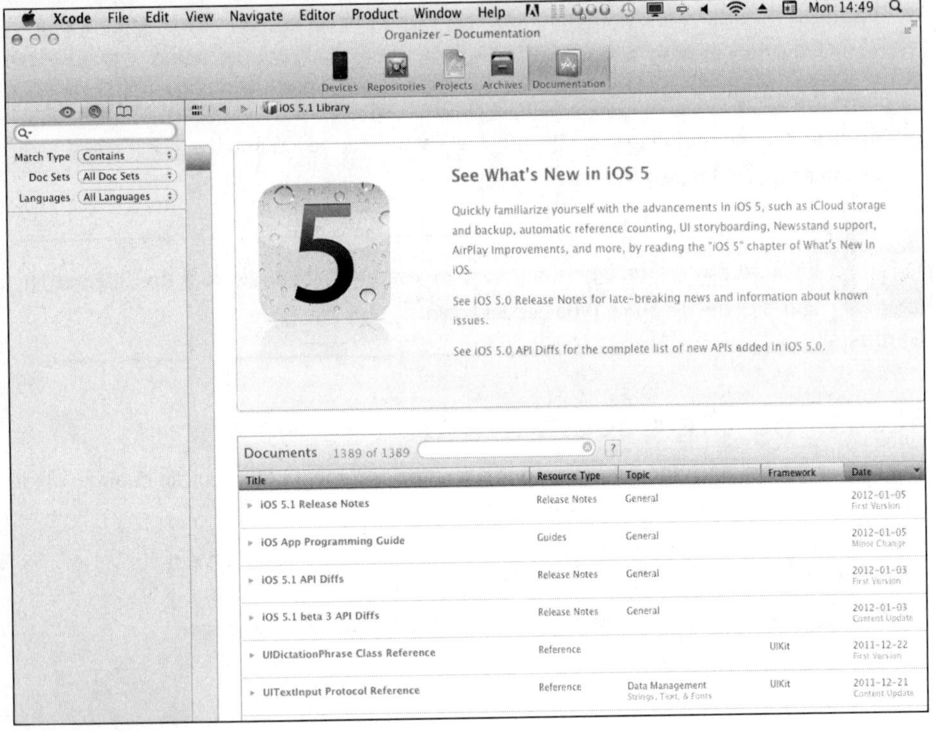

2.19 Accessing the Organizer search tool.

Caution

The version of the documentation in the Organizer is a changeable hybrid of offline and online documentation. When there's a new version of iOS, it's not unusual for the documentation to be temporarily inaccessible in the first beta version. It's also not unusual for new features to remain undocumented until later betas.

Accessing the documentation from a web browser

The online Developer Library in the iOS Dev Center is web-based, so you can access it from any web browser. The Organizer doesn't support tabbed browsing, so this is a particularly useful and productive option. You'll often have 10 or 20 class references open at the same time in multiple tabs, with further browsing of Guides, How-Tos, and other non-Apple resources in other windows. Using a web browser makes it possible to create a bookmark library that survives Xcode updates.

Although it's difficult to search for some of the resources online, it's easy to find class references. Simply search for the class name. Search engines usually return a link to Apple's documentation pages as the first hit, as shown in Figure 2.20. In this example, searching for UISlider—the class that creates and manages a slider on the screen—returns a link to the online version of the UISlider Class Reference document.

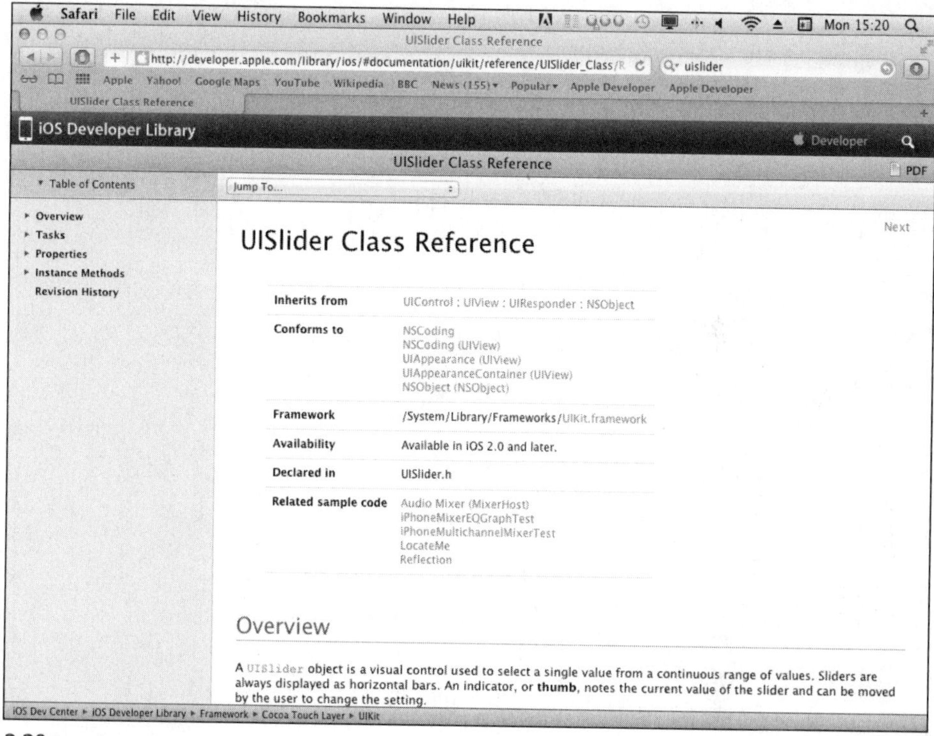

2.20 Searching the web when you know the name of a class usually returns a link to the Class Reference document.

Getting Further Help

The web is a vast resource, and it includes many postings, tutorials, and examples that you can use to save yourself time. Help from these non-Apple sources isn't optional: It can be a huge time-saver for you as a new developer, because you can explore sample projects and in-depth discussions at every level.

To find examples and tutorials, search the web. For example, to find out more information about using sound in iOS, search for "iOS sound tutorial," as shown in Figure 2.21. You'll occasionally need to narrow the search by including the word "dev" or "developer" in your search string.

Most common search topics return a good selection of hits. Some are complete worked solutions with sample code, while others are video- or web-based tutorials. All are likely to be easier to follow than Apple's own documentation.

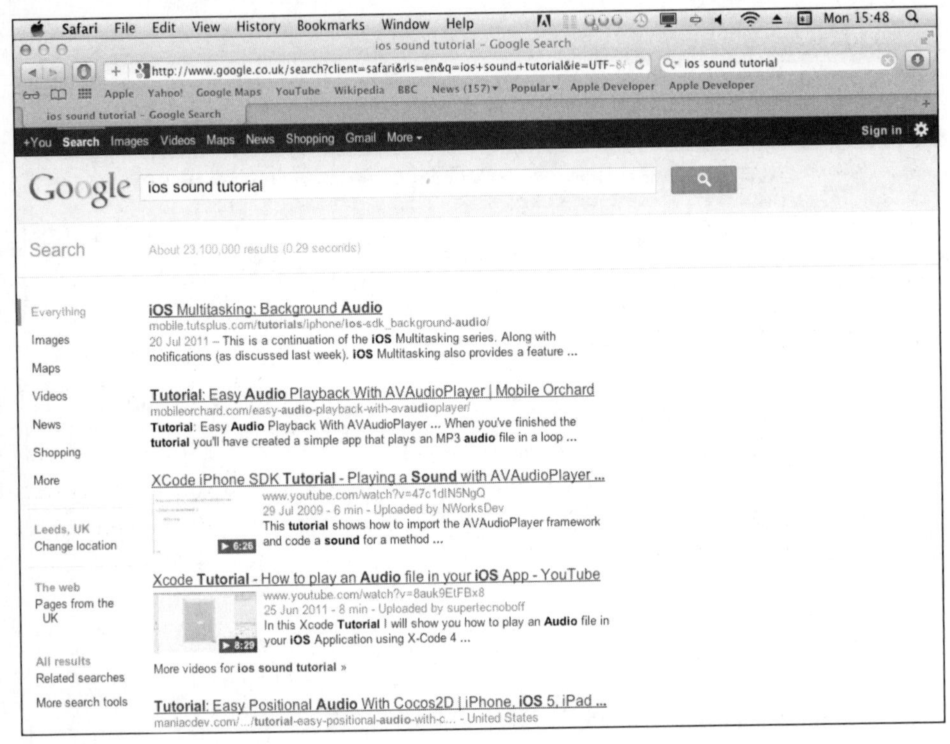

2.21 Finding useful tutorials online.

Two other sources are useful for more experienced developers:

- **StackOverflow.** This message board is used by professional developers who ask questions and solve each other's problems. Beginners are welcome as long as they don't ask very basic questions with answers that are easy to find online. You can read previous discussions without having to take part in current ones. Find it at http://stackoverflow.com/.
- **github.** This is a code repository with many iOS projects in various stages of development. Code is often public, so you can download projects, read the source code of other developers, and build projects to see what they do. Find it at https://github.com/.

Between them, these online sources can save you weeks when you're getting started.

Putting It All Together

Now that you've been introduced to help for iOS, you can develop a problem-solving strategy. Not all problems can be solved in the same way, but you'll find the following steps useful:

1. **Decide what features you want to add to your app.**
2. **Look through the topic and framework lists to find some frameworks that may include the classes you need.** Looking through the Guides and How-Tos is also useful. You won't usually find a complete solution, but you may find some pointers to relevant classes.
3. **Review the sample code to see if a full or partial solution already exists.**
4. **Run general and specific (class-based) web searches looking for message board comments related to your task and sample code.** Don't forget to check for possible third-party frameworks.

At this point, you should have enough information to begin solving your problem. The first few iterations will be challenging because you'll be learning the core techniques used in iOS, while also trying to master more advanced features. After a while, you'll no longer need help with the basic features, and you can concentrate on learning about new classes and techniques.

Now that you're ready to begin experimenting with code, it's time to learn how to build a sample application.

How Do I Build and Run an Application?

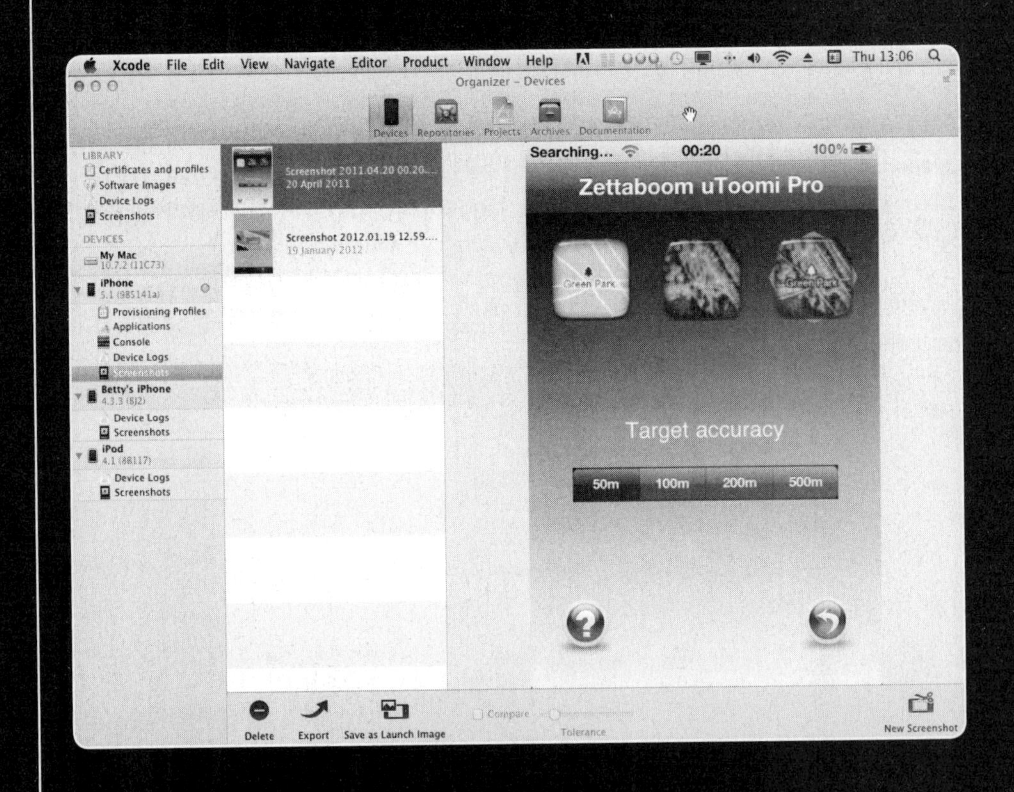

1 2 3 4 5 6 7 8 9 10 11 12 13

App development comes alive when you begin to build and test your own apps. Xcode includes a selection of simple app templates to help you get started. The official documentation includes hundreds of sample projects, and you can find many more projects online—all free. Building and running them in the Simulator is easy, but getting them running on a real device is only slightly more difficult—and more rewarding.

Building Applications

As you learned in Chapter 2, Xcode is primarily a tool for converting source files—code, media files, design templates (nib files), and other components—into an app package.

Experienced developers can customize the build process almost indefinitely. But newcomers should postpone exploring the more advanced features until they've mastered the basics of development. This is easy to do because the essentials of the build process are very simple: Just click the Run button in the main toolbar, and wait a while.

There are some minor details to master, even at the beginner level. Let's explore them now by creating a very simple app. This app does nothing; it's a dummy app shell with no working features, but it demonstrates how to convert source files into a working app, and how to run that app in the Simulator.

Creating a new project

To create a new project, follow these steps:

1. **Launch Xcode, if it isn't running already.**
2. **Select File ➪ New ➪ Project from the main menu.**
3. **Click the Application item under the iOS header at the top left, as shown in Figure 3.1.**
4. **Click the Single View Application item near the top right to highlight it.** This step selects one of the *Application Templates*—ready-made starting points for various types of apps. You'll find more about the templates later in this chapter.
5. **Click Next.**
6. **Type a product name.** This name appears under the app when it's installed on an iOS Device. It's also used by Xcode as the project name, and it automatically prefixes some of the files in the project. Keep the name short, and don't include spaces. Here, we've used MyFirstApp, as shown in Figure 3.2.

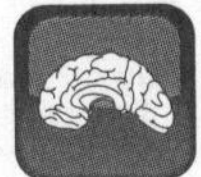

Genius

As you'd expect, if you click the Mac OS X header and select Application, Xcode creates a new Mac app. Naturally, you can run a Mac app on your Mac, but you can't run a Mac app on an iOS device because the structure and contents aren't compatible. You may want to try this option anyway, just to see what happens.

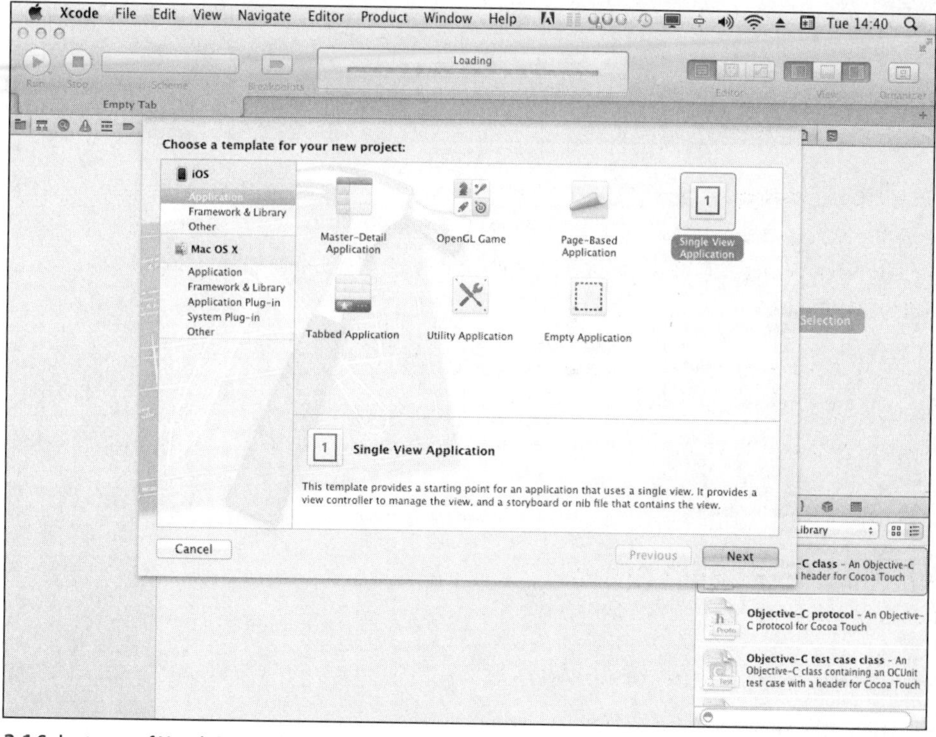

3.1 Select one of Xcode's standard preset app templates.

7. **Type a company identifier.** This should be of the form "com.[companyname]." If you enrolled in the developer program as a company, type the name here prefixed by "com." If you enrolled as an individual, type the name you want to use to identify your apps, such as your full name without spaces.
8. **Watch how Xcode creates a *bundle identifier* from the two fields you entered.** The bundle identifier is an essential part of the app store submission process and is described in Chapter 13. You can ignore it until then.
9. **Ignore the Class Prefix field.** We'll get back to this shortly.
10. **Don't change the Device Family menu.** It defaults to iPhone, which is what we want for this first project.
11. **Make sure the Use Automatic Reference Counting option is checked and the other options aren't checked.**
12. **Click Next.**

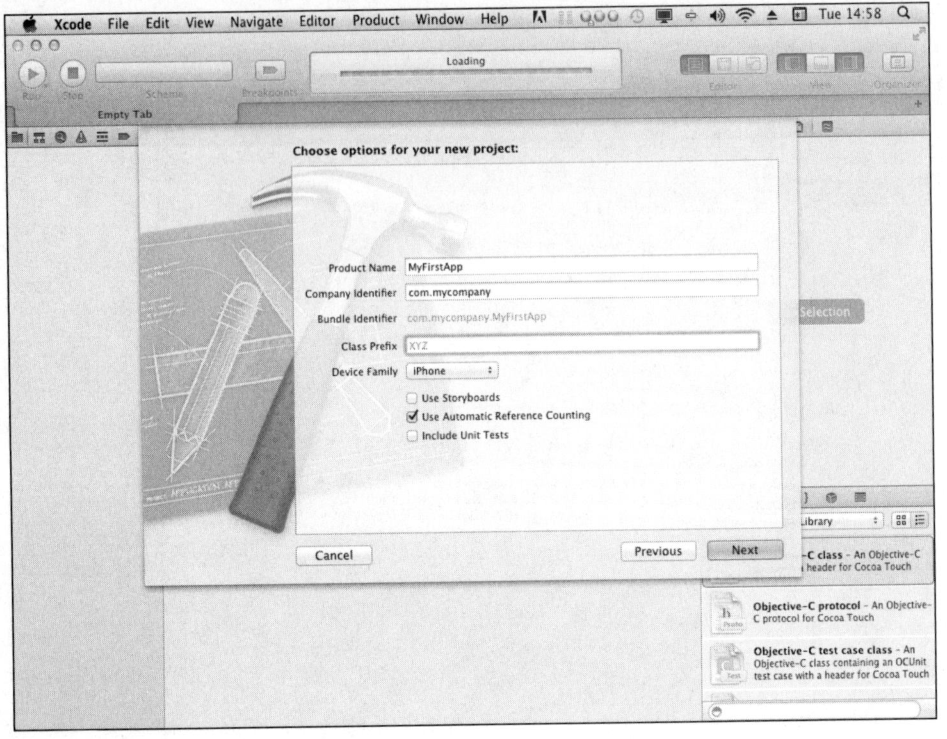

3.2 Fill in basic options for a new app.

13. **Click New Folder, and create a new folder for your projects, as shown in Figure 3.3.** It's up to you where to put the folder and what to call it. If you're planning to release apps through the app store, it's a good idea to have at least two folders—one for experiments and one for production development. Optionally, you also may want to create a third folder for projects created by other developers and downloaded from the Internet.
14. **Leave the Create local git repository for this project option unchecked.**
15. **Click Create to write the project files to disk.** Xcode creates a new project folder with a selection of essential files in the folder you nominated.

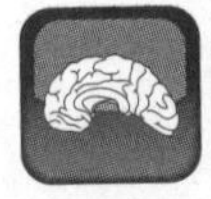
Genius

For clarity, Xcode creates a new folder for each project automatically. But to minimize disk sprawl and to keep your projects organized, it's useful to keep these project folders grouped inside a few folders of their own. A useful tip is to create them on the root folder of your system disk, because this makes them easy to access. For extra convenience, you can drag the folders to Finder's sidebar after you create them.

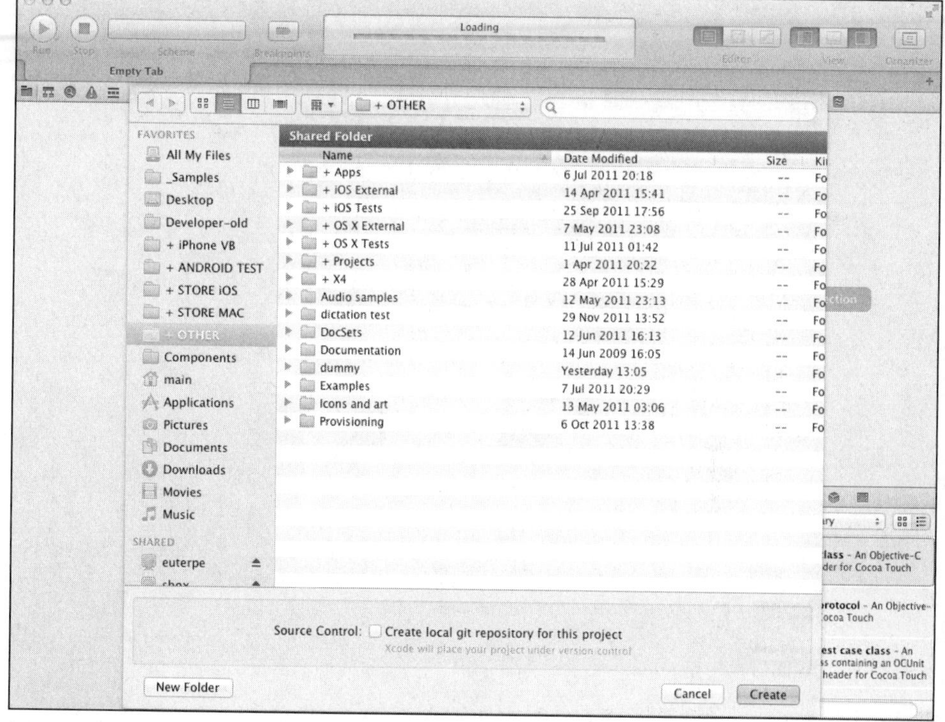

3.3 Create and select a new folder for your app projects.

Building a project

The files created for the project are shown in Figure 3.4. Note that Xcode defaults to showing you the Project Build Settings, which were introduced in Chapter 2.

We'll look at the files in the project in more detail shortly. First, let's build this project and launch it in the Simulator.

To build a project, follow these steps:

1. **Click the Scheme menu in the Toolbar, and make sure the iPhone Simulator is selected.** This menu includes the version number of the current SDK.

Caution

Be sure to click to the right of the chevron/arrow in the menu. If you click to the left of the chevron, you see a menu that takes you to Xcode's *scheme editor*. The editor is an advanced feature for users who want to customize the build process. Don't try to access it now.

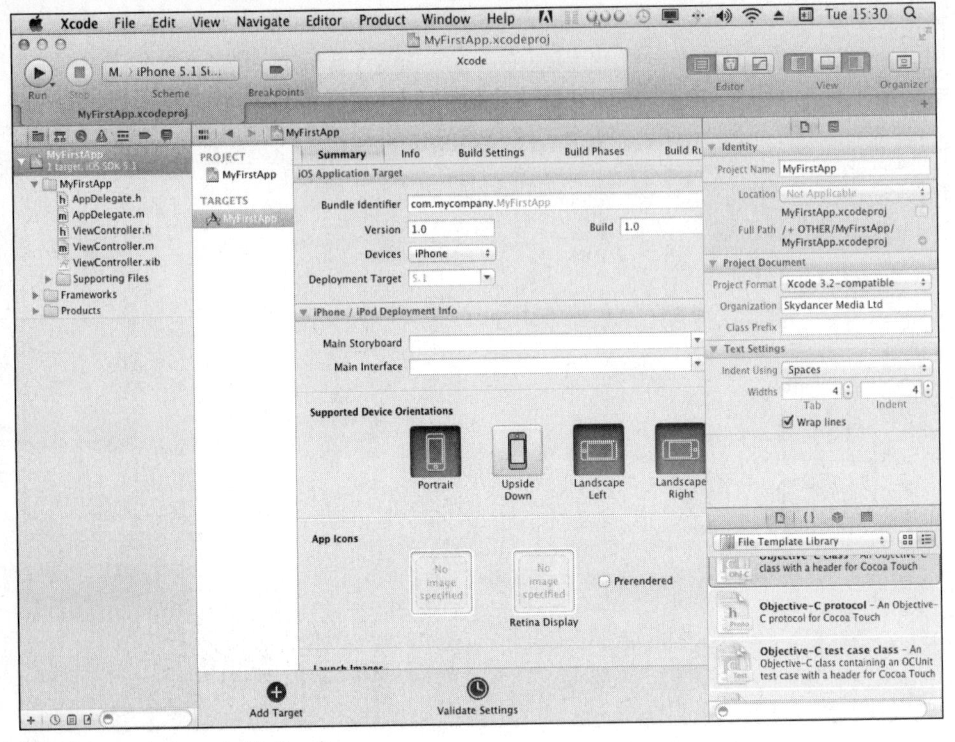

3.4 A new project created in Xcode.

2. **Click the Run button at the top left.**
3. **Watch the progress indicator in the toolbar, as Xcode builds the project.**
4. **When the build is complete, you'll see a Build Succeeded graphic flash onscreen for a couple of seconds.**
5. **Xcode launches the Simulator automatically, if it isn't running already.** Note that while it usually takes a few moments for the Simulator to launch, it can sometimes take a minute or two, especially when memory is low.
6. **The app is copied to the Simulator and run automatically, as shown in Figure 3.5.** The status message in the Toolbar status window is updated accordingly. It can take another minute or two for the Simulator to start the app and display it.
7. **Click the Stop button in the Xcode toolbar to end the run.** The app stops running in the Simulator, but the Simulator itself continues running, with a simplified version of the usual Springboard icon list. As you work with more apps, they're copied to the Simulator "desktop" and you can click them to launch them manually.

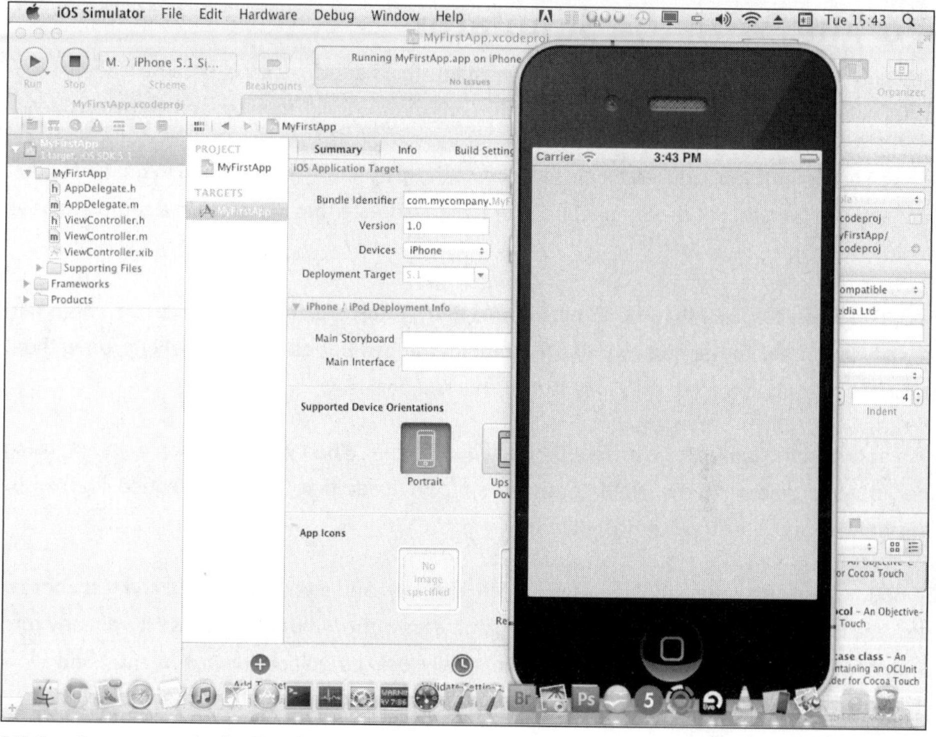

3.5 Run the new app in the Simulator.

Although the app does almost nothing (it draws a plain gray background), it is a full-fledged iPhone app.

You can't sell it. In fact, you probably can't even give it away. And its icon is blank, although you'll discover how to fix that in Chapter 10.

You can, however, use it as a base for further development, as long as you understand the limitations of the Simulator.

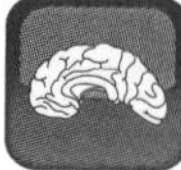

Genius

Xcode uses *incremental compilation* to speed up builds. The first time Xcode builds an app, it processes every file in the project. Subsequent builds process only files that have been changed. So you'll find that if you change a single file as you work, builds can be almost instant. This feature is automatic, so you don't need to do anything to make it work for you.

Working with the Simulator

Although the Simulator is convenient, it isn't a substitute for live device testing, because it doesn't support special features including GPS, Bluetooth, the compass, the accelerometer, and the gyroscope.

In fact, very limited support is available for most of these options—just enough to guarantee that your app won't crash. But the Simulator doesn't try to emulate these features in a comprehensive or detailed way.

Another key difference is that the Simulator runs much faster than real iOS devices do. This is particularly important for games, sound, and graphics-intensive apps. They're likely to run without stalling in the Simulator, but they may stutter on a real device.

Also note that the Simulator is an independent application. When you kill an app manually using the virtual home button, the Simulator doesn't inform Xcode that testing has ended. For consistency, always use the Stop button in Xcode.

Sometimes the Simulator simply doesn't launch correctly. And if you try to build and test another app, you'll see a message saying that Xcode can't access the Simulator because it's already running. When this happens, quit the Simulator manually (use the Quit option in its menus) and allow Xcode to re-launch it.

Finally, the iPhone and iPad Simulators share the apps you build. If you use the Home option, you'll see the same list of icons in both. Unfortunately, you can't switch between simulated devices while the Simulator is running.

Basically, the Simulator is good for designing and building app UIs. It's also useful for network- and Internet-based apps. It's less ideal for testing animated games or apps that use any of the specialized hardware in real iOS devices.

Understanding Xcode's Project Templates

Although you can build an app from scratch by adding files to an empty project, it's faster and more productive to flesh out a ready-made app skeleton.

Xcode includes a selection of app templates to get your projects started. The templates don't do much, but they create a very basic app that you can expand by adding more features.

Creating iPhone, iPad, and Universal projects

Figure 3.6 shows the new project options page, highlighting the menu that selects whether your new project will run on an iPhone, an iPad, or both platforms. (The iPhone option is compatible with iPod touch devices.)

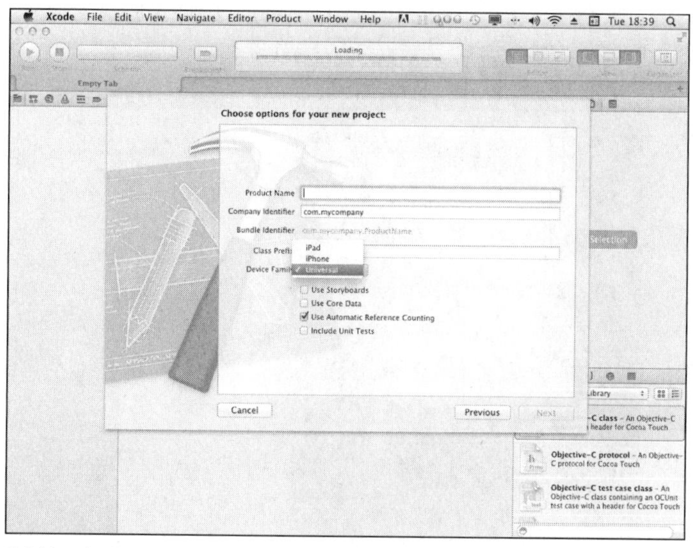

3.6 Use the Device Family menu to select the target device.

The structure of iPad and iPhone templates is very similar. But the graphic design template—the nib file, introduced in preceding chapters—is configured differently to match the differing display resolutions of each device.

If you select the iPad option from this menu, you must select the iPad Simulator when you build and run it. This loads your app into a larger simulated iPad, shown in Figure 3.7.

In the figure, we've launched MyFirstApp in the iPad Simulator. The frame in the center appears only when you run an iPhone app in the iPad Simulator. True iPad apps fill the whole window.

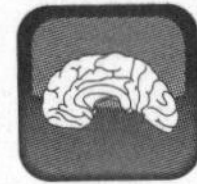

Genius

You can scale the size of the iPad window by selecting Window ➪ Scale in the Simulator menu, followed by 100%, 75%, or 50%. The current version of the iPad Simulator doesn't have a home button. To access the software equivalent, select Hardware ➪ Home.

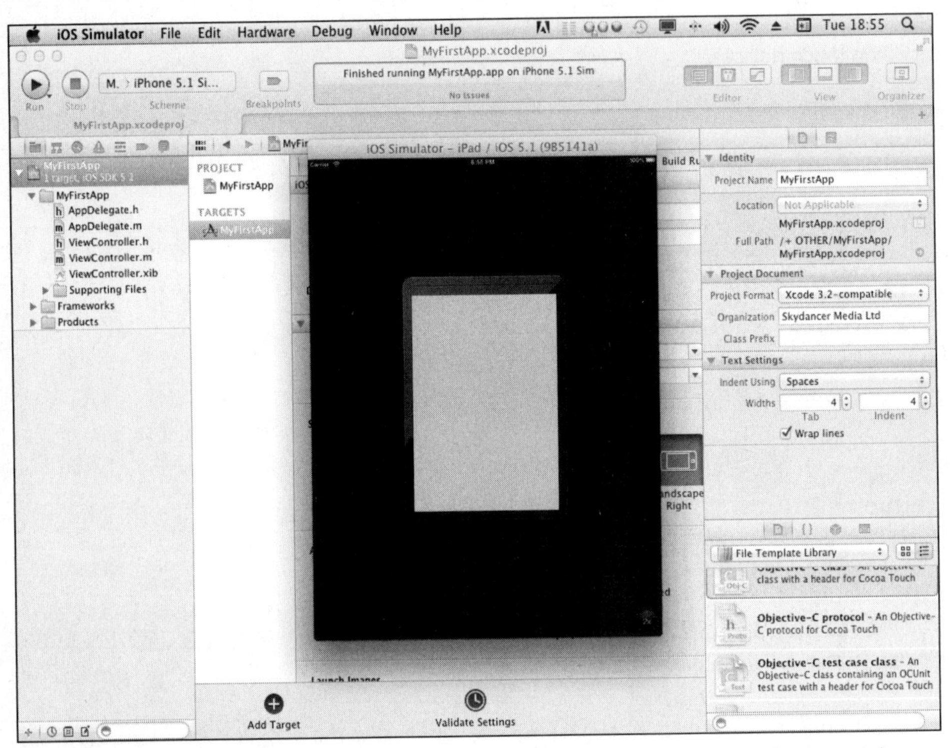

3.7 Running MyFirstApp in the iPad Simulator. Because it's an iPhone app, it runs in its own mini-window in the center of the screen.

These are the rules for compatibility between devices:

- **iPhone apps.** These run in the iPhone Simulator and in the iPad Simulator inside a frame. (You can use a "2X" button in the iPad Simulator to double the size of the iPhone app window. This is a simple zoom effect found on the iPad itself. It doesn't double the effective resolution.)
- **iPad apps.** These run in the iPad Simulator only. For iPad apps, Xcode won't let you select the iPhone Simulator from the Scheme menu.

- **Universal apps.** Universal apps include two separate design/layout (nib) files—one for the iPhone and one for the iPad. This makes universal apps compatible with both platforms.

Caution

Universal apps can be confusing initially. When you add design elements to one nib file, the changes aren't automatically copied to the other platform. This can leave you wondering why the iPhone Simulator is showing your edits, but the iPad Simulator isn't. Remember this key point: *You must add design elements to both files by hand.* A universal app is really two different apps in a single package. Code features can be shared, but the files that control the design and layout are separate.

Exploring the app templates

Each template shown in Figure 3.6 (earlier in this chapter) is designed to help you get started with a certain type of project. These projects aren't the only possible app configurations, but they're a useful starting point for certain common types of apps.

Caution

The templates that follow are included in Version 4.3 of Xcode. Apple occasionally changes, renames, or updates the templates as new features appear in iOS. The templates in later versions of Xcode are likely to be similar, but they may not be identical.

Master-Detail Application

On an iPhone, this template creates a single scrollable window with an empty table. On an iPad, the "detail view" shows a main content window with an optional table. The table slides in from the left, as shown in Figure 3.8. It can be hidden when not needed.

This template is ideal for apps that use a menu structure to select and display data. The code includes some, but not all, of the features needed to display a table using a class called UITableView. You must add further features to manage editing by hand.

Note

When you create a Master-Detail application, the project options include a check box for Core Data. Core Data is a complex data management framework that can be included in iOS apps and is often used with tables—although it isn't obligatory, and you can fill tables with data from other frameworks and classes. Core Data is too complex for an introductory book, but you can find more details online or in a more advanced book, such as *Cocoa* in Wiley's Developer Reference series.

OpenGL Game

OpenGL is a very complex framework used for games, advanced animations, and other graphics. The OpenGL Game template creates a *context*—an area of memory that can be displayed onscreen. It also displays two animated rotating cubes, as shown in Figure 3.9.

Like Core Data, OpenGL is a complex framework whose details are outside the scope of this book. iOS supports a simplified version of the framework called OpenGL ES, optimized for mobile devices. OpenGL ES is well documented online, and there are plenty of beginner tutorials that you can explore. But unless you want to get started with advanced game development, it's better to spend more time on app development essentials before trying to master it.

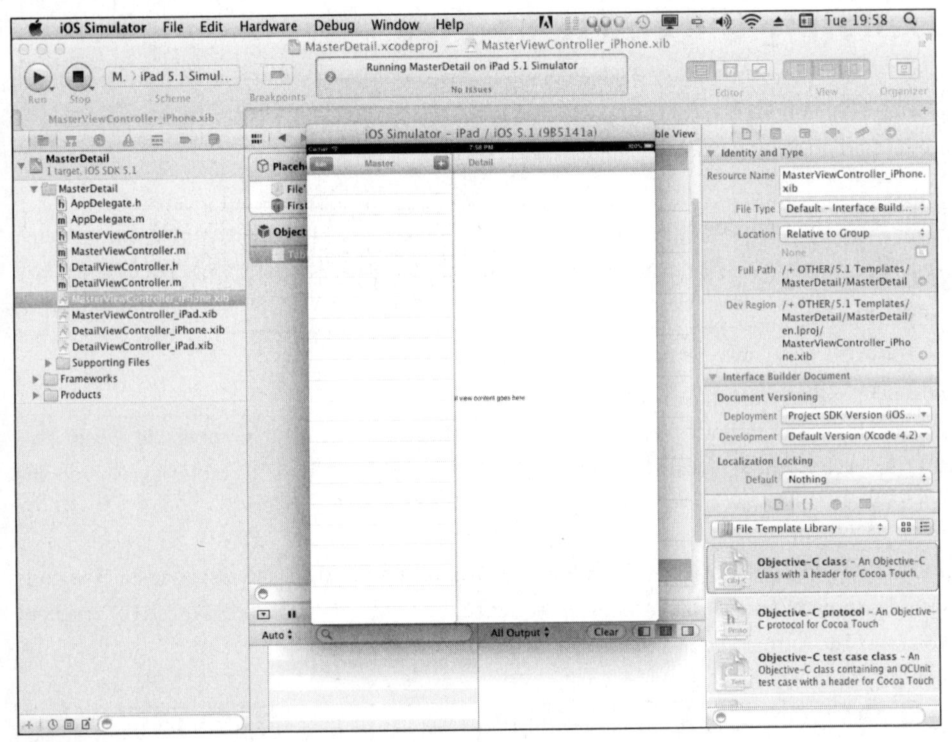

3.8 The Master-Detail template running in the iPad Simulator.

Note

There are simpler ways to create graphic effects in iOS! OpenGL ES is ideal for complex 3D animations, but it's possible to create simpler games—even ones with 3D effects—without it.

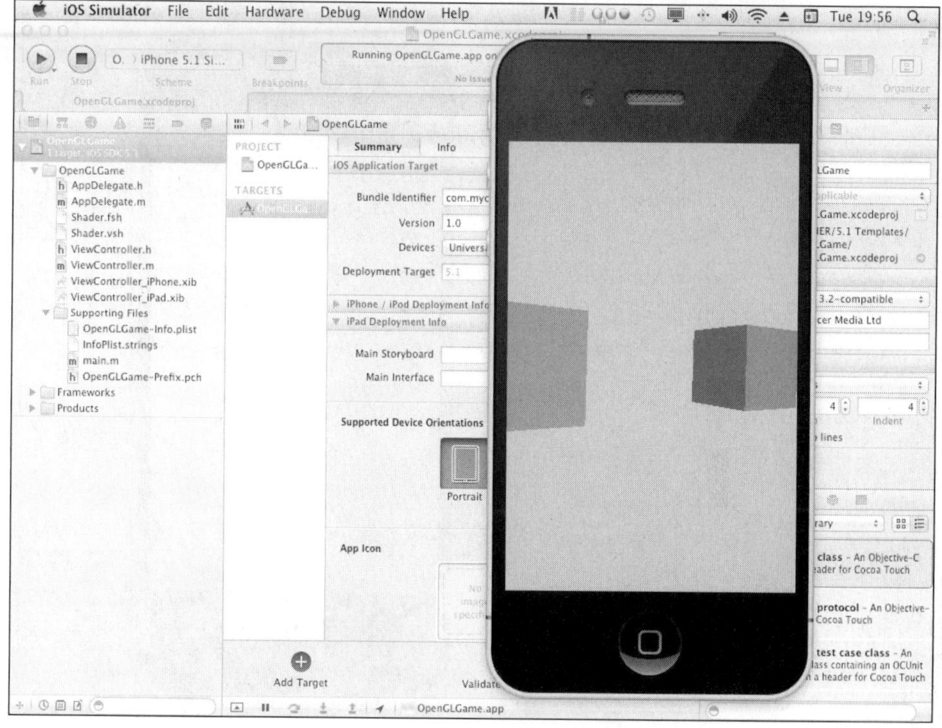

3.9 The OpenGL Game template, which displays two animated rotating cubes.

Page-Based Application

This template simulates a book with pages that you can turn by touching and dragging, as shown in Figure 3.10. The page effects are created automatically by feeding data to a class called UIPageViewController. The default data in the template shows empty pages headed by a list of months. Your code must fill in the pages with other data. Text is relatively easy to add. More complex code can display animations or video.

Single-View Application

We've already experimented with this template and used it to create a very simple app with a static gray background.

Technically, this template creates an app with a single *view*. In app jargon, a view is an object that appears in the display and can draw on the screen. Views are managed by a *view controller*—an invisible object that loads and unloads views from memory as they're needed, manages screen rotation, and so on. Optionally, a view controller can be programmed to switch between views—with animation effects, if you want them—in response to some user action.

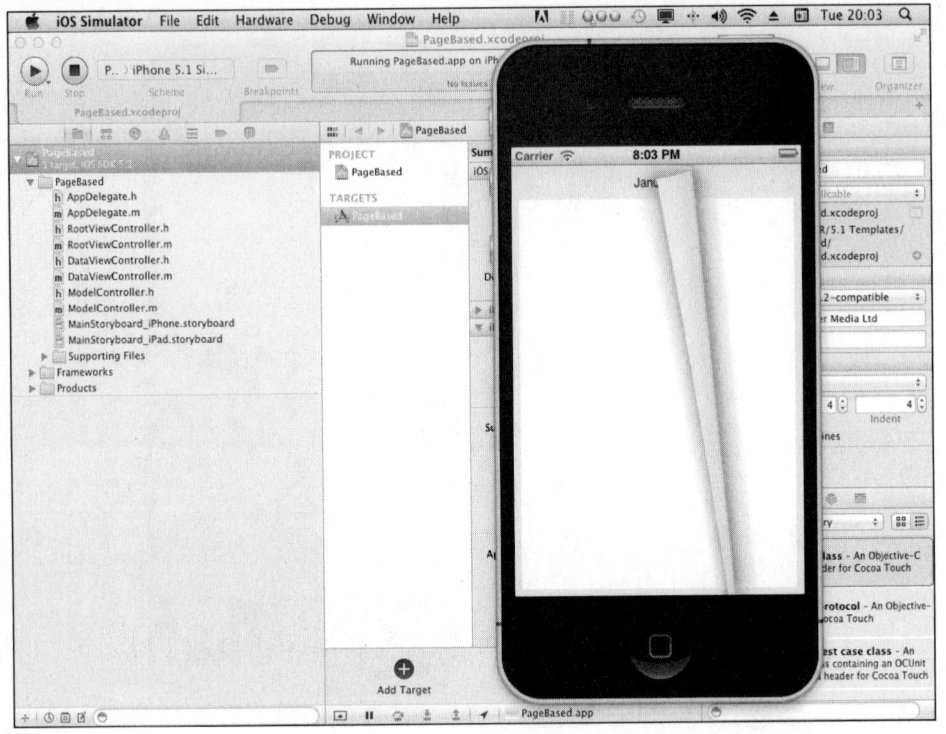

3.10 The Page-Based Application template creates a book-like app with simulated pages.

This app is a good generic blank canvas for an app. But its features are minimal, so you must do lots of work to add further views, view controllers, and UI objects.

Note that if you check the Use Storyboards box in the template options, the app creates storyboard files instead of the usual nib files, as shown in Figure 3.11. Storyboards are a relatively recent innovation, and they are designed to make it easier to create apps that display multiple screens. (Don't worry if you don't understand what this means in practice; you'll read more about views, controllers, storyboard, and nib files in later chapters.)

Tabbed Application

This template creates an application with two views selected by a button tab at the bottom of the screen, as shown in Figure 3.12.

The app loads both views when it launches, and then it creates a tab controller to manage them, using a class called UITabBarController. The controller switches the views automatically when the buttons on the tab are touched. You don't need to add further switching code, but you can customize the icons that appear on the tab in Interface Builder.

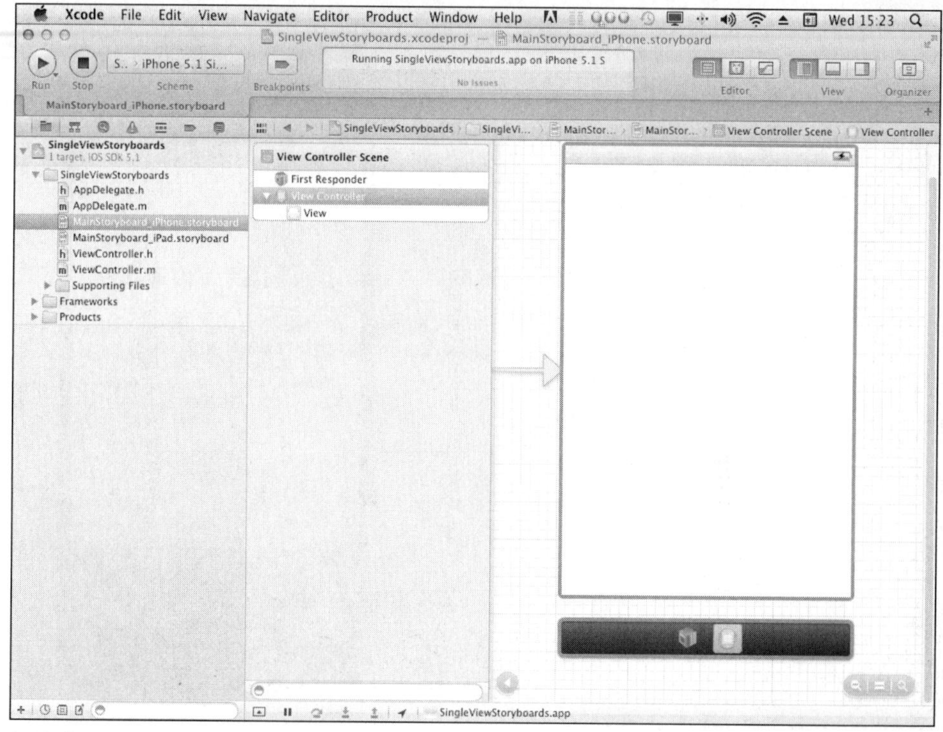

3.11 The Single-View Application template can create apps that use Apple's new storyboards for simplified page layout and switching.

You can add further views by adding more view controllers with an associated nib file and modifying the code slightly. Many apps use a tab bar in this way, so this is a very common app format. But be aware that loading too many views into memory at the same time will use lots of memory, so some care is needed. (More memory-efficient techniques are possible, but this template doesn't use them.)

Utility Application

This template creates two different apps. On the iPhone, it creates an app with a blank main screen and a flipside screen with a Done button. Touching the information icon at the bottom left of the main screen rotates the display to reveal the flipside view. Tapping the Done button flips the display back to the main view.

On the iPad, the app displays a title bar with an info button, instead of an info icon. Tapping the button displays a *popover*—a small pop-up window, shown in Figure 3.13. Tapping the Done button in the popover hides it by fading it out. You can also hide the popover by tapping anywhere outside it.

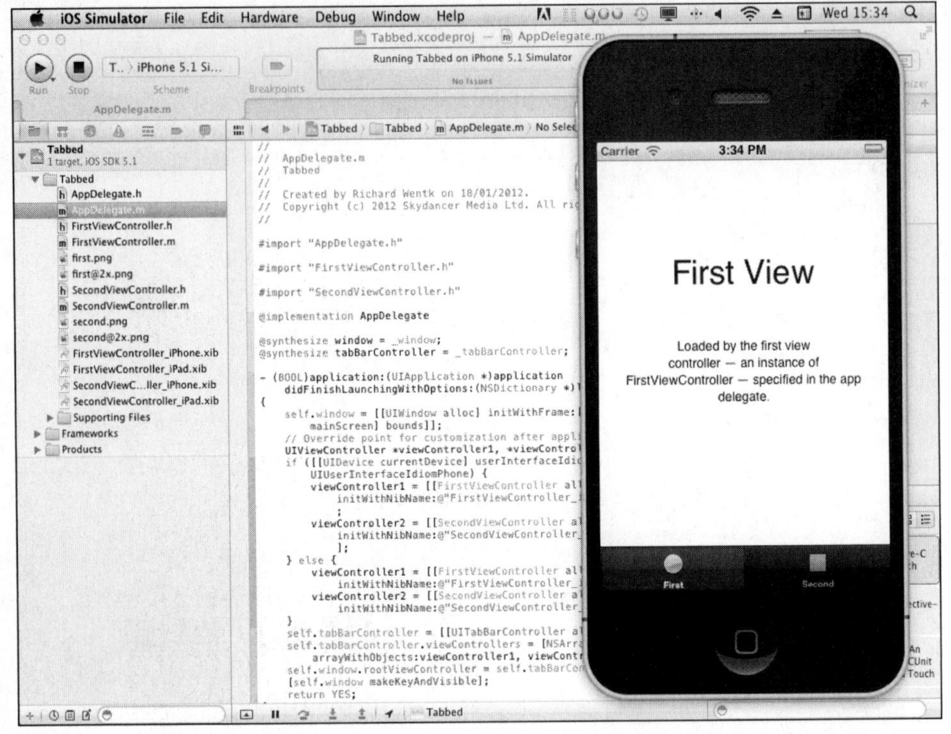

3.12 The Tabbed Application template creates an app with simple tabbed view switching.

Note that, for consistency, the flipside/popover view embeds the Done button in a *Navigation Bar* object using a class called UINavigationBar. A navigation bar is similar to a tab bar, but it appears at the top of the screen and is less flexible, with only two possible buttons and a title. It's often used with table view objects to create a hierarchical menu the user can move through.

Note

The nib file that creates the flipside/popover view is shared between the iPhone and iPad versions of this app. But on the iPhone, most apps that use a flipside view won't add a navigation bar. It's more usual to save space by inserting a back button (labeled Done, OK, Back, and so on) in the view itself.

Empty Application

In spite of the name, the Empty Application isn't empty. It includes a window object (UIWindow) that appears as a white background, as shown in Figure 3.14. It doesn't include any views or view controllers.

Experienced developers can use this template to create an app with an unusual or heavily customized configuration. Because it's so minimal, it isn't a good starting point for beginners.

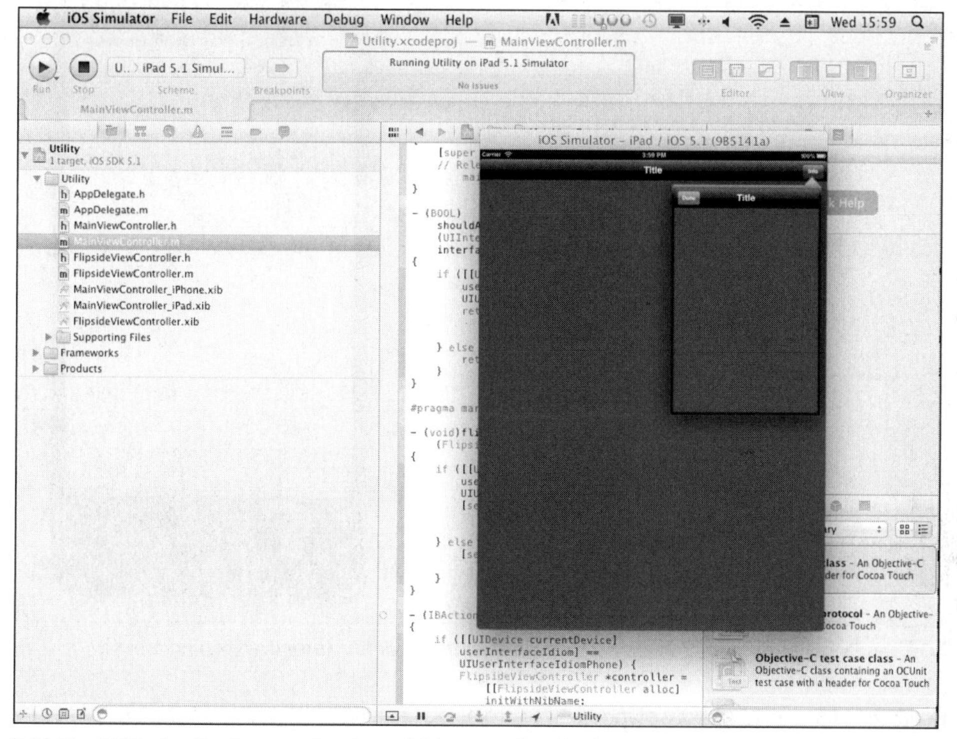

3.13 The Utility Application template is useful for apps that display a supporting window or view of optional features, such as preferences or other app options.

Note

In app design, the window object is a placeholder for views and view controllers. Although it has a colored background and you can add UI elements to it, it's better to manage views by adding a view controller object. UIWindow has limited features. UIViewController is far more sophisticated and powerful.

Customizing and expanding templates

As you gain more experience creating apps, you'll find that your own app designs don't match the standard templates. It would be useful to customize the template list; unfortunately, there's no easy way to do this. (It is possible, but it's a complex process.)

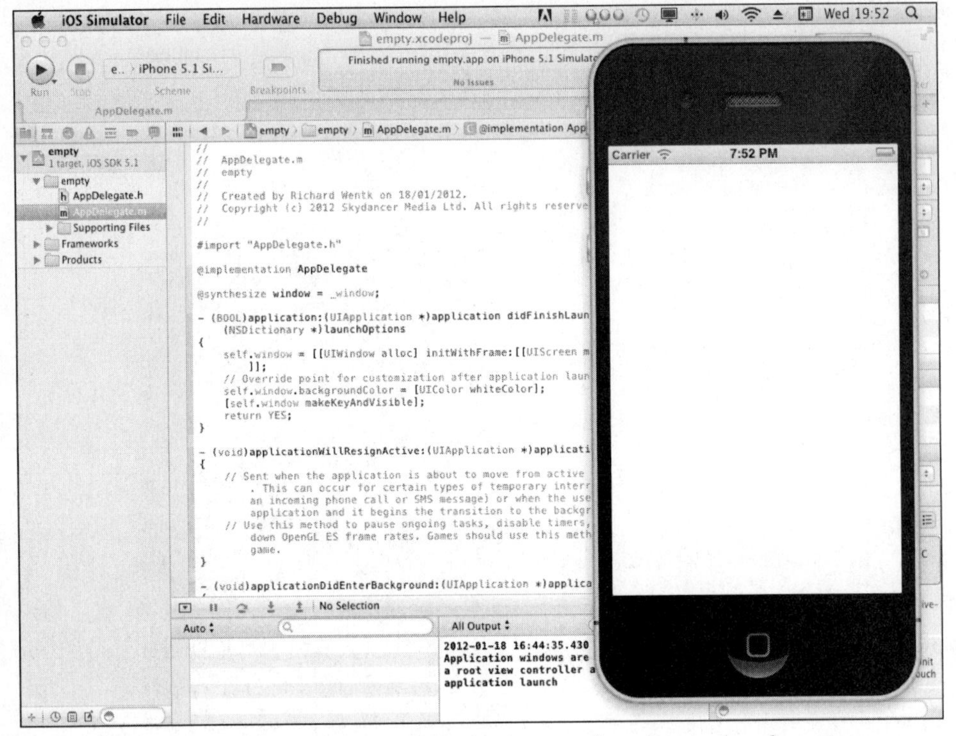

3.14 The Empty Application template is useful for beginners or for customized configuration.

However, you can create your own template projects as follows:

1. **Create a new project with one of the existing templates.**
2. **Customize it to order, adding the new features and code you need.**
3. **Save it to a special folder you create.** You can even call it /My Templates.
4. **When you want to use a template, duplicate the project folder in Finder and move the copy to your working directory.**

Caution

If you copy a custom template you'll need to change some of its build settings. This isn't a completely trivial process—it's outlined in Chapter 13—but depending on the features you use in your templates, it will take you less time than starting from an Apple template and making the same changes to it every time.

Caution

Note that you can't simply open a project and Save As… to create a new project. The way Xcode manages files makes this impossible—or at least, too difficult and complex to be practical.

Keep in mind that practical apps usually include a combination of features from the templates. It's not unusual to begin with the Single-View Application template, add a table object to its view, and create a flipside view for the app preferences.

Genius

Don't let the templates mislead you into thinking apps must be structured in set ways. When you start app design, it's useful to begin with the templates to minimize the work you have to do. Eventually, you'll understand how to design and assemble apps with almost any configuration. Freeform app design is an intermediate skill, but it's something you should work toward because it expands your creative options.

Building Apps from Sample Code

You can learn so much by building complete sample projects in Xcode. Unlike the templates, sample projects are either complete apps with all features present or demonstration projects for specific features. Use them to understand how apps are constructed and to view working code.

You can find sample code in two places:

- **In the documentation.** These projects are created by Apple's internal developers and support staff.
- **Online.** These projects are created by both amateur and professional developers outside Apple.

Building sample projects from the documentation

Sample Code is one of the resource types introduced in Chapter 2. You can access it in two ways:

- **From the Organizer in Xcode.** With this option, sample projects are loaded into Xcode with a single mouse click, as shown in Figure 3.15.
- **Online.** When you access the documentation online, sample projects are downloaded, usually as zipped files. Finder unzips files automatically.

Both options save the project files into a designated folder. You can run sample projects from your /Downloads folder, but it's often more useful to move them to a different folder reserved for third-party projects.

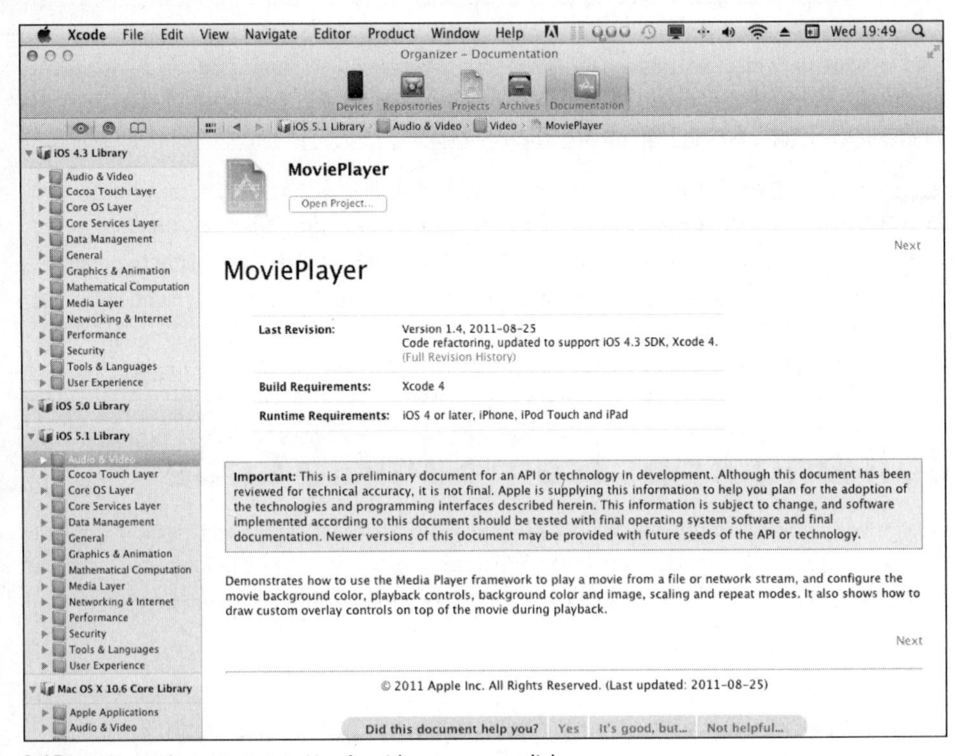

3.15 Load sample projects into Xcode with one mouse click.

Loading projects from the Organizer

Let's look at the first option in more detail. Follow these steps:

1. **Click the Organizer button at the top right of the main Xcode toolbar.**
2. **Click the Documentation icon.**
3. **Scroll down to find the version of iOS in the list at the left.**
4. **Optionally, you can click one of the topics under the version header to filter the list.** Not all topics include sample code, but most do.
5. **Click the Resource Type tab at the top of the main document list to sort the documentation by resource type.**
6. **Scroll down to the view the available sample projects.**

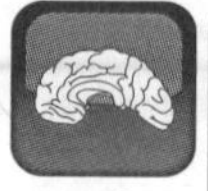

Genius

If you want to view all sample projects, you can also click Sample Code in the Resource Types at the left of the main window.

7. **Pick a sample project that interests you.** Click it to open it. You'll see a brief description (refer to Figure 3.15).
8. **Click the Open Project button under the project title at the top left.**
9. **Select a Folder to save the project into.** After saving, the project loads automatically into Xcode.
10. **Click the Run button at the top left to build the project.**
11. **You may see a message showing incompatibilities between your version of Xcode and the SDK, and the version used to create the project, as shown in Figure 3.16.** Xcode does a reasonable job of fixing incompatibilities automatically, so click the Perform Changes button. (Xcode makes a *snapshot*—a saved version—of the project when you do.)

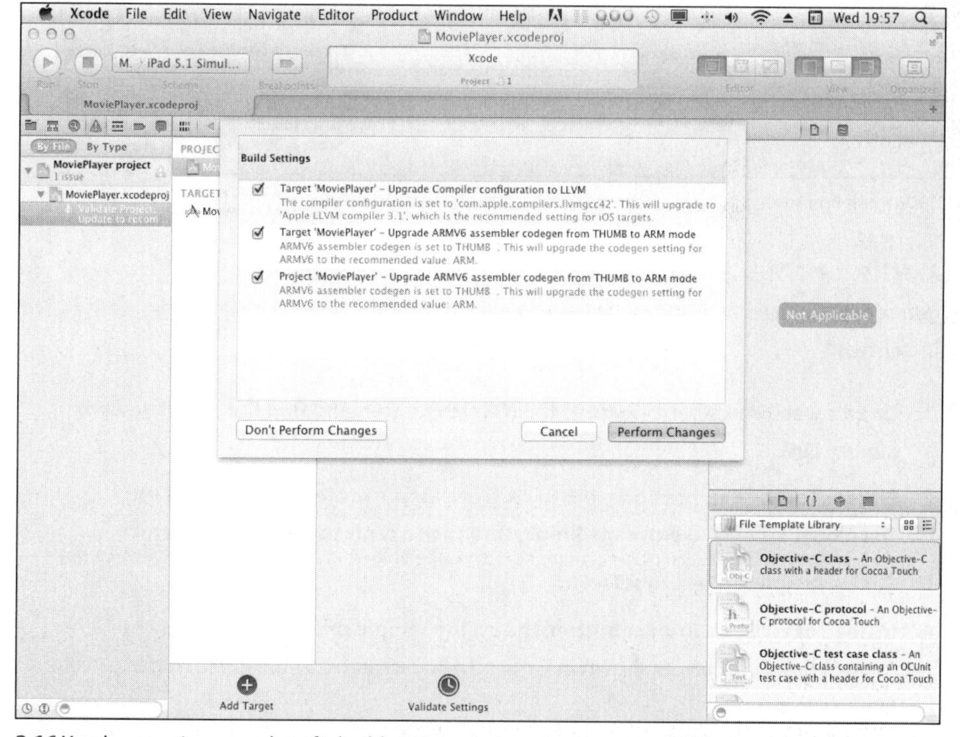

3.16 Xcode sometimes needs to fix build settings and version incompatibilities in older projects.

12. **Click Run again.** This time, the project should build and run without errors, as shown in Figure 3.17.

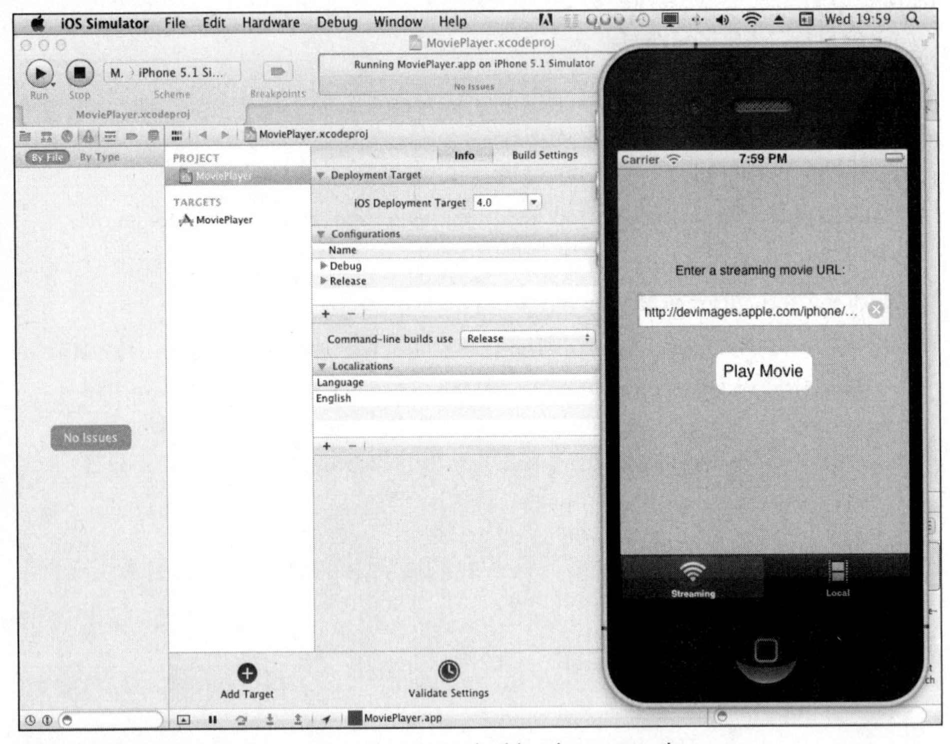

3.17 After it completes a fix, most sample projects build and run correctly.

Loading projects from the online documentation

The process for selecting and downloading online sample code is similar, with a few critical differences:

1. **Open a web browser, navigate to the iOS Dev Center, and find the iOS Developer Library Link.**
2. **Either click the Sample Code link to view all sample projects, or click the iOS Developer Library to enter the library and click a topic to narrow your search.**
3. **Click a sample project to select it.**
4. **Instead of an Open Project button, the online sample projects have a Download Sample Code button, as shown in Figure 3.18.** Click it to download the zipped project files to a folder.

5. **After downloading and unzipping, launch it with File ➪ Open in Xcode and navigate to the .xcodeproj file.** (Don't double-click the .xcodeproj file. If you have two versions of Xcode installed, it may launch the wrong one.)

6. **Online sample code includes a Table of Contents with a list of files in the project.** Click these files to preview them in your web browser.

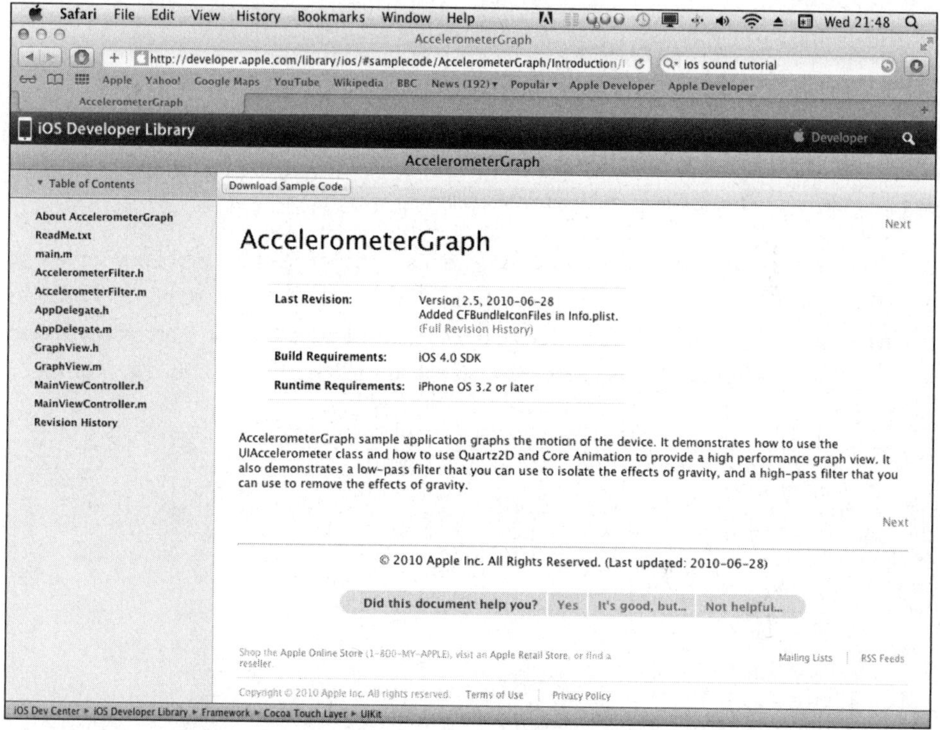

3.18 Sample code online appears in a slightly different format to the sample projects listed in the Organizer Documentation.

Note

Some of the earliest third-party apps in the App Store were based on Apple's sample projects, usually with slightly modified graphics. It isn't a good idea to upload a literal copy of a sample project for sale, because Apple's sample code is copyrighted by Apple. But there is precedent for using code from sample projects in creating third-party apps, provided that it adds basic and essential features. The code examples are often used more or less "as-is," since there's no need to reinvent the wheel.

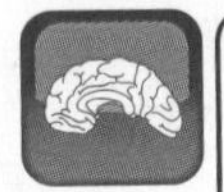

Genius

There's plenty of overlap between online and Organizer sample projects. But note that some projects appear only in one collection or the other, so it's always useful to search both.

Building sample projects from other sources

Many online tutorials include a link to sample project code. This is usually available as a Zip file, and you can download the file, unzip it, and load the .xcodeproj file into Xcode in the usual way.

Some projects include links to an online repository such as github (https://github.com). One of the advantages of github is that it manages online access automatically. Every project has its own web area, and the files in the project can be viewed online.

It's possible to load projects directly into Xcode from a repository, but the process is somewhat complex. For now, you'll find it easier to click the ZIP button available on each project's page, as shown in Figure 3.19. This button automatically creates a zipped file with the most recent version of the code and downloads it to your Mac. You can then unzip the project and load it, as usual.

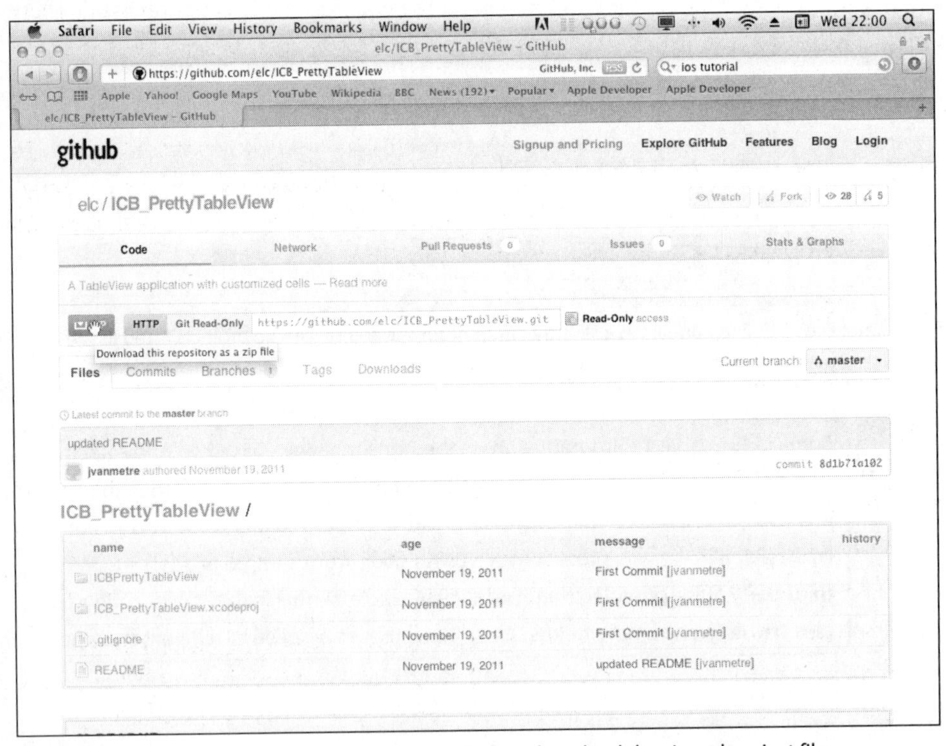

3.19 Use the ZIP button on a project stored on github to download the zipped project files.

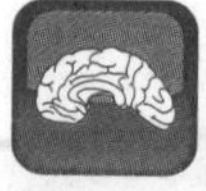

Genius

Tutorials sometimes compress project files using an alternative compressed format called RAR. Finder doesn't handle RAR files automatically, but you can install a free application called UnRarX (www.unrarx.com) to add RAR support.

Building Apps for Test Devices

So far, we've learned how to build projects for the Simulator. Dedicated developers test their projects on one or more test devices because this is the only way to access advanced hardware features and check app performance.

Live testing is limited to developers who enroll in the iOS Developer Program, which was introduced in Chapter 1. If you want to use live testing and haven't yet enrolled, go back to Chapter 1 and read the instructions before continuing.

Understanding certificates and provisioning

Live test privileges and app store access upload privileges are granted through a security system. The system is really designed to manage team development. Team administrators can use it to control which team members can use live testing and which members are allowed to submit finished apps to the app store.

The security system is complex and uses four files to control access to testing and distribution. To set up access, you must use a section of the developer website called the iOS Provisioning Portal, shown in Figure 3.20. After you log in to the iOS Dev Center as a developer, you can access the iOS Provisioning Portal by clicking a link near the top right of the page.

The four files are:

- **A Certificate Signing Request (CSR).** This file contains a digital key. You create it on your Mac to confirm your identity.
- **A Developer Certificate.** This file gives you live testing privileges. Xcode doesn't allow you to test apps on iOS devices without it.
- **A Distribution Certificate.** This file gives you access to the App Store. A version is bundled with your app to confirm your developer identity.
- **A Provisioning Profile.** This file is installed on test devices. It includes your digital key and a time limit. If the profile is valid, Xcode allows you to build your app, install it on your test device, and run it. After the time limit expires, your test app stops working.

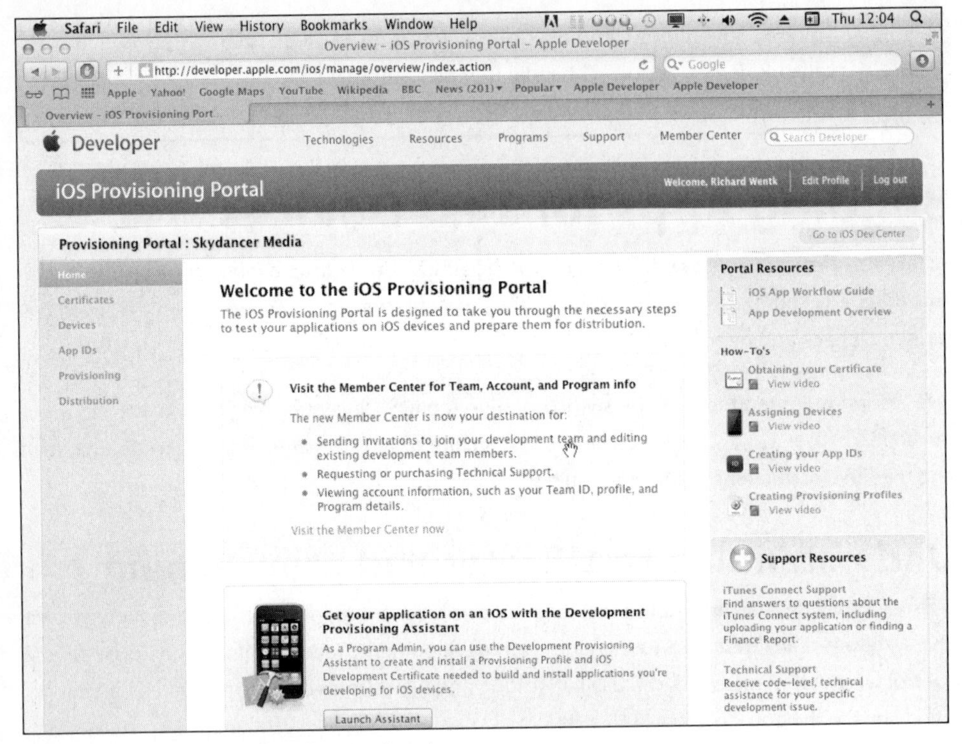

3.20 A first look at the iOS Provisioning Portal.

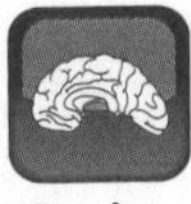

Genius

An extra complication is that distribution and development certificates use *App IDs*. An App ID uniquely identifies either a single app or a group of related apps. Chapter 13 contains more about App IDs, but you don't need to worry about them yet, because Xcode device management automatically creates a temporary ID for device testing.

Creating certificates and provisioning profiles

You *can* create certificates and profiles manually and install them in Xcode by hand. But it's a time-consuming process, and it's been simplified and partially automated in more recent versions of Xcode.

To create a developer certificate and a provisioning profile, follow these steps:

1. **Log in to the iOS Dev Center.**
2. **Navigate to the iOS Provisioning Portal.**

3. **Click the Certificates link from the list at the left.**

4. **Click the How To tab.**

5. **Follow the instructions to create, submit, and approve a Certificate Signing Request, as shown in Figure 3.21.** This step identifies your Mac and your identity to the portal. Don't follow the steps to create and install a Development Certificate.

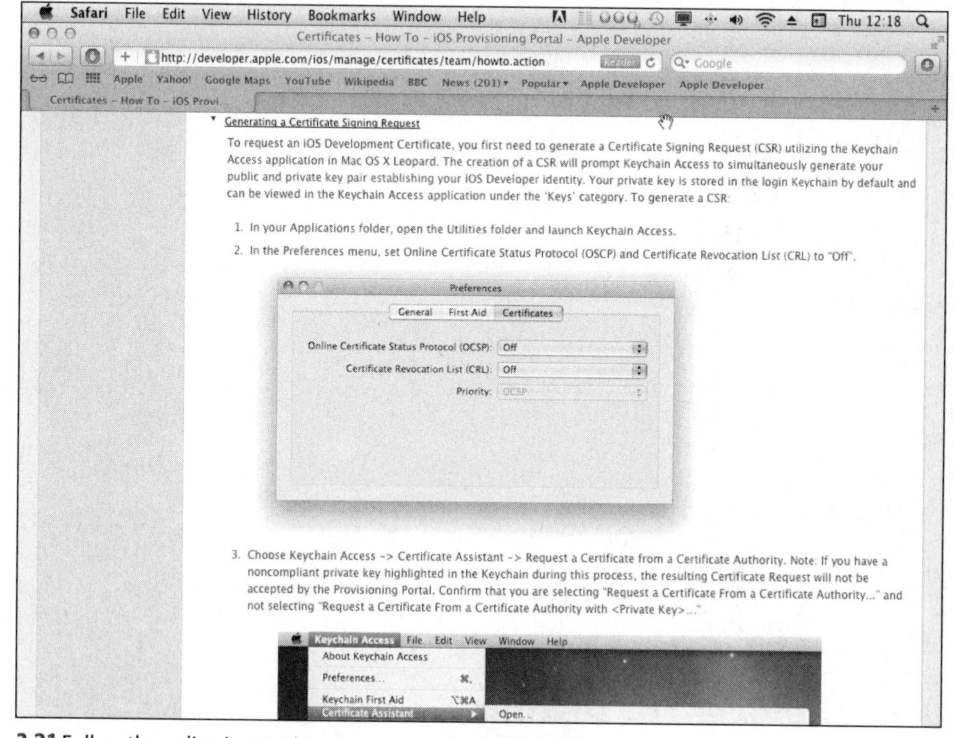

3.21 Follow the online instructions to create and submit a CSR.

6. **Launch Xcode.**

7. **Click the Organizer button at the top right of the toolbar to open the Organizer.**

8. **Click the Devices tab.**

9. **Connect your device using the standard USB cable.**

10. **Wait until Xcode recognizes the device.** Xcode may download some data from the device.

11. **Click the Add to Portal button near the bottom left of the Devices window.** Xcode connects to the Internet, asks you to log in with your developer credentials, adds the device to your list of test devices on the Provisioning Portal, creates development and distribution certificates, downloads them, and installs them, as shown in Figure 3.22.

You should now be able to use your device for live testing. The device appears in the Scheme menu in the main toolbar. Select it before building to install a build on it.

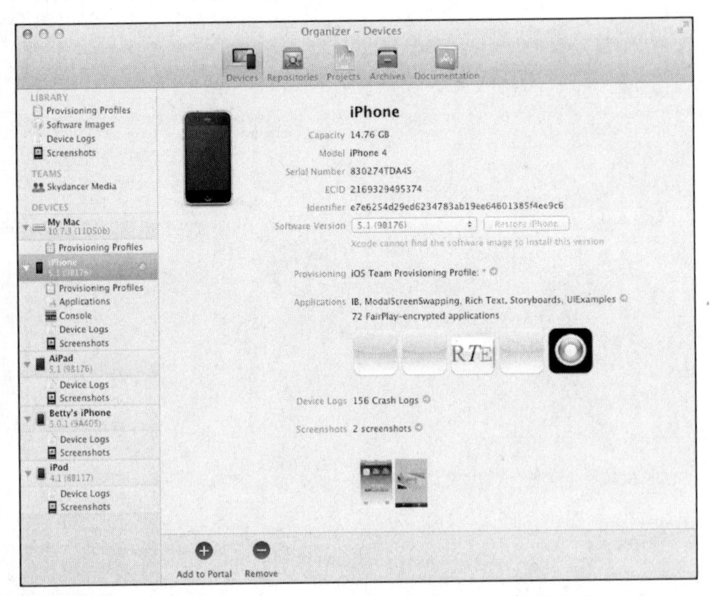

3.22 Set up a device for live testing in the Devices page of the Organizer.

Using devices for testing

If your device uses a passcode, you must unlock it before Xcode can install your test app.

Note that Xcode takes significantly longer to launch an app on a test device than it does to launch the Simulator. So it's efficient to use live testing only when you really need it. For basic UI development, use the Simulator.

Note

For clarity, it's worth repeating that *you can't use live testing to permanently install custom apps on your devices.* Test apps are linked to a provisioning profile, and after the profile expires, the apps no longer work. The only way to install your apps permanently on your devices is to have them accepted in the App Store. You can then download them as if you bought them. (The App Store includes a free promo code system, so you're not forced to buy your own apps.)

Genius

The Devices page has some cool features. Click the Provisioning Profiles option to delete old profiles after they expire. You can also view device logs and crash reports, and you can even create screenshots of your app as it's running.

What Are Applications Made Of?

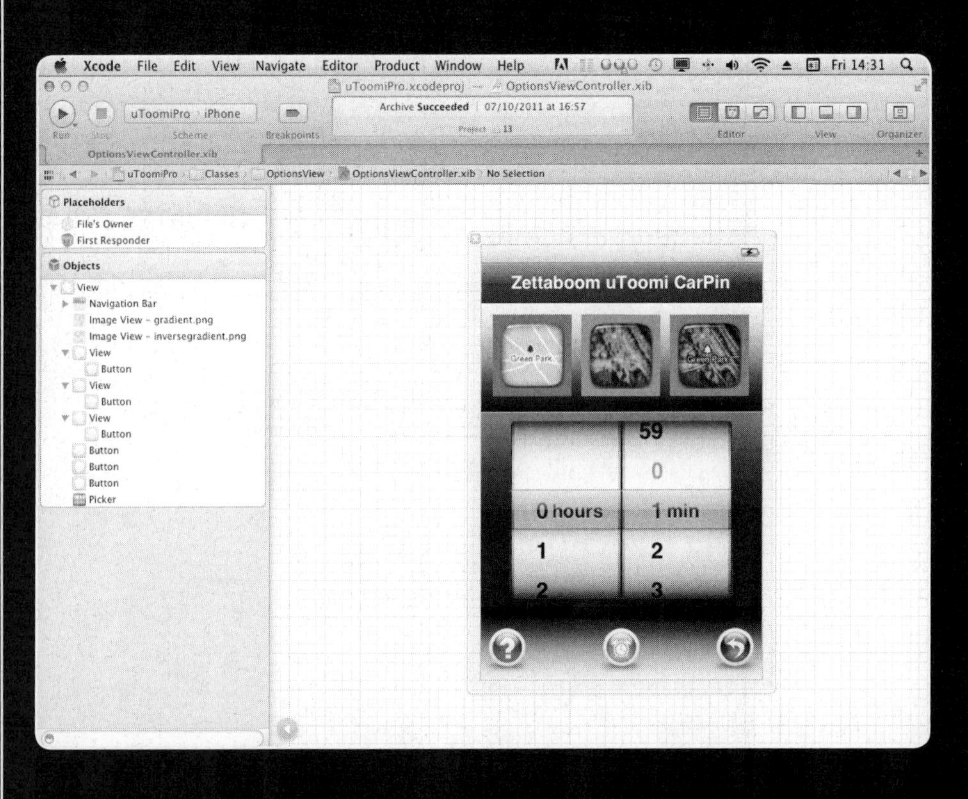

1 2 3 4 5 6 7 8 9 10 11 12 13

Applications are made of code behind a user interface (UI). iOS uses a message-driven system to ask your application for a response at critical moments. App code is a collection of message handlers that creates these responses. The structure of an app links messages to visible screen content. Messages from the UI trigger events in the app. Screen content is dynamic and can be animated or changed as needed.

Understanding Applications

Now that you know how to build applications, let's look at the ingredients of an application in more detail. As mentioned in Chapter 3, applications are built from a kit of parts called objects. iOS includes a vast selection you can use in your app. You can—and often do—customize objects to add extra features.

Technically, iOS is an *object-oriented* system. This doesn't just mean that iOS uses standardized and customizable kit parts. It also defines how iOS exchanges information with your app and how iOS and your app communicate with each other.

Let's look at what this means in practice. Follow these steps:

1. **Launch Xcode, if it isn't running already.**
2. **Create a new project using the SingleView Application Template.** The name doesn't matter. If you saved the project when you created it in Chapter 3, you can reload it instead of creating it again.
3. **If it isn't already open, click the reveal triangle to the left of the top group in the Project navigator, as shown in Figure 4.1.** You'll see four files: one pair labeled with the word "AppDelegate" and the other with ViewController. These two files hold the core of the app.
4. **Click the ViewController.m file to load it into the editor.**

You'll see the code in Figure 4.1. In the rest of this chapter, we'll outline what the code does—without looking at it in too much detail.

Understanding messages

Apps are *message based.* You must understand how messaging works before you can understand app design.

iOS uses a *question-response* model. Whenever anything significant happens, when something is about to happen, or when iOS needs data from your app, it sends one of the objects in your app a message, as shown in Figure 4.2.

Your app can choose to respond to the event, or it can ignore it. If your app doesn't include a message handler for an event, it's ignored automatically. Your app can also send messages to iOS—for example to ask iOS to create an object in memory or to start a hardware service like the GPS (Global Positioning System) location tracking.

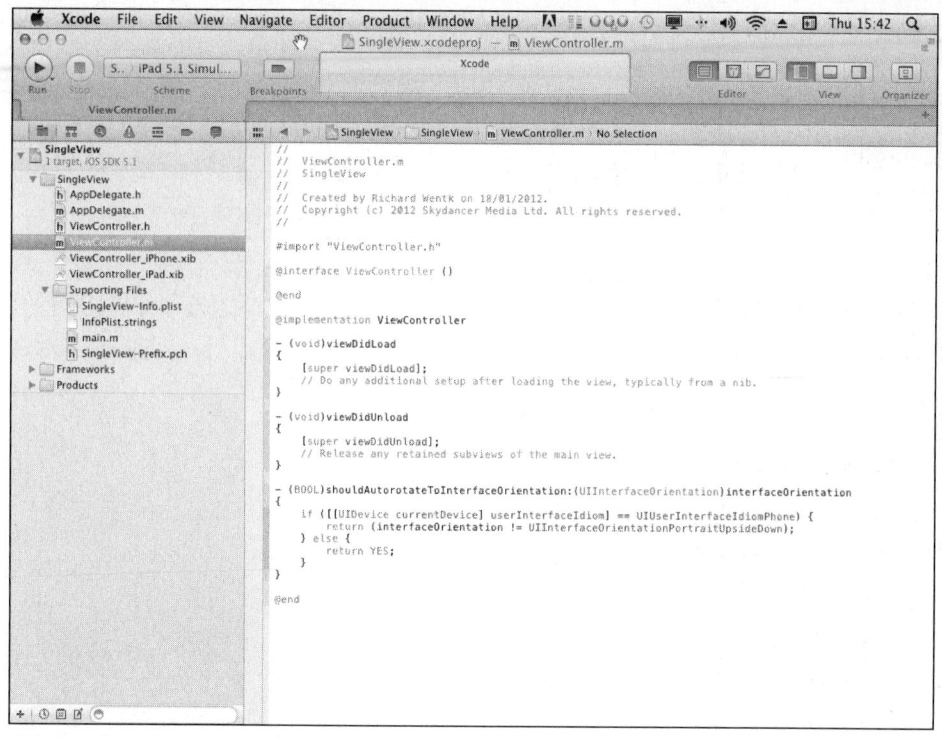

4.1 A first look at the code in an app.

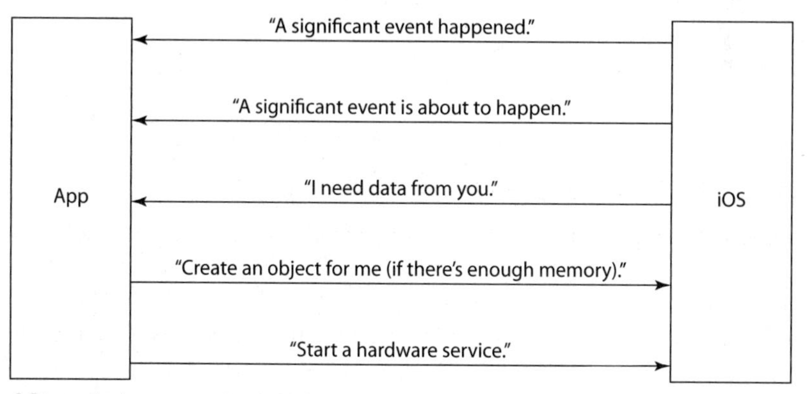

4.2 Introducing messaging in iOS.

Sometimes a message is a request for data. Your app must respond with a useful value or with an object that iOS needs to perform a task.

Objects in your app can message each other. They can even message themselves. For example, many objects in your app may need to know that iOS has sent an "out of memory" error message. iOS sends only a single message, but your app can send further messages to itself to spread the word.

The way to get anything done in your app is to use messages.

Caution

It's important to understand that message-based programming means that code doesn't start at the top of a file and work its way through the file in sequential order. Files in Xcode are long lists of message handlers. Each handler is independent. It can be triggered at any time. The order of the handlers doesn't affect how the app works.

Using messages in practice

Let's look at messaging in more detail with some examples. iOS sends to your app a message when:

- The app has finished loading.
- The initial screen has appeared.
- The user touches the screen.
- The user moves his finger after that initial touch.
- The user lifts a finger from the screen.
- The user taps a button or control. (Note that this isn't the same as touching the screen outside a button.)
- The user lifts her finger from a button or control.
- Your app runs out of memory.
- The GPS hardware generates a location update.
- iOS requests data for a cell in a table.
- A web page or other download you requested has finished.
- A web page or other download hasn't completed because of an error.
- The user has rotated the device, and iOS wants to know if it should rotate the display.

This isn't a complete list of the messages iOS can send. In reality, there are tens of thousands of possible messages. But this list summarizes the most common messages that apps need to work with.

Understanding code

We'll look at messages in more detail later in this chapter. But first, we'll make a brief detour into coding.

Figure 4.3 hides the files shown in Figure 4.1 to concentrate on the code inside a single object. The code in the figure is part of the app's *view controller*—the object that manages the items that appear onscreen and respond to user actions.

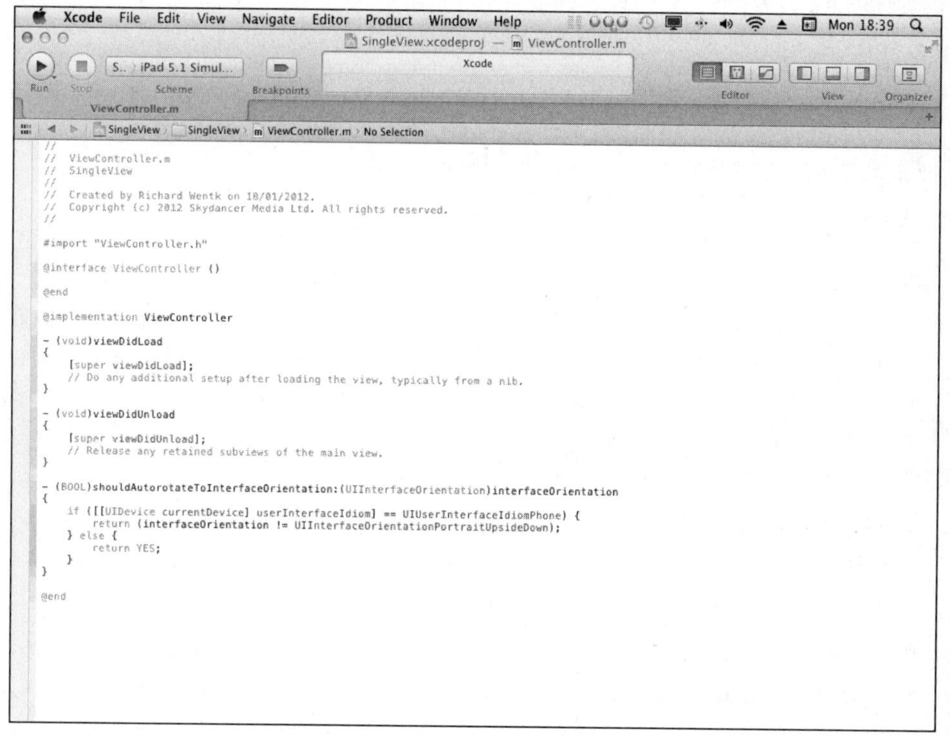

4.3 Another look at some real message handlers.

iOS apps are typically defined using a *programming language* called Objective-C. Code is a series of instructions. A programming language defines how you create those instructions.

In practice, code is made of English-like words—"if," "do," and so on—surrounded by punctuation marks. There are hundreds of programming languages. Each uses words and punctuation in a different way.

Human languages can have dense, ambiguous meanings. But code is *task-based.* All code is a series of well-defined instructions. A complete app has hundreds of lines of code, but each line does something simple, specific, and unambiguous.

What are programming languages?

Programming languages don't just define the words and symbols you type to create instructions; they also force you to think about problems in certain ways. In practice, a programming language defines the *mental models* you use. Objective-C makes you solve problems with objects and messages. Other languages force you to work with other mental models.

Some languages use a very literal model based on the hardware—the processor and memory—of a computer. Others use very abstract models that have no obvious connection with real hardware.

Objective-C is part of the C language family. C is an older language that was designed to be close to real computer hardware for speed and efficiency. C is just abstract enough to create code that can work on many different computers without modifications. This made C extremely useful. It's still popular with developers who use it to create code for all kinds of applications. (If you have a network router or cable/ADSL modem, the code that makes it work probably was written in C or a language in the C family.)

Technically, Objective-C is a *superset* of C. You can use C in your apps, and parts of iOS and OS X still use C code. The more advanced features in both iOS and OS X use objects, messages, and other features that are unique to Objective-C.

The features of C were defined by its creators—Brian Kernighan and Dennis Ritchie—in a book called *The C Programming Language*. The book is a reference guide rather than a beginner's tutorial, but if you're serious about app development, it's worth buying a copy. You can also look for it online.

More advanced developers can also use a language called C++ (pronounced C plus plus) in their apps. C++ is a different superset of C. It's popular and powerful, but mixing Objective-C and C++ code in the same app can be tricky, so we won't look at that option in this book.

You don't need to know the history of C or Objective-C to use either effectively. For beginners, the easiest way to understand programming is to learn the words and syntax—the ways in which words and symbols can be combined—to perform standard tasks.

Note

For a quick preview of C syntax, look at Appendix A.

In this chapter, the only syntax you need to learn is that each message handler starts with a "-" (hyphen) character. The code that defines the instructions for the handler is between the curly brackets {…} after the message name. Each separate instruction—called a statement—ends with a ";" (semicolon).

Here's an outline of a typical message handler:

```
- (stuff) messageName: moreStuff
{
    codeToDoUsefulThings;
}
```

In the example in Figure 4.3, the message handlers do very little, so there's barely any code. In a finished app, the handlers can be many lines long before the final closing curly bracket.

Note

You'll often see lines of plain English in code, preceded with a double slash "//." In Xcode, they're displayed in green text. These lines are *comments*. Comments aren't computer instructions; they're included as text to explain how the code works. When you start writing your own code, you'll find it's useful to add comments as you go, because they can be an essential memory aid. Larger blocks of comment text sometimes appear between /* and */ characters.

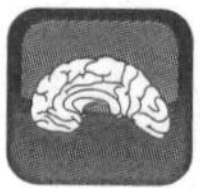

Genius

stuff and moreStuff are explained in Chapter 5. As a preview, data comes in different formats, such as single text characters, strings of text, numbers, simple yes/no values called Booleans, objects, and others. moreStuff defines the kind of data that is passed to your message handler. stuff defines what kind of data the message handler returns when it's done. Messages that accept data have a colon after the name. Most messages do, so when you read the documentation, it's more usual to see "messageName:" than "messageName."

In the same way that iOS sends messages to your app, your app can also send messages to iOS. Here are some tasks your app can perform with messages:

- Create an object in memory.
- Delete an object from memory.
- Create a timer.
- Load an object or other information from a file.

- Swap between screens, with optional animation.
- Request messages and data from the GPS, accelerometer, gyroscope, Bluetooth, camera, or other hardware feature.
- Stop messages from a hardware feature, or turn it off to save battery power.
- Change the size or position of a visible object on the screen.

Figure 4.4 shows some examples taken from a finished mapping app. In this example, the message handlers are more complex and include code that sends messages to iOS.

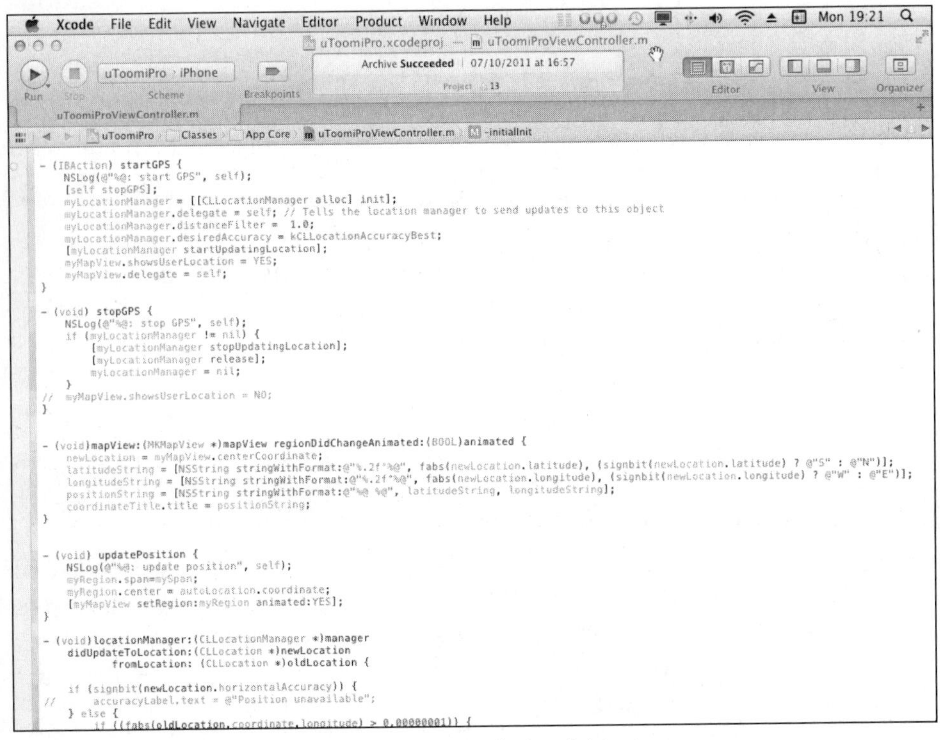

4.4 Looking at the message handlers in a view controller in a finished app.

The code for the startGPS message handler runs when the user taps a button onscreen. The next few lines create an object in iOS called a *location manager* to receive information from the GPS, setting the required accuracy. Next, they direct messages from the location manager to the current object. Finally, the app sends a message to the location manager to tell it to start working. The other message handlers (stopGPS and so on) stop the GPS, manage map updates, and add other related features.

Note

Don't worry about trying to follow the code in detail. The critical features are explained in later chapters.

Understanding messages in objects

How does iOS know where messages should be sent? How do you know which messages an object can handle? And what happens if iOS sends your app a message and you haven't created a handler for it?

For objects in the iOS toolkit, you can find the answers in the documentation. Each object's class reference lists the messages the object can receive. Figure 4.3 shows part of the class reference document for the UIViewController class. The *Tasks* heading lists two types of information. Items prefixed with a "-" (hyphen) are messages the object can receive. Items without a prefix are called *properties* and define the data stored by each object.

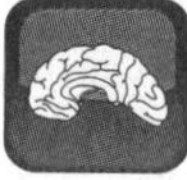

Genius

If you look through a few class references, you'll see some messages are prefixed with "+" (plus) instead of "-" (hyphen). There are some technical differences between these message handlers; they're explained later in this book.

If you look back to Figure 4.3, you'll see that handlers for some of the messages that appear in this list (viewDidLoad and viewDidUnload) are defined in the code. When iOS sends these messages to your app's view controller, the code under the message name between the curly brackets runs.

If a message doesn't have a handler, your app ignores it. Most messages generated by iOS are ignored in this way. For example, Figure 4.3 doesn't include a handler for the viewWillDisappear message. Because there's no handler for this message, it does nothing in the template app.

Note

Messages from iOS are routed automatically to the object responsible for handling them. This is a feature of iOS. iOS keeps track of an app's structure and makes sure that objects in the app are sent the messages they can handle.

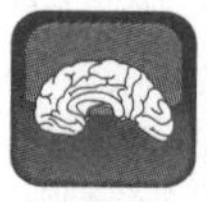

Genius

The ViewDidLoad message handler is often used for setup code in an app.

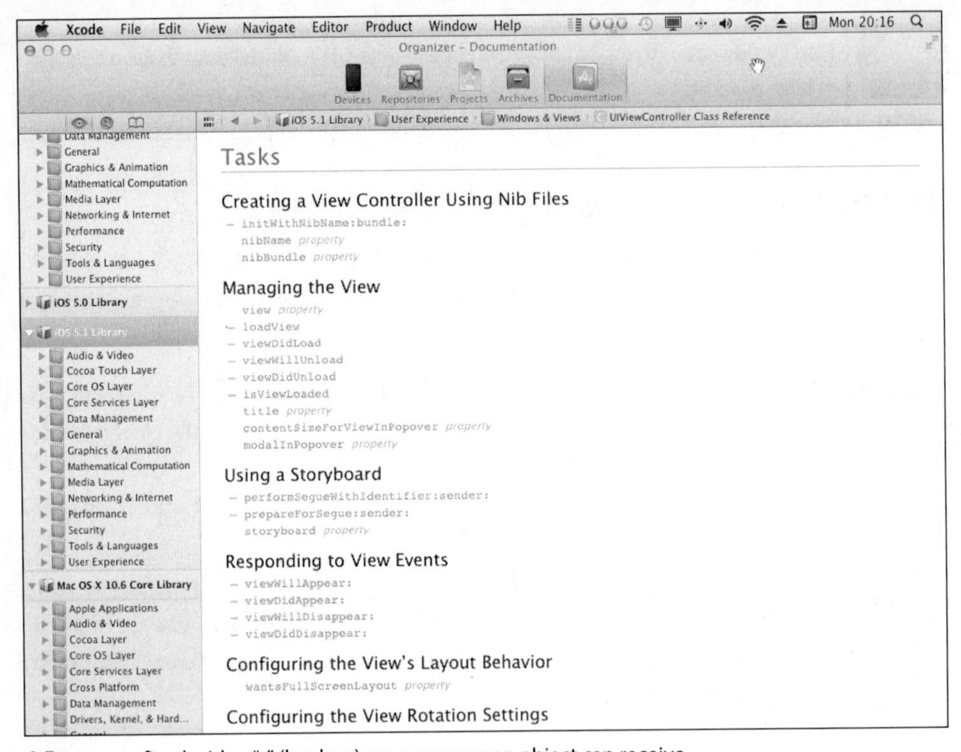

4.5 Items prefixed with a "-" (hyphen) are messages an object can receive.

Building apps from messages

Here's a critical point: If your app *did* need to do something before the view (the contents of the screen) was about to disappear, you could add a handler for the viewWillDisappear message. Code in the handler would run when the view was about to be hidden.

This is one of the key things you need to remember about app development. An app is really just a long list of message handlers. To add features to your app, look through the class documentation for each object you use, add the message handlers you need, then fill out each handler with the instructions you want your app to perform when that message arrives.

Note

For clarity, there's a subtle difference between hiding a view and unloading it. Unloading a view deletes it from memory. If you want to show it again, you must reload it and redisplay it. Hiding a view keeps it in memory, but moves it out of sight in case you want to display it again later.

iOS doesn't throw out messages at random. Messages are generated for four reasons:

- **Something has happened.** The user may have tapped a control, the app has reached a certain point while starting up, or a hardware device has reported a new value.
- **Something is about to happen.** iOS warns your app when it's about to do something your app may want to know about—for example, when iOS is about to rotate the display.
- **Should something happen?** In a few circumstances, iOS asks your app how to respond. For example, you may not want your app to rotate to the upside-down orientation. iOS sends a message to your app asking for a yes/no value for each orientation before attempting the rotation.
- **iOS needs data from your app.** Some features in iOS work only if your app feeds data to iOS through a message handler.

The syntax for these options looks similar. There's no technical distinction between them. But it's useful to know the different circumstances in which different messages are generated, because different messages are handled by different objects in your app.

If you don't understand how apps are structured, it can be difficult to understand where to find the message handlers you need.

Understanding App Structure

Although there are many possible ways to structure an app, all apps share some common elements. They're shown in Figure 4.6.

Here's how each object in the structure handles messages:

- **iOS sends app-level messages to the Application Delegate object.** These messages arrive as the app is launched and loaded, when it's moved to the background after the user presses the Home button, or when some other app-level event happens, such as a low memory condition.
- **The App Delegate includes a window object.** In iOS apps, the window object is just a placeholder for other content. It doesn't have a frame around it, it can't be moved, and it doesn't have open/close/minimize/maximize buttons. It has a small repertoire of messages, but they're not often used.

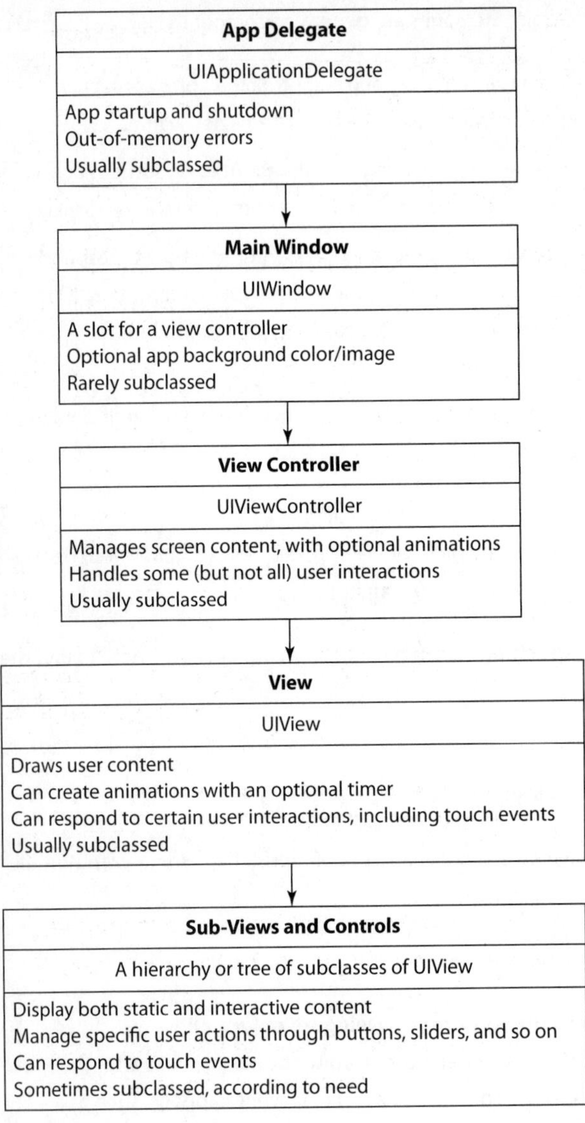
App Delegate
UIApplicationDelegate
App startup and shutdown
Out-of-memory errors
Usually subclassed
Main Window
UIWindow
A slot for a view controller
Optional app background color/image
Rarely subclassed
View Controller
UIViewController
Manages screen content, with optional animations
Handles some (but not all) user interactions
Usually subclassed
View
UIView
Draws user content
Can create animations with an optional timer
Can respond to certain user interactions, including touch events
Usually subclassed
Sub-Views and Controls
A hierarchy or tree of subclasses of UIView
Display both static and interactive content
Manage specific user actions through buttons, sliders, and so on
Can respond to touch events
Sometimes subclassed, according to need

4.6 An outline structure of an iOS app.

- **iOS sends screen control and animation messages to the View Controller object.** The View Controller loads and unloads screen content as the app runs, with optional animations. It can also respond to user touch events from the screen, and it manages screen rotations.

- **View objects are arranged in a hierarchy.** Views are objects on the screen that create useful content, including background images, buttons, timer displays, and so on. There's typically a single main view and various subviews. The subviews are often *controls*—objects that respond to use actions.
- **Both the View Controller object and iOS can send messages to the views onscreen.** The view controller can hide, show, move, resize, modify, and animate view objects. It can load them and unload them from memory. It can rotate them when the user rotates his device. View objects can also respond to user touches. Some of these features are created by sending messages to iOS, others by adding custom code to your app.

Note

View Controller objects come in different flavors. There's a single generic View Controller class called UIViewController and various specialized view controllers that manage toolbars and tab bars, tables, pop-ups, and so on. The specialized controllers have all the features of UIViewController with a few unique extra features of their own.

Understanding message timing

When an app launches, iOS sends a series of messages as certain stages of the launch sequence complete. When the app quits, iOS sends an equivalent series of messages that the app can use to quit cleanly.

In outline, a simplified version of the startup sequence looks this:

1. **iOS loads the app.**
2. **It sends a message called applicationDidFinishLaunchingWithOptions: to the App Delegate.** You can use this message to add your own setup features for the app—for example, to load preferences or other essential data.
3. **Apps usually load the nib file (the contents of the first screen) at this point.** This is a slightly complex process. The nib includes the default view controller object, which automatically loads the first views.
4. **When the view controller has finished loading the view, iOS sends the viewDid-Load: message to the view controller.** At this point, you can do further setting up in viewDidLoad:.
5. **The app starts waiting for user actions.** The app is now running.

In the SingleView template, applicationDidFinishLaunchingWithOptions: includes some default code, as shown in Figure 4.7. This code does the following:

1. **It asks iOS to create a window object.**
2. **It checks whether the code is running on an iPhone or iPad and loads the corresponding nib file.** The nib file holds the view controller and its views, so they load with the nib file.
3. **It slots the view controller object into a special slot in the window object.** This guarantees that the next step displays the views.
4. **It sends a message to the window object to tell iOS to bring it to the front of the other content and make it visible.**

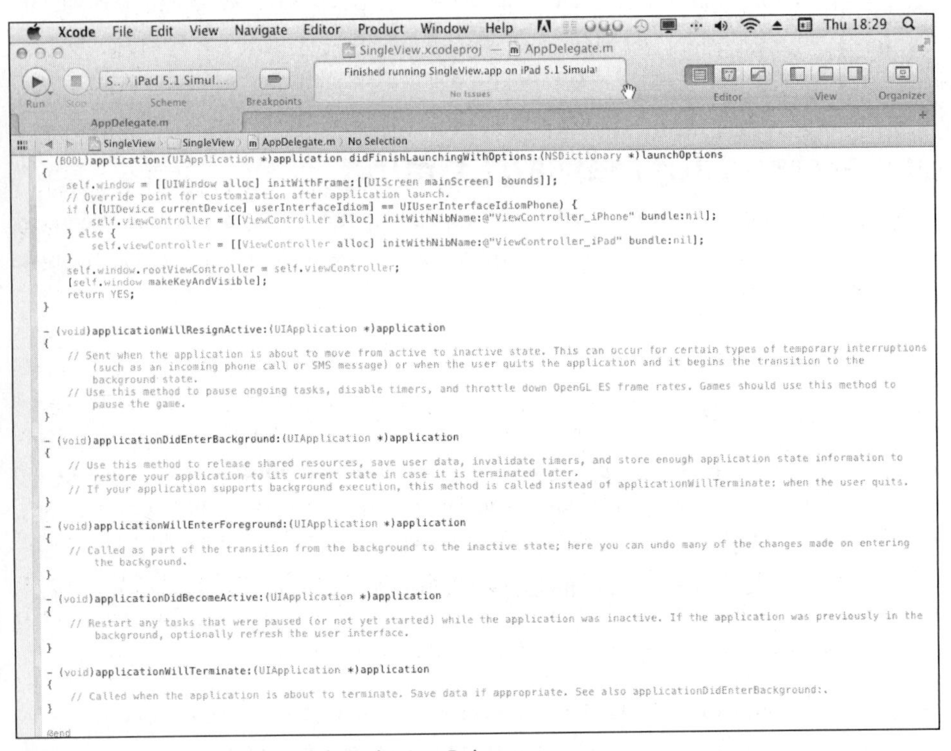

4.7 App startup and shutdown code in the App Delegate.

Working with message timing

You can see that this is a complex process. Here are some points to watch for:

- **You can create objects in two ways: by asking iOS to create them in memory or by loading them from a nib file.** This confuses many beginners. Either method works, but there's a critical difference: If you load an object from a nib file, you can preload it with data you define using Interface Builder. For example, you can set the size and position of views and controls. Objects created in memory have default values that need to be set up with extra code.
- **Message sequencing is tricky.** The viewDidLoad: message arrives in the middle of applicationDidFinishLaunchingWithOptions:, because it's sent after the nib file loads. You might expect the order to be different, but viewDidLoad: is sent *inside* application-DidFinishLaunchingWithOptions:. If you add setup code to either handler, you need to understand when it runs.
- **Startup messages arrive in strict sequence.** Other messages can arrive at any time. For example, the applicationWillResignActive: message can arrive at any moment. The code for this handler must be able to pause the rest of the app, and the rest of the app must be robust enough to survive being paused.

Message sequencing can sometimes be a problem. It's standard practice to add a log message—a line of code that sends a message to the debugging window in Xcode—at the start of many message handlers. You can use these messages to check that the sequence of events matches your expectations.

You should also pay attention to the shutdown messages toward the end of the App Delegate. iOS supports *task switching.* When the user quits an app, it stays in memory in case it's needed again. Certain apps—those that stream audio or use the GPS—can work behind the scenes. If an app isn't used for a while, iOS eventually dumps it from memory.(For details, see Chapter 11.)

Each of these options is supported with a different message from iOS. The handlers toward the end of the App Delegate include comments to help you understand when each message is triggered. But they don't contain any useful code. Typically, you'll need to shut down some of the features in your app and release some objects when these messages arrive.

Introducing Views, Nib Files, and Storyboards

So far, we've looked briefly at the code in an app. Now let's look at views in more detail. Go back to the template you loaded earlier in the chapter. Open the Project navigator, if it isn't already open. Click the ViewController-iPhone.xib file to load it into Interface Builder.

After a pause during which Interface Builder loads from disk (wait patiently if nothing seems to be happening), you'll see the layout shown in Figure 4.8. In the figure, we've closed the Project navigator at the left to maximize the useful space.

Caution

Don't forget that nib files have a .xib extension, not .nib, as you might expect. In fact, nib files *used to* have the .nib extension, but the extension was changed a few versions of Xcode ago. Technically, nib files now store object details in a format called XML (eXtensible Markup Language). The extension probably doesn't stand for "XML nib file," but it can be useful to pretend that it does.

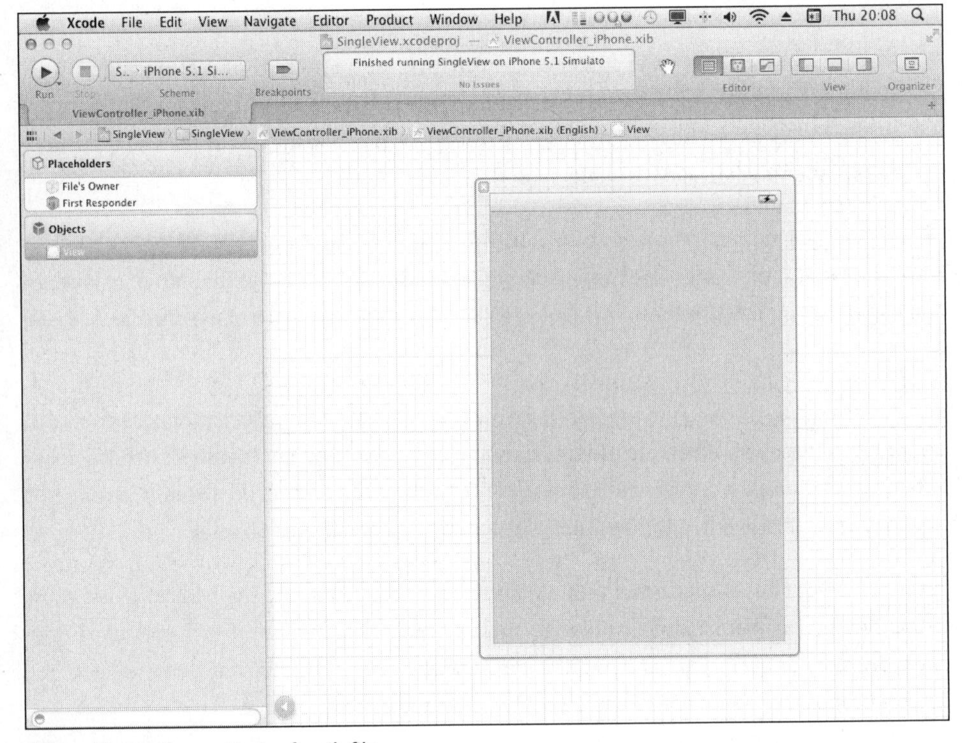

4.8 Looking at the contents of a nib file.

Looking at nib files

In previous chapters, you learned that nib files are used to lay out and manage the UI (User Interface) of an app. UI design is a three-stage process:

1. **Use Interface Builder in Xcode to lay out the content of each screen.**
2. **Add code to link "live" objects to message handlers.** Objects that are decorative, such as a static background or illustrative graphics, don't need a message handler.
3. **Add code to send messages to objects.** For example, if your app includes a map, you may want to send the map object a message to update the displayed location.

Note

In app jargon, messages sent by UI objects are called *actions*. Messages are sent to UI objects via *outlets*. (Interface Builder includes special editing features for actions and outlets.)

It's not unusual to repeat these stages, adding more features as you go or perhaps redesigning the UI to improve it.

Actions and UI message handlers are described in later chapters. Let's explore the first part of the process: adding views and controls to a UI.

Adding objects to a UI

To add objects to a UI, follow these steps:

1. **Open a nib file in Interface Builder, as described earlier in this chapter.**
2. **Click the Utilities button near the top right to show the Utilities pane.**
3. **Click the Object library icon in the divider near the middle of the pane.** The icon looks like a small cube.
4. **Optionally, drag the divider up the pane to show more objects, as shown in Figure 4.9.**

Note

As you can probably guess from the name, the Objects library holds a list of objects that you can add to a UI layout. Scroll down the list to see all the objects. Not all objects have a visible representation that appears onscreen. For example, the *gesture recognizers* aren't designed to be visible; they simply generate messages when the user moves her fingers in a certain way. Don't forget that IB can load *any* object. It's not limited to objects with visible content.

5. **Drag a Switch object from the library onto the gray mockup area in the middle of the screen.** Don't release it yet…

4.9 Looking at the list of objects that can be included in a nib file.

6. **Move it side to side and up and down.** You'll see guidelines appear when the switch is centered horizontally and/or vertically, as shown in Figure 4.10.
7. **Release the switch when it's centered.** Note that the centering is optional and for display only. If you want to place the switch at the top right, you can do that too, but it's useful to know the centering and alignment guidelines exist.

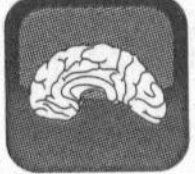

Genius

If there's more than one object in the UI, the guidelines appear on object centers and edges as well as the UI centers.

If you build the app now, you'll see that when it launches, the blank gray screen now includes the button you added. The button is functional—you can flick it on and off—but the app doesn't include any code that responds to it, so it does nothing. We'll discover how to wire up a UI with some actions later in this book.

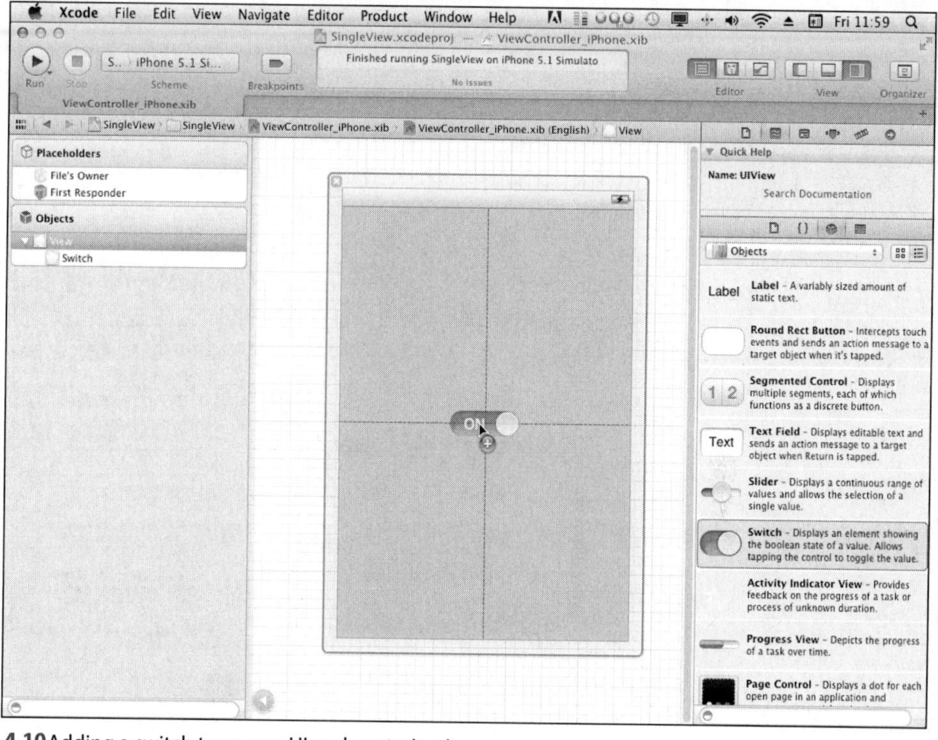

4.10 Adding a switch to an app UI and centering it.

Optionally, you can add more objects to the UI to experiment with layout and alignment. Figure 4.11 shows the UI with a static label and a date-picker object. The button and label have been moved to make the design look more symmetrical and pleasing. If you build the app again, you'll see these new objects have been added to the UI.

Understanding the view hierarchy

If you look at the left of the IB window, you'll see a sub-pane called Objects. The main view appears here, and the objects you added appear indented under it.

This indentation is important: The view *contains* the objects indented under it. The objects in each view are arranged in a hierarchy, like an upside-down tree with a single root and many branches, each of which can have sub-branches of its own.

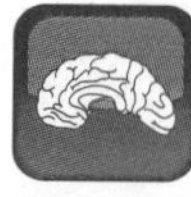

Genius

Technically, the objects are stored in an array that is part of the data managed by the view. View objects—including controls—inside a view are called *subviews*. They're stored in the array.

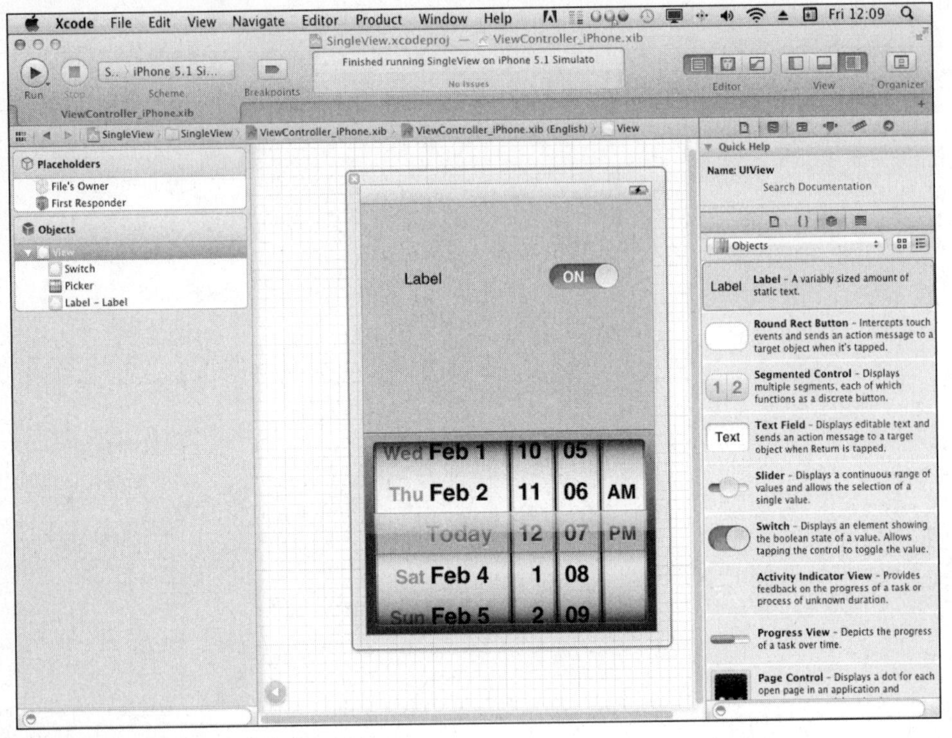

4.11 Expanding the UI with further objects.

The sequence defines the front-to-back order. Objects towards the the bottom of the list overlap objects above them.

In a more complex UI, the indentation can become much more complex. You can place views inside other views—for example, to create a virtual window with animated objects or video content inside a static frame. The objects inside the second view will be indented again, and they'll be stored in the data managed by the second view.

Modifying views and the view hierarchy

In simple apps, the view hierarchy is static. It loads and appears, and the user interacts with it. But it doesn't change. In practice, this means you can ignore it.

More advanced developers can modify views and the view hierarchy to order in three ways. As a developer, you can do the following:

- **Add or remove objects from the hierarchy.**

- **Modify a view.** This includes changing its color, size, position, and so on. For certain views, it can also mean adding a background image. And for controls (which are also views), it can mean changing the visible state of a control—for example, changing a switch from On to Off.
- **Draw custom graphics inside a view.** There are many ways to do this. Some view types can display a graphic loaded from a file. Others support a range of custom drawing options. The key feature is a message handler called drawRect: that is run automatically by iOS when the view loads. Code to draw custom graphics goes inside drawRect:.
- **Animate a view.** Views include built-in animation features. You can animate views directly by changing their properties, but you can also trigger a selection of preset animation effects that are built into iOS.

Figure 4.12 shows the reference documentation for the UIView class that manages view modification. You send the messages shown in the figure to access and modify the hierarchy. In practice, you write code that sends a message to the target view, and iOS modifies it according to your instructions.

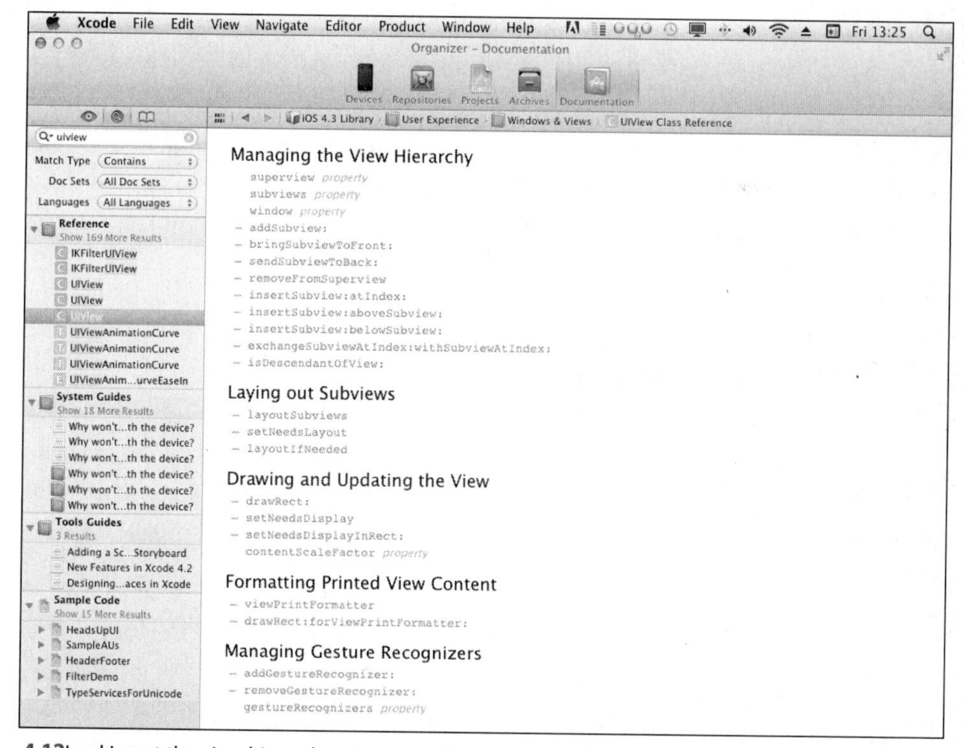

4.12 Looking at the view hierarchy management messages in the documentation.

View modification is more of an advanced topic, so ignore it for now if it seems like too much information to take in on a first reading. The key point is that screen content doesn't have to be static. You can modify it by sending messages to a view to animate it or modify its visible properties. You can also rearrange the view hierarchy, moving views, adding them, and removing them as needed.

Note

You'll find an example of an app with multiple screens in Chapters 10 and following.

Understanding Views and Controllers

A key point to remember now is that view controller objects *manage* views. Views draw content, but user interaction and screen swaps are best handled by a view controller.

A single view controller is always loaded at startup, with a default screen of content defined in its nib file. Often, this view controller stays in memory and manages animated changes to further screens.

To add further screens, add further view controllers to your app. Each view controller is created with an associated nib file. To design the content for those screens, edit the corresponding nib file.

To switch between screens, add code to either the master view controller or the other view controllers, depending on the design of your app. The code loads a view controller and its associated nib file. The view content is added "free" when you load the controller.

You *don't* load views directly from a nib file when you swap screens. You load a view controller object, and the view controller loads the view.

Introducing storyboards

Screen swapping can feel clumsy and overly complex, so in iOS 5 Apple added a new feature called *storyboards*. A storyboard graphs the relationship between screens—or more accurately, it graphs various possible paths through a collection of view controllers. Animations are defined in the storyboard.

Figure 4.13 shows a simple example with two screens. We'll work through a hands-on example of design with storyboards in Chapter 10.

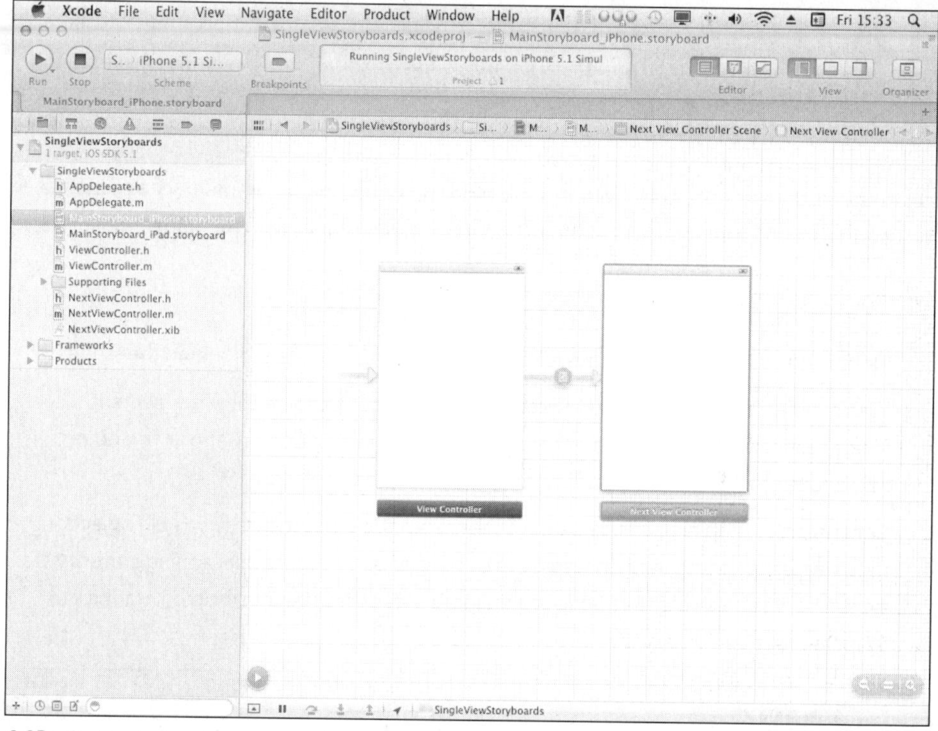

4.13 A first look at a storyboard with two view controllers.

Introducing Model-View-Controller (MVC)

iOS is designed to be efficient and to use as little memory as possible. It's good practice to keep as few objects in memory as you can.

This particularly applies to views. In practice, you have to do extra work to create the illusion of an app that holds more information in memory than it really does.

For example, you might expect a virtual book app would keep every page in memory at the same time. In fact, it's more usual to only load a few pages (the current page, the previous page, and the next page) and use animation effects to suggest that the other pages are also available. When the user turns a page, the app releases one page from memory and loads the next one.

In iOS development, this process is given a special name. It's an example of a design pattern—a way of thinking about app design. The pattern is called Model-View-Controller (MVC).

Caution In the official documentation, MVC is presented as a useful goal, but it's almost impossible to understand why it matters. Even experienced developers have trouble making sense of Apple's presentation.

An important goal of MVC is to keep as little redundant information in memory as possible. In practice, this means your app uses a bare minimum of objects to represent a bigger pool of data.

MVC is built into the design of many view controllers. It has three elements:

- **Model.** This part stores data. With MVC, data is kept out of sight and behind the scenes.
- **View.** This is the visible view of the data. For maximum efficiency, the view element, which can include multiple view objects, should use as little memory and as few objects as possible.
- **Controller.** This object pulls data out of the model and plugs it into the visible objects in the view. Optionally, it may do some format translation—for example, adding currency symbols before numbers in a table in a financial app, or resizing or cropping graphics to fit them onscreen.

Using MVC

A key feature of MVC is that views don't access the model directly. Both data and views are managed by a controller.

Suppose your app uses a table. In iOS, the table display object—UITableView—displays a series of cells. Figure 4.14 shows a typical example: the iPhone preferences app.

A user can drag a finger to scroll through the cells. Without MVC, all the cells would be prefilled with information from the user preferences. This could slow down the load time of the Preferences app and wouldn't be memory efficient.

4.14 With MVC, only visible objects are kept in memory.

With MVC, UITableView knows how many cells are visible. As the user scrolls through the table, cell objects are *reused*. When a cell scrolls off the screen, it's moved to a small pool where it can be recycled before the next cell appears. Then it's filled with new data and made to reappear at the other end of the table. This creates an illusion of one long table using a small number of cell objects.

You'll find the same principle elsewhere in iOS. For example, map pins are independent of pinned locations. When a map is scrolled, pins are reused if they scroll outside the visible area. This minimizes the number of pin objects in memory and makes it possible to display maps with thousands of pinned locations using a handful of pin objects.

MVC can seem overly complex when you first encounter it. But it offers real advantages over more straightforward display options.

Working with MVC messages

If you've never used MVC, it's natural to expect that visible objects are created and displayed in a loop, with a clear order.

This isn't how MVC works. In practice, MVC uses question-response messages to ask your app for data to display, but only when it needs to.

Figure 4.15 shows the code that manages a table in the Master Detail Application template.

The critical message handler here is called cellForRowAtIndexPath:. iOS sends this message to your app when a cell is about to scroll into view.

The code in this handler manages cell recycling, fills a cell with text to represent the current date and time, and returns the cell to iOS for display. iOS then adds the cell to the top or bottom of the table, as needed. Cell insertion and display as the table scrolls are automatic.

Even if you don't understand the details of this example (it may be too much to take in on a first reading), keep in mind that you'll find MVC used throughout iOS. Objects are only displayed when they need to be. Your app needs to handle messages from iOS that ask for data, but these messages arrive just before iOS needs the data, not when the surrounding view appears.

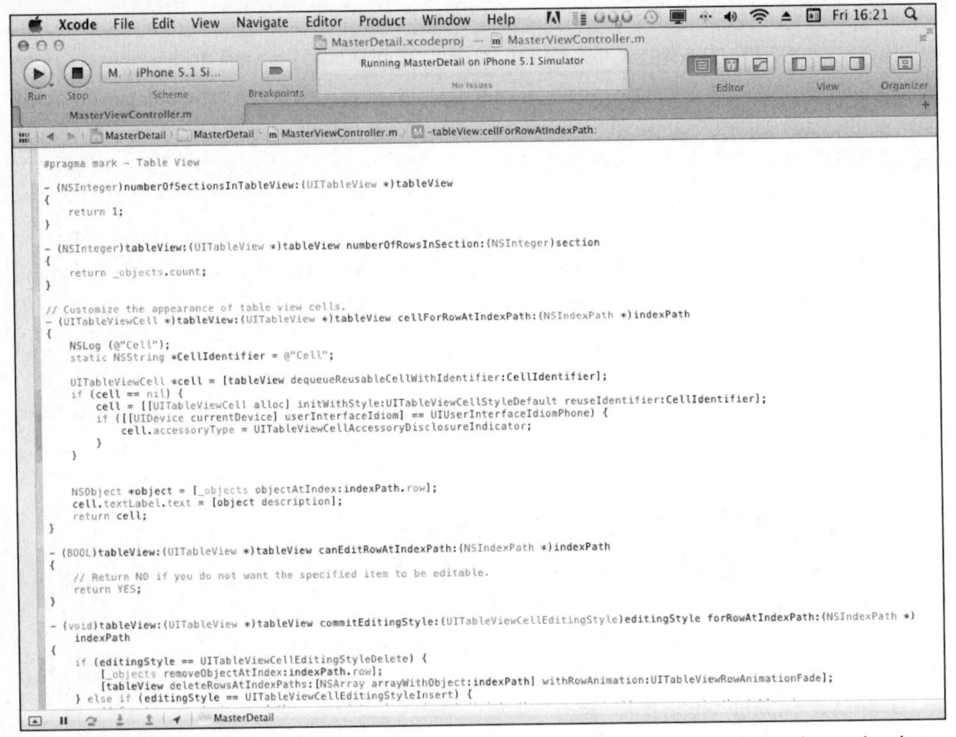

4.15 Table management code. MVC means that cells are recycled and filled with new data only when iOS decides they need to be.

Appreciating Graphic Design

You need to understand the mechanics of UI design—views, controllers, and nib files—to build a working app. To build a *successful* app, you must make the UI appealing and easy to use.

Apps that use the default objects in the Xcode library don't stand out in the App Store. For maximum impact, you should customize the look of your app with creative use of color, text fonts, logos, and custom design elements. Aim for a consistent color scheme, and use original graphics where you can. Don't be afraid to borrow ideas from your favorite apps.

The ideal UI is so simple that it doesn't require instructions. Aim to eliminate redundancy, so users have to do as little as possible to perform the task they want. Keep the app concept as simple and clear as you can, so it's obvious how the different features of the app work together.

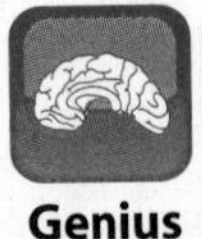
Genius

It's a good idea to use icons instead of text labels in your UI. Icons and graphics have international recognition. Text labels have to be *localized*—translated into different languages—as described in Chapter 11. This can create lots of extra work.

If you're not a designer, you can find many online sources that offer original free backgrounds and graphics for iOS. Search for "iOS graphics" to find examples. If you have a development budget, consider hiring a professional graphic designer.

Customizing graphics takes time, but the results can be worth it. Figure 4.16 shows one example: Zettaboom's Usha link sharing app, which uses both stock and custom graphics to create a distinctive visual feel.

4.16 Creating a simple but intuitive interface with graphics and minimal text.

Summarizing UI Creation

You've learned a lot in this chapter, so let's end with a summary.

- Apps are made of message handlers.
- iOS sends messages to your app when significant events happen or are about to happen.
- iOS also sends messages to your app when it needs data or to ask if your app supports a feature, such as screen rotation.
- Objects in your app can message iOS to ask for objects, data, or services.
- Objects in your app can message each other and themselves.
- An app UI is made of visible objects that generate messages when the user interacts with them.
- For each screen in the UI, a view controller manages UI content and most of the user interaction, while visible UI content is made of views, subviews, and controls and saved in a nib file.
- A technology called MVC is used to minimize the number of visible objects held in memory.

How Do I Create Code?

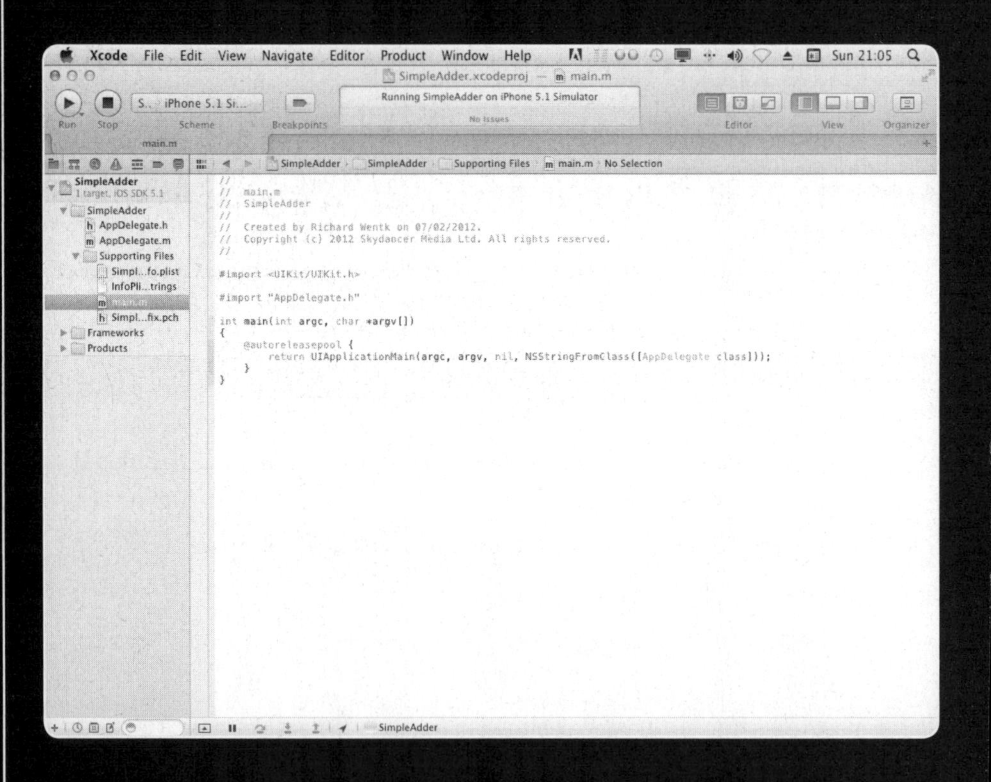

Apps are coded using a mix of C and Objective-C code. Some features in iOS use C instead of Objective-C. Although app developers don't need to be experts in C development, a basic working knowledge is essential. This chapter introduces the fundamentals of C and demonstrates a few of them in a very simple C application. It also introduces the key features of code editing and explains how to create debugging information and display it in Xcode's Debug window.

Introducing Code Design

Apps are built of two kinds of raw material: data and instructions for managing and processing data.

Computers are powerful because they're good at working with many different kinds of data. As a developer, you can make your app work with text, numbers, sounds, graphics, animations, nib files, web pages, and so on.

This flexibility is created by a useful illusion. Inside every computer, all data is binary—patterns of 1s and 0s. The patterns are processed by relatively simple instructions. Because computers can follow hundreds of millions of instructions every second, it's possible to create complex effects from simple building blocks.

In theory, a developer could build a working app by typing millions of 1s and 0s into a file and uploading it to an iDevice. In practice, it's much easier to let the computer *compile* a list of instructions and data definitions into binary.

This means there's less work for you to do. You create your app by typing instructions using C and Objective-C code. Xcode then takes your instructions and builds an app from them.

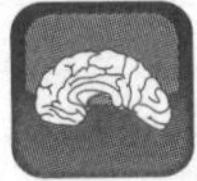
Genius

The very earliest computers were literally programmed with binary. Programmers worked out binary patterns on paper and entered 1s and 0s directly into memory using a bank of switches. (Software was rather less complicated then.)

Organizing data

As a developer, you perform two tasks as you create an app.

- **Organize the data in your app.** This means defining the numbers, text, objects, and other elements your app uses as it works.
- **Define the instructions that work on that data.** As we saw in Chapter 4, this means creating message handlers for many possible events.

The complete set of data definitions and instructions are your app's code.

Some developers believe that organizing data is almost as important as processing it. Messy and confusing data designs make it harder for you to create the instructions that process the data. Your app will be less likely to work reliably. You'll find it's harder to fix problems and more difficult to make changes if you try to update basic features. Conversely, simple and elegant data designs make the rest of the development process seem easy.

Mixing C and Objective-C

In this chapter, we introduce some of the basic features of code design in C, including the raw materials you can use to organize data and process it in your app.

Because apps are a mix of C and Objective-C code, and because some features of iOS use C code, you must understand some of the basics of C before you can start creating apps.

Basically, you use C code for the following:

- **Basic arithmetic**
- **Basic counting**
- **Simple collections of data**
- **Very simple text management.** This includes format conversion—for example, specifying the number of decimal places that appear when you display a number.
- **Simple comparisons and tests.** These tests are called *conditionals.* You can use them to select code based on the result.
- **Simple loops.** You can repeat a section of code a set number of times, or until a condition becomes true (or false.)
- **Simple text output to the Debug window.** Typically, you use this for testing and remove the test code before releasing your app.

Objective-C is more complex and powerful. It's typically used for the following:

- Creating and using objects
- Handling messages
- Creating and processing complex collections of data
- Managing screen content
- Working with formatted text (in a specific font, size, color, and so on)
- Creating animations
- Playing and recording media, including video, sound, and photos

Most apps mix C and Objective-C code seamlessly. Often, a skeleton of C code that defines the order of events, covered in a flesh of Objective-C objects. Other features—both instructions and data—use C or Objective-C, as needed.

Editing and Building Code

In a typical app, code is split across multiple files. We'll look at the organization of the files later in this chapter and the next one. But with the exception of nib files, which were introduced in Chapter 4, all code files are text. You edit them by selecting a file in the Project navigator so that it appears in the Editor pane and typing text into it.

The Editor isn't a conventional word processor. It's designed for code editing, and it includes useful tools for highlighting errors as you type, and while the app is being tested, as shown in Figure 5.1. It also includes a feature called *Code Completion* that tries to guess what you're trying to type, so it can fill in the rest of your typing for you to save time.

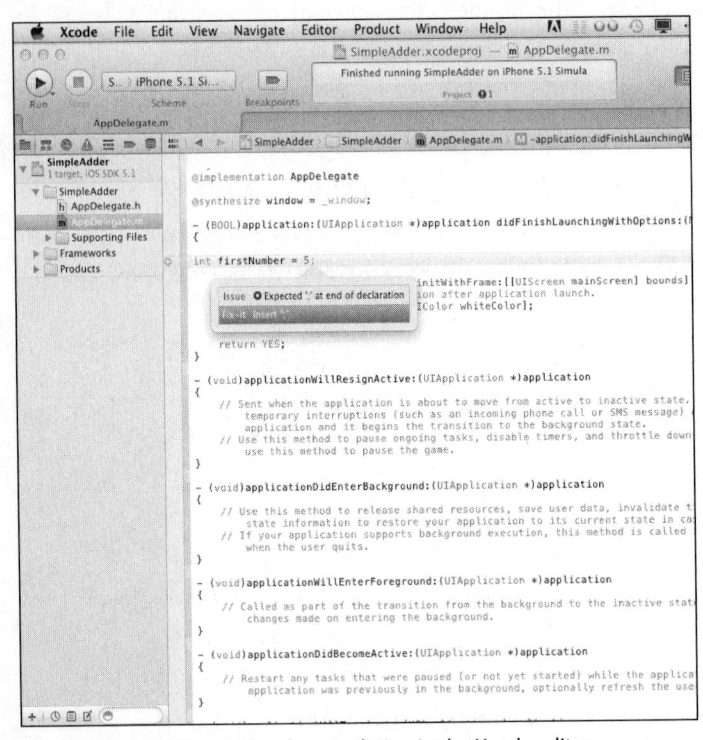

5.1 Error highlighting and code completion in the Xcode editor.

Understanding Errors and Warnings

Code is complex, and most code has errors. Two types of errors can occur:

- **Compile-time errors.** These are also known as build-time errors. Xcode finds them while it builds your app.
- **Run-time errors.** These occur after the app builds. Ideally, you try to catch them while the app is being tested, but it's not unusual for apps to be released with run-time errors.

Understanding compile-time errors

Compile-time errors are basic errors in code. They're the equivalent of obvious mistakes in English. When Xcode reports a compile-time error, it's telling you that some part of your code doesn't make sense and that you must fix the error before it can build the project.

The Editor looks for obvious errors as you type. Figure 5.1 shows an example: a missing semicolon. (You'll find more about semicolons in code later in this chapter.)

The error is indicated with a red marker to the left of the code. Note that Xcode includes five features to help you code correctly.

- **Xcode tries to anticipate the code you want to type as you type it.** To accept a guess, press Enter. Otherwise, keep typing to see more accurate guesses. If there are multiple fields in a guess, you can tab through them. You can also select the correct code from a floating menu, if it appears there. (It won't if you're doing something unexpected.)
- **Code is indented automatically.** Indentation (distance from the left side of the screen) is cosmetic only, but it does make code easier to read by grouping related code vertically. The automatic indentation in Xcode isn't bulletproof, and sometimes you need to help it by entering extra tabs yourself. But it does attempt to keep your code looking good.
- **Errors are shown immediately.** Distractingly, you'll see errors marked before you've finished typing the correct code. Ignore the temporary errors. Wait to see if any are left after you've finished typing a line, statement, or a block of code.
- **If you click an error marker, you see a more detailed description of the error.** The description is terse, but it tells you more than a red warning marker does.
- **Suggested fixes are shown for some errors.** This is a feature called Fix-It. You can click a suggestion to accept it. Xcode modifies your code automatically.

Caution

The Fix-It suggestions are very basic. They can help you fix very simple and obvious errors. But Xcode isn't smart enough to understand your code in detail, so sometimes the suggestions are misleading or just plain wrong. As you become more experienced, you'll stop making basic errors and use Fix-It less and less.

Understanding warnings

Some compile-time errors aren't serious enough to stop Xcode, but are worth reporting; for example, Xcode warns you if you create an object but never do anything with it. These errors are called *warnings.* Xcode flags them with a yellow triangle symbol. In theory your code shouldn't generate warnings. But some warnings are overly cautious, and many warning messages make sense only after you gain some experience. A good strategy is not to worry about warnings for your first few practice apps. Once you get comfortable with app basics, you can start learning the extra details that make it possible to write warning-free code.

Understanding run-time errors

Run-time errors are more subtle than build-time errors. You may encounter two types:

- **Crashes.** Your app stops running because it tries to do something impossible or forbidden, known as a *fatal error*. For example, your app may have tried to access memory that doesn't exist. Xcode reports a crash by highlighting a line of code in green with a message from iOS—typically either SIGTERM or EXC_BAD_ACCESS, as shown in Figure 5.2.
- **Logical errors.** The app runs, but some features don't work as they should. Xcode doesn't report these errors. You must use the built-in debugging and testing tools to track them down.

When you see a crash, the line in the code marked by Xcode may not be the location of the original error. Figure 5.2 shows a simple error: an attempt to access memory that an app isn't allowed to access. In this example, the line is marked correctly.

But some errors are more complex. They can propagate through your app and cause a fatal error elsewhere in the code. Xcode always shows the location of the fatal error condition—the point at which your app attempted to do something it couldn't. This may not be the location of the original error.

Note also that SIGTERM or EXC_BAD_ACCESS don't necessarily tell you much about the error. When you see one of these errors, you'll need to use one of the debugging tools to work through your code step by step to try to find the mistake.

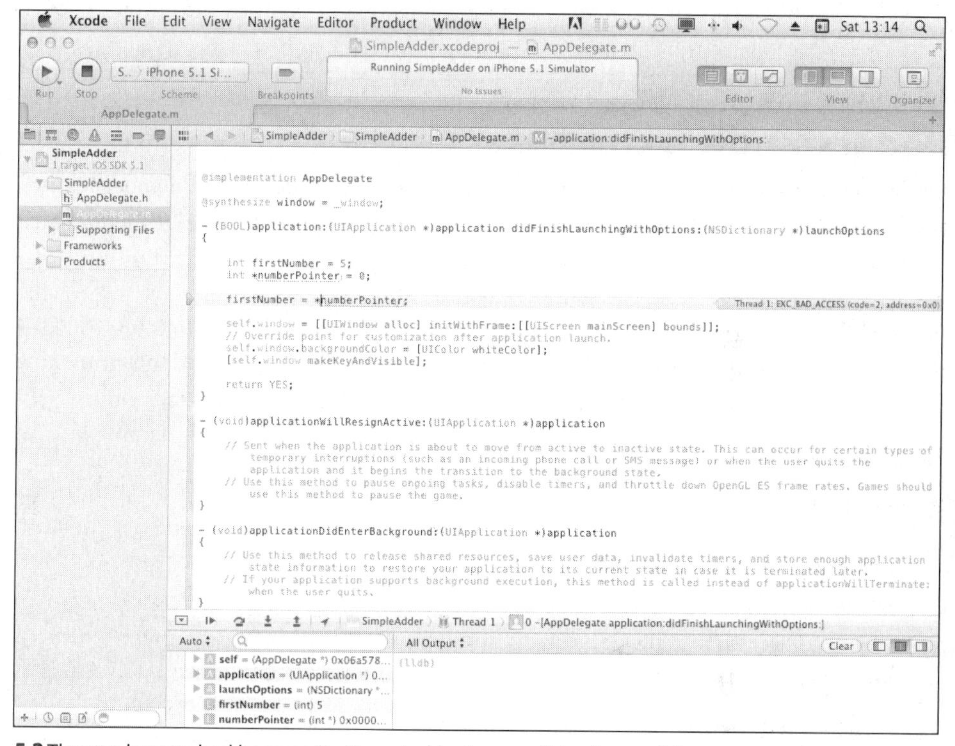

5.2 The app has crashed because it attempted to do something impossible.

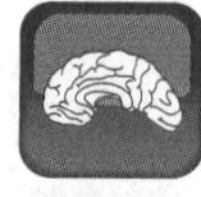

Genius

> It's completely normal to make lots of mistakes when you begin coding. You not only have to learn the features of C and Objective-C, you also have to avoid basic misspelling and remember extra basic details about the special punctuation symbols used in code. Eventually, you'll develop coding habits that avoid the most common errors. But this takes most developers—even professionals—a while.

Understanding the C Language

C is an old-fashioned programming language that is closely modeled on computer hardware. To use C successfully, you must know a little about how computers work.

Note

This chapter isn't a complete introduction to C. It's a simple primer that introduces many key features and gives you enough detail to understand the many more comprehensive tutorials you can find online. It takes most developers a few weeks to master the essentials of programming, and months or even years to become effortlessly fluent.

Understanding computers

A computer is a machine that stores and processes binary patterns. All the numbers, letters, images, web pages, sounds, and other information you work with (or play with) are represented by collections of binary digits (bits), each of which holds a single 1 or 0.

You can't do much with a single bit, so bits are grouped together. The most basic grouping is a *byte*—eight bits in a row. Any group of two more bytes in a row is called a *word,* as shown in Figure 5.3. Different computer systems use different word lengths. In iOS, words are 32-bits long.

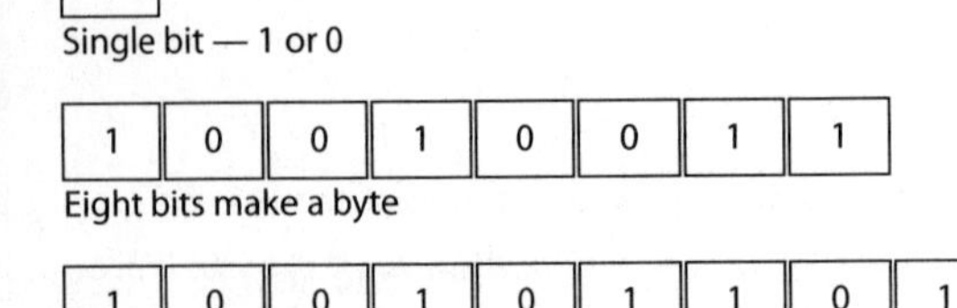

5.3 Bits, bytes, and words—the most basic binary groupings.

Caution

In computer jargon, a word isn't a word of text. It's simply two or more bytes taken together.

A single bit has two possible values: 1 and 0. Two bits have four values: 00, 01, 10, and 11. Every time you add a bit, you double the number of possible values. To find the number of possible values for a given number of bits, calculate it as a power of 2. For example, 16 bits has 2^{16} possible values, which is 65,536.

Note

It's almost impossible for humans to read binary. For convenience, it's traditional to pack binary into a denser format called *hexadecimal* (or *hex*). Conventional decimal numbers are base 10. This means numbers are represented with 10 symbols (0 to 9). Hex is base 16, with 16 symbols (0 to 9, A to F). The counting system is similar to decimal, but instead of adding an extra digit at the front of a number when you reach 10, you keep counting through A to F and add an extra digit when you reach 16, which is "10" in hex. Hex numbers are often prefixed with "0x". Sixteen in hex is "0x10".

Representing data in C

Although you can work directly with bits, bytes, and words in C, it's more usual to work with *fundamental data types*—C representations of numbers and text. In practice, most information reduces to numbers and text characters. The numbers and text are usually grouped into more complex structures, but there isn't much else going on under the hood.

Understanding Computer Hardware

Although computers include screens, disk drives, and other hardware, the two most critical components are a processor and a memory.

Computer memory is like a very long series of numbered pigeonholes, each of which stores a single byte. Each byte has a unique *address,* numbered sequentially from 0. Traditionally, addresses are shown in hex.

The memory holds all the data your application uses, as well as iOS itself. The same memory holds data and instructions. They're usually kept in separate areas of memory, but these areas can be anywhere in the millions of pigeonholes that are available.

The processor pulls bytes and words from memory by fetching ("reading") them from their addresses; combines them in various ways to perform arithmetic, compare values, and so on; and reports the result, usually by putting ("writing") more bytes and words back into memory.

To speed up this process, computer hardware often reads and writes whole words instead of single bytes. In iOS, the words are 32 bits long.

This may seem a complex process, and in some ways, it is. Computer languages like C and Objective-C exist to simplify it for you. They hide the complexity of the binary and give you a more straightforward mental model to work with.

You could design your own schemes for packing numbers and text into binary patterns, but for everyone's convenience the designers of C have already done the job for you. Using fundamental data types saves you design time, and it also means you'll be using the same definitions as other developers.

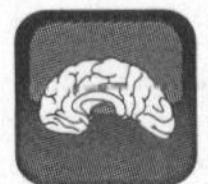

Genius

If you tell other developers how you organize data in your app or discover how they organize data in their apps, you can share files and information. Some developers share this information readily.

Using text in C

In C, text is stored in bytes. Western alphabets are represented with a single-byte system called ASCII (American Standard Code for Information Interchange), which uses standardized single-byte codes to represent lowercase and uppercase letters and common punctuation. Non-Western alphabets used a more complex multi-byte system called Unicode. Unicode can support foreign characters from Chinese, Japanese, Arabic, and other languages.

Text is often collected into *strings,* which are letter sequences arranged sequentially in memory, as shown in Figure 5.4. Strings are *terminated* with 0x00—a special zero character that marks the end of the string.

T	e	x	t	0
0x54	0x65	0x78	0x74	0x00

5.4 A string of characters spelling the word "Text" using ASCII codes.

Note

If you want to know more about ASCII and Unicode, search for them online. Both are international standards, so for example, the letter "A" is always 01000001. iOS can support both ASCII and Unicode text. Some features in iOS assume one or the other, so it's useful to know which formatting you're dealing with.

Note

Text in C is often terminated with an *escape sequence*—a special character preceded by a "\" (slash). For example "\n" starts printing any following text on a new line. Escape sequences are used for special characters and for other text effects. They're not often needed in Objective-C. You can find a complete list of escape sequences online with a web search.

Using numbers in C

Numbers are more complex than text. Numbers can be positive or negative, they may have a decimal point, and they may need to include a certain number of digits to guarantee accuracy or cover a certain range. (How many bits are needed to represent a trillion?)

For efficiency, numbers in C can be represented in more than one way. Numbers used in financial apps need a decimal point and many digits of accuracy. Numbers used in scientific or engineering apps often need an even wider range and greater accuracy. But apps can also use simple integers (whole numbers) because integer arithmetic is always much faster than arithmetic on numbers that include a decimal point.

Note

> Note that numbers in C *aren't* represented as text strings. Although it's possible to write software that takes a string like "1234.567" and converts it into binary, this turns out to be very slow and inefficient. It's much quicker to pack numbers into various byte combinations. The processor inside an iDevice can perform arithmetic on many of these byte combinations directly.

Table 5.1 shows the data types you'll use most often.

Table 5.1 Common C Data Types

Type	Size	Range	Notes
`unsigned char`	8 bits	0 to 255	Short for "character." Mostly used for ASCII characters, but can also be used for small numbers.
`char`	8 bits	-128 to 127	The first bit defines whether the number is positive or negative.
`unsigned int`	32 bits	0 to 429467295	Short for "integer," a whole number.
`int`	32 bits	-2147483648 to 2147483647	The first bit defines whether the number is positive or negative.
`float`	32 bits	1.17549435 * (10^{-38}) to 3.40282347 * (10^{+38})	Short for "floating point number," a number with a decimal point.
`double`	64 bits	2.2250738585072014 * (10^{-308}) to 1.7976931348623157 * (10^{+308})	Short for "double precision floating point number."

There are some ad hoc rules for using numbers and characters:

- **Use char for characters.** Don't use it as a simple counter.
- **Use int to count and for basic integer arithmetic.** It's faster and more efficient than char, and you're less likely to run off the end of the available counting range.
- **Only use signed int if you're certain you need negative values.**
- **float isn't very precise.** It has about seven significant figures of accuracy. This is good enough for basic arithmetic where extreme accuracy doesn't matter—for example, the position of objects in a game.
- **Use double when you need extra precision.** If your app does lots of math, using doubles will make it run slowly. Use float when you can and double only when you have to.

Creating a Simple App in C

Now that you know something about representing data, you can create a very simple app to add two numbers together.

C includes a basic system for getting data from the user into an application. iOS isn't compatible with this system, so we're going to cheat and define the numbers inside the app itself and then print the results to Xcode's debugging window.

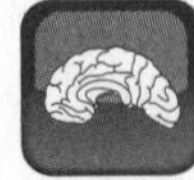

Genius

Technically, we're using the internals of the App Delegate object as a testbed for C code. In practice, most iOS apps are a mix of C and Objective-C, so this isn't a very strange thing to do. (It is possible to create and run a C-only application in Xcode without embedding the code inside an object. But the details would be distracting and wouldn't help you with app design, so we won't take that approach in this book.)

Adding code

To create this app, follow these steps:

1. **Launch Xcode if it isn't running already.**
2. **Create a new application using the Empty Application template.** Follow the instructions in Chapter 3. Save it as SimpleAdder.
3. **Navigate to the AppDelegate.m file in the Project navigator.**
4. **Click the file to load it into the editor.**
5. **Find the applicationDidFinishLaunchingWithOptions: message handler.**

6. **Add the following code after the first curly bracket:**

```
int firstNumber = 5;
int secondNumber = 8;
int outputNumber;
```

7. **Add the following code on a new line after the line with [self.window makeKeyAndVisible];:**

```
outputNumber = firstNumber + secondNumber;
NSLog(@"Result: %i", outputNumber);
```

Your code should look like the text in Figure 5.5.

8. **Build and run the App.**
9. **If the Debug window doesn't appear at the bottom of the screen, click the Debug view button near the top right of the main toolbar.** The result should look like Figure 5.6.

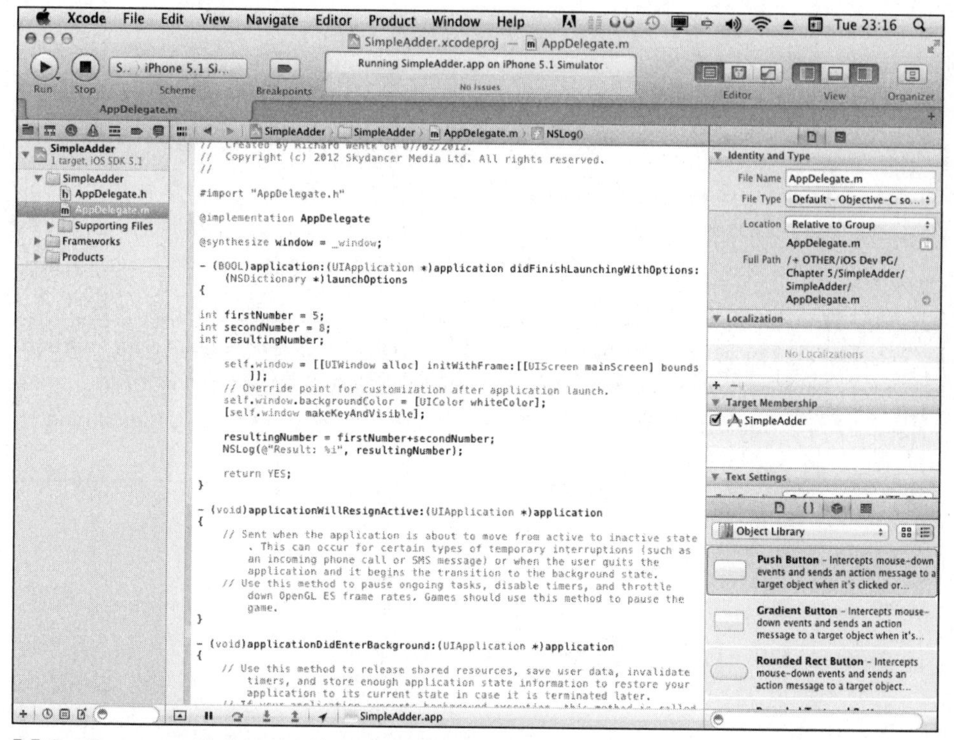

5.5 Creating a very simple app with very simple C code.

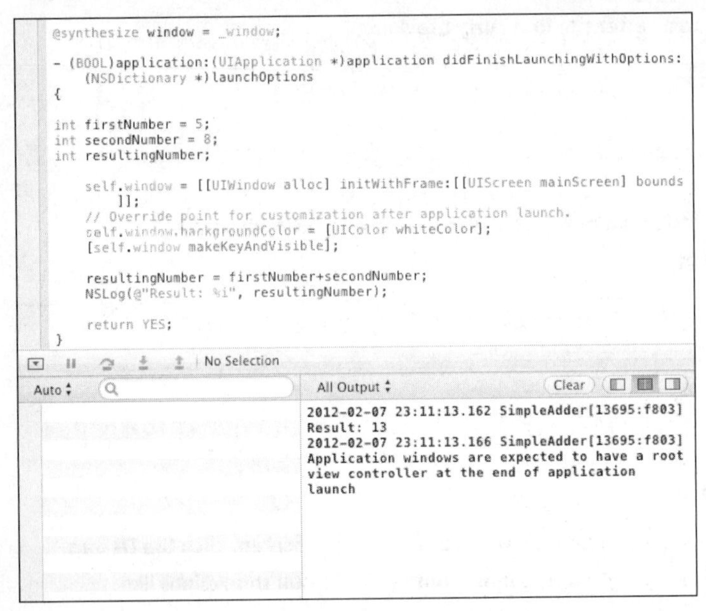

```
@synthesize window = _window;

- (BOOL)application:(UIApplication *)application didFinishLaunchingWithOptions:
    (NSDictionary *)launchOptions
{

int firstNumber = 5;
int secondNumber = 8;
int resultingNumber;

    self.window = [[UIWindow alloc] initWithFrame:[[UIScreen mainScreen] bounds
        ]];
    // Override point for customization after application launch.
    self.window.backgroundColor = [UIColor whiteColor];
    [self.window makeKeyAndVisible];

    resultingNumber = firstNumber+secondNumber;
    NSLog(@"Result: %i", resultingNumber);

    return YES;
}
```

No Selection
Auto
All Output
Clear
2012-02-07 23:11:13.162 SimpleAdder[13695:f803]
Result: 13
2012-02-07 23:11:13.166 SimpleAdder[13695:f803]
Application windows are expected to have a root
view controller at the end of application
launch

5.6 Our simple app added two whole numbers together.

If this is what you saw, congratulations! You've just created your first iOS app.

As you've likely guessed by now, you change the numbers assigned to firstNumber and second-Number, run the app again, and your app will add them.

Let's look at what the code does in more detail. Remember from Chapter 4 that code in the applicationDidFinishLaunchingWithOptions: message handler runs when the app launches. So the code we've added runs automatically before the rest of the app starts.

Note

When you build the Empty application template, Xcode produces an error message because it can't find a view controller object. Because we're creating a very simple app without a UI, we don't need a view controller. So you can ignore the warning; it doesn't apply to this app.

In this code, we've done four things:

- **Reserved memory for some data.** Specifically, we're using ints to store some numbers.
- **Given each item in memory a name, so we can refer to it.**

- **Inserted code to add two numbers together and store the result in another item.**
- **Added code to display the resulting item in the debug window.**

This looks like very simple code, and it is. But lots is happening behind the scenes.

Managing data

Data is stored in *variables.* Before you can use a variable, you must *declare* it—give Xcode some basic information about it. Whenever you use a variable in your code, Xcode checks that you have declared it. If you haven't, it reports a compile-time error.

A variable has three elements, with an optional fourth element that can be added if it's needed:

- **A data type.** When you declare a variable, you start your definition by telling Xcode its type. This tells Xcode how much memory to reserve for the variable. As you use the variable, Xcode keeps track of its type and complains if you try to combine it with an incompatible type—for example, by attempting arithmetic on a char and a float.
- **A name.** We define this by typing a name in Xcode.
- **An address in memory.** Xcode calculates the address for you when you build an app. If you don't need to know the address, you can ignore this element because it just works.
- **Optionally, an initial value.** We can define this if we need it. If we don't define it, it's likely (but not guaranteed in all circumstances) that the initial value will be zero.

This line of code:

```
int firstNumber = 5;
```

...is the same as telling Xcode the following:

- **We want to reserve memory for an int.**
- **The int is called firstNumber.**
- **Its initial value is 5.**

Note

Each complete line of code is called a *statement.* In C, statements end with a semicolon (;). Some statements are spread over multiple lines, so you don't *always* add a semicolon at the end of a line.

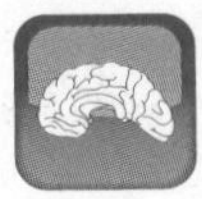
Genius

When Xcode builds an app, it builds a table with the name of every variable and every memory address. This table is used in debugging; it's how the debugger knows where to find the data in memory for each variable.

Naming variables

Although you can name variables with single letters, it's more useful to type a complete descriptive name because it makes your code easier to follow.

In iOS apps, variables are named using camelCase. There are no spaces in compound words. The first letter is lowercase. The first letter of each subsequent word is uppercase: firstNumber, secondNumber, and so on.

camelCase isn't enforced by Xcode. In theory, you can name variables as you like. But it's good practice to follow the convention. If you ever need to share your code with other developers, they'll find it easier to read if you do. (For further details see the "Introducting Coding Guidelines for Cocoa" document in the documentation.)

Caution

Computers are utterly unforgiving about inconsistent spelling. You *must* spell a variable's name the same way throughout your code. If you make a spelling mistake, Xcode assumes you have an undeclared variable and reports a build error. Note that the spellings are arbitrary. Xcode doesn't care if you spell English words correctly, but it does care if you change one of the letters in a variable name.

Note

In apps that use *x* and *y* coordinates, such as games, it's not uncommon to skip the capitalization for variables with names like firstx. Names like firstX look clumsy and can be difficult to follow. C code in other contexts sometimes uses Pascal case, with all first letters capitalized. Don't let this put you off from using camelCase in your own apps.

Displaying variables

In a commercial app, you would display information by sending it to an onscreen object. This works well, but it requires extra setting up.

In this app, we'll use a simpler option: the NSLog feature built into iOS. NSLog doesn't write to the screen. Instead, it sends text to the Xcode Debug window. Users can't see NSLog messages, but if you open the Debug window, you can watch the messages as they arrive.

NSLog is powerful, but it's also quite complex, and you need to learn how it works before you can use it. Here's a sample line of code:

```
NSLog(@"Result: %i", outputNumber);
```

Let's break this down into sections.

- **NSLog.** This tells Xcode that the rest of the line is an attempt to display information in the Debug window.
- **@"Result:** This part of the statement is called a *string literal.* iOS displays the string "Result:" without changing it. When you have many NSLog statements in an app, you can use this feature to label them so you can tell them apart in the Debug window.
- **%i":** This is a *format specification,* which is always prefixed by a percent (%) character. "%i" tells NSLog that you're trying to display an int. NSLog uses this information to interpret the bytes in memory according to the format you select.

Caution

If the format specification doesn't match the variable type, you get a meaningless result. In extreme cases, your app may crash.

- **outputNumber.** This is the variable you're attempting to display. Try replacing resultingNumber with firstNumber or secondNumber. You'll see that NSLog displays their values instead.

In addition to these elements, there's **(@"** at the start of the statement and **)** at the end. There's also a comma between the literal/format and the variable to be displayed. These are important symbols. You must include them, or the code won't work.

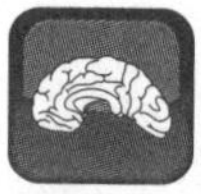
Genius

Try replacing %i with %x. You'll see the result displayed as a hex number—"d" in this example, which is hex for 13. Appendix A has a list of format modifiers that you can use with NSLog.

Note

C includes a simpler version of NSLog called printf. You should use NSLog in your apps instead of printf, because only NSLog can print information about objects.

Working with memory

In both C and Objective-C, you have to tell Xcode that you want to reserve memory. This means you must define variables before you can use them in your code.

For simple C variables, memory is reserved automatically. You don't need to worry about this part of the process; it just works.

However, sometimes you need to know where in memory your variables live. (This can be particularly useful in Objective-C.)

Change the last line you entered to the following. Don't forget to include the ampersand (&) in front of resultingNumber:

```
NSLog(@"Result: %p", &resultingNumber);
```

Build the app, and you'll see that the Result line in the Debug window shows a long hex number, as shown in Figure 5.7. You've now changed your code to find and display the memory address of resultingNumber. The ampersand (&) symbol tells Xcode to give you the memory address of a variable instead of the value it holds. The "%p" format specifier tells NSLog to display this address as a long hex number—0xbfffde90 in this example.

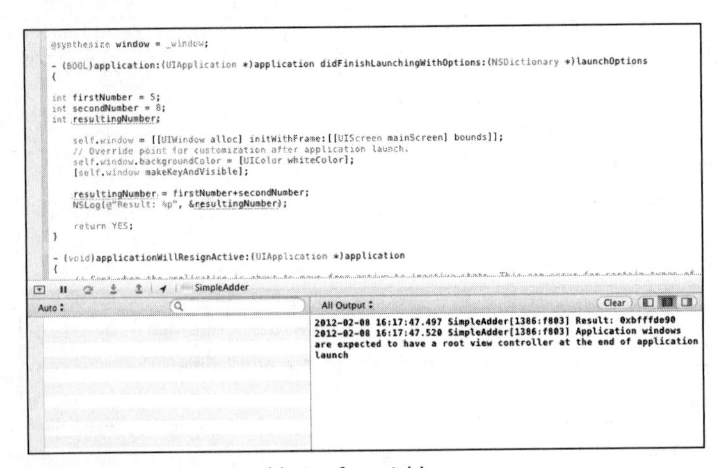

5.7 Finding the memory address of a variable.

Note

The exact value you see probably won't be the same because it depends on how much memory your Mac has and how many applications you have open.

Introducing pointers

It's often useful to access variables through their memory address. Instead of using a fixed name, you use another variable that holds the address of the variable.

This is so useful that both C and Objective-C have a special data type that holds memory addresses; it's called a *pointer,* because it points to a memory location.

You might expect a pointer to be a generic 32-bit memory address. In fact, pointers in C point to a specific data type, so you can have a pointer to an int, a pointer to a float, and so on.

This may seem overcomplicated, but it makes it possible to do arithmetic with pointers; if you have ints in a list and want to access the next one, C automatically knows how many bytes to add to a memory address.

Pointer types are also very important in Objective-C. In fact, you can access objects only through their pointers.

Pointers are prefixed with an asterisk (*) character. You declare a pointer to an int like this:

```
int *intPointer;
```

You can now experiment with pointers and memory addresses. Figure 5.8 shows one possible example of what you can do. You should be able to work out what the code does from the preceding few sections.

Note

Notice how adding 1 to intPointer adds 4 to the memory address it points to, because an int is four bytes long. Adding 1 to the memory address would be incorrect. The pointer would point to one of the bytes *inside an int.* The result would be meaningless.

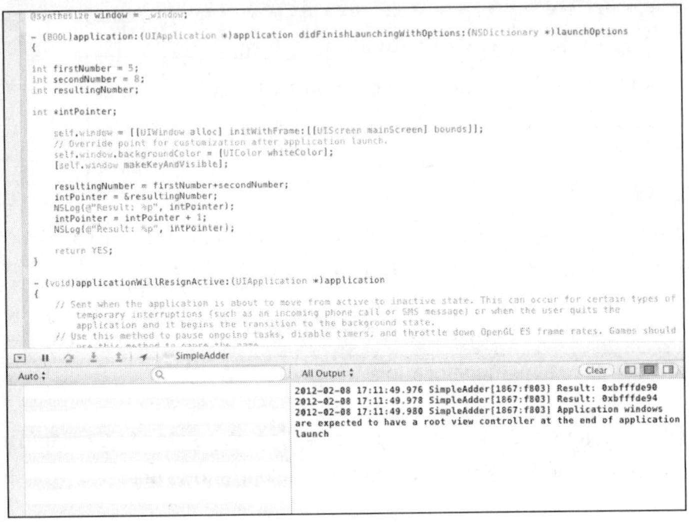

5.8 Using a pointer to work with memory addresses.

Grouping data

It's often useful to group the basic data types into more complicated structures. The two most useful compound data types in C are *arrays* and *structs.*

Introducing arrays

An array is a list of data arranged in sequential order, as shown in Figure 5.9. Each item in the array has an index, numbered from 0 up.

Index	Items
0	First item
1	Second item
2	Third item
...	...
n	(n + 1) item

5.9 An array is a list of items, accessed with an index.

Arrays have a type for the same reason pointers do. Knowing the type makes it possible for C to work out how many bytes of memory each item in the array needs. The index is *not* a simple byte counter.

You declare an array like this:

```
int anArray[numberOfItems];
```

numberOfItems sets the size of the array. The size is fixed when the array is created. You can't make simple C arrays bigger or smaller while your app is running, so it's good practice to make the number of items as big as you need.

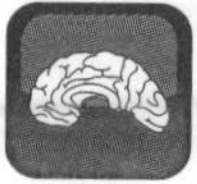

It's possible to create resizable arrays in C, but it's a complex process. You don't usually need to do it in an app, because Objective-C includes a more sophisticated kind of array you can use instead. It's described later in this book.

You access items in an array like this:

```
anArray[index];
```

As you've probably guessed, the index is just the item number. The index can be a constant like this:

```
anArray[3]; //Always accesses the fourth item in the array
```

or a variable, like this:

```
anArray[itemNumber];  //The value of itemNumber selects an item
```

Arrays are often used to store text strings. It's common practice to access a text string using a pointer to the first character in the array:

```
char *textString = &textArray;
```

It's possible to set itemNumber beyond the end of the array. If you try to access an array with an index outside its range, your app will crash.

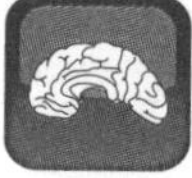

Arrays can have more than one dimension. In fact, they can have as many dimensions as you need—for example, int array ticTacToe [3][3]. A multidimensional array has one index for each dimension.

Introducing structs

It's often useful to create records that hold multiple data types in a single structure. For example, a patient record in a hospital might include age, height, weight, sex, a hospital reference number, and so on.

To create grouped data, use a C feature called a *struct,* which is short for structure, like this:

```
struct  patientRecord {
char    *patientName;
int     patientAge;
float   patientWeight;
int     patientID
};
```

After you have defined a struct, you can use it like any existing data type. To declare a variable with your new struct, do this:

```
patientRecord aPatient:
```

You can even create arrays of structs:

```
patientRecord allPatients[1000];
```

To access elements inside the struct, use *dot notation* like this:

```
aPatient.patientAge = 134;
aPatient.patientWeight = 500.0;
thisID = aPatient.patientID;
```

Making decisions

Your code must be able to make decisions automatically. In practice, this means testing variables to see how their values compare with some other value and then picking code accordingly.

Tests are called *conditionals*. Conditionals are used to select different code if a test is true or false. They're also built into loops, which repeat code until a condition becomes true (or false.)

Conditionals look like this:

```
(<value or variable> <conditional test> <compared value or variable>)
```

Table 5.2 shows a list of the tests you can use.

Table 5.2 Conditionals

Conditional code	Meaning
`==`	True if equal. (You must use *two* equals signs. Using a single equals sign will set the test variable to a new value and will always return true, which is never what you want.)
`!=`	True if not equal
`>=`	True if greater than or equal
`>`	True if greater than
`<=`	True if less than or equal
`<`	True if less than
`&&`	True if both values are true
`||`	True if either value is true
`!`	True if a value isn't true. (This can be more useful than it sounds. It's often useful to do something if a condition isn't true.)

In practice, conditionals are embedded in other statements. For example, you can use the "if" statement to select between two options:

```
if (firstNumber == 3 && secondNumber == 10)
   thatNumber = 5;
else
   thatNumber = 10;
```

The English equivalent is "if firstNumber is 3 and secondNumber is 10, then make thatNumber 5. Otherwise, make thatNumber 10."

Appendix A includes a summary of the most useful statements you can use with conditionals.

Repeating code

Code that repeats is called a *loop* (because it loops back on itself). There are three options in C:

- **The for loop.** This is usually used to repeat code a set number of times.
- **The do loop.** This loops until a condition is true. The code inside the loop runs at least once.
- **The while loop.** This loops while a condition is true. The conditional test happens first, so the code inside the loop may not run.

A sample for loop looks like this:

```
for (int i = 0; i<10; i++) {
    doStuff...
}
```

This code sets a counter int to 0 and repeats the doStuff code as long as i is less than 10—that is, 10 times, counting from 0 to 9 inclusively. (The "i++" statement means "add 1 to i"; there's more about this idiom later in this chapter.)

You can find examples of the other loops in Appendix A.

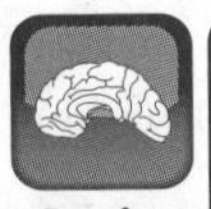

Genius

Technically the for loop is redundant. You can create the same result using a while loop. But for loops can make your code easier to read, and advanced developers can use more complex initialization and conditional code to create more sophisticated results.

Note

You can jump out of a loop or conditional by using "break", which skips the rest of the loop and conditional and continues running the code immediately after it.

Re-using code with functions

It's often useful to take a piece and make it reusable from different parts of an app. In C, you can do this by *declaring a function.*

A function has two elements:

- **The prototype.** This includes the return data type, the function name, and the input data type (or types).
- **The definition.** This includes the code that you want to reuse.

Here's a simple prototype:

```
int addTwoInts (int, int);
```

And here's a matching definition:

```
int addTwoInts (int a, int b)
{
   return a+b;
}
```

Here are the key points you should remember about functions:

- **Prototypes and definitions can be defined almost anywhere.** They don't have to be close to each other. They don't even have to be in the same file.
- **The prototype defines the function name and the data types it works with.** The input and output variables aren't named in the prototype.
- **The definition defines the variable names.**

Note

The names are valid only inside the function. You can repeat the names inside the function elsewhere—for example, in another function that multiplies two numbers.

- **The code in the definition is placed between curly brackets.**
- **The value after "return" defines the result of the function.** In the example, the return value is "a+b."
- **If a function doesn't return a value, its type is "void."** Use "void" for functions that do something useful but don't calculate a single returned value. (For example, you might want a function that steps through every item in an array and runs some code on each one. There's no single return value, so void is appropriate.)
- **The returned data type must match the function type.** This may sound complicated, but it simply means that if the function is supposed to return an int, you must give the return statement an int. Likewise for other data types. Pointers are allowed.
- **Any code after "return" is ignored.** Xcode literally skips over it.

Figure 5.10 shows a revised version of our simple app with a function prototype and definition at the top of the file. The function is used later in the code to perform the addition. As you can see, the result is the same.

Some functions return an int as a success/fail indicator. Traditionally, 0 indicates that a function completed its task successfully. Anything other than 0 indicates there was an error.

Understanding scope

When you declare a variable inside a conditional or loop, it's available only to the code immediately around it. So if you declare an int i in a for loop, that int *disappears* once the loop completes.

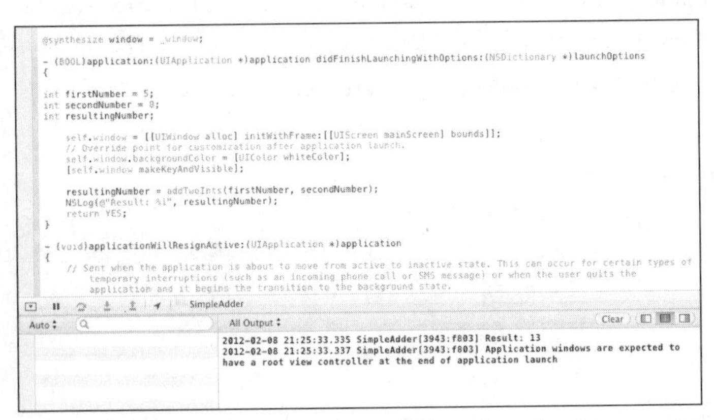

5.10 Modifying the test app to perform addition using a function.

Similarly, if you declare variables inside an if statement, those variables exist only inside the statement.

This is called *scope*. Every variable has a scope. In outline, there are three scopes:

- **Inside a conditional or loop.**
- **Inside a function.** (Or inside a method in Objective-C.)
- **Inside a file.**
- **Anywhere.** These are called *global variables.*

This becomes more important in Objective-C. But the simple rule-of-thumb method is that if you want to use a variable in a file, declare it at the top of the file. Variables inside functions/methods or conditionals are temporary and will be trashed without notice.

Caution

You can use global variables in C—do a web search for the "extern" keyword for more details. Global variables are possible in Objective-C, but strongly discouraged. You're supposed to use objects instead—which are described in the next couple of chapters.

Using other C idioms

Here's a selection of other C idioms you should know.

Bitwise operations

You can use *bitwise* operations to manipulate binary patterns directly. Bitwise operations don't work on floats or doubles.

Some operations combine the bit patterns in two variables:

- **AND.** This sets an output bit if the corresponding bit in BOTH the input variables is on.
- **OR.** This sets an output bit if the corresponding bit in EITHER input variable is on.
- **Exclusive OR.** This sets an output bit if ONE of the bits in the input variables is on, but not if both are on.

Others work on a single variable:

- **Right shift.** This shifts all the bits to the right; it takes an int to specify the number of places to shift.
- **Left shift.** This shifts all the bits to the left; it takes an int, as above.
- **Invert.** This flips 1 to 0, and vice versa.

Table 5.3 lists the bitwise operations you can use and the symbols you include in your code when you want to use them.

Table 5.3 Bitwise operations

Operation	Meaning
&	Bitwise AND
|	Bitwise OR
^	Bitwise Exclusive OR
<<	Left shift
>>	Right shift
-	Invert

Note that shifting one place to the left is equivalent to multiplying by 2. Shifting two places to the left is equivalent to multiplying by 4. Shifting one place to the right is equivalent to dividing by 2. And so on.

```
int i = 16;
int j = i << 1;    // j is 32
int k = i << 2;    // k is 64
int l = i >> 1;    // l is 8
int m = i >> 2;    // m is 4…
```

Manipulating numbers

Assuming we have declared an int called i, we can add one to it like this:

```
i = i+1; // This is the obvious way to add 1 to i
```

You can also do any of the following:

```
i += 1; //A shorter way to add 1 to i
i++;    //An even shorter way
++i;    //Another shorter way
```

The first shortcut works with all other arithmetic operations and bitwise operations. The last two shortcuts support only addition and subtraction.

The last two examples are subtly different when they appear in a longer statement such as this:

```
arrayIndex [i++] = otherArray[q];
```

The ++i version adds one to i before the code does anything else. The i++ version waits until the rest of the statement is complete and then adds one to i.

Note

You don't have to use these shortcuts, but you will find them in sample code created by other developers.

Converting between types

Remember that integer arithmetic works only on whole numbers. When you divide integers, there's no fractional part.

```
int a=5;
int b=3;
int c= a/b; //c is 1
```

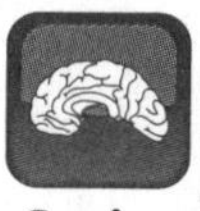

Genius

The percent (%) symbol is used for modulo division, which returns an integer remainder. For example, 5 % 3 is 2.

You can convert between types using a *cast*. To use a cast, place the type in brackets before an existing variable.

```
int a=5;
int b=3;
float c = (float) a/(float) b; // c is 1.666667
```

a and *b* are still ints, but the two casts temporarily upgrade them to floats for that one statement.

Using the standard library

C includes a standard library of functions, with a few hundred predefined functions you can use in your code. The functions include math, text string management, data checking, random number generation, and many others. For example, you can use a function called isdigit() to check if a character is in the range 0 to 9.

iOS has its own vastly extended version of the standard library, described in *manual pages* in the documentation, often shortened to "man pages."

You can view the complete list of iOS man pages by opening the main developer library page, clicking System at the bottom of the list at the left, and selecting iOS Manual Pages from the Documents list, as shown in Figure 5.11.

You do *not* need to remember this vast list. In practice, most of the functions are so obscure and highly specialized that you're very unlikely to use them. But it's useful to know how to do basic math, how to generate random numbers, and how to apply basic tests to characters and other data.

If you have a copy of *The C Programming Language*, the critical functions are listed near the back.

Note

This chapter has introduced you to lots of information. Unless you have a superhuman memory and a four figure IQ, it's unlikely you'll remember all of it. Don't worry if it takes some time to understand the key points. If you're finding it too much to take in, try exploring C features one at a time and experimenting with them. (And if you don't yet have a copy of Kernighan and Ritchie's *The C Programming Language*, now would be a very good time to acquire one.)

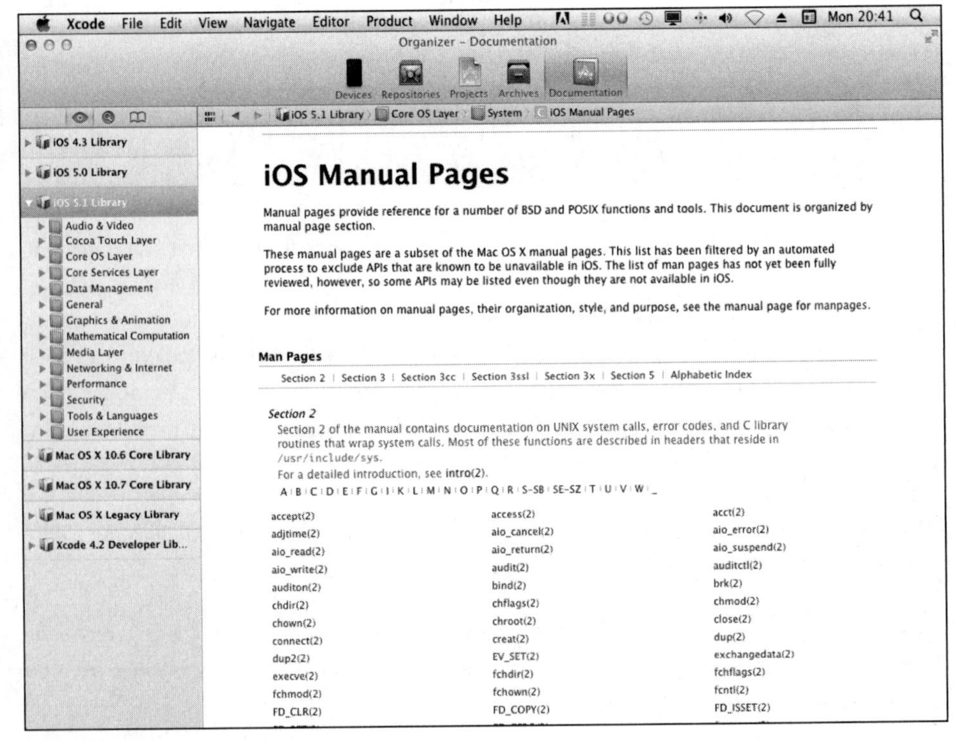

5.11 Introducing the iOS C Library functions.

How Do I Use Objects in My Code?

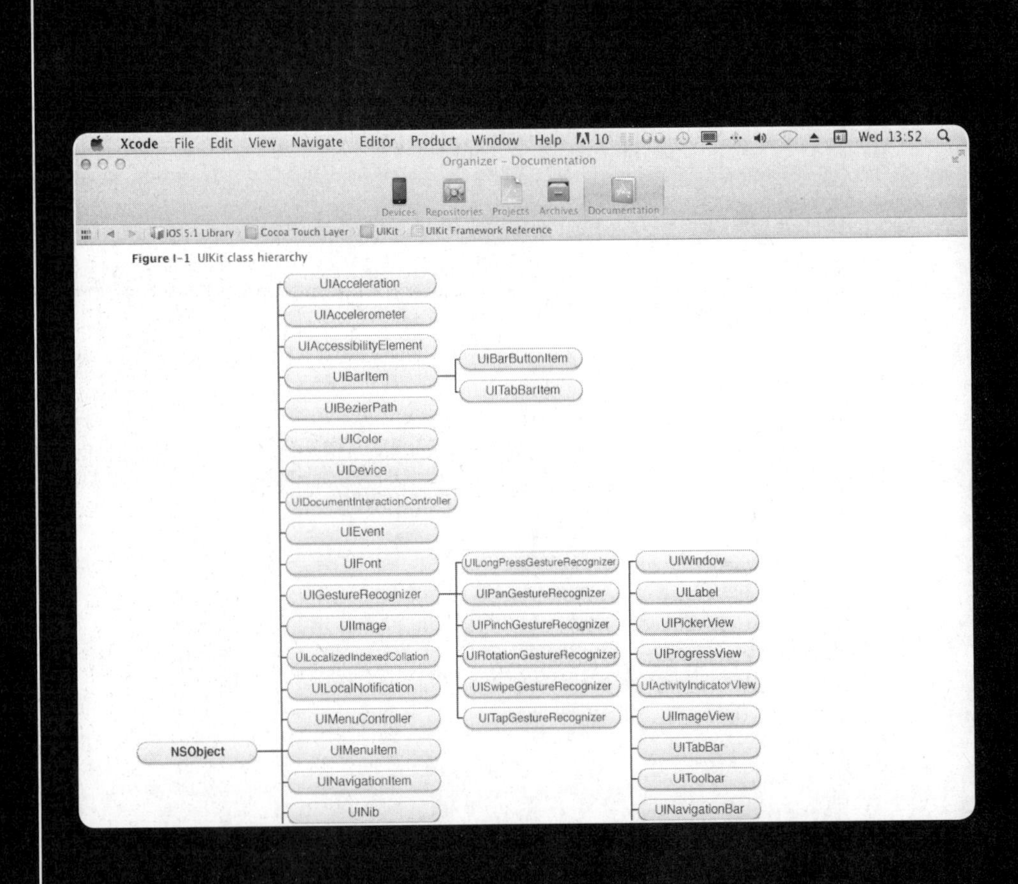

1 2 3 4 5 **6** 7 8 9 10 11 12 13

Objective-C is very different from C. The code looks similar, and many apps combine elements of both languages. But using Objective-C makes you think about the design of your app in a more abstract way that is less tied to computer hardware. Objective-C is a much looser language than C, and you can use its features to change how your app responds to events as it runs. With Objective-C, the goal isn't just code that works; the goal is intelligent code with a wide range of possible behaviors. You can use Objective-C to create simple, linear code, but its powerful features can help you add smarts to your apps.

Moving from C to Objective-C

At first sight, Objective-C code is very similar to C code, with a few extra punctuation marks and symbols. But because Objective-C uses objects, you must think about app design in a different way.

To develop a C application, you organize your data and create functions to process the data. The mental model you use is close to that of real computer hardware. You design structures that hold data in memory and process them with instructions that run in a fixed order.

To develop an Objective-C application, you pick objects from the iOS "kit of parts," customize them as needed, and link them by adding code to send messages. Events no longer happen in a fixed sequence, because Objective-C code is event-driven. App design focuses more on behaviors and less on data management, although you still have to include some of the latter in your app.

Caution

Some online descriptions of Objective-C bury you in jargon, with words like "polymorphism," "dynamic typing," and "dynamic binding." These are complicated words for simple ideas. But they're not often explained clearly, and you don't need to know what they mean to use Objective-C successfully.

Note

Many of the frameworks in iOS include both C and Objective-C features. It's not unusual to find helper functions and basic data structures defined in C, and in parts of iOS you can find objects embedded in C data structures. You need to be familiar with C to use these options. You should always look in the Framework Reference list for any framework you use to see which functions and data structures have already been defined for you.

Thinking with objects

Using objects means thinking about app design in a way that's less tied to computer hardware. Objects lend themselves naturally to the kit-of-parts model. They're also intuitively closer to the experience of objects in the physical world.

Imagine a racing game. Each car is an object. These are some possible properties of a car:

- **Position.** For a simple two-dimensional game, this will include *x* and *y* coordinates.
- **Speed.** More technically, this will be a velocity with at least two dimensions.
- **Graphical state.** Perhaps you want your car to explode when it leaves the track or collides with another car.

These are possible methods for our car example:

- **Update the position.** You might use this method to place the car on a starting grid.
- **Update the velocity.** You might use this method to find the current position and then update the position using the previous method.
- **Change the graphics.**

Crucially, the entire game can be an object. It might include the following methods:

- **Update all velocities.** This method might update all positions too.
- **Test for collisions.**
- **Update the score.**

Instead of thinking in terms of functions and data, you can design your app as a set of properties and behaviors. This has two benefits:

- **Code becomes modular and reusable.** After you have a method for updating the position of a single car, it's very easy to create code to update the position of every car.
- **Objects hide complexity.** When you're thinking about your game as a whole, you can make a list of the things you want your cars to do and outline your game code very quickly. You can then fill in the details for the car object. Crucially, you don't need to worry about fine details while you're sketching the big picture. Similarly, you can ignore the bigger structure of your app while you create the internal code for each object.

The down side is that you often need to spend more time designing the structure of your app before you begin coding. But if you can keep the structure clear and simple, you'll save time overall. You'll also make fewer mistakes.

Understanding classes

Methods and properties are defined in the *class definition* for the object. In the same way that C includes fundamental data types, Objective-C includes classes. Each type of object has its own class definition. The class provides an empty template that defines how data is organized in the object and which behaviors (methods) it supports.

In the documentation, the useful parts of a class are defined under the Tasks heading. Figure 6.1 shows the task list for the MPMoviePlayerController class. You've seen similar pages earlier in this book. But now that you understand properties and methods, you can see that both are summarized here. If you scroll down, you'll find that each item in the list is described in more detail—usually tersely—in a further section under the Tasks list.

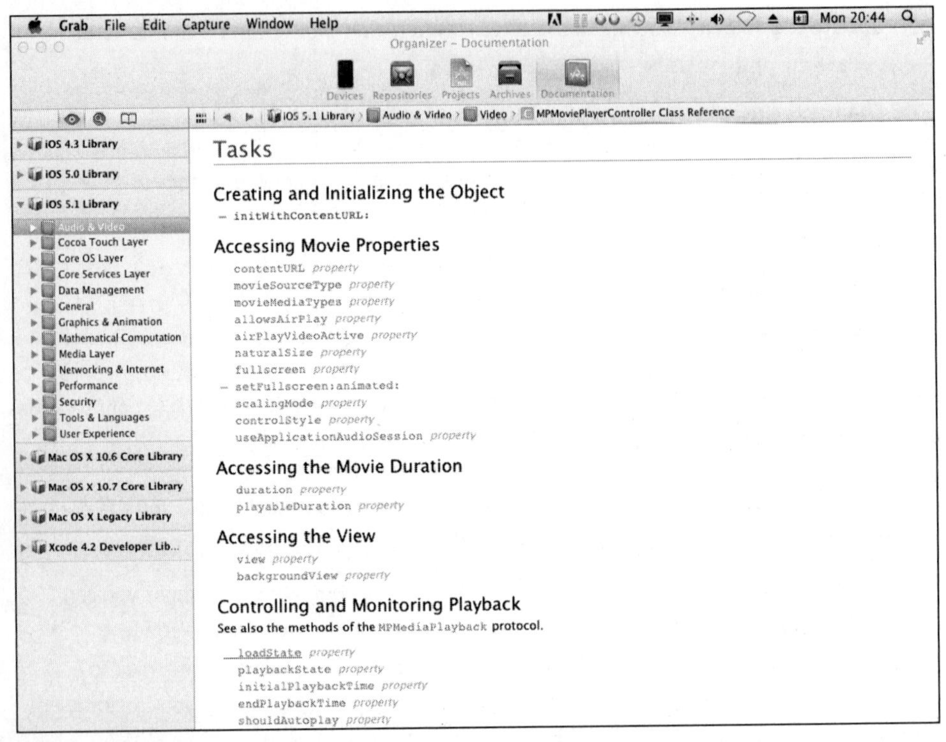

6.1 Looking at a class in more detail.

Note

A class is a template for an object of a given type. Objects in memory are *instances* of the class. The distinction is clear, but in practice it isn't unusual for it to become slightly fuzzy: In Objective-C, everything can be an object.

This list of methods and properties *completely defines the class*. Some features may not work as you expect because of design quirks, but the Tasks list is the definitive document on the features of the class.

In most apps, you use some classes as-is, creating objects without modifying them. The objects include the properties and methods shown in the documentation. But you can also *subclass* (customize) objects to extend or change their methods or properties.

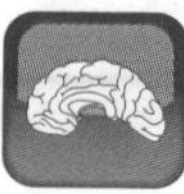

Genius

Why are properties included as tasks? It's natural to think of properties as variables rather than behaviors. But in Objective-C, properties are accessed indirectly through messages. So it makes sense of a sort to think of them as tasks. If this point isn't clear, you can ignore it. "Tasks" are only listed in the documentation. If you'd prefer to think of the task list as a useful summary of the features of a class, you won't miss any essential details.

Understanding inheritance

All iOS objects, including ones you define yourself, are subclasses of a single object called NSObject. All the classes in iOS are organized in a hierarchy rather like an inverted tree. NSObject is at the top of the tree. Various subclasses are one level down. These subclasses are subclassed in turn.

The complete tree structure has hundreds of classes and many levels. You don't need to remember the shape of the tree or the position of the classes in it. But you need to know about *inheritance.*

Inheritance means that when you create a subclass, it inherits all the features of the classes on the branch above it, all the way up to NSObject.

Note

The class above a subclass is called the *parent class* or *superclass.*

Figure 6.2 shows the class reference for the UIStepper class, which displays a +/- button on the screen. Near the top of the page is an "Inherits from" field. This entry tells you that UIStepper not only supports the properties and methods listed in its class reference, it *also* supports the properties and methods of the following classes: UIControl, UIView, UIResponder, and NSObject.

This point is critical, and it can be immensely confusing for newcomers, because *inherited properties aren't listed in the UIStepper class reference.* The list of superclasses is the only clue you get that other properties and methods are built into a class.

When you see an inheritance list like this, you should read the documentation for every class in the inheritance list. It's the only way to find the full list of properties and methods that are included in a subclass.

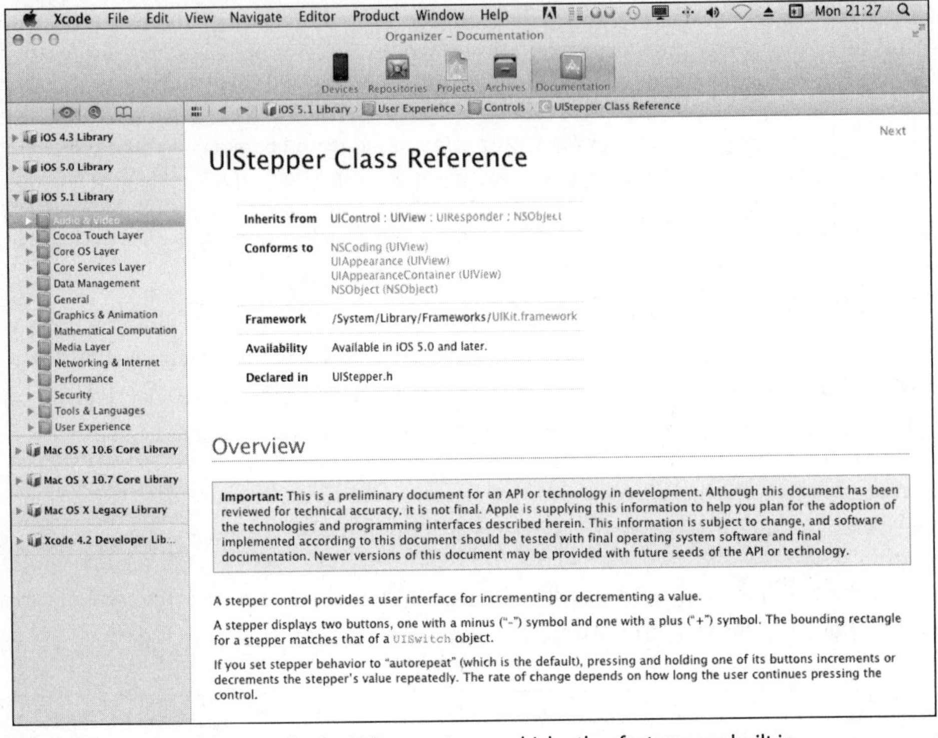

6.2 Looking at the inheritance list for UIStepper to see which other features are built in.

Let's look at an example. Figure 6.3 shows the task list for UIControl, which is the parent class of UIStepper. You can see there are plenty of extra features that manage touch events and other user actions. They're built into UIStepper, but they aren't listed in the UIStepper documentation; if you never look at the features of its superclasses, you'll never know they're there.

Exploring messaging and behaviors

In C, you write or read data in a struct by accessing it directly. In Objective-C, you send an object a message asking it to set a property or return a value.

You can use this option in a very simple way. Writing methods that set or get properties is a chore, and Objective-C includes a feature called @synthesize that automates this process for you. It literally generates the code you need to access properties, leaving you free to concentrate on the design of your app.

But you can also create your own methods, with more advanced features. For example, when you update the position of one object in a game, you might want your code to redraw some graphics or update some other data.

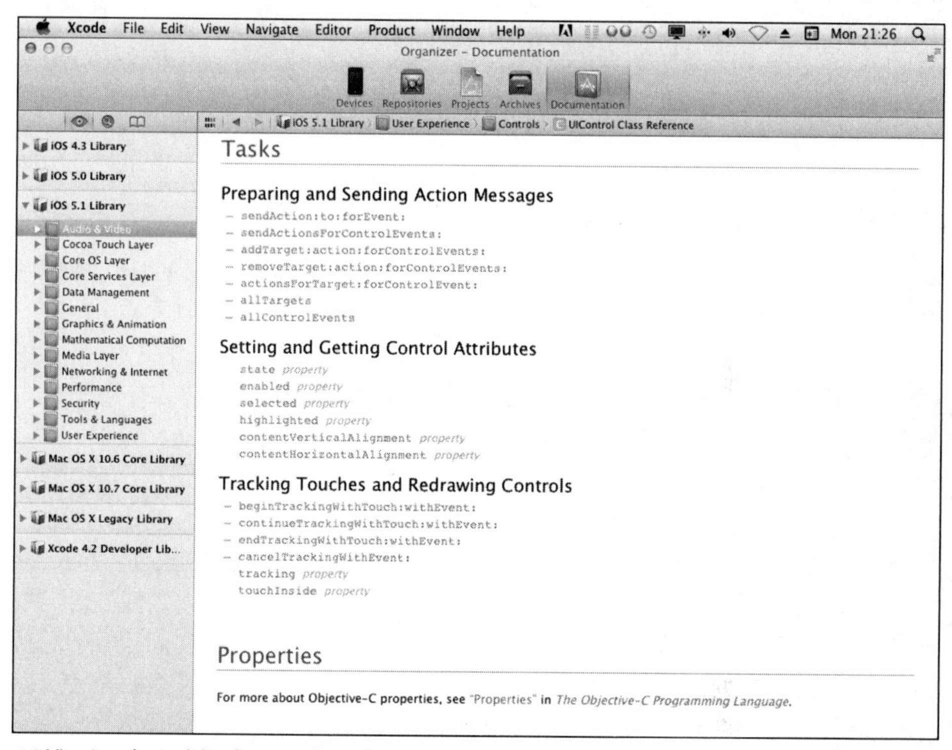

6.3 Viewing the task list for one of UIStepper's superclasses.

Objective-C supports more advanced techniques that can monitor a property value and trigger a method whenever it changes. Objects can "watch" properties in other objects and respond automatically when they're updated.

This makes Objective-C immensely powerful. Changing a property in one object can start a series of events that modifies the entire state of the app. For example, your app might download data from the Internet. Instead of explicitly sending a list of messages to various objects when the download completes, you can create objects that monitor the download and respond automatically when the downloaded data is available.

Put simply, objects can be intelligent. They can respond with complex behaviors to changes in their own properties, and they can monitor properties in other objects and respond automatically.

These advanced features are optional, and if you're new to Objective-C, they can seem abstract and difficult. But they're available if you need them, and it's useful to start thinking in a more abstract way as soon as you can. You'll find you can imagine code that is more sophisticated than is possible with C, but easier to understand.

Introducing Objective-C Code

The essential features of Objective-C are very easy to use. The idioms are simple and intuitive, and you'll likely find they're easy to remember.

Working with messages and properties

The code for sending a message to an object, which is equivalent to running a method in an object, looks like this:

```
[anObject aMessage];
```

This simply sends aMessage to anObject.

You can nest messages, like this:

```
[[anObject aMessage] anotherMessage];
```

This code sends aMessage to anObject and then sends anotherMessage to the result.

If aMessage takes some input values or objects, the code looks like this:

```
[anObject aMessage: anInput with:anotherInput andPossibly: moreInput];
```

"with" and "andPossibly" are part of the method name. They're set when you (or Apple) define the method. (Some methods have very long lists of inputs.)

If aMessage returns a result, you can do this:

```
aResult = [anObject aMessage];
```

aResult is *typed;* when you declare aResult in your code, it's type must match the type returned by aMessage. However, if you don't know the type or if you don't care about the type, you can use a generic catch-all type called id:

```
id aResult = [anObject aMessage]; //This always works. (But it isn't always
   useful.)
```

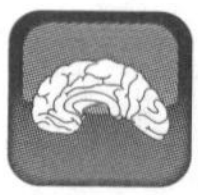
Genius

Using id is particularly helpful for managing UI events. Sometimes you want a single method that can handle events from multiple UI objects of many different types. id makes it possible to do this, because it works as a placeholder for inputs of any type.

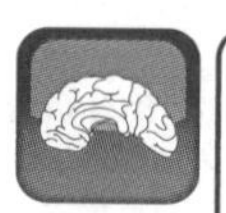
Genius

Objects can send messages to themselves. You can use this feature to trigger one method from another. Just replace the object name with the word "self." The rest of the syntax is the same.

To access a property in an object, use this idiom:

```
anObject.aProperty
```

Because objects can contain other objects and structures, you can extend this as needed:

```
anObject.anObjectInsideIt.aProperty
```

You can use "=" to assign values to properties.

```
anObject.aProperty = someValue;
```

Some objects also use set/get to access properties. This option is slightly old-fashioned now, but you will see the following in the Apple class references:

```
[anObject setAProperty: someValue];
aValue = [anObject getAProperty];
```

An important difference between C and Objective-C is that properties can store simple C data types or object pointers.

This is a small point with big consequences. When you assign a simple C value with "=", you're actually duplicating the data in memory. When the operation is over, you have two separate variables in two memory locations.

```
int a = 3;
int b = a; //b = 3. The memory address of a is different to the address of b.
```

When you assign objects with "=", you're copying the memory address stored in a pointer, which acts like a "handle" for the object.

This doesn't copy the object. It stays in a single block of memory. After the "=" statement, you can now access it through two pointers instead of one.

In other words, you still have *one* object in memory. But there are now two references to it. If you modify the object, you can access the change through either reference. *You don't have two independent objects.*

```
anObject.aProperty = 1;
anotherObject = anObject;       //This copies a pointer, not the object data
anotherObject.aProperty = 2;    //anObject.aProperty is also 2 now!
```

Figure 6.4 illustrates the difference. The key point to remember is that "=" doesn't copy objects. If you want to have two separate copies of an object, you must duplicate the object data. (You can use a method called copy, which is built into all objects in iOS.)

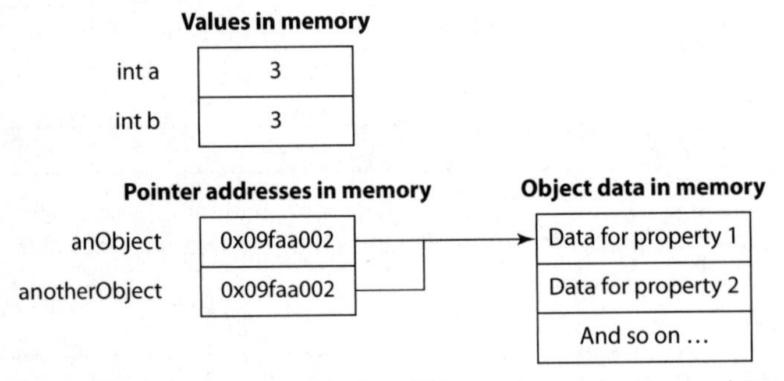

6.4 Simple C assignments copy data. Object assignments copy a pointer to an object, *not* the object data.

Caution

Because objects can contain other objects, copying can become complicated. To guarantee the operation works correctly, developers often have to create a custom version of the copy method for objects they create. Don't assume that copy "just works" without testing it thoroughly first.

Creating objects

In Chapter 4, you learned that you can create some of the objects in your app by including them in a nib file that loads when the app launches.

You can also create objects using code. The standard code looks like this:

```
ClassName *anObject = [[ClassName alloc] init];
```

This is a single line of code, but it does a lot. It sends a message called alloc to the class you want to create. The class assigns some memory for the object and returns a pointer to it, which is called anObject.

The code then sends a message called init to the new object. init initializes the object. This makes sure the object is ready to be used. (It doesn't usually set useful default values; you have to do that in your code.)

Caution

If iOS can't create an object—perhaps because there isn't enough free memory—it returns a "nil pointer." Robust code checks for this condition by comparing anObject to nil. (Many developers write lazy code that assumes the operation worked.)

Defining Classes in Your App

Before you can create objects in memory, you have to decide what they should do in your app. You can then add class definition files that define the features of your new objects.

This is a multi-stage process. Follow these steps:

1. **Decide what you want the class to do.** Sometimes this question has an obvious answer; all apps have an App Delegate and most have at least one View Controller, so most apps include these objects. Other objects, such as those for video and sound support and extended graphics, are optional, and you must find them and add them as needed. (Don't forget that you can search online for sample code.)

2. **Look through the documentation to find an existing iOS class that matches your needs.**

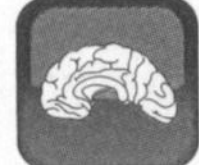

Genius

A useful timesaver is to look for sample code to see which objects Apple and other developers have used to add a feature. You can take these "recipes" and modify them. This is quicker than creating code from scratch.

Note

The iOS kit-of-parts objects solve specific problems and add specific features such as styled text, video, Twitter support, and so on. If your app has some unique requirements—for example, if it's an original game—it's likely you'll have to use the more generic *data collection* objects in iOS and build your own code around them. These objects include object arrays, object dictionaries, and other complex data storage options, and they're described in Chapter 7. For graphics, you can use one of the standard graphics classes such as UIView and add your own custom graphics code.

3. **If the class isn't part of the standard three iOS frameworks, add the framework manually to your project.** There's more about this later in this book. In this chapter, we'll use objects in frameworks that are already included in all the templates.
4. **Decide if you want to subclass the class.** If it already does everything you want, you can use it unmodified. If it doesn't, you can add new features. Some classes such as View Controllers are almost always subclassed.
5. **To subclass it, add a couple of files to your project and add code to define the custom features.** You've now created a new class specification. There's a practical example later in this chapter.

Note

Some of the templates perform this step for you. For example, most templates come with a subclassed View Controller and already include the files to support it. But if you add further view controllers, you must add files for them manually.

6. **Add code elsewhere in your app to create one or more instances of the object.** Technically, you ask iOS to reserve memory for an object and initialize it. iOS returns a pointer. You use the pointer to access the properties and methods in the object.
7. **Use the object.** You can now access its properties and send messages to it to trigger its methods.

Note

If you subclass an object included in a nib file, you have to tell Interface Builder to use the subclass instead of the default unmodified object. This is a simple process: After you've finished creating subclass files, you select the new class name from a menu. It's easy to forget this step and wonder why your UI is ignoring the new customized features, but you'll be reminded about it in Chapter 8.

Using premade subclasses

As noted earlier, some of the templates create subclasses for you. When we looked at the project templates in Chapter 3, we took these files for granted. Now we can understand that they're subclassed for us, ready to be customized with code.

Note

Functionally, there's no difference between a premade subclass and one you add manually. The only difference is practical; in the templates, Xcode saves you a couple of steps by creating these files for you when you make a new project. When you need a subclass elsewhere in an app, you have to create it yourself.

Let's look at these subclasses in detail to see how they're put together.

Create a new project using the SingleView template. As you'll remember from Chapter 5, this template creates two premade subclasses: the AppDelegate and the View Controller. Each subclass is defined by two files that appear in the Project navigator, as shown in Figure 6.5:

- **The interface.** This file has a .h extension.
- **The implementation.** This has a .m extension.

Subclassing works the same way, whether we use premade subclasses in a template or add our own files manually. The interface and implementation files define the features of a subclass. So we'll look at both in detail.

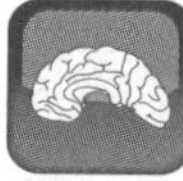

Genius

The dual-pane Assistant feature in the Xcode Editor comes into its own when you work with classes. The Counterparts option automatically displays the interface file in the other pane when you select the implementation for editing, and vice versa. Being able to see both files at once can save you lots of time and confusion.

Understanding the interface file

As the name suggests, the interface file defines the features of a class that are visible to other objects. It includes a list of the methods and properties included in the class. But it doesn't include any of the code that makes these features function.

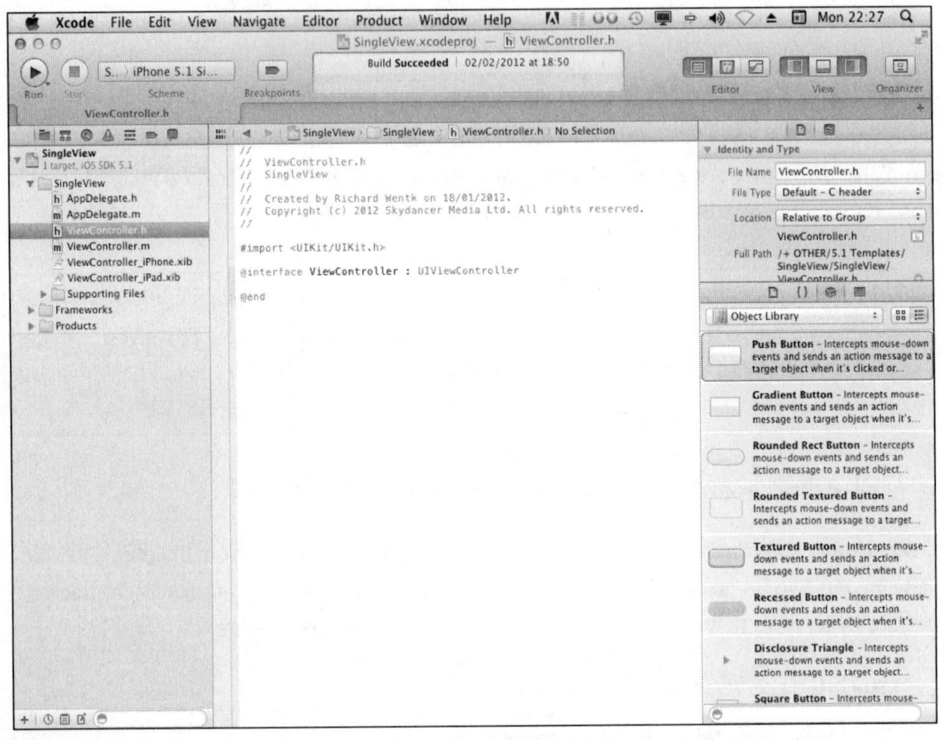

6.5 Looking again at the AppDelegate and ViewController files in the SingleView template.

Note

In Objective-C, methods have a *signature* instead of a prototype. The signature works in a similar way: It names the features of the method without including code, but it includes the input variable names rather than just their types. (As elsewhere in Objective-C, don't think of the word "signature" in its literal English sense; there isn't much of a link between the two meanings.)

The methods and properties are the key features in the file. But they're surrounded by extra items that help Xcode build the file correctly. These items must be included, because Objective-C expects them.

Looking at an interface file

An interface file includes five elements. Figure 6.6 shows one example: the interface file of the App Delegate class.

Some elements are *directives*. Directives work rather like code statements, but they're included to manage parts of the build process. This includes telling Xcode where the file content starts and ends, and where Xcode can find supporting files elsewhere in the project.

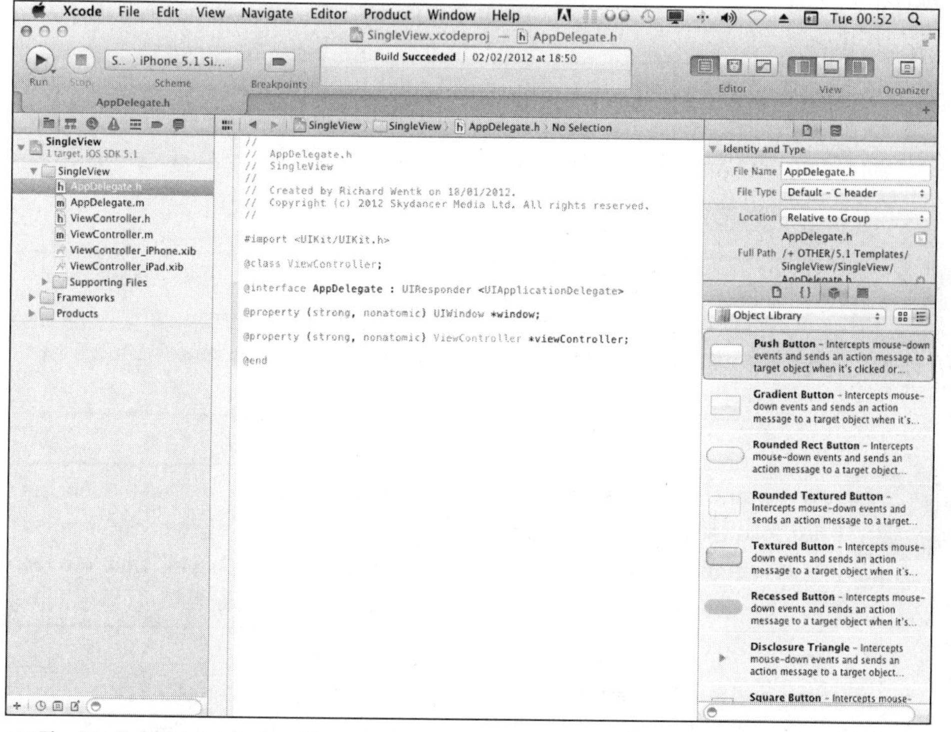

6.6 The AppDelegate's interface file.

From top to bottom these are the elements:

- **A comment header and copyright notice.** This is optional and for human readers only. Xcode creates the copyright notice automatically. You can add further comments of your own to this notice.

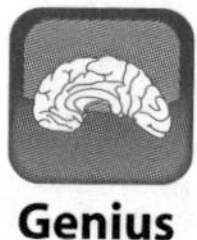

Genius

Xcode imports the name and company name from the Me card in Address Book. This feature is not at all obvious and almost completely undocumented.

- **One or more #import directives.** Xcode refers to these as it builds your class. Put simply, if you use objects or features from an external class anywhere in the class you're defining, you must tell Xcode where to find their interface files. (For C code, these files are known as header files.) If you don't do this, Xcode can't find the definitions it needs to build your app.

Note

You'll sometimes see the "@class" directive in headers. This tells Xcode that the class will have an #import directive in another file—usually the implementation.

- **An @interface directive.** This does two things, with a third option. It defines the name of the class, and it specifies the parent class. Optionally, you can add one or more *protocols* to the definition.

Note

Protocols are packaged bundles of optional methods that the class *adopts*. They're not built into the class; they're bolted on like an extension. You can add code for the methods included in the protocol, as needed. You'll find more about protocols later in this chapter.

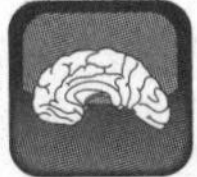

Genius

As you can probably guess, the @interface directive places the name of the subclass first, followed by a colon, and then followed by the name of the parent class it inherits its features from. Sometimes you'll want to set the parent class by hand. You can do it by simply retyping the name of the parent class after the colon.

- **@property and method definitions.** These are the meat and potatoes of the class—the features other objects can access. The template files explored in this chapter don't include any methods, but you'll see examples later in this book that show how methods are defined.

Note

The words "strong" and "non-atomic" are memory management options. There's more about them in Chapter 9.

- **@end.** This directive marks the end of the header file. It should be the last thing in the file.

Looking at an implementation file

Click the AppDelegate.m file in the Project navigator to see the AppDelegate's implementation file, which is shown in Figure 6.7.

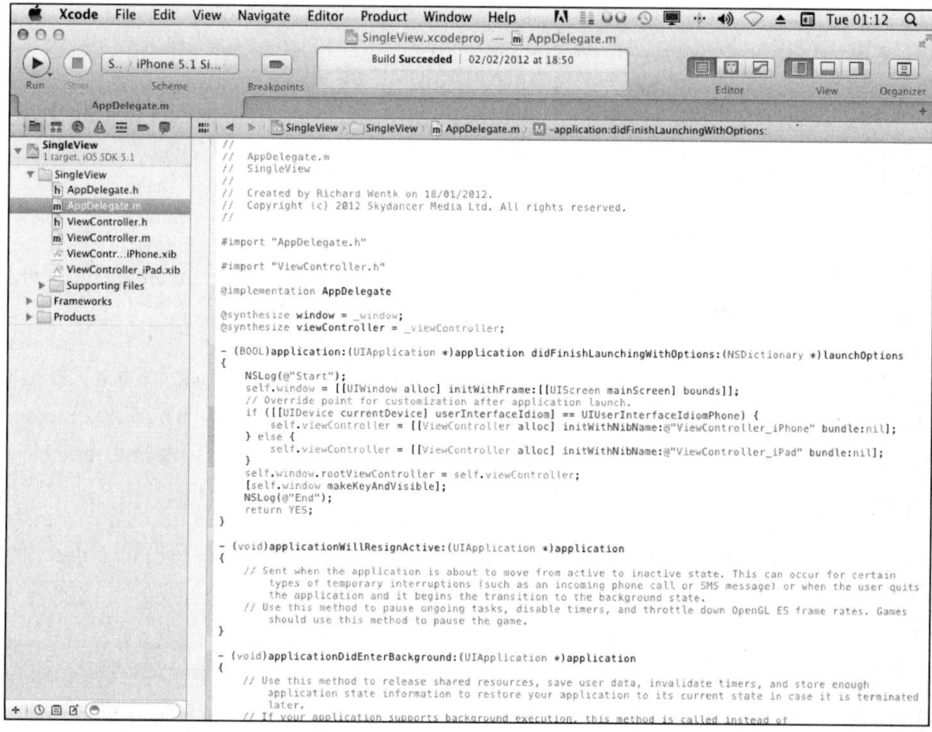

6.7 The AppDelegate's implementation file.

You've already seen this implementation file in earlier chapters. Let's look at it in more detail. These are the elements:

- **Another copyright notice.** Like the notice in the header file, this is generated automatically. The two notices are independent. If you change the comments in one file, the other isn't updated.
- **An @implementation directive.** This tells Xcode that the following code defines the implementation for the named class.
- **A @synthesize directive.** There's more about this in the next section.

Note

You can also declare variables in this section. You can use them in any of the methods in the implementation file, but they won't be visible to other objects. The *scope*—see the previous chapter—includes the entire class.

- **A list of methods, with code.** Methods look like C functions. They start with a "-" (hyphen) symbol, but otherwise they're formatted like a function, with a return data type, a name, and a list of data that is "plugged into" the method before it runs.
- **An @end directive.** This ends the file.

Using @synthesize

Remember that in Objective-C, you can't access properties directly. So you must create setter and getter methods to read and set property values.

The @synthesize directive makes this easy by creating the correct code for you. To use it, simply type "@synthesize" on a line below the @implementation directive, and follow it by one or more of the properties listed in the interface. You can list multiple properties on the same line, separating them with commas. (Don't forget to include a semicolon at the end of the list!)

You *must* synthesize every property in the class if you want it to be accessible to other objects. It's easy to forget this, but when you do, Xcode flags the error so you can fix it.

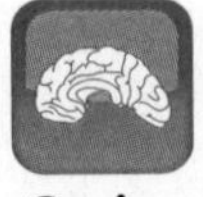

Genius

Don't use @synthesize without thinking. Sometimes you'll still want to create your own setters and getters, because in some applications, you want an object to do something extra, such as updating a set of related values, when a property is read or written. This is a key feature of Objective-C: *A simple value update can trigger a complex sequence of events.*Search online for "@synthesize custom setter" for examples. Setter/getter methods must start with "set" or "get" followed by the class name. The first letter of the class name must be capitalized.

Adding your own subclasses

If a template doesn't include the subclass you want, you must add it yourself. Follow these steps:

1. **Select File ⇨ New ⇨ File… from the main Xcode menu.**
2. **Select iOS Objective-C class, as shown in Figure 6.8.** Click Next.

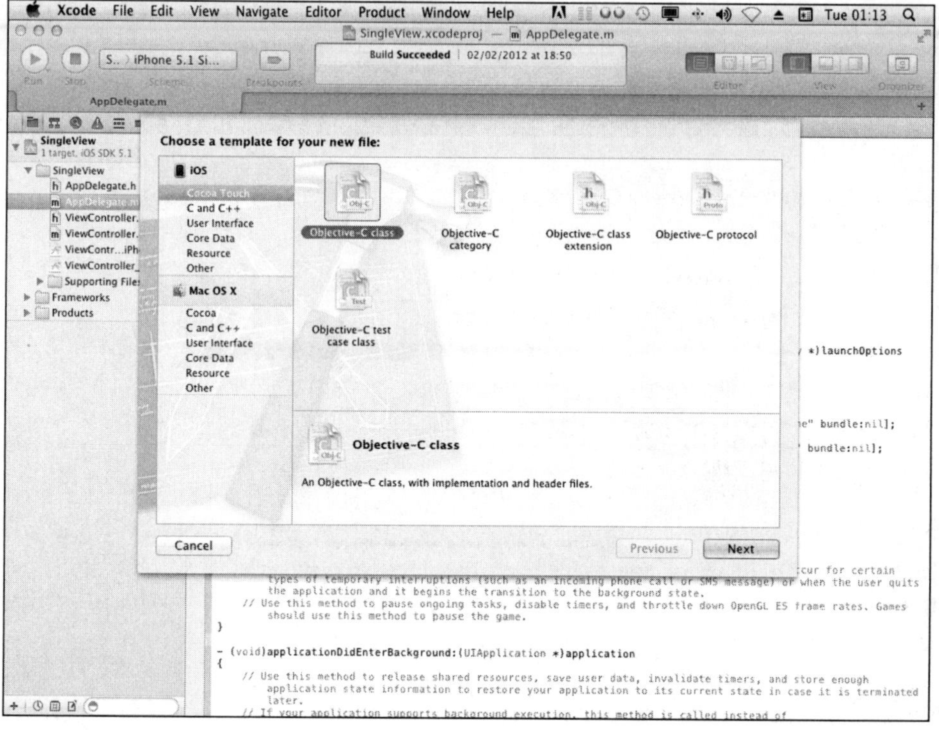

6.8 Naming a subclass.

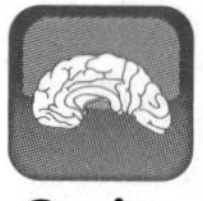

Genius

Some developers prefix their class names with their initials. If you are creating many classes as part of a framework, you can also prefix the name with a two- or three-letter mnemonic of the framework name. Names are partly cosmetic, but your code will be easier to read if you pack as much information into the names as possible.

3. **Type a name into the Class field.** It's a good idea to pick a short but descriptive name.
4. **Use the "Subclass of" menu to select a parent class, as shown in Figure 6.9.** If the parent class you want to customize doesn't appear in the list—it probably does, but you'll need to scroll down—you can type in the name by hand.
5. **If you are subclassing UIViewController, you can choose to add a nib file, with an option to make it iPad compatible.** Select these options by checking the relevant boxes. They're grayed out for other classes.
6. **Click Next.**

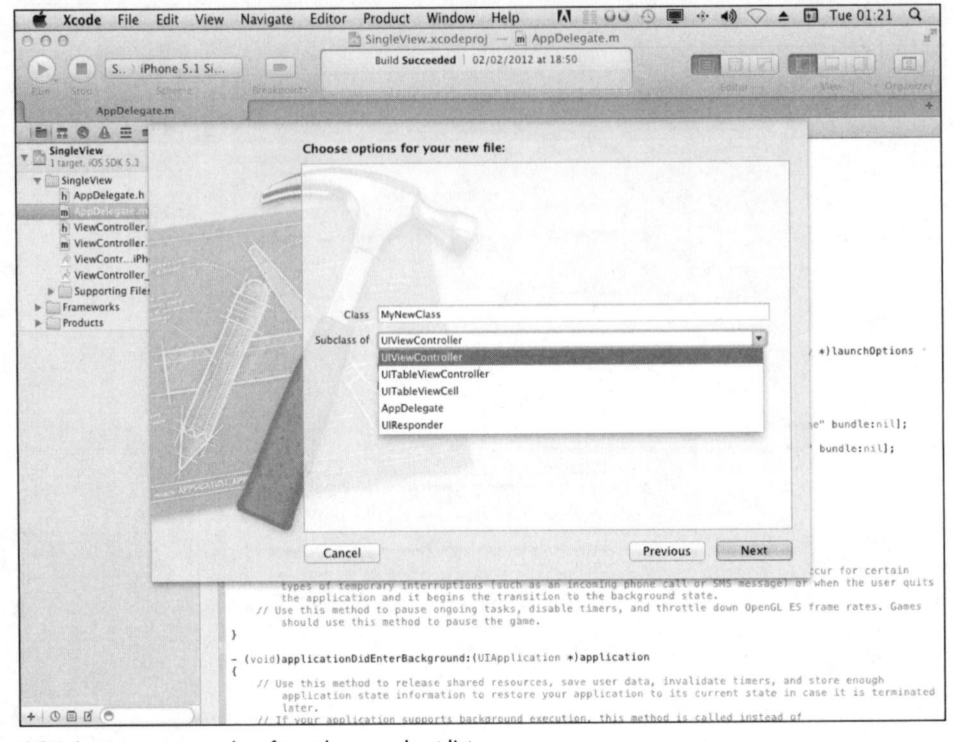

6.9 Selecting a parent class from the very short list.

7. **Select the target folder for the new files.** This is usually the project folder. But don't forget that you can place the files anywhere on disk. Xcode's file management system will still include them in the project.
8. **Click Create.**

Xcode adds the new files to the project, and they appear in the Project navigator. Figure 6.10 shows the project after we've worked through this process a couple of times to add two new classes: MyNewClass and MyViewController.

These files aren't empty; the content depends on the parent class you select. If you subclass NSObject, you get a bare minimum of directives as shown in Figure 6.10—just enough to create the class, but with no useful code. You'll get a similarly minimal pair of files when you subclass most parent classes.

The parent classes that you can select in the menu in the preceding Step 4 are special cases. When you add them to a project, they arrive with extra prewritten code that sketches some of the most useful methods in the parent class.

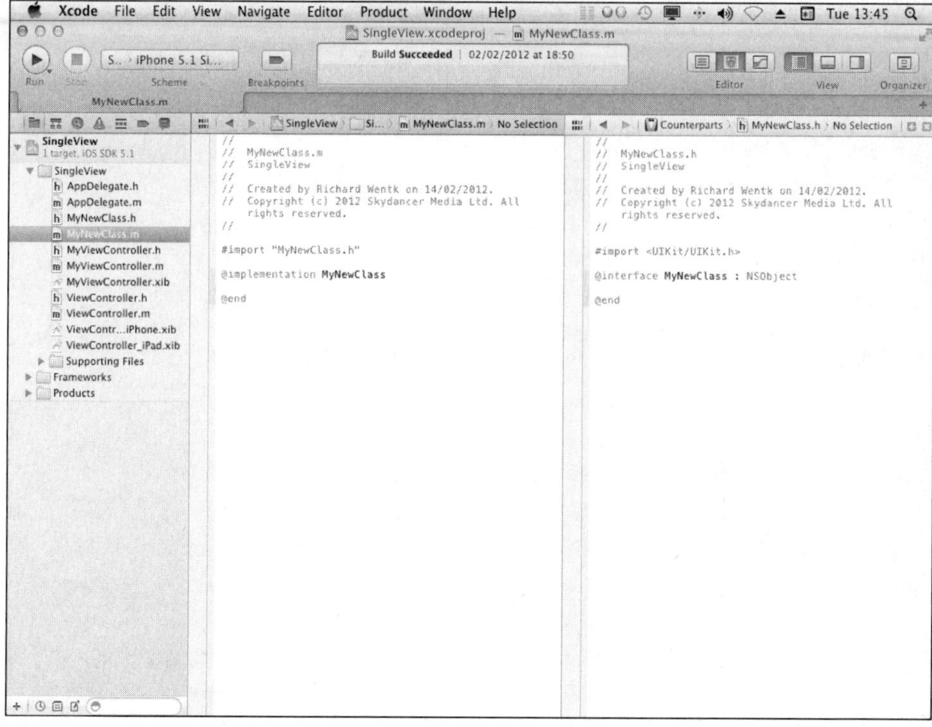

6.10 Subclassing NSObject. There's not much to see here.

Figure 6.11 shows the default contents of MyViewController, our subclass of UIViewController. As you can see, some of the methods are already included.

Caution The default code is *not complete*. You still have work to do to add the features you want. You may even want to delete some of the default methods if your code doesn't use them. The default code is just a sketch to get you started. (This is a particular issue when subclassing UITableViewController. The default code crashes!)

Using subclassing

When you create a subclass, you can do the following with it:

- Add new properties.
- Add new methods.
- Override existing methods.

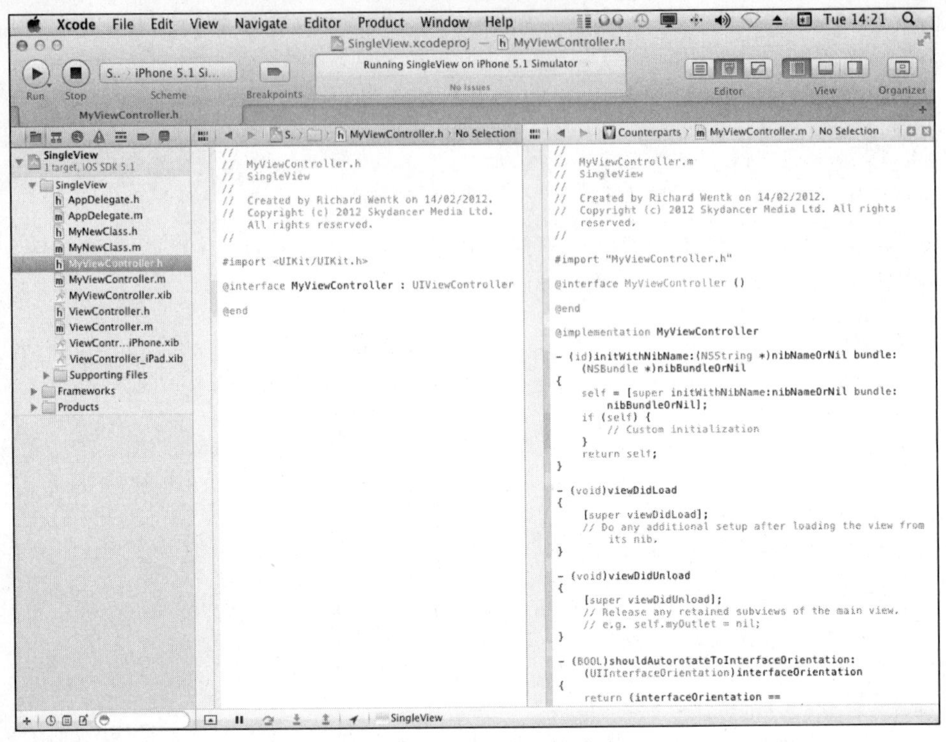

6.11 Subclassing UIViewController. Some code is already included.

Note

Remember that because of inheritance, you don't need to reinvent the wheel in your subclasses. Your subclass already includes a good selection of properties and methods. Subclassing means adding new properties or methods or changing existing methods. It doesn't mean designing a new class from the ground up.

Adding features

When you subclass a View Controller, you typically add properties and methods to manage screen content. For example, if you include a switch in your app, you must include a handler method for messages sent by iOS when the switch is changed. If you include one of the text interface objects built into iOS, you'll want to include a text string object that can store the current text.

Basically, every active object onscreen (excluding static decoration) needs a handler method that responds to user events, a property that stores data for the object, or both. Complex objects may need multiple methods and properties.

The design of other objects is more open-ended. It's up to you to design and add the properties and methods you need. For example, the driving game example earlier in this chapter might include some of the methods and objects we looked at, or it might not. Your design could be completely different.

Overriding methods

All iOS classes include a selection of predefined methods. You can find these methods in the Tasks list for the class.

When you add a custom method to a class, you can design it to your own specification. But when you override a method, you have to start from the definition that already exists in iOS.

Caution

What happens if you try to override a method that doesn't already exist in a subclass? Nothing at all. This matters because most of the existing methods in iOS objects *receive messages from iOS*. If you try to add a method that doesn't already exist in a subclass, iOS treats it as a new method—and ignores it. You can send messages to it from your own subclasses, but it won't receive any messages from iOS.

You can override existing methods in two ways:

- **Some methods are designed to be overridden.** They're available in iOS, but they're included as *stubs*—empty placeholders that do nothing until you add your code. drawRect: in the UIView class and the various touch management methods in iOS work like this. They're deliberately left empty so you can create your own versions.
- **Other methods are designed *not* to be overridden.** You should override them only if you know exactly what you're doing. Most methods are like this, so overriding the standard features of iOS is best left to experts.

To override an existing method, follow these steps:

1. **Find the method in the documentation.** After a while, you'll learn the names of some of the most useful methods, so you can skip this step.
2. **Create your method using one of these options:**

   Copy the method signature from the documentation, and paste it into your subclass.

   Or…

   Type the first part of the method name, and use Xcode's auto code-completion to fill in the rest of the details for you.

3. **Type a left-facing curly bracket under the signature and Return.** Xcode adds a closing curly bracket automatically.
4. **Add your own code between the curly brackets.**

Exploring touch messages

Let's work through an example—an app that includes code that responds to touch events.

From what you know about View Controllers, you might expect touch management to be included in the UIViewController class. It is…almost. It's actually defined in the parent class, which is called UIResponder.

This means all subclasses of UIResponder respond to touch events. How do you know what the subclasses are? Usually, there's no easy way to find this out. But because UI management is so important, Apple has included a useful diagram of subclasses in the UIKit framework reference, partly shown in Figure 6.12.

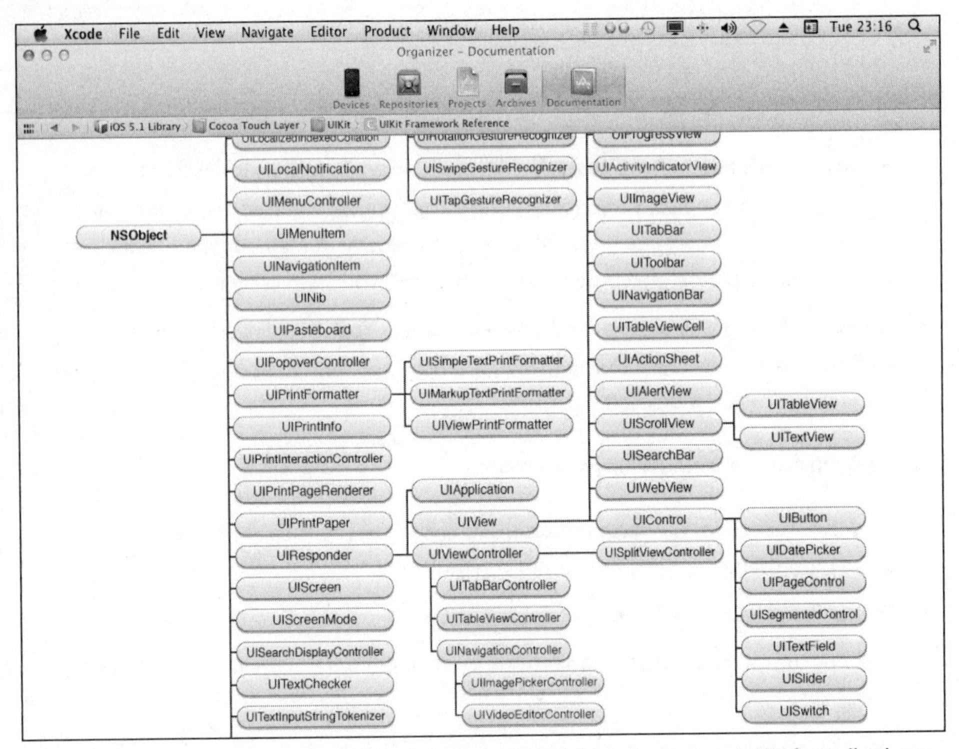

6.12 The UIKit framework class diagram. UIResponder is sixth from the bottom in the first tall column.

Caution

Most frameworks *don't include a diagram like this.* You can easily find the superclasses of a class from the "Inherits from" entry in its class reference. But you won't usually find a convenient list of subclasses. This isn't often a problem. Sometimes it would be a useful thing to have; without it, you'll have to spend some time trying to find existing subclasses.

This diagram tells you that UIApplication, UIView, UIViewController, and all their subclasses in turn can all be made to respond to touch events. If you create your own subclass of any of these classes, you can include touch event methods, and they'll receive touch messages from iOS.

Getting started

To get started with our app, follow these steps:

1. **Open the Organizer window, and select the Documentation.**
2. **Search for UIResponder.**
3. **Scroll down to the Tasks list.** You'll see a list of methods for handling touch events and motion (shake) events, as shown in Figure 6.13.

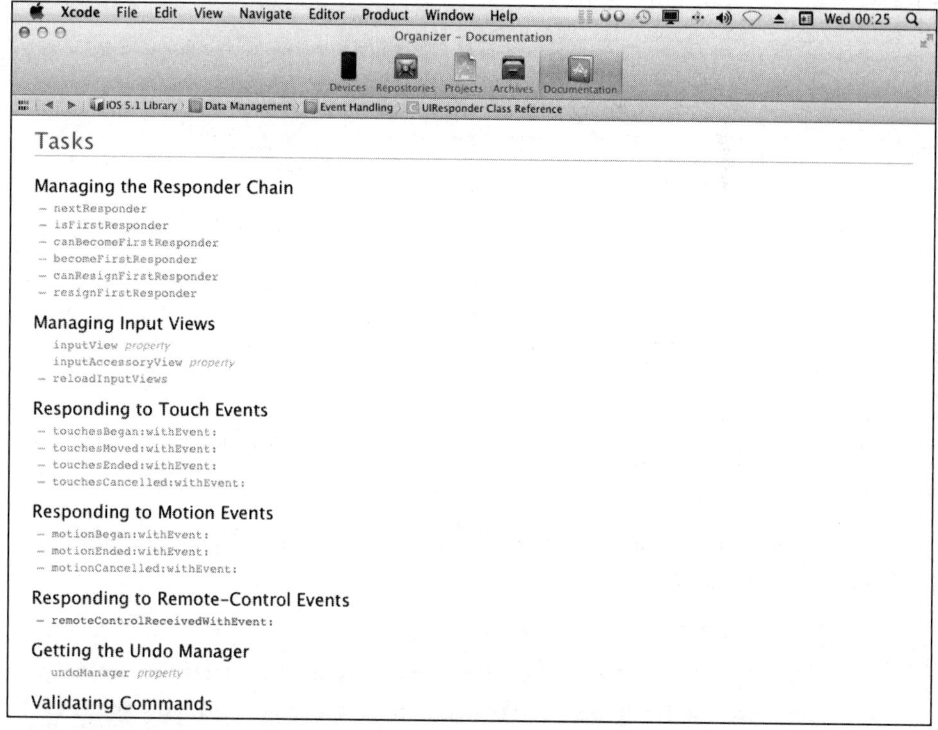

6.13 Finding the touch event methods in the Tasks list for UIResponder.

4. **Consider how the touches might work.** With some background reading, you'll discover there are four separate messages: one sent when a touch begins, one sent when it continues (or moves), one sent when it ends and the user lifts a finger from the screen, and one sent when iOS cancels existing touches because of some external event.

5. **Click the touchesBegan:withEvent: link in the list to view the documentation for this method, which is shown in Figure 6.14.** Usually (as here) there's extra detail that you don't need, and it can be distracting on a first reading. The critical information here is the method name and its return type, which is (void). Optionally, you can now copy and paste the method signature.

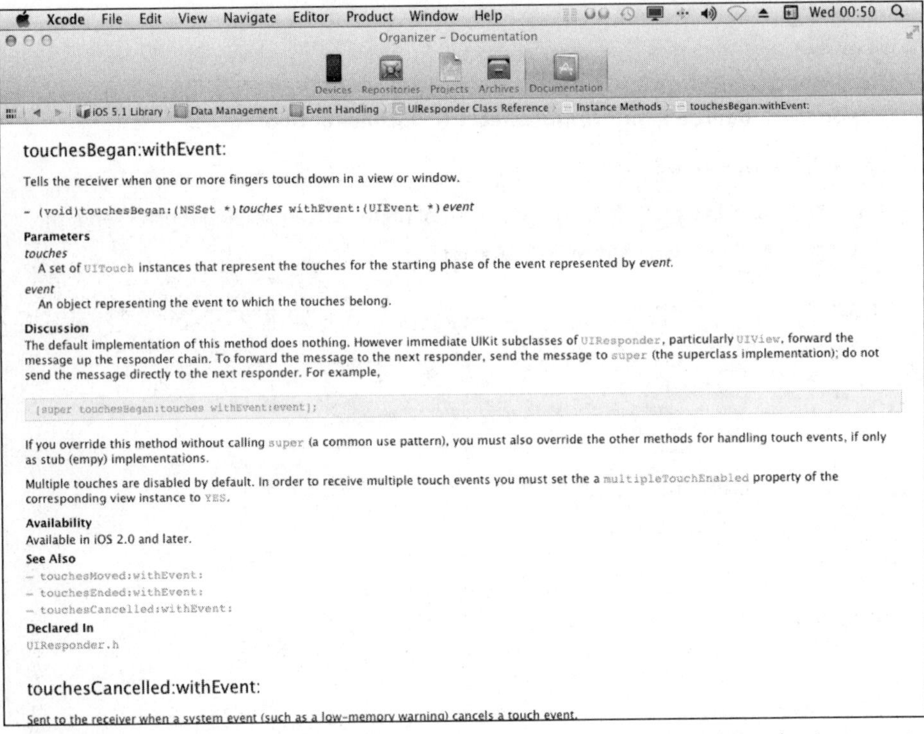

6.14 Looking up a method. You'll need to note the name, and you may want to copy the signature at the start of the entry.

6. **Create a new project using the SingleView application template, using the instructions from Chapter 3.** Save it as TouchEvents.

7. **Click the ViewController.m file to load it into the editor.**

8. **A line or two down from the @implementation directive, either paste the method signature you copied in Step 5 or type "-(void) touchesBegan:" and allow Xcode to fill in the rest.**

9. **Type Return.** If you used Xcode's automated code feature, type it again to move the cursor to the next line.
10. **Type "{" to open a curly bracket.** Xcode adds the closing "}" bracket automatically.

You have now overridden the default touchesBegan: method. Your version doesn't do anything yet, but you've taken a first step toward creating an app that responds to a user's actions.

To finish, add the following line between the curly brackets.

```
NSLog(@"Touched");
```

Build and run the app. The code should look like Figure 6.15. If you open the Debug window, you should see that the app is generating "Touched" messages whenever you tap the screen. (If you're testing the app in the Simulator, click the Simulator window with the mouse.)

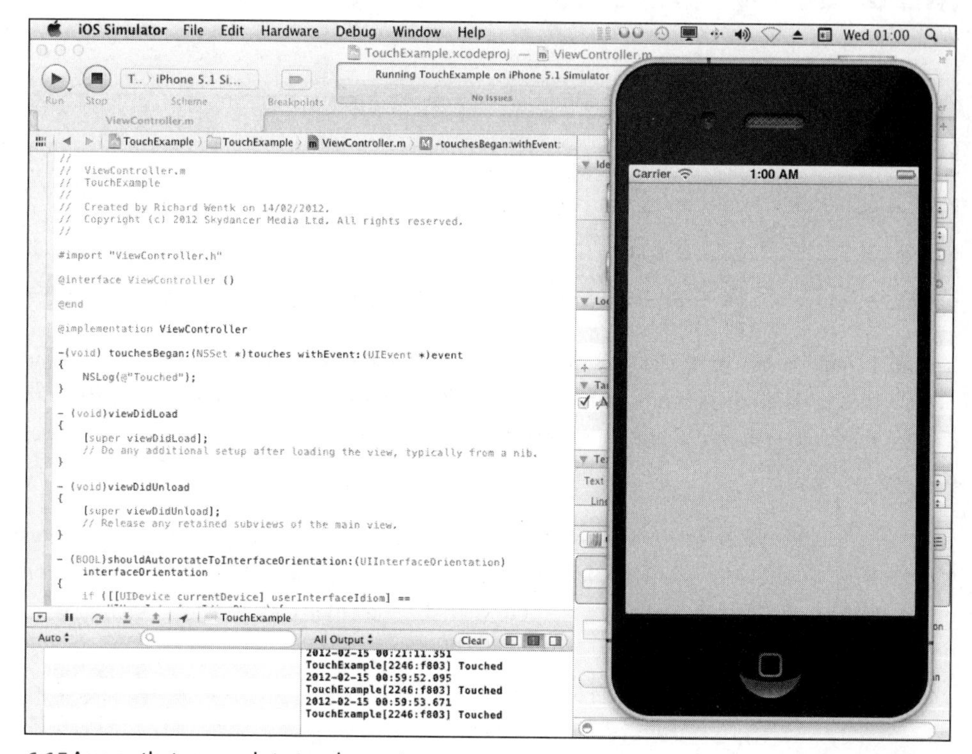

6.15 An app that responds to touch events.

As an exercise, add code for the other touch events: touchesMoved:, touchesEnded:, and touches-Cancelled:. See when they're triggered.

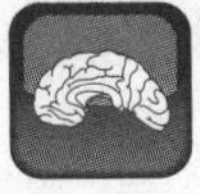

Genius

There's more to learn about touch events. If you look at the method signature, you'll see that the message arrives with a payload of two objects: an NSSet that includes one or more touch objects, and a UIEvent object that includes further information about the time of the touch event. In a commercial app, you can read the properties of these objects to find the touch coordinates, the number of touches, the type of touch (single or multi-tap), and the time of the event. You'll find more about this in Chapter 8.

Going Deeper with Objective-C

Objective-C includes some unique code idioms. You'll see them used regularly, so you should be familiar with them. Here's a partial list of the most important idioms. Others are introduced later in this book.

Introducing selectors

A selector looks like this:

```
@selector(methodName:)
```

You can also declare a selector as a variable, like this:

```
SEL thisIsAMethod = selector(doSomething:);
```

Selectors aren't complicated; they're similar to pointers, but they point to a method instead of an object. They're one of the more useful features in Objective-C, because you can use them to change the method that's triggered by some event while the app is running. (Most languages don't let you do this.)

For example, when you create a timer object, you use a selector to specify the method it triggers when it fires, as shown in the NSTimer documentation in Figure 6.16. Some of the animation objects in iOS use selectors to trigger a method when the animation completes.

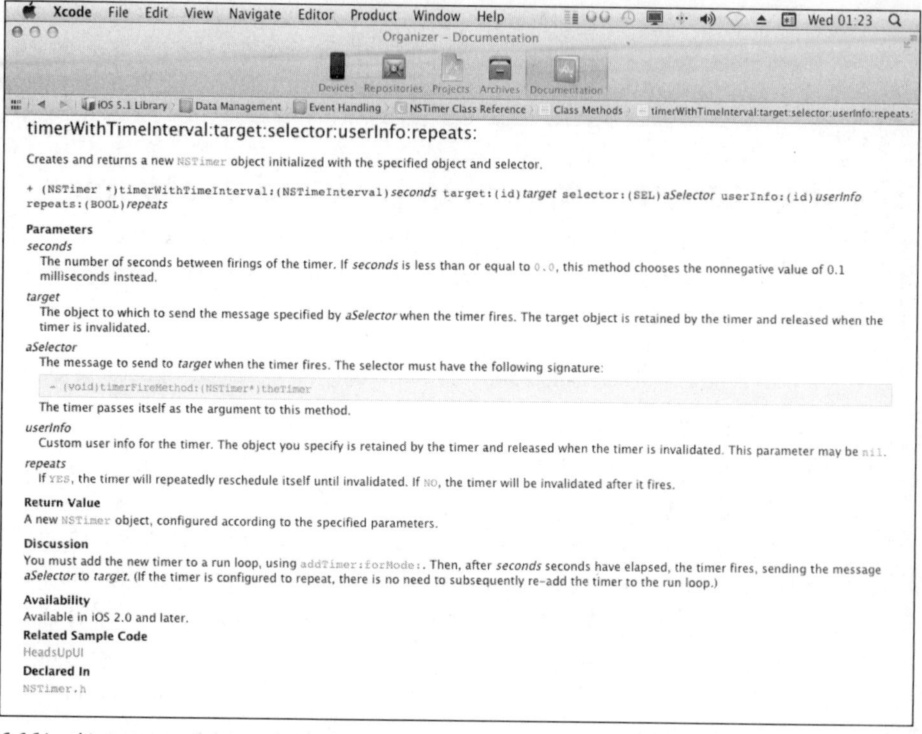

6.16 Looking at one of the methods that sets up a timer in iOS, using the NSTimer object.

Using Target-Action

Selectors are part of a system called target-action. This is another uncomplicated part of iOS, though the official documentation tries hard to persuade you otherwise.

Target-Action simply means you can specify a target object as well as a target method. In the timer example, you plug a pointer to your target object into a property called "target." When the selector is triggered, it runs in the object you select.

Target-Action makes Objective-C very flexible. You can literally rewire your app as it runs, directing different messages to different objects as needed. Objects can trigger different behaviors at different times; for example, buttons in a game can trigger different behaviors as the game progresses.

Caution

Note that if a target object doesn't include the target method you set, your app crashes.

Getting started with delegates and protocols

Delegates are used throughout iOS. Objects can pass messages to other objects instead of attempting to process them internally. They can literally delegate the message to a helper object, which processes it as needed.

This is the official definition of delegation, and it's almost completely misleading, because iOS uses delegates in a very specific way.

In practice, delegation works with two elements:

- **A delegated object.** Objects that support delegates have a property called "delegate." To direct delegate messages to an object, assign its pointer to this property. You can even assign "self" to make an object send delegate messages to itself.
- **A delegate protocol.** As introduced earlier in this chapter, a protocol is a library of useful methods that an object can "adopt." Adopting a protocol is equivalent to adding all the methods in the protocol to the object's interface. Instead of typing in all the method signatures, you simply add the name of the protocol, and Objective-C merges them into your class definition. You can then override them if you need to or ignore them if you don't.

Many protocols are bundles of delegate methods. They appear in the documentation with the word "Delegate" added at the end. All the frameworks in iOS include their own protocols that can be used with the objects in the framework. If you look at the main reference page for a framework, you'll see a list. Figure 6.17 shows part of the list in the UIKit framework.

Delegates are often used for the following applications:

- To trigger an event before some other event
- To trigger an event after some other event
- To send data to iOS when it requests it
- To enable or disable some behavior

For practical code, see Chapter 9.

Class methods

Classes are also objects in their own right. They don't have accessible properties, but some classes support *class messages:* If you send the class a message, it will respond in a useful way:

```
[AClass aClassMessage];
```

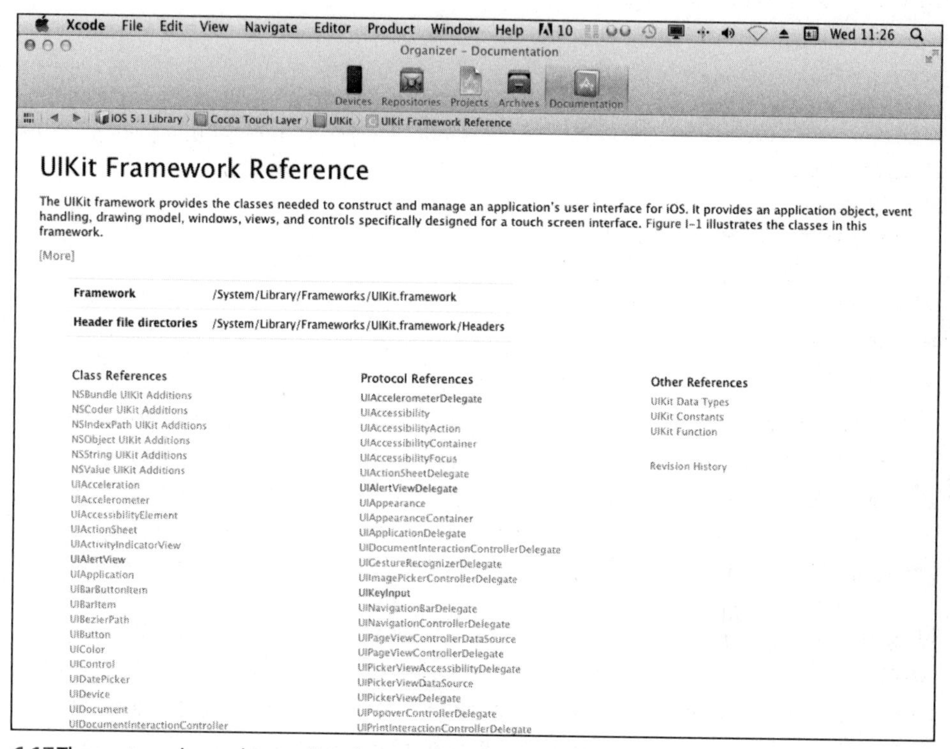

6.17 The center column shows a list of protocols included in UIKit. Note how some are labeled as delegate protocols.

A class message signature starts with a "+" character instead of a "-". Where they're available, they're listed in the class reference documentation.

Applications vary. Objects are created by sending a class message to the NSObject class rather than to a generic object. And some animation effects can be managed by sending messages to the UIView class instead of a specific UIView. Figure 6.18 shows the relevant part of UIView's Tasks list.

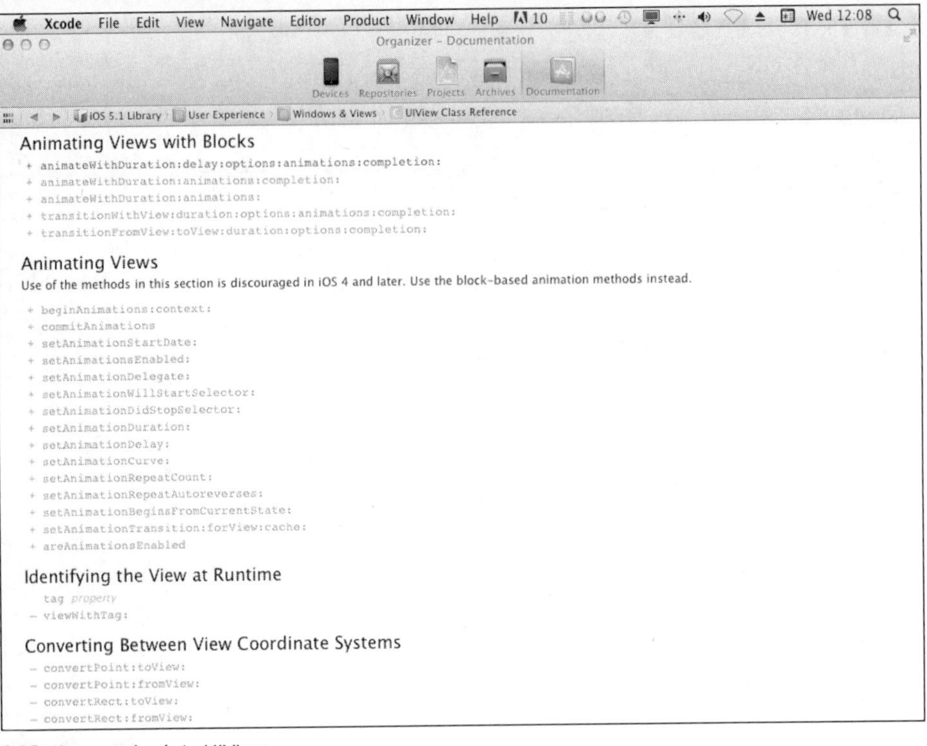

6.18 Class methods in UIView.

Note

This chapter has been heavy on theory. You'll find practical examples of code that uses the features and idioms of Objective-C throughout the rest of this book.

How Can I Use Objects to Manage Data and Schedule Events?

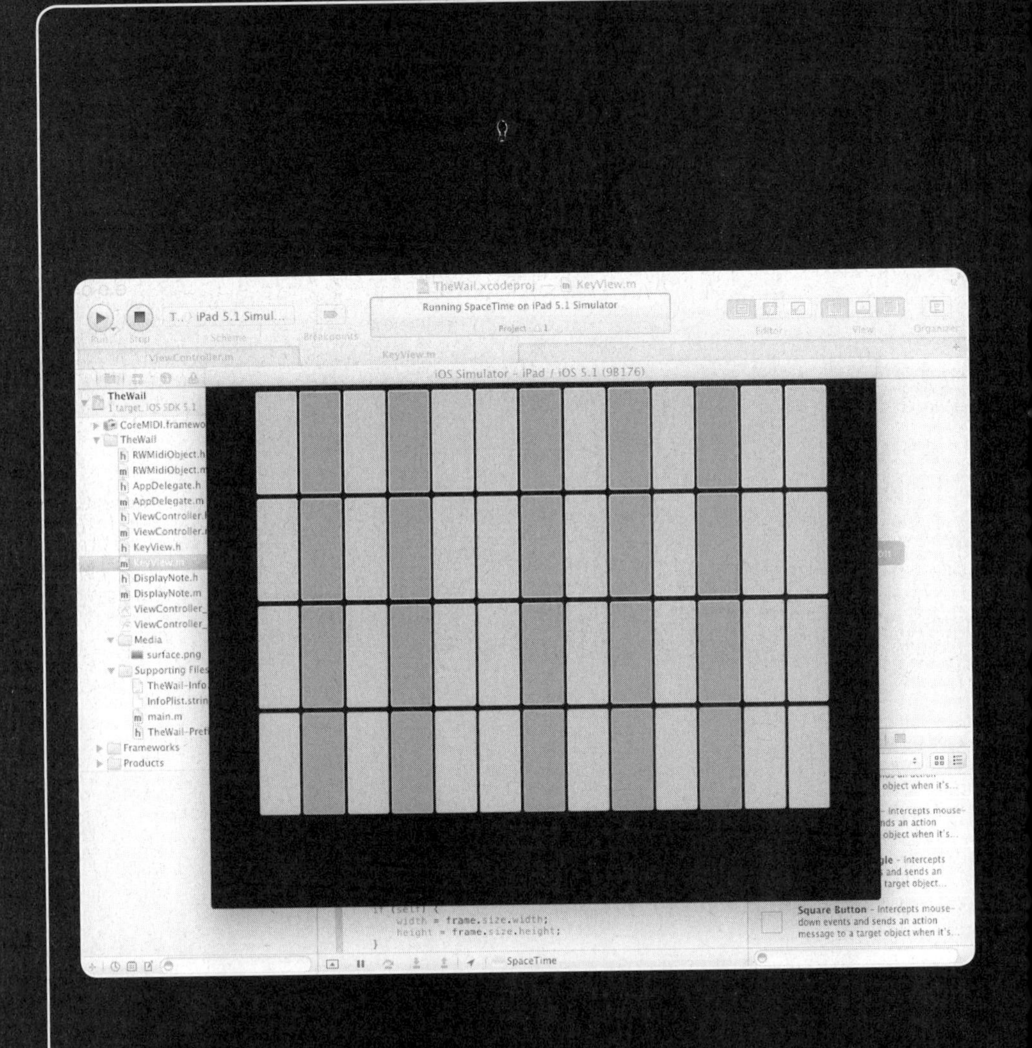

1 2 3 4 5 6 7 8 9 10 11 12 13

Data is at the heart of every app. Whatever an app does, it must organize and manage data efficiently. iOS includes a selection of data collection objects that make it relatively easy to collect, count, list, search, and filter data. These objects are powerful, with many methods, but their features are elegant and subtle. This chapter introduces the iOS data collection objects and includes a brief introduction to some possible applications. It also explains how you can control the timing of events with timers and delayed methods.

Managing Text with NSString

Text is one of the most useful data types. The main iOS class for working with simple text is NSString. Although it does a simple job, it's a huge class with a vast collection of methods, some of which are shown in Figure 7.1.

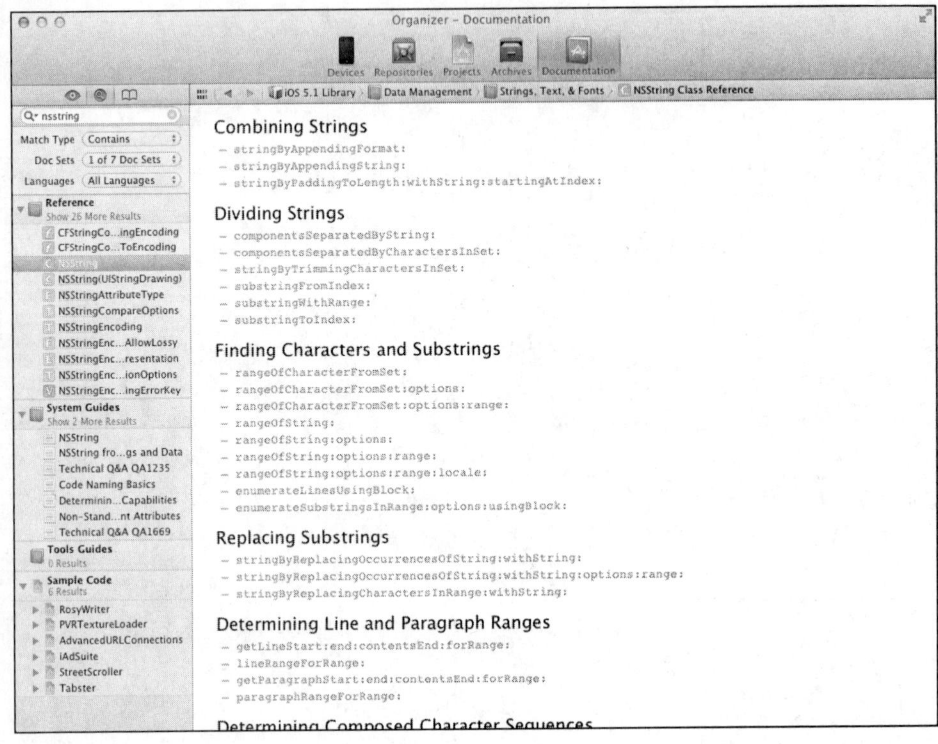

7.1 Just a few of the many methods built into NSString.

Creating a string

In spite of its complexity, you'll likely use only a handful of the available methods in most projects.

To create a string, do this:

```
NSString *aNewString = @"A new string";
```

You don't need to use any of the more complex methods.

To duplicate a string, *don't* do this:

```
NSString *string2 = string1;
```

As usual, this copies the pointer, not the data, and gives you two references to one object. Do this instead:

```
NSString *string2 = [NSString stringWithString: string1];
```

The stringWithFormat: method is widely used, because it can format text using standard NSLog format specifiers, like this:

```
NSString *aNewString =
   [NSString stringWithFormat: @"This is a string: %@, and this is a float: %f",
   anotherString, aFloat];
```

"%@" is replaced with the contents of anotherString, and "%f" is replaced with the contents of aFloat, formatted as a floating point number. (Details of key format options are listed in Appendix A.) You can use this method to concatenate multiple strings with optional separator characters:

```
NSString *aNewString =
   [NSString stringWithFormat: @"Here are three strings in a row. One has a
   space in front of it: %@%@ %@", string1, string2, string3];
```

Comparing strings

Another standard operation is string comparison. You *can't* do this:

```
if (string1 == string2)…
```

This operation compares pointers and ignores the content of the strings. (If the pointers are the same, the strings are identical. But usually you want the operation to compare two different strings.)

Do this instead:

```
if ([string1 isEqualToString: string2])…
```

Caution

You must include the square brackets: You're running a method called "isEqualTo-String" on a string object.

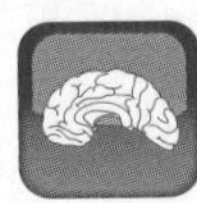
Genius

NSString doesn't support complex text effects, such as styles and fonts. The relatively easy way to add these effects is to use a class called NSAttributedString, which combines text with formatting information. For more details, see the Attributed Strings Programming Guide in the Documentation. For more complex effects, including styled page layout, you can use a framework called Core Text, which has many features but is too complex for this book (and indeed for most developers.)

Managing Data Collections

It's often useful to collect objects together and work with them as a group. For example, if you have a collection of views in a UI design, performing some operation on all of them can be useful.

iOS includes three *data collection objects* that store other objects. You'll see these objects used throughout iOS. When iOS needs to pass a collection of data to a method in your app, it often arrives wrapped inside one of these objects. You'll find you regularly use these objects to manage data collections of your own.

There are three object types, and they organize the data in different ways, as follows:

- **NSArray.** Each object in the collection is numbered sequentially with an *index,* which starts at 0.
- **NSDictionary.** Each object is associated with a unique *key,* which can be a text string or some other object.
- **NSSet.** Objects aren't ordered, but you can retrieve objects from the set, and you can test whether an object is included in the set. Testing is quite speedy: It's faster than for the other collection objects.

Figure 7.2 shows the Class Reference for NSArray. If you're familiar with arrays in C, you can see that NSArray is far more powerful. You can search for objects in the array, create an array from a list of objects, and load array data from a file or a web URL. You can also sort the contents of an array, perform a method on every item in the array with a single operation, and write the entire array to a file with a single line of code.

Data collection objects don't just store data. You can also use them to manipulate data in powerful but accessible ways.

Caution

Data collections objects are complex and sophisticated. The information in this chapter is an extremely brief introduction, and it won't turn you into an instant master of data collections. To get the most from these objects, look through their class references, see how they're used in sample code, and take the time to experiment with them. They're not difficult to work with, but you may need to expand your ideas about how data can be processed and organized, especially if you already have a background in C.

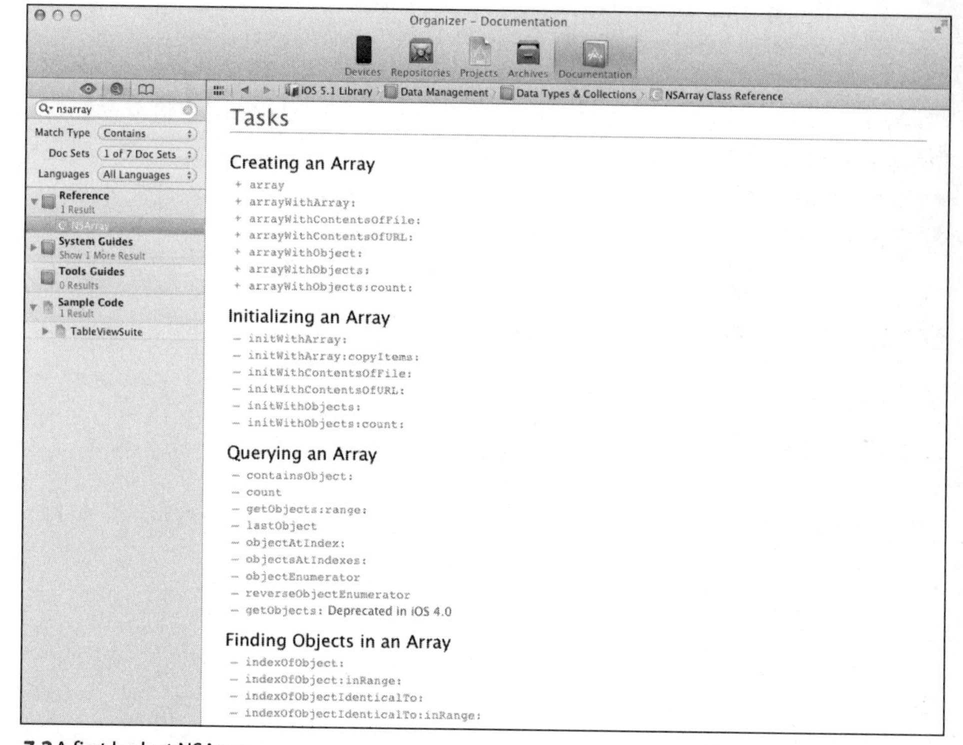

7.2 A first look at NSArray.

Here's sample code to create an array of two objects:

```
NSArray *aNewArray = [[NSArray alloc] arrayWithObjects: object1, object2, nil];
```

You must end the list with "nil." The objects can be of any type.

To access the objects, use this code:

```
anObject = [aNewArray objectAtIndex: anIndex];
```

anIndex is an integer. (Technically, it's an NSInteger, which is more or less equivalent to a C-type int.) Indexing starts at 0. With two objects, anIndex can be 0 or 1.

Caution

NSArray is unforgiving. If you try to access it with an index that's bigger than the number of items, it crashes your app.

Note

"nil" is used as a list terminator. If you want to create an empty object as a placeholder, use the NSNull class. Specifically, you can create a null object with [NSNull null].

Understanding mutable collections

One of the most unusual quirks of standard data collections is that they're *read-only*. When you create a collection, or when iOS sends one to your app, you can read information from it. But you can't change it. The standard collection objects don't include methods for modifying the data they hold.

If you want to modify the data in a collection, you must use the *mutable* versions of these objects:

- NSMutableArray
- NSMutableDictionary
- NSMutableSet

These versions are subclasses of the main collection objects, so they support their powerful searching, sorting, and processing features. But they include extra methods for adding and removing objects from the collection, shown in Figure 7.3.

You can create these objects as empty containers in the usual way, like this:

```
NSMutableArray *myMutableArray = [[NSMutableArray alloc] init];
```

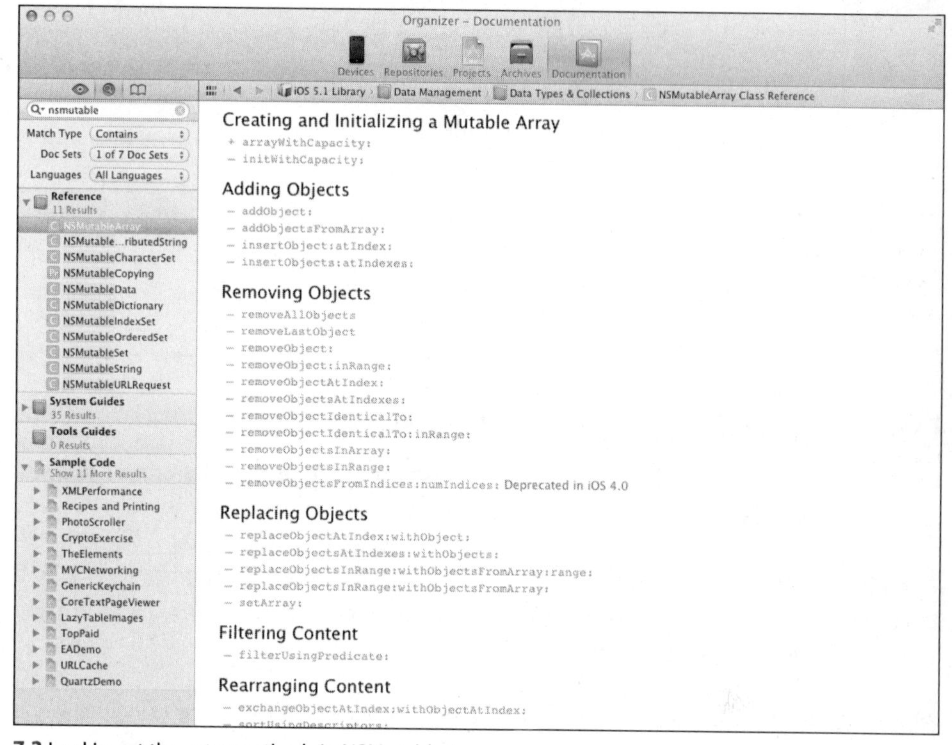

7.3 Looking at the extra methods in NSMutableArray.

You can then use the various addObject: and insertObject: methods to add objects, and you can use removeObject: methods to delete objects. You can also use a removeAllObjects method to clear the collection.

Note that although you can specify a capacity when you create a mutable object, this isn't a fixed limit. The size of a mutable object expands or shrinks as you add and remove objects, up to the available memory.

Note also that NSMutableArray doesn't allow gaps in the indexing. You can't insert an object at index 50 if you don't already have objects at indexes 0 to 49.

When you use the addObject: method, the object is always added at the top of the array and given the highest possible index. When you insert an object at a smaller index, the index of objects above it is increased by one. When you remove an object, the index is decreased by one.

Note

Why are collections read-only? For two reasons: speed and security. There's a small speed advantage in using a non-mutable collection. Mutable objects must do extra work to manage a collection. Also, read-only objects are inherently secure. If the data is coming from outside an app, apps can't change it.

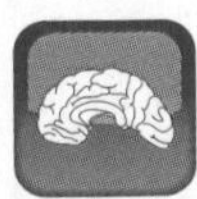
Genius

You can also"modify" data collections by copying them. NSSet and NSArray include methods that copy an existing set or array to another array. Optionally, you can add further objects to the copy. But if you need mutability, it's usually easier to start with a mutable object.

Understanding "objectification"

Data collection objects can store only other objects. They can't store more basic data types, such as ints, floats, and C strings.

This often causes problems, because apps regularly need to store and manage basic data. To fix this issue, iOS includes a selection of objects that take a basic data type and convert into an object. You can then store the object in a collection.

When you retrieve the object, you can convert it back into its original data type using the various conversion methods built into these "objectification" classes.

- **NSNumber.** This is a wrapper object for numbers, including ints, floats, Booleans, and other numeric types.
- **NSValue.** This is a more general wrapper for data and data structures of all kinds. Although it's more powerful than NSNumber, the code needed to make it work is slightly unusual and specialized.
- **NSData.** This is a general blob of binary data copied from a file or from memory. NSData is really meant for raw binary files and buffers, but if you know the size of a data structure, you can use NSData to pack it into a collectable object.

Using NSNumber

NSNumber is very easy to use. To create an NSNumber from a number, do this:

```
NSNumber *myFloatObject = [NSNumber numberWithFloat: 0.1234];
```

Naturally, you can replace "0.1234" with a float variable.

Figure 7.4 shows the Class Reference with the methods and data types you can use.

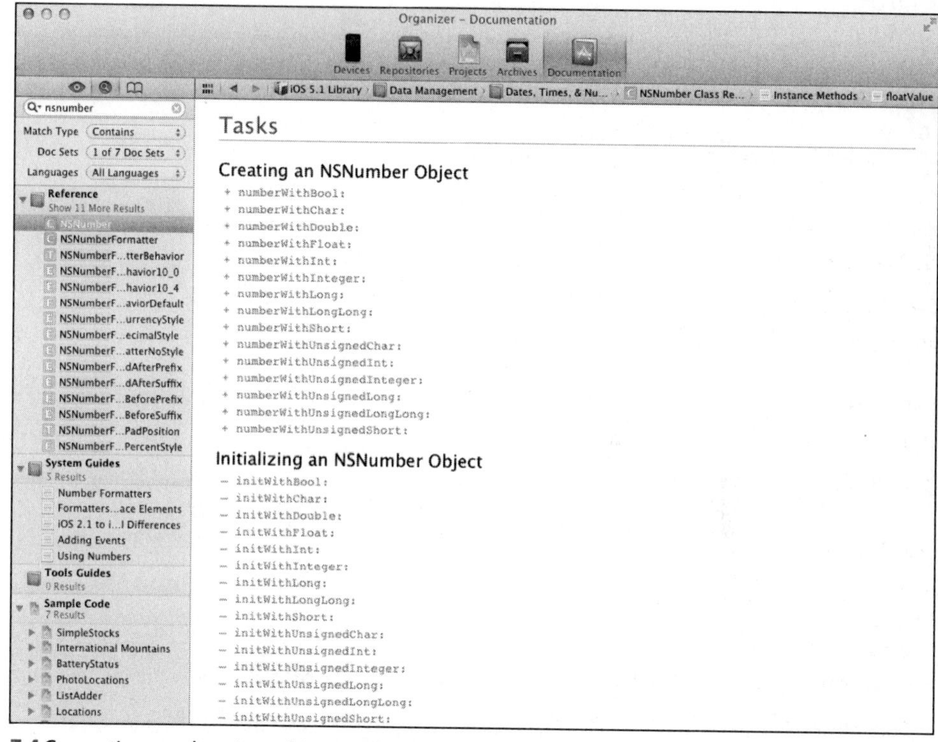

7.4 Converting numbers into objects with NSNumber.

To recover the number, do this:

```
aFloat = [myFloatObject floatValue];
```

You don't need to match types before and after "objectification" because NSNumber converts between input and output types automatically, like this:

```
NSNumber *myFloatObject = [NSNumber numberWithFloat: 3.14159];
anInt = [myFloatObject intValue];
//anInt = 3
```

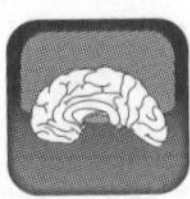

Genius

There's a special subclass of NSNumber called NSDecimalNumber that can store numbers with up to 38 significant figures and an exponent of -128 to 127. In addition to storing numbers, it's also useful for calculator apps.

Using NSValue

NSValue is more complex. It's really a wrapper for object pointers rather than a wrapper for object data, and it stores the *name* of the data type using a compiler directive called @encode. This may seem intricate, but you can persuade NSValue to "just work" with some simple boilerplate code.

Figure 7.5 shows the standard methods. You can see that pointer types are built into the class. Other types require more work.

Here's an example that can encode a float. (You'd usually use NSNumber to do this, but the code is similar for other data types.)

```
float aFloat = 3.14159;
NSValue *aValueObject = [NSvalue value: &aFloat withObjCType:@encode(float)];
```

Remember the following:

- **Specify a pointer to the data type, not the usual reference.** This usually means prefixing it with "&" to get the memory address.
- **The "withObjCType: @encode()" part of the statement is boilerplate.** Use it as is.
- **Include the name of the data type between the round brackets.**

Retrieving the value is less straightforward, because you create a statement that assigns a result to the right instead of to the left—or in English, you specify a target pointer at the *end* of the statement, instead of the start.

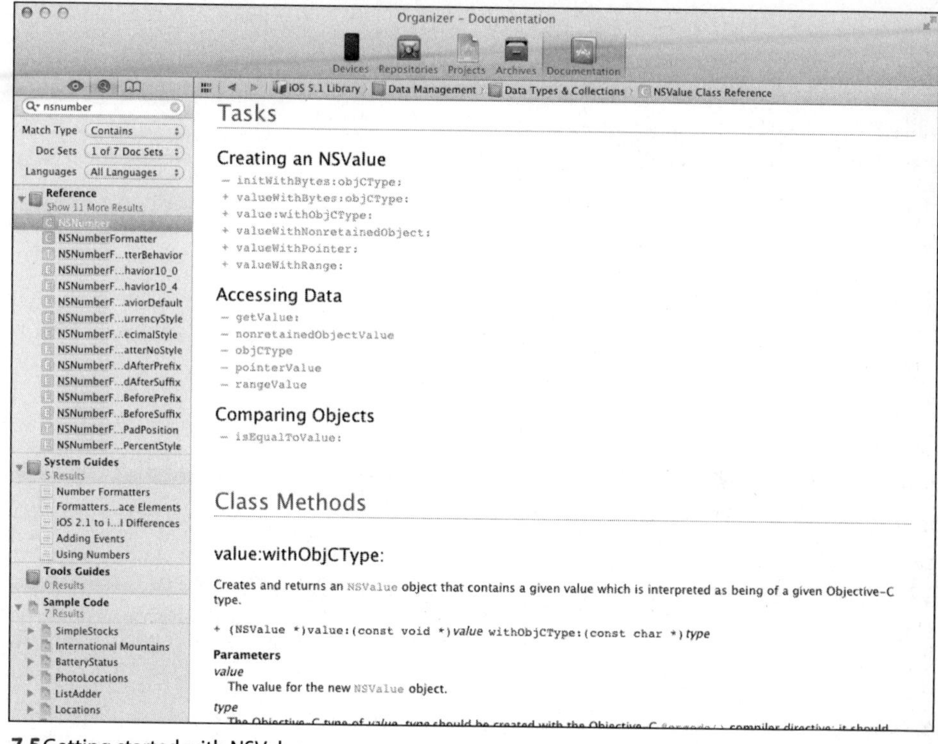

7.5 Getting started with NSValue.

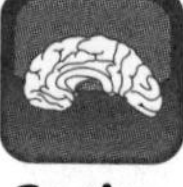

Genius

NSValue supports a useful set of extensions that create value objects from geometrical objects, including points, rectangles, size objects, edge insets, and so on. You can find them in the NSValue UIKit Additions Reference. They're very useful if you need to store geometric information in a data collection—and much easier to use than plain vanilla NSValue methods.

This example writes the value to aFloat:

```
[aValueObject getValue: &aFloat];
```

In normal Objective-C, this would send the getValue message to aValueObject passing &aFloat as a parameter.

That's also what happens here—kind of. But the result is that aFloat now references the original data, which recovers the original value.

Using NSData

NSData is even less specific than NSValue. You give it a memory address and a length, and it wraps whatever binary data it finds at the address into an object. Unlike NSValue, you don't need to specify a data type.

NSData is specialized and not very useful in simple apps. In more advanced applications, it can be used with a class called NSCoder, which converts the contents of any object into binary so it can be saved to a file and reloaded later. If the object contains other objects, they must be able to respond to NSCoder internally.

NSCoder is complex, and a full introduction is outside the scope of this book. For more details, see the companion Cocoa Developer Reference title.

Understanding key-value coding (KVC)

KVC isn't a complicated technique, but it's often poorly explained, which makes it seem more challenging than it really is.

In practice, KVC describes two loosely related techniques. They're often grouped together, but looking at them separately is more useful.

Caution

> Apple's introduction to KVC is almost impossible to understand—even if you already understand KVC.

Basic KVC

The first technique is general, so you can use it with any object. You've learned that you can access object properties using dot notation, like this:

```
aProperty = anObject.nameOfProperty;
```

With KVC, you can also access object properties like this:

```
aProperty = [anObject valueForKey: @"nameOfProperty"];
```

And you can set properties like this:

```
[anObject setValue: aValue forKey: @"nameOfProperty"];
```

Compared to dot notation, this seems pointlessly wordy. It's also dangerous; if anObject doesn't have a property called "nameOfProperty," your app crashes, as shown in Figure 7.6. Using KVC makes it more difficult for Xcode to check that your code is correct.

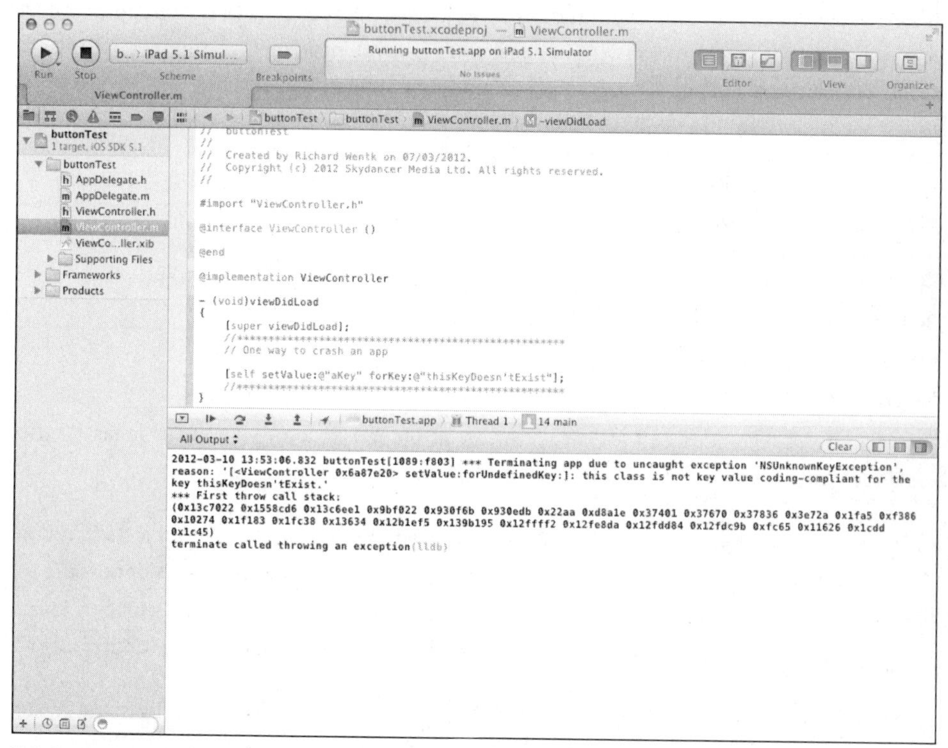

7.6 Crashing an app by asking it to use a ViewController to access a key it doesn't recognize.

Note

In the jargon, a crash is called "throwing an exception." Crash messages are often somewhat obscure. The error message for a key-related crash says that the target class isn't key-value coding compliant for the given key. In English, this simply means "I couldn't find that key, and I don't know what to do next."

Why bother with the extra complication? Because you can replace @"nameOfProperty" with a string object, like this:

```
NSString *thePropertyName;
<…some code that sets or selects thePropertyName goes here…>
aProperty = [anObject valueForKey: thePropertyName];
```

You can now select the property you want to access at run-time by creating a string object with the property name wherever you decide which property to access. Your chosen property isn't hardwired into your code, so you can change it whenever you need to.

This kind of KVC is often used in intermediate and advanced apps. You don't need to use it in a simpler app, but it's useful to remember that it exists.

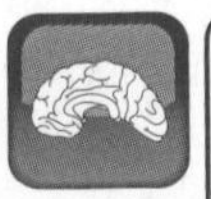
Genius

You can nest KVC to access sub-properties. Technically, you don't access a key; you access a *key path*. You don't need to think about this extra detail in simple apps.

Using KVC with NSDictionary

The second KVC technique isn't *technically* KVC at all. But it uses some very similar ideas. It's used exclusively with NSDictionary.

NSDictionary has many applications, but it's often used to define settings for objects that don't have fixed properties. For example, audio and video objects may have hundreds of possible settings, and the list may change as technology develops. It would be wasteful, and probably impossible, to create audio and video objects with properties to match each possible setting.

It's more efficient to have a free-form way of listing settings, accessing them by some related value—typically, a name, but potentially any relevant object.

NSDictionary supports both name-linked and object-linked storage. You can pair objects with name strings, or you can pair objects with other objects. It's more intuitive to think of keys as text labels, but it's more powerful to think of them as generic objects.

For example, in an address book, you can pair addresses with names. But if you create an object for each individual, you can use it to hold supporting data such as birthday information. Potentially, you can even pair dictionaries with other dictionaries and store the pairs in a third dictionary.

Because of its versatility, you'll find NSDictionary used as a data store throughout the more complex classes in iOS.

Note

Technically, name strings in iOS are already objects, so the first option is redundant. But it's included because it simplifies the code in certain applications.

Because NSDictionary takes pairs of data items rather than single items, it's often populated with two arrays of existing objects, like this:

```
NSArray *keysArray = [NSArray arrayWithObjects: key1, key2, nil];
NSArray *objectsArray = [NSArray arrayWithObjects: object1, object2, nil];
NSDictionary *thisDictionary =
          [NSDictionary dictionaryWithObjects: objectsArray forKeys: keysArray];
```

To return an object for a key, do this:

```
id returnedObject = [thisDictionary objectForKey: aKey];
```

In most apps, you'll know the class of the returned object ahead of time. But if you don't, you can use id as the usual placeholder type. All data collection objects support multiple object types in the same collection, so it's easy to collect a grab bag of miscellaneous objects of varying classes.

If you use valueForKey: instead of objectForKey:, aKey must be an NSString:

```
id returnedObject = [thisDictionary valueForKey: aString];
```

Caution

In spite of the name, valueForKey: isn't directly related to NSValue.

Basic key-value access is the simplest feature built into NSDictionary. Figure 7.7 shows some of the other key-value methods that are available. You can copy all keys and/or values into an array, enumerate the dictionary by keys or values, and sort or filter the dictionary by keys using your own custom methods. You can find example code for these methods online.

Using NSSet

Because NSSet isn't ordered, its behavior isn't well-defined. You can retrieve an object from a set using the anObject method, like this:

```
id returnedObject = [aSet anyObject];
```

Object selection isn't guaranteed to be random. It isn't guaranteed *not* to be random. The documentation for NSSet says that it returns whichever object is most convenient!

If you need to access objects in a set in a more predictable way, you may want to copy the objects in the set to an array using the allObjects method, like this:

```
NSArray *newArray = [aSet allObjects];
```

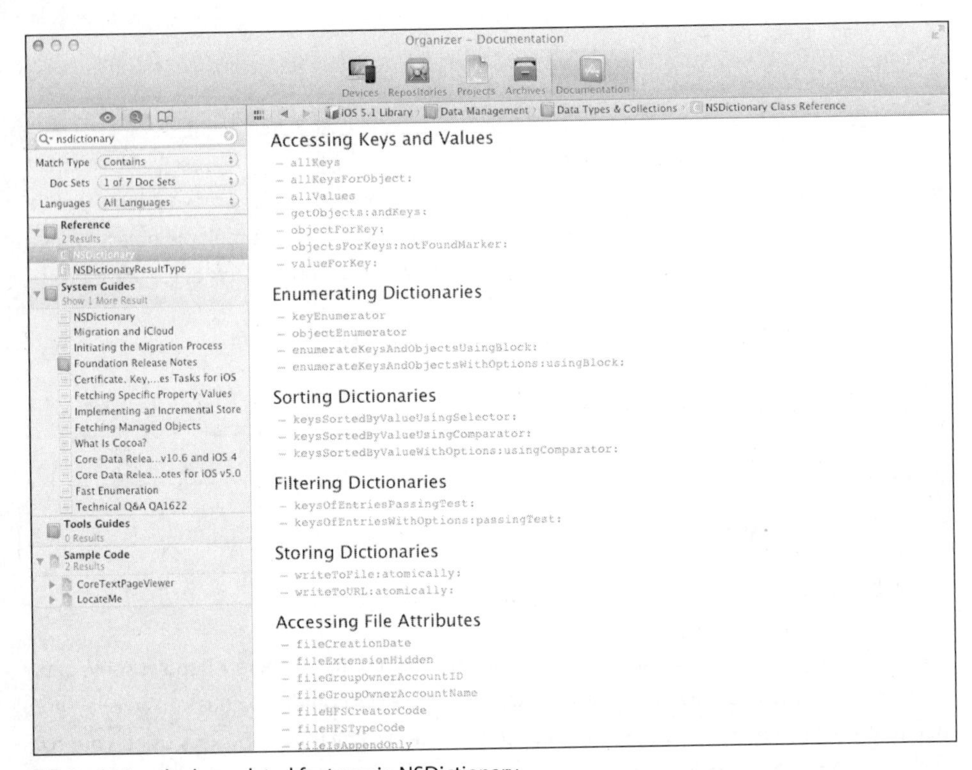

7.7 Exploring the key-related features in NSDictionary.

The order in which the objects appear in the array isn't defined. (It still isn't random.) But after objects are in an array, you can access them in a reliable and repeatable way through their indexes.

To search a set for an object, do this:

```
id returnObject = [aSet member: objectToSearchFor];
```

If the object exists in the set, returnObject is set to objectToSearchFor. If it doesn't, returnObject is set to nil.

If you just want to know whether an object is in the set, use containsObject:, like this:

```
BOOL yesOrNo = [aSet containsObject: objectToCheck];
```

Figure 7.8 shows that NSSet also offers a unique set of comparison options. You can check whether a set contains another set, or you can collect objects that appear in two different sets.

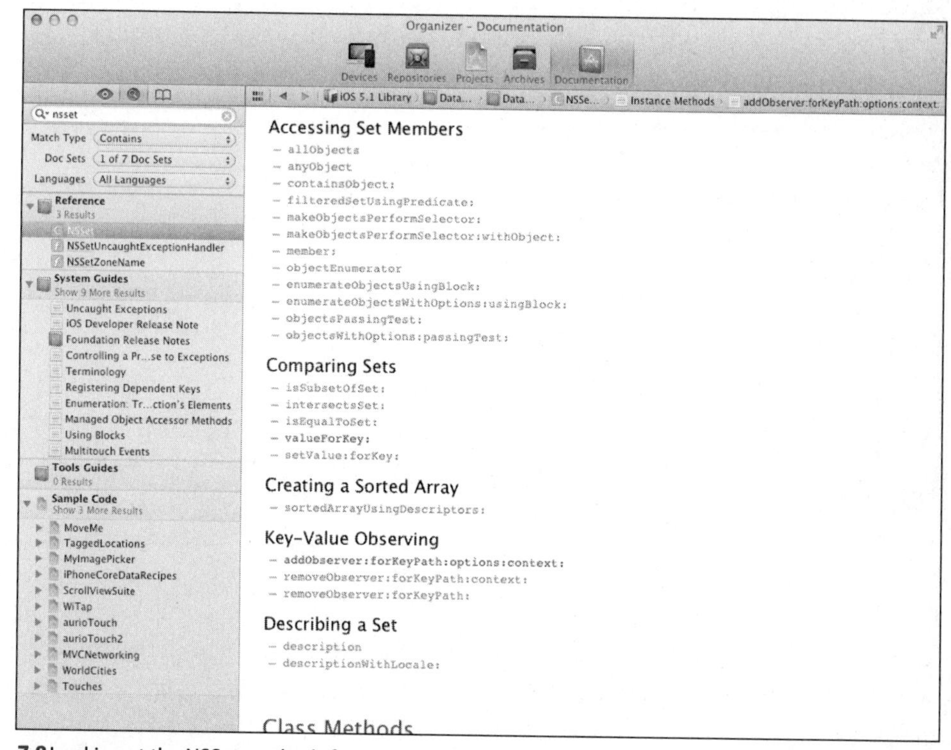

7.8 Looking at the NSSet methods for comparing sets.

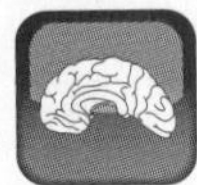
Genius

NSSet also supports KVC. The valueForKey: method builds a new set by enumerating the objects in the set and running valueForKey: on each one. If an object doesn't return a value for a key, it's ignored in the new set. (Enumeration is a quick way to step through each object in a collection and run some code on it. It's described in the next sub-section.)

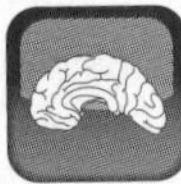
Genius

NSSet has an unusual subclass called NSCountedSet. A counted set stores objects like a set, but each object is associated with a counter that counts the number of times that object was added. You can use NSCountedSet for histograms and other statistical applications.

Processing objects in collections

Chapter 6 introduced for loops that use a counter. *Fast enumeration* is a similar but simpler technique for objects in a collection. It works like this:

```
for (id thisObject in aDataCollectionObject)
{
     ...do things to thisObject...
}
```

All the data collection objects include a property called count that holds the item count. With fast enumeration, you don't need to count the objects in the loop: It runs automatically until all the objects have been processed.

If you know the type of thisObject ahead of time, you can replace id with the type. If you don't, id works as a placeholder.

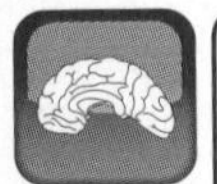
Genius

Fast enumeration isn't just convenient; it's also fast, as the name suggests. It can enumerate the items in a collection more quickly than a traditional for loop.

Running methods on objects in a collection

Another useful method available in all data collection objects is makeObjectsPerformSelector. It's even simpler than fast enumeration, and it runs the same method on every object with a single line of code, like this:

```
[aCollectionObject makeObjectsPerformSelector: @selector(aMethod)];
```

You can define aMethod elsewhere in your code in the same object that includes the line above. (You can't use this option to run a method in another object directly. There's no reason not to include a call to another method in another object in aMethod, if you need one.) A related method passes an object as a parameter:

```
[aCollectionObject makeObjectsPerformSelector: @selector(aMethod:) withObject:
   someOtherObject];
```

With this variation, aMethod should look like this:

```
-(void) aMethod: (id) someOtherObject
{
...Do something
}
```

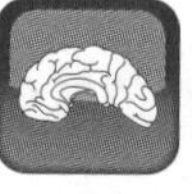

Genius

Because you can pass only a single object to aMethod, the options may appear limited. In practice, this object is often a data collection itself. So you can pack lots of information into a single method call.

Checking method availability

If a collection holds objects of different classes, you may need to check that your defined method is implemented in all of them before you attempt to process a collection with a single operation. You can use the respondsToSelector: method to check whether an object can perform a method:

```
if ([anObject respondsToSelector:@selector(aMethodName)])...
```

This gives your code a chance to check that your app isn't about to crash because it wants an object to run a method that doesn't exist.

If you need to check the class of an object before continuing, do this:

```
Class *thisClass = [anyObject class];
```

"Class" is actually an Objective-C class! It isn't a text string, so you can't compare it to a string. However, you can do this:

```
if (returnedObject isMemberOfClass: [AClassName class])…
```

A related method checks whether the object is a member of a class *or any of its parent classes:*

```
if (returnedObject isKindOfClass: [AClassName class])…
```

Key-value observing (KVO)

Key-value observing is an intermediate technique. KVO allows objects to watch each other—or specifically, to watch each other's properties.

Caution

KVO is a mixed blessing. It makes it very easy for objects to respond intelligently to each other. For example, if a user updates the preferences in an app, you can use KVO to force every object that refers to the preferences to update itself automatically. But it can also make for obscure code, because it becomes harder to see how objects are connected.

In outline, KVO works like this:

1. **The observer object sends the watched object a message setting up KVO.** The message includes the name of the property/key that will be watched and options that define whether messages include the old and/or new values of the watched property.
2. **When a property is updated, the watched object sends the observer a message with its own name, the property/key name, and a dictionary of information about the update.**
3. **The observer can observe more than one object.** All update messages are processed in a single method. So the observer begins by pulling the name of the observed object and the updated property/key out of the incoming message. Optionally, it may also check the contents of the dictionary.
4. **The observer uses the object name and property/key name to select the code that runs.**

To set up KVO, the code looks like this:

```
[objectToWatch addObserver: objectThatWatches
               forKeyPath: @"keyToWatch"
                  options: NSKeyValueObservingOptionOld |
   NSKeyValueObservingOptionNew
                  context: NULL];
```

If you run this method in the observer object, you can replace "objectThatWatches" with "self." You can use the options to select whether the update message includes the previous "old" value, the current "new" value, or both—as here.

When you run this method, objectToWatch starts monitoring keyToWatch. If its value changes, it automatically sends objectThatWatches an update.

To receive messages in the watcher object, add this method to it:

```
-(void) observeValueForKeyPath: (NSString *) keyPath
                      ofObject: (id) object
                        change: (NSDictionary *) change
                       context: (void *) context
{
     if ([keypath isEqual: @"keyToWatch"] && (object == objectToWatch))
     {
        ...doStuff...
     }
}
```

If you set up only a single observed object and a single observed keypath in your app, you can skip the test and just doStuff. Otherwise, you should include the conditional to check which object and key generated the message. To process multiple objects and keys, add multiple conditionals.

You can turn off KVO like this:

```
[objectToWatch removeObserver: watchingObject forKeyPath:"@"keyToWatch"];
```

When you run this method, the watched object stops sending update messages to the watching object.

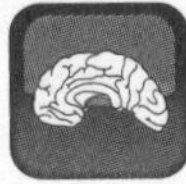

Genius

Objects can watch themselves. This might seem useless, but it allows an object to respond whenever another object updates the value of a property. You can create the same result with custom setter methods, but with KVO, you can add or remove the observation as needed.

Caution

KVO isn't fast, so don't set up tens of watched properties in applications where speed matters.

Scheduling Events

You may want to add a timer to an app or to include a delay so a message is sent after a predetermined time. iOS includes basic timers and supports more complex scheduling options.

Caution

Timers have obvious applications—clocks, counters, sequence controllers—but occasionally, you'll need to delay an event to give some other event time to finish. If your app seems to need this, you may need to rethink how it's designed. Some time-based features in iOS, such as the animation classes, can automatically trigger a method when they complete. It's better to make events happen in a clear order than to include arbitrary delays that guesstimate how long a process will take to finish.

Simple delays are built into iOS. You don't need to create a timer to use them; you can trigger a method after a delay with a single line of code. Although you can use timer objects to achieve the same result, the single-method option is easier to work with.

Creating a simple delay

To trigger a method after a delay, do this:

```
[targetObject performSelector:
          @selector(delayedMethod:) withObject: someObject afterDelay: a
  Delay];
```

If you don't want to pass an object to the delayed method, replace "someObject" with "nil." aDelay is a float—technically, an NSTimerInterval—set in seconds. You can use this feature with any method in any target object. Figure 7.9 shows a simple example. A method is used to log a message. The method is run twice—first by calling it directly and the second time by using performSelector and specifying a delay.

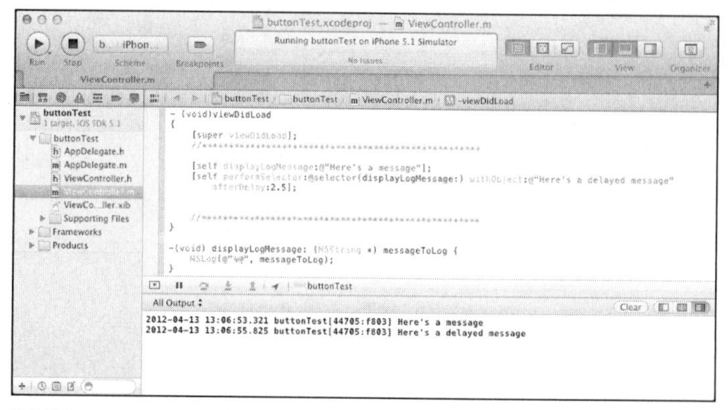

7.9 Triggering a method after a delay.

Creating a simple timer

Use NSTimer to create timer objects. The most useful method is scheduledTimerWithTimeInterval. Use it like this:

```
NSTimer *aTimer = [NSTimer scheduledTimerWithTimeInterval: timeInSeconds
            target: targetObject
          selector: @selector(methodToRun)
          userInfo: anOptionalObject
           repeats: YES]; //Or NO for a one-off delay
```

The method fired by the timer should look like this:

```
- (void) methodToRun: (NSTimer *) theTimer
{
    doStuff...
}
```

Figure 7.10 shows a simple counter. The method fired by the timer increments a counter variable and logs the result.

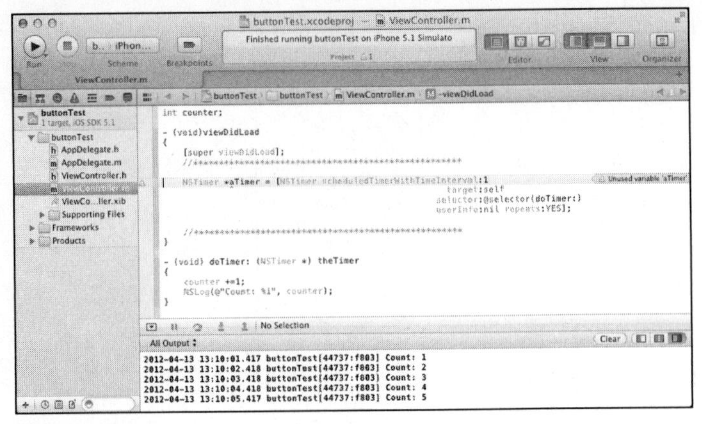

7.10 Creating a simple counter with a timer.

To remove and stop a timer, use a method called invalidate.

```
[aTimer invalidate];
```

If any objects are likely to access the timer after it has been invalidated, it's useful to zero the pointer to the timer object like this:

```
aTimer = nil;
```

If your app attempts to access an object that no longer exists, it crashes. If it accesses a nil object, nothing happens.

Scheduling an event at a future time

You can create an NSDate object to specify a time and date in the future. (In spite of the name, NSDate specifies a date *and* a time on that date.) For example, you can use the dateWithString: method, like this:

```
NSDate *aDate = [NSDate dateWithString: @"2015-01-16 17:45:56 +0000"];
```

The format for the string *must* be "YYYY-MM-DD HH:MM:SS ±HHMM". This is the international standard format for date events. The last field defines an offset from Greenwich Mean Time.

You can then create a timer object that fires on that date/time:

```
NSTimer *aTimer = [[NSTimer alloc] initWithFireDate: aDate
                                            interval: timeInterval
                                              target: targetObject
                                            selector: @selector(timerMethod:)
                                            userInfo: nil
                                             repeats: YES or NO];
```

Caution

Of course, if your app isn't running, the timer won't fire! To get around this, you can use *notifications*, which are introduced briefly in Chapter 11.

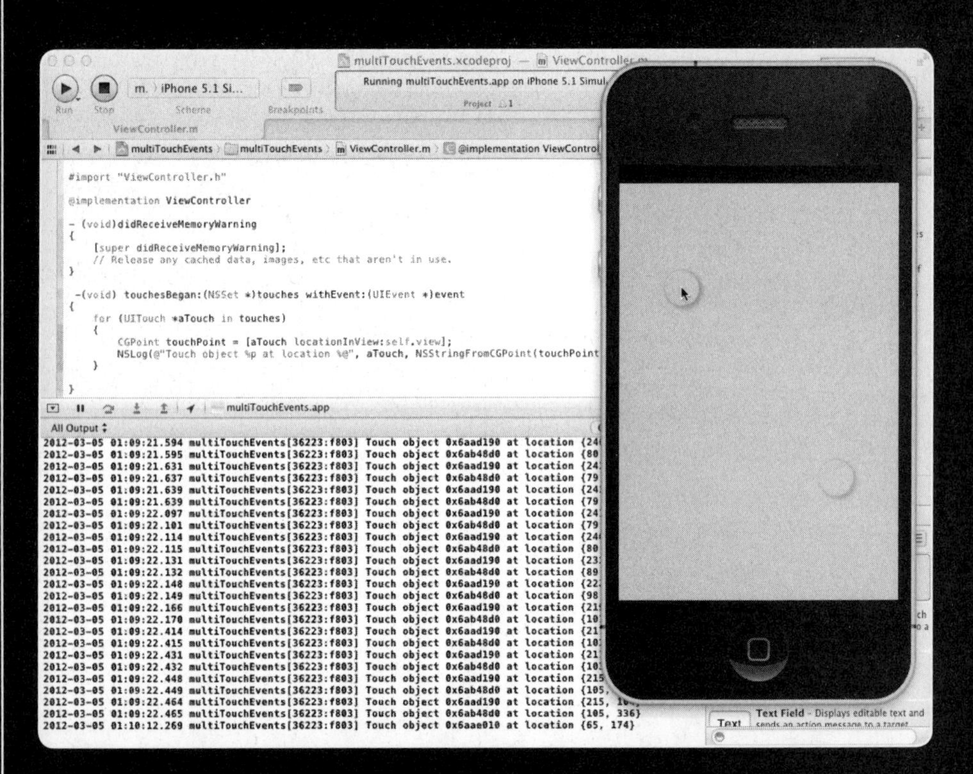

multiTouchEvents.xcodeproj — ViewController.m
Run
Stop
m. 〉iPhone 5.1 Si...
Scheme
Breakpoints
Running multiTouchEvents.app on iPhone 5.1 Simul
Project 1
ViewController.m
multiTouchEvents 〉 multiTouchEvents 〉 ViewController.m 〉 @implementation ViewControl
#import "ViewController.h"
@implementation ViewController
- (void)didReceiveMemoryWarning
{
[super didReceiveMemoryWarning];
// Release any cached data, images, etc that aren't in use.
}
-(void) touchesBegan:(NSSet *)touches withEvent:(UIEvent *)event
{
for (UITouch *aTouch in touches)
{
CGPoint touchPoint = [aTouch locationInView:self.view];
NSLog(@"Touch object %p at location %@", aTouch, NSStringFromCGPoint(touchPoint
}
}
multiTouchEvents.app
All Output
2012-03-05 01:09:21.594 multiTouchEvents[36223:f803] Touch object 0x6aad190 at location {24
2012-03-05 01:09:21.595 multiTouchEvents[36223:f803] Touch object 0x6ab48d0 at location {80
2012-03-05 01:09:21.631 multiTouchEvents[36223:f803] Touch object 0x6aad190 at location {24
2012-03-05 01:09:21.637 multiTouchEvents[36223:f803] Touch object 0x6ab48d0 at location {79
2012-03-05 01:09:21.639 multiTouchEvents[36223:f803] Touch object 0x6aad190 at location {24
2012-03-05 01:09:21.639 multiTouchEvents[36223:f803] Touch object 0x6ab48d0 at location {79
2012-03-05 01:09:22.097 multiTouchEvents[36223:f803] Touch object 0x6aad190 at location {24
2012-03-05 01:09:22.101 multiTouchEvents[36223:f803] Touch object 0x6ab48d0 at location {79
2012-03-05 01:09:22.114 multiTouchEvents[36223:f803] Touch object 0x6aad190 at location {24
2012-03-05 01:09:22.115 multiTouchEvents[36223:f803] Touch object 0x6ab48d0 at location {80
2012-03-05 01:09:22.131 multiTouchEvents[36223:f803] Touch object 0x6aad190 at location {23
2012-03-05 01:09:22.132 multiTouchEvents[36223:f803] Touch object 0x6ab48d0 at location {89
2012-03-05 01:09:22.148 multiTouchEvents[36223:f803] Touch object 0x6aad190 at location {22
2012-03-05 01:09:22.149 multiTouchEvents[36223:f803] Touch object 0x6ab48d0 at location {98
2012-03-05 01:09:22.166 multiTouchEvents[36223:f803] Touch object 0x6aad190 at location {21
2012-03-05 01:09:22.170 multiTouchEvents[36223:f803] Touch object 0x6ab48d0 at location {10
2012-03-05 01:09:22.414 multiTouchEvents[36223:f803] Touch object 0x6aad190 at location {21
2012-03-05 01:09:22.415 multiTouchEvents[36223:f803] Touch object 0x6ab48d0 at location {10
2012-03-05 01:09:22.431 multiTouchEvents[36223:f803] Touch object 0x6aad190 at location {21
2012-03-05 01:09:22.432 multiTouchEvents[36223:f803] Touch object 0x6ab48d0 at location {10
2012-03-05 01:09:22.448 multiTouchEvents[36223:f803] Touch object 0x6aad190 at location {215
2012-03-05 01:09:22.449 multiTouchEvents[36223:f803] Touch object 0x6ab48d0 at location {105,
2012-03-05 01:09:22.464 multiTouchEvents[36223:f803] Touch object 0x6aad190 at location {215,
2012-03-05 01:09:22.465 multiTouchEvents[36223:f803] Touch object 0x6ab48d0 at location {105, 336}
2012-03-05 01:10:12.269 multiTouchEvents[36223:f803] Touch object 0x6aae010 at location {65, 174}
Text
Text Field - Displays editable text and

1 2 3 4 5 6 7 **8** 9 10 11 12 13

Apps need users, and designing an app's UI is a major part of the app development process. iOS stands between the design and your app, sending messages to your app when the user interacts with the screen and sending messages to the screen when your app responds. To make a UI live, you must link your code to the objects that appear on the screen. You can use Interface Builder to create and edit links. IB includes some useful automation that simplifies the process for you. But before you can use it, you must learn how messages pass in both directions and discover what linking means in practice.

Understanding User Interaction

Typically, a user taps on the screen to make something happen in an app, and the app responds by updating the content of the screen. It may also perform other tasks, such as downloading data from the Internet, getting the current device location, and so on.

Interaction is usually manual, but it can also be automated with timers, delayed messages, and other scheduled events. In this chapter, we'll look at manual interaction—capturing and processing events generated by a user.

Introducing actions, outlets, and responder events

iOS includes three systems for dealing with manual interaction:

- **Actions send messages to objects in your code.** Action messages can be created by onscreen controls and by external events.
- **Outlets control the properties of onscreen objects.** You can use properties to change the appearance and content of objects on the screen as your app runs.
- **The responder system sends messages to objects that volunteer to receive them.**

Let's look at what this means in practice.

Working with actions, outlets, and responder events

In an app, you typically design a UI with a number of *controls*—buttons, sliders, text boxes, and so on—and then *connect* the action messages sent by the controls to the code in your app. IB includes tools to make this easy. When the user interacts with a control, it sends a message to a method in your app, which can then respond as needed.

Outlets send information the other way, from your app to the screen (or more specifically, to controls; technically the controls don't have to be visible on the screen, although usually they are). You typically use outlets to update the properties of onscreen objects—to modify their appearance or update the data they display.

The responder system works independently. iOS sends touch and motion (shake) events to the *responder chain*—a list of objects that may respond to them. There's no direct link between touch events and specific objects. They're processed by whichever object grabs them first.

Working with Action Messages

When a user interacts with an object, it sends an *action message* to an object in your code—usually the current view controller.

iOS includes a standard repertoire of action messages. The list is defined in a class called UIControl and appears in Figure 8.1. Buttons, sliders, text fields, and other standard UI objects are all subclasses of UIControl, so they inherit the items in this list. Most of this list is built into Interface Builder, so you can access it directly when you design your UI.

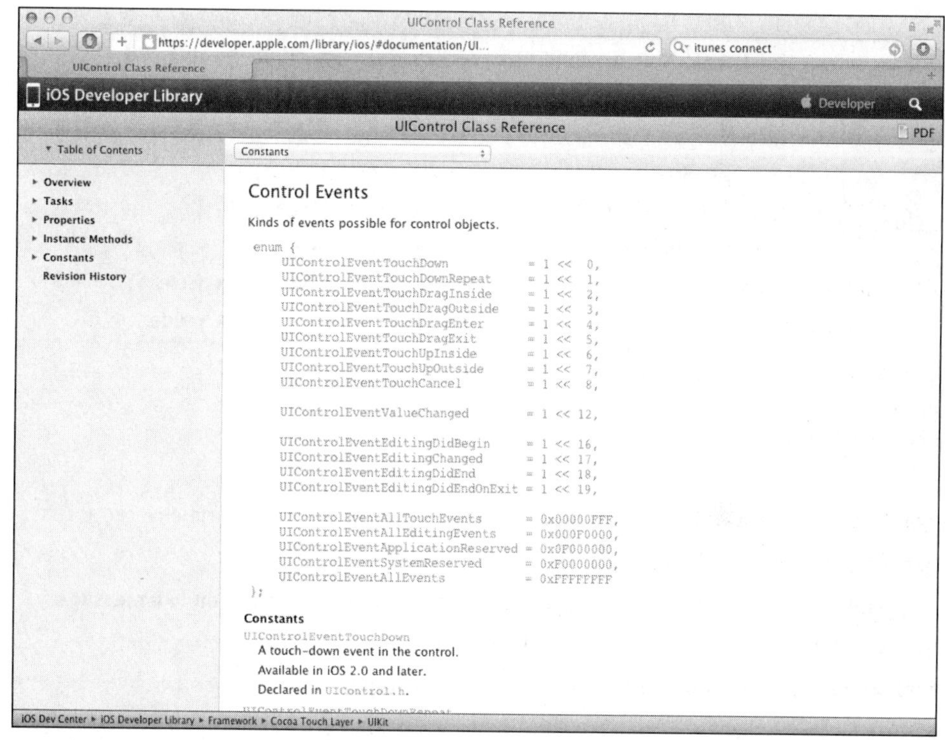

8.1 A first look at UIControl messages.

Caution

It makes no sense for a slider to send a UIControlEventEditingDidBegin message, because sliders aren't editable. Don't be confused by this. The same list is available for all objects, but that doesn't mean all objects can send every kind of message. It's up to you to work with the messages that make sense for each kind of control.

Note

An enum is simply a list of named items. Internally, each name in the list is associated with a value. This makes it possible to use names in your code instead of numbers—which makes your code easier to read. You'll often see message names and constant values defined in this way. (The numbers are almost always arbitrary, so you can ignore them. But extra points if you understood that "1<<0" is C code for bit 0 i.e. 1; "1<<1" means bit 1 i.e. 2; "1<<2" means bit 2 i.e. 4, and so on!)

Working with action messages in IB

Let's create a simple app that logs a message when a user taps a button. Create a new SingleView Application project, using the instructions in Chapter 3. Save it as "SimpleButtonLogger."

Note

iPhone and iPad apps handle messages in exactly the same way. The only difference is that the iPad has a bigger screen, so you can fit in more controls. For simplicity, we'll create this project as an iPhone app. It takes up less screen space than the iPad equivalent, making it easier to work with. But you use exactly the same techniques to create an iPad project. And for a universal project, you typically create two different UI designs—although they may use the same event handling code.

We'll follow these steps to create the app:

1. **Add a button to the view using IB.**
2. **Customize the look of the button.** This step is optional, but most commercial apps customize their buttons.
3. **Link the UIControlEventTouchDown event generated by the button to a message handler method in the view controller.**
4. **Add code to the message handler to log button taps.**

Let's look at each step in detail.

Adding a button to a view

Follow these steps:

1. **Click the ViewController.xib in the Project navigator file to load IB.**
2. **Click the Utilities button to show the Utilities pane, if it isn't already visible.**
3. **Click the Cube icon at the top of the lower pane to select the Object library.**

4. **Optionally, click the Objects menu and select the Controls item.** This filters the object list so it shows controls only.

5. **Click the Round Rect Button object, and drag it onto the view, as shown in Figure 8.2.**

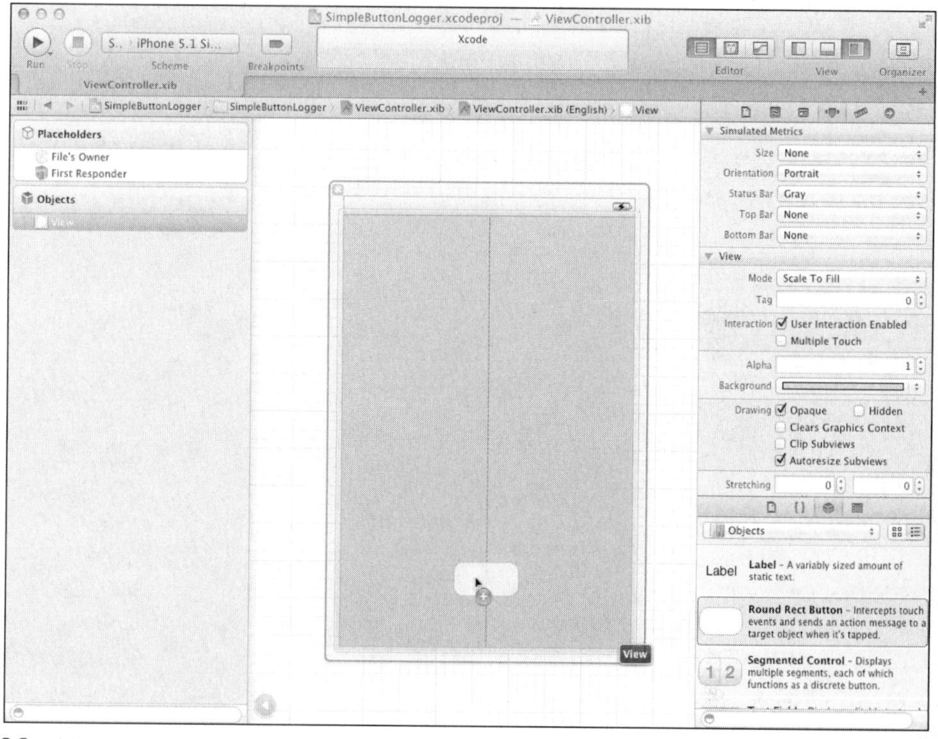

8.2 Adding a button to a view.

6. **Optionally, use the alignment guides to center the button in the view.** The button position isn't critical in this example app. But it's worth experimenting with the guides again to remind yourself what they do.

Customizing the appearance of a control

Most controls have various customization options. Basic customizations include size and labeling. More advanced customizations include colors, fonts, and original graphics.

Note

The standard controls aren't very exciting visually. Most developers customize them for maximum visual impact, even though customization can take as much time and effort as the code. In this example, we'll look briefly at the customization options and then look at them again in more detail in Chapter 10.

1. **Double-click the button, and type "Tap" to label it.**
2. **Optionally, click an edge or corner handle on the button to resize it, as shown in Figure 8.3.** Note how a floating window displays the width and height of the control. You may want to re-center the button after you change the size.

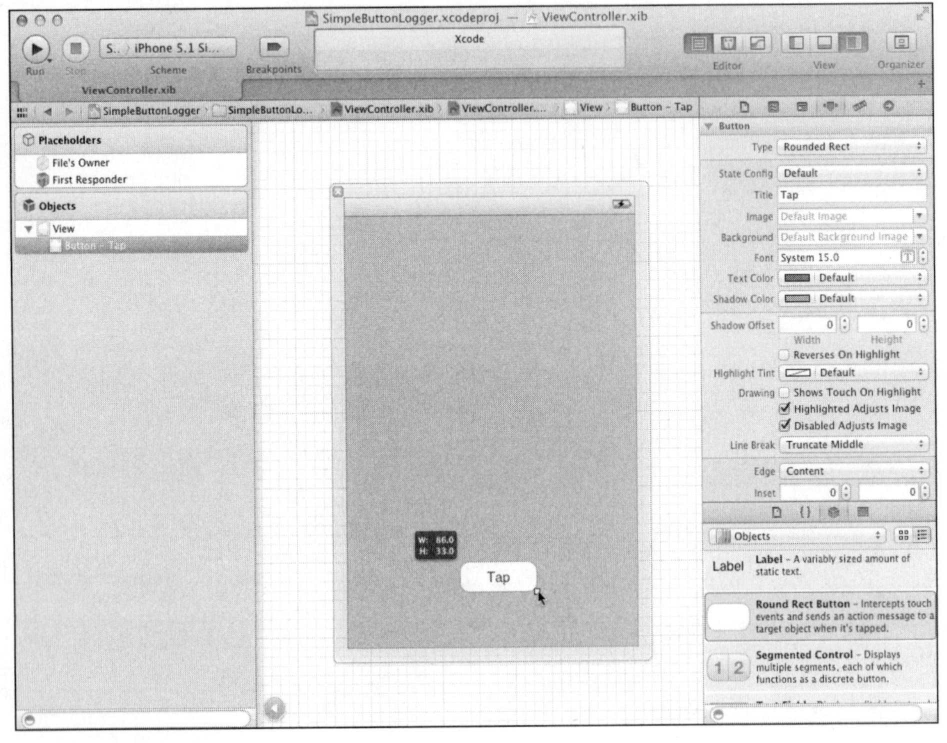

8.3 Resizing the button.

3. **In the top pane, click the third icon from the right to show the Attributes Inspector pane.** The icon looks like a shield in front of a rectangle.
4. **Optionally, experiment with the settings in the Attributes inspector, which is shown again in Figure 8.4.** Although there are many settings, there's much you *can't* do. For example, you can't change the background color of this type of button. However, you can change the text size and alignment, and you can add a drop shadow to the text.

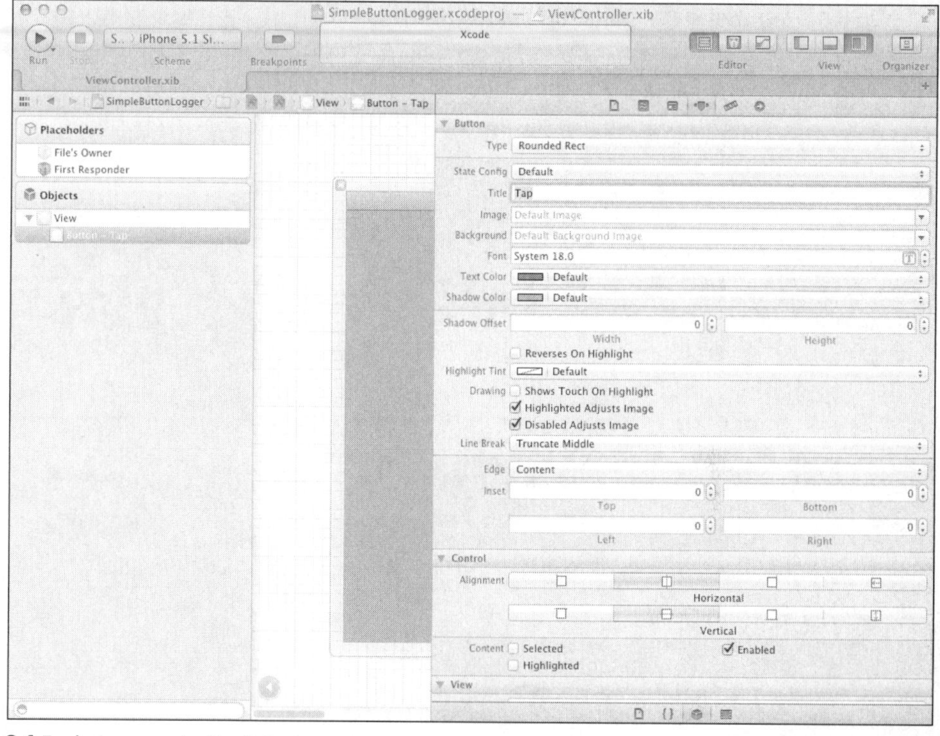

8.4 Exploring a control's attributes.

Caution

In practice, you have almost infinite control over the appearance of a control. Unfortunately, many possible options don't appear in the Attributes inspector. So although you can do almost anything with controls, you have to add the eye candy elsewhere in your code. Some advanced developers create their own controls from scratch—a time-consuming process.

Note

As you can see, the Attributes inspector has lots of options. They're not documented very thoroughly in the official documentation, so the best way to find out what they do is to experiment with them. Documenting all the options for every possible control would fill a book.

5. Optionally, experiment with the Size inspector, shown in Figure 8.5. The icon looks like a badly drawn ruler. You can set the size and position of the control numerically here. Use the origin box and the Layout Rectangle option to select the reference point for the position settings. You can also use this inspector to define how the control's position changes when the view is rotated. (For details, see Chapter 10.)

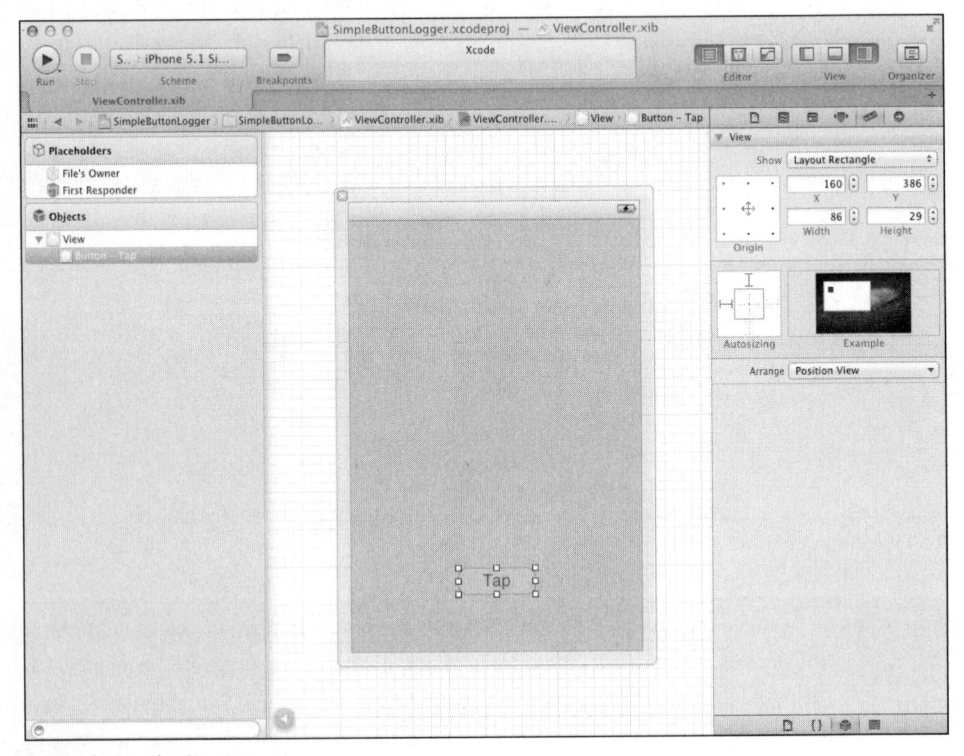

8.5 Exploring the Size inspector.

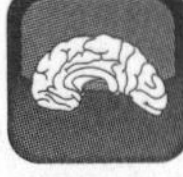

Genius

The items in the Arrange menu in the Size inspector provide quick and easy layout shortcuts. You can center any object, change its size so it fills the view, and align multiple selected objects with each other. It's worth remembering this menu; it can save you lots of layout time.

Creating event handlers in code

IB includes a handy helper feature that can insert basic event handlers into your code. To use it, follow these steps:

1. **Select the Assistant editor from the toolbar at the top left so you can see two files at the same time.**

2. **Use the Counterpart feature to show the view controller implementation file in one pane and the nib file in the other, as shown in Figure 8.6.** It doesn't matter which file is on the left and which is on the right. (Note that in the figure, we've hidden the Navigator and the Utilities pane to leave space for both files. You don't need to do this if you have a much larger monitor.)

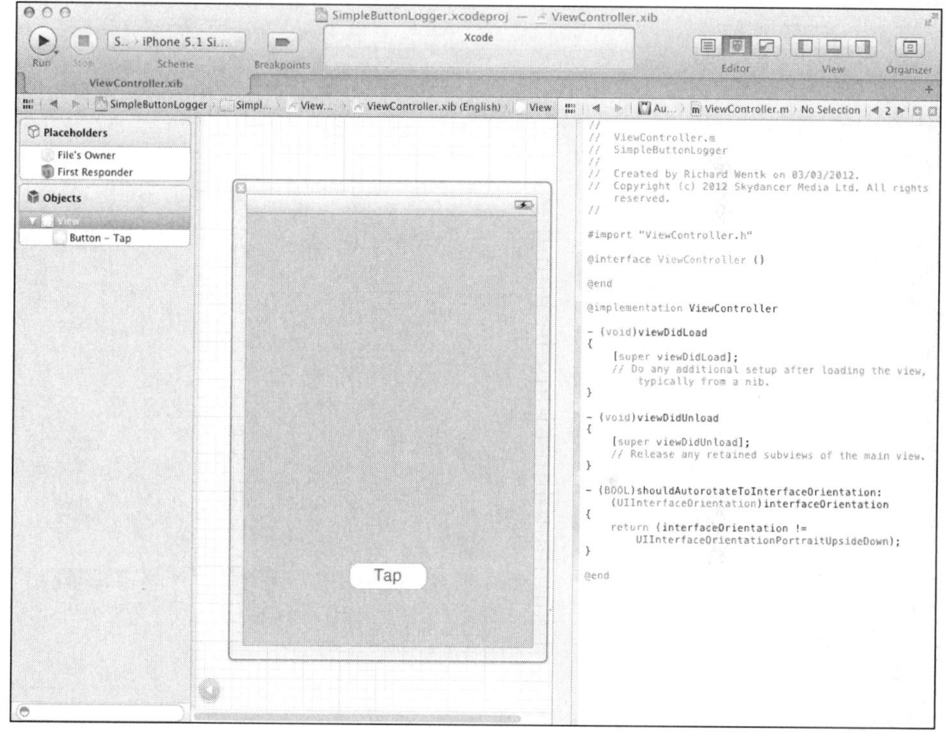

8.6 Setting up the editor area to show a view controller and its associated nib file.

3. **Click the button to select it. Hold down the Ctrl key, and drag the mouse from the button to the view controller pane, as shown in Figure 8.7.** You'll see a marker labeled "Insert Action." It follows the mouse as you move it up and down the implementation file.

4. **Release the mouse in the space between any of the existing methods.** In this example, we'll create the message handler under the last method, above the @end directive.

Note Where should you create the method? Remember, the order of the methods in the implementation file doesn't matter. But it's useful for clarity to group related methods together. Some developers place control handlers at the end of the implementation. Others place them at the beginning. Pick a position that works for you, and use it consistently.

5. **In the dialog that appears, fill in the Name field with "buttonWasTouched."**

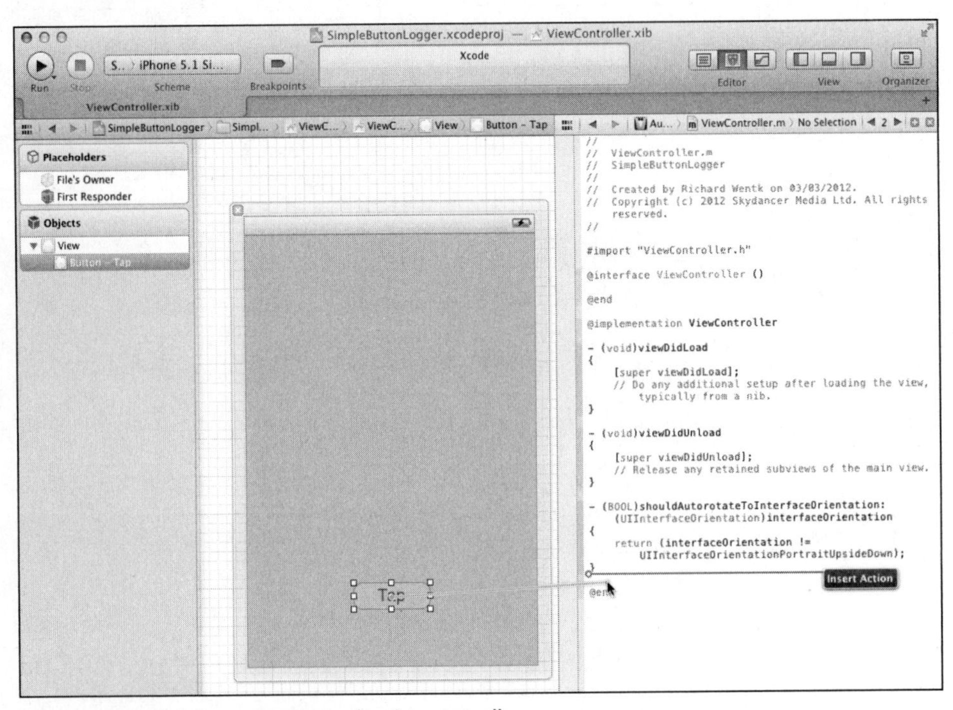

8.7 Dragging a link from a button to the view controller.

6. **Select the Touch Down option from the Event menu.** Doing this automatically selects the UIControlEventTouchDown message for this handler and ignores other events. The dialog box should be filled out as shown in Figure 8.8. Ignore the other options for now.
7. **Click the Connect button at the lower right of the dialog box to create a message handler.** Xcode automatically inserts code for the handler into the implementation file, as shown in Figure 8.9.

Note When you use this technique, code is inserted only into the implementation file. For a more advanced technique that inserts code into both the header and the implementation files, see later in this chapter.

8. **Optionally, right-click the button in the nib file.** You'll see the floating dialog box shown at the right of Figure 8.9. The Touch Down message from the standard list is shown connected to the buttonWasTouched: method in File's Owner.

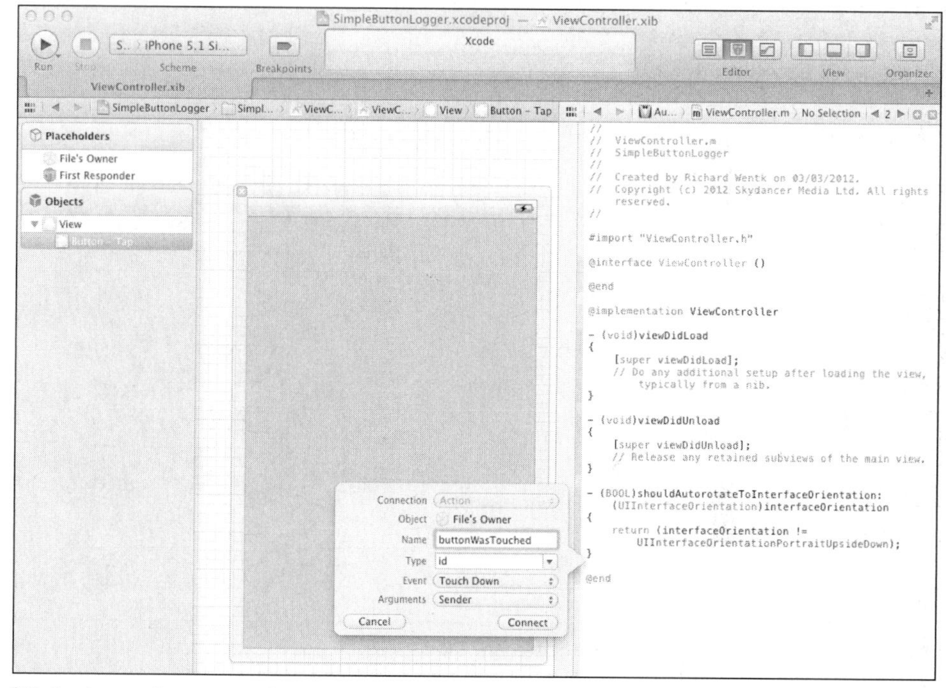

8.8 Getting ready to create the action handler.

Filling in an event handler

It's up to you to create the code that goes into an event handler. This is the creative part of app design—deciding what you want your app to do and creating code to make it happen.

In this example, we'll add a simple log message to check that the button works as advertised. Add the following line of code between the curly brackets of the new method, as shown in Figure 8.10.

```
NSLog("@Button was touched");
```

The figure also shows the result: A message is logged to the debug window when the user taps the button. (In the Simulator, click the button to test it.) The rest of the view does nothing.

Editing action connections

The automated connection tool built into IB is very useful, but sometimes you need to create new connections or delete existing ones.

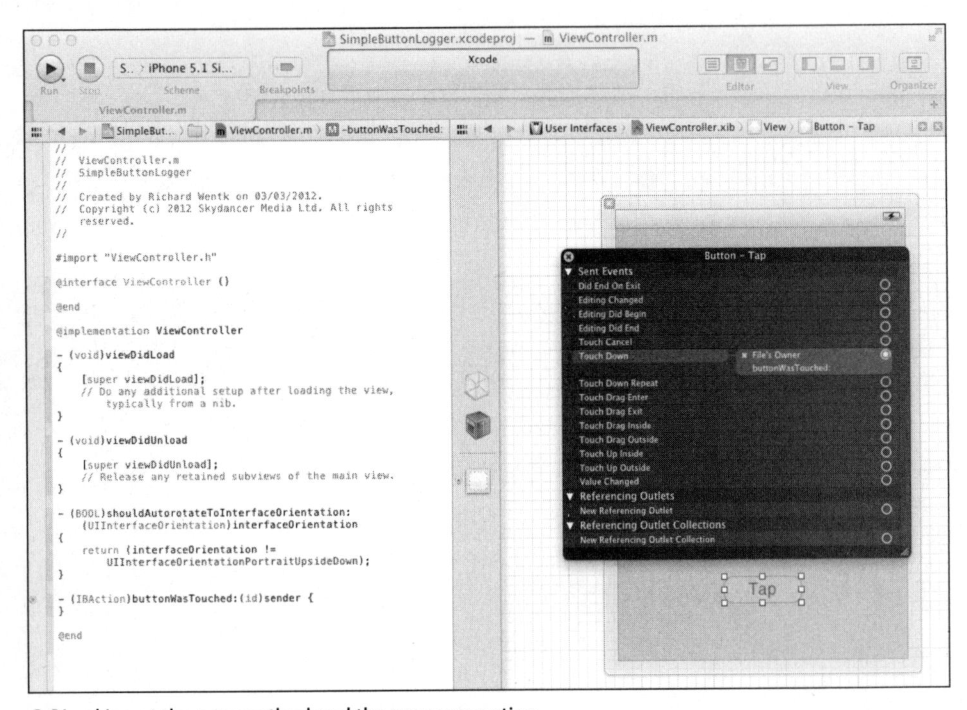

8.9 Looking at the new method and the new connection.

Deleting a connection

Follow these steps:

1. **Set up the editor window to display the nib file you want to change.**
2. **Right-click the object you want to disconnect.** You'll see the floating list of connections.
3. **Click the small cross on the connection to delete it, as shown in Figure 8.11.**

Note that deleting a connection doesn't get rid of the corresponding code. The message handler IB added to your code remains in place—but it's never triggered, because it never receives any messages from the UI.

Note

When a handler is connected, you'll see a filled dot in the breakpoint gutter to the left of the code. When a handler is disconnected, the dot is empty.

Creating connections manually

Although the automated code creator is handy, you may still want to make connections manually.

You can connect a method to an object or connect an object to a method. The two options give slightly different results, and it's important to understand how they differ.

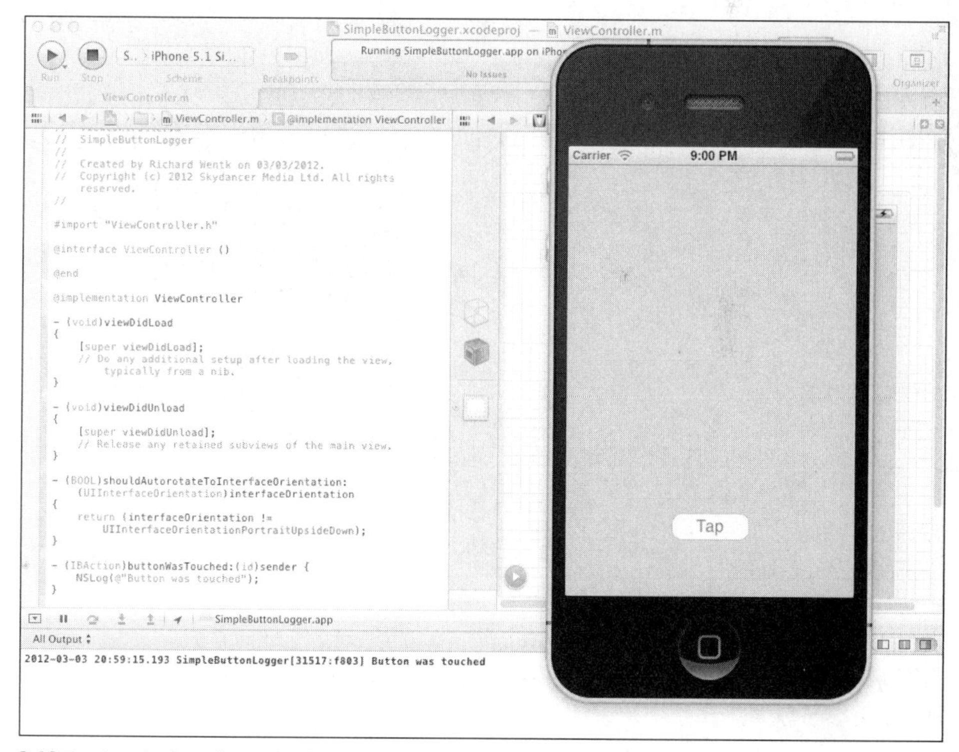

8.10 Testing the handler with a log message.

Note that IB can only connect methods that begin with "-(IBAction)." If you've already created a suitable method using IB's code creator, you can reuse it. You can also create a custom method by typing "-(IBAction)" by hand. (The signature usually ends with"(id) sender," which is described later in this chapter.)

If your method signature is correct, Xcode shows an empty dot in the breakpoint gutter to the left of the code.

You can also connect multiple objects to a single method. This can be a good way to make a simple but powerful UI. As you'll see later in this chapter, you can use the information passed in "(id) sender" to discover which object sent the message.

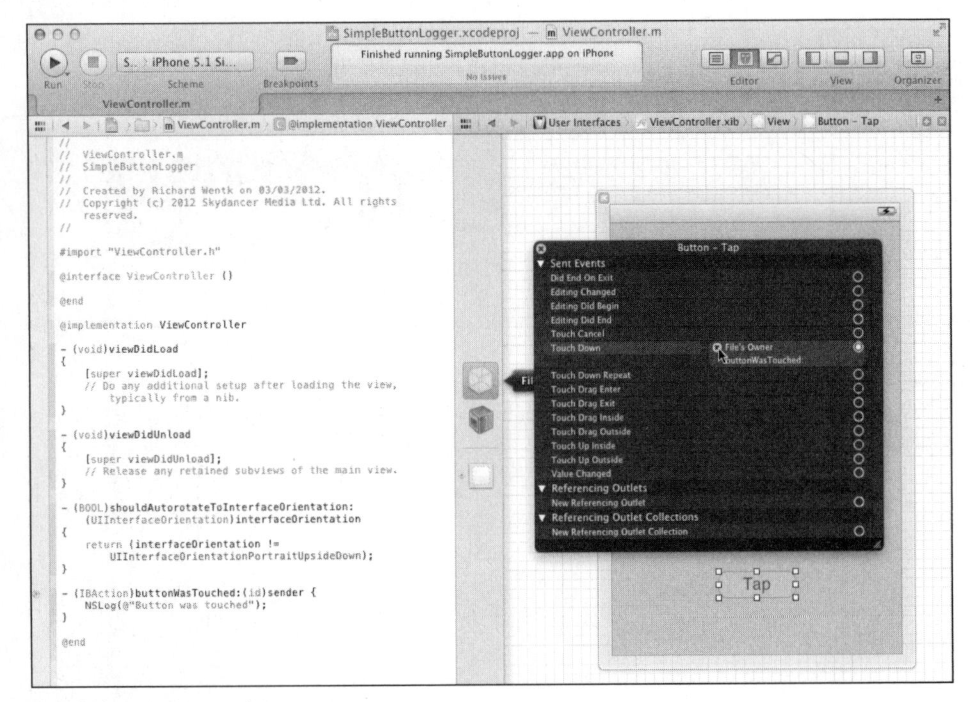

8.11 Deleting a connection.

Connecting a method to an object

Follow these steps:

1. **Arrange the Editor panes so you can see the method you want to connect in one pane and the nib file with the object you want to connect it to in the other.**

2. **Click the empty dot next to the method in the code.**
3. **Drag a link from the dot, and release the mouse pointer on the object, as shown in Figure 8.12.**

If you create the link correctly, Xcode fills the dot. If you right-click the object, you'll see the connection listed in the floating window.

A critical feature of this linking method is that Xcode *chooses the action message sent by the object.* You're not presented with a choice because Xcode selects a default action for you.

This isn't always a good thing. For a button, the default action is Touch Up Inside; in other words, the message is sent when the user taps the button and then lifts her finger while it's inside the button boundary.

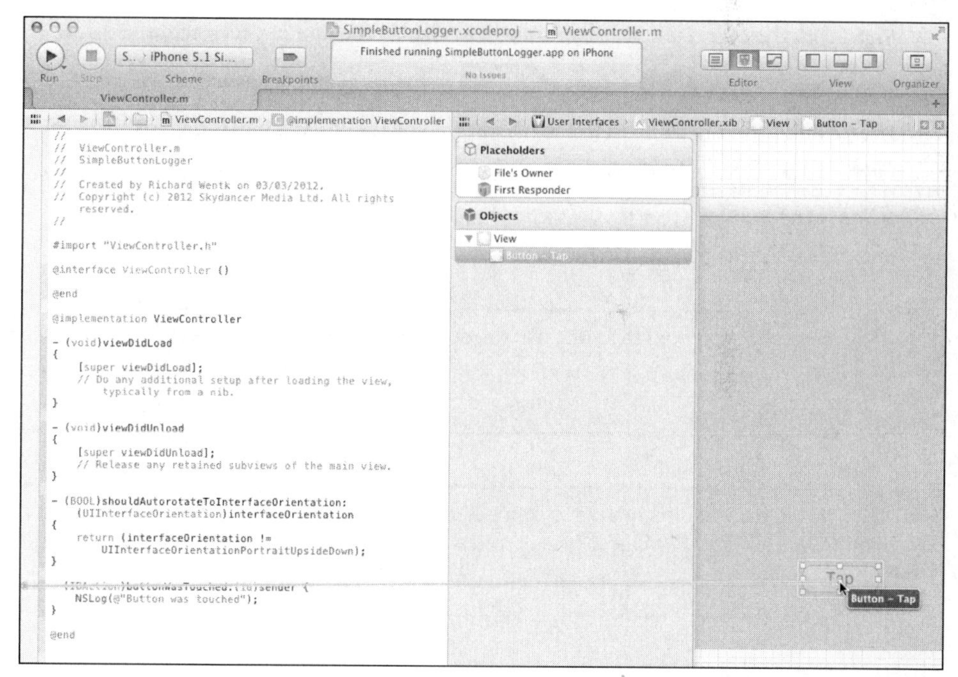

8.12 Linking a method to an object.

Some developers prefer to use the Touch Down action, which is sent as soon as the user taps the button. This matches the behavior of buttons in the physical world that usually respond when they're pressed, not when they're released.

The official Apple guidelines for UI development are described in a document called the Apple Human Interface Guidelines. In this case, the guidelines disagree with using Touch Down, because the delayed option gives the user a chance to move his finger outside the button area to cancel the action.

Whichever option you prefer, this connection option doesn't give you a choice.

Connecting an object to a method

If you want to select the action message sent by an object, use this alternative technique.

Follow these steps:

1. **Arrange the Editor panes so you can see the method you want to connect in one pane and the nib file with the object you want to connect it to in the other.**
2. **Right-click the object you want to connect to display the floating connection window.**
3. **Click the white circle to the right of the action message you want to use.**
4. **Drag a link from the circle to the method that will handle the message, as shown in Figure 8.13.**
5. **Release the mouse.** Xcode creates a connection, fills in the dot to the left of the code, and displays the connection in the floating window.

Caution

Note that you drag the link onto the code, not onto the dot to the left of the code. When the mouse pointer is in the right place, a translucent light blue box outlines the method.

Note

You can use this technique to connect multiple action messages from a single object to the same method. You can also use it to connect multiple messages from multiple objects to the same method.

Understanding (id) sender

When you create a connection using Xcode's code generator, the dialog box (refer to Figure 8.8) gives you the option to select a type for the method and an argument. Typically, you select "id" for the type and "sender" for the argument.

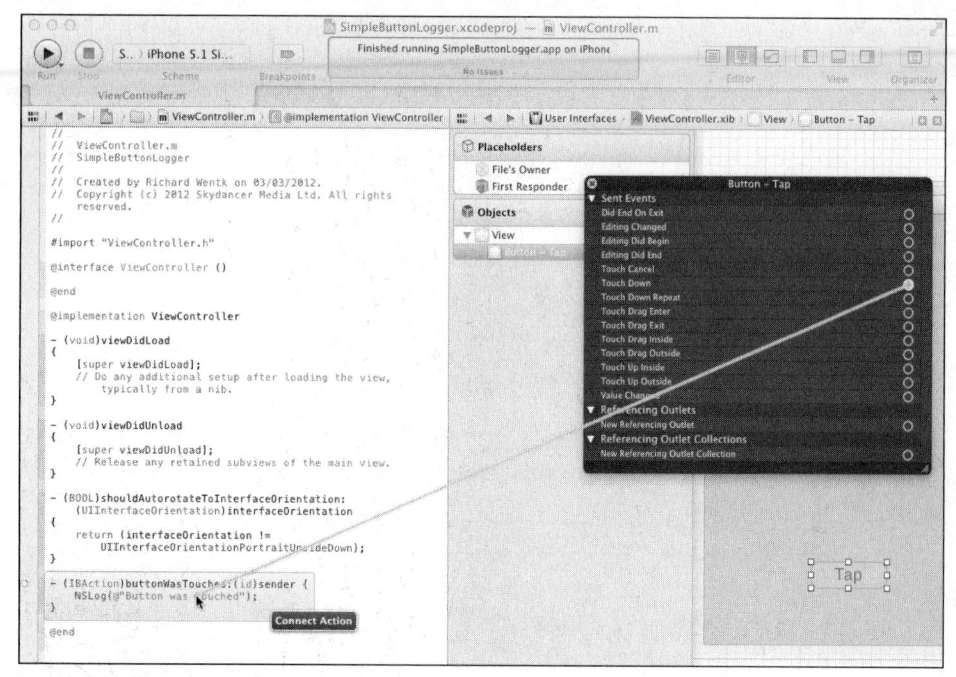

8.13 Connecting an object to a method.

Note

In developer-speak, an argument has nothing to do with a vigorous disagreement. An argument—sometimes called a parameter—is an extra item of data passed to a method or function. The method or function can use it as needed. If it doesn't need it, it can ignore it.

Here's why: The argument is a pointer to the object that generated the message. Because you may not know the type of the object ahead of time, it's handy to use Objective-C's placeholder "it doesn't matter what type this is" id type.

If you've set up your UI so that messages can arrive from more than one object, you can compare the pointer with your object pointers to discover which object sent the message.

```
if (sender == buttonOne)
    doSomething;
else
    doSomethingElse;
```

Another very common technique casts (id) sender to a known object type. This makes it possible to access that object's properties and methods. If you don't include the cast, Xcode doesn't know what type of object you're trying to use, and it doesn't let you access its features.

```
// Do this only if you know the sender is a UIButton

// This line tells Xcode that the sender object is a UIButton
UIButton *thisButton = (UIButton *) sender;

// You can now access the properties and methods of the button
if (thisButton.state == UIControlStateSelected)
     doSomething; //Do something only if the button is now selected
```

Note

The possible states for a control are listed in the UIControl Class Reference as another enum.

Creating and Using Outlets

Where actions receive messages, outlets link code to an object on the screen. After you create an outlet, you can use it to read and set the object's properties. In this example, we'll create an outlet to a *text field*—a small text box—and use it to change the text in the box when a button is tapped.

To work through the steps, you can either carry on using the project created earlier in this chapter or create a new project and repeat the steps you followed to create a button with a connection to an (IBAction). We'll use the button message handler to trigger a change in the text.

Creating an outlet

Follow these steps:

1. **Starting with the previous project or a duplicate, select a text field from the Object Library in the Utilities pane, and drag it onto the view in the nib.** Optionally, you can use the guide lines in IB to center the text field. The nib file should look like Figure 8.14.

Note

Review the steps earlier in this chapter if you're not sure how to find the Object Library and drag objects from it into a view.

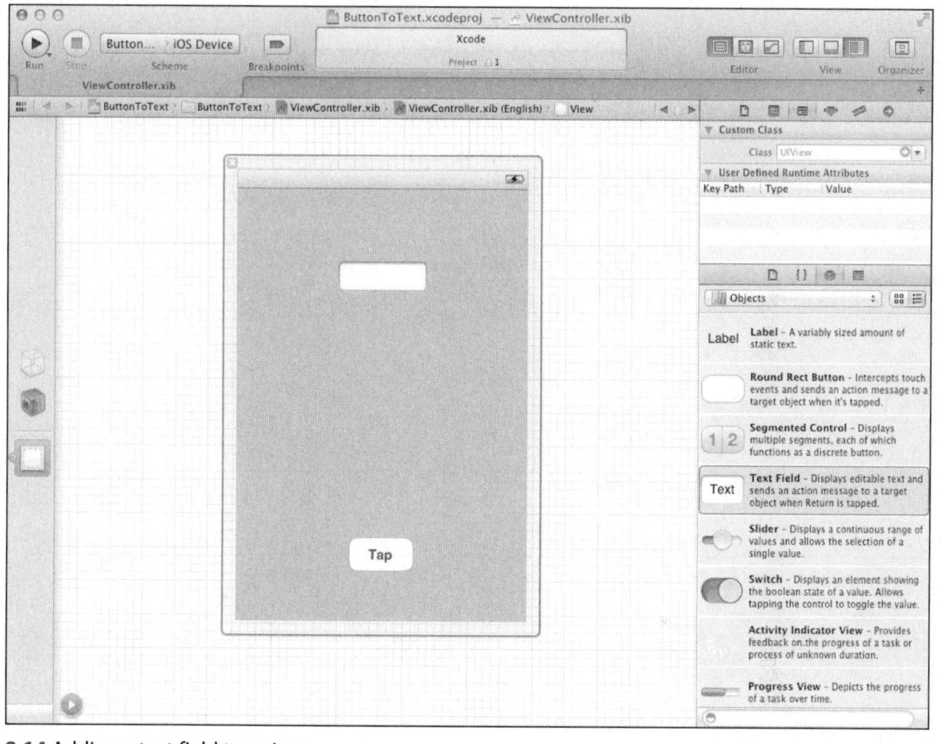

8.14 Adding a text field to a view.

2. **Arrange the editor windows so you can see the ViewController header file in one pane and the corresponding nib file in the other.**
3. **Hold down the Ctrl key and drag a link from the text field to the @interface section of the header file, as shown in Figure 8.15.**
4. **Release the mouse.** You'll see the dialog box shown in Figure 8.16.
5. **Type "textField" into the Name field.** Leave the other options unchanged.
6. **Click the Connect button at the lower right of the dialog box to create the outlet.**

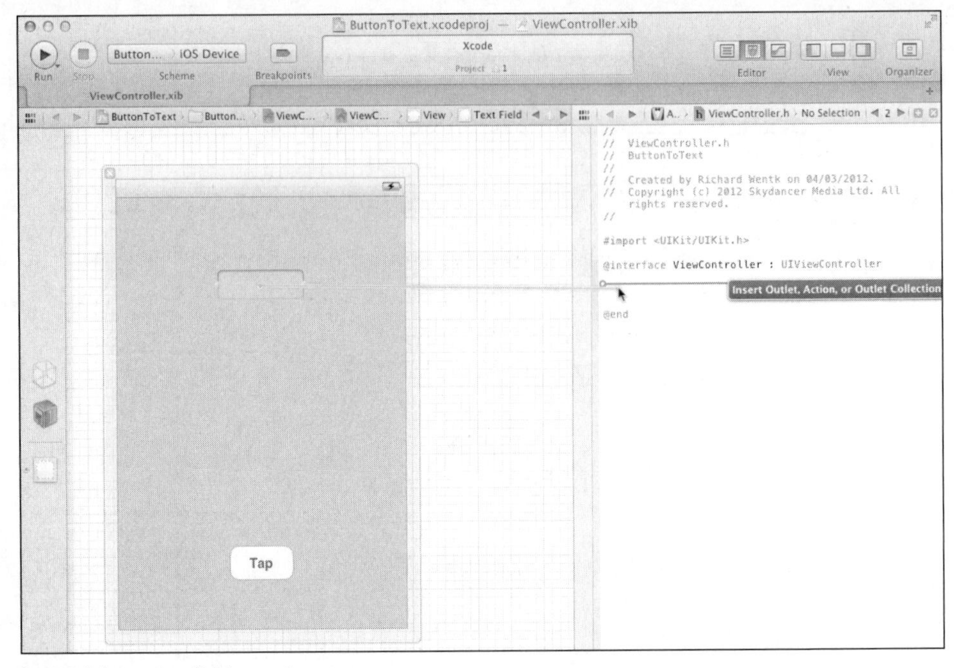

8.15 Adding a text field to a view.

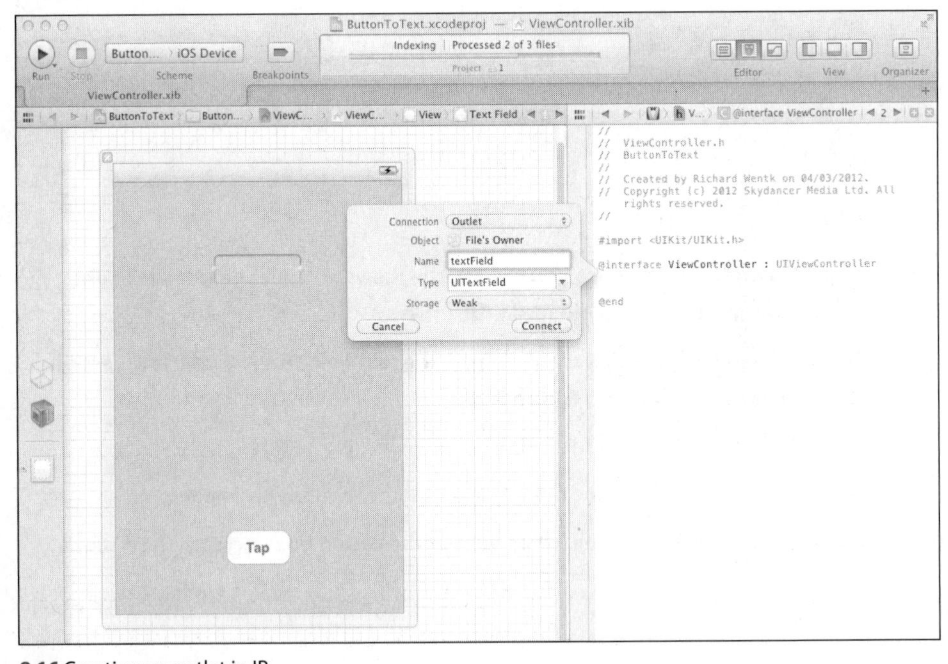

8.16 Creating an outlet in IB.

The outlet is now ready to use. If you look at the header file, the implementation file, and the nib file, you'll see the following changes have been made:

- **A new property called "textField" has been added to the header file.** It's tagged as an "IBOutlet" and has a filled connection circle to its left.
- **A line of code to @synthesize textField has appeared in the implementation file.**
- **A line of code setting textField to nil has been added to the viewDidUnload method.** This is a safety feature; it guarantees that the text field will be released from memory, and that further attempts to access textField will do nothing after the surrounding view has been released from memory.
- **The floating connection window for the text field now shows a new "Referencing Outlet."** You can see the changes in Figure 8.17.

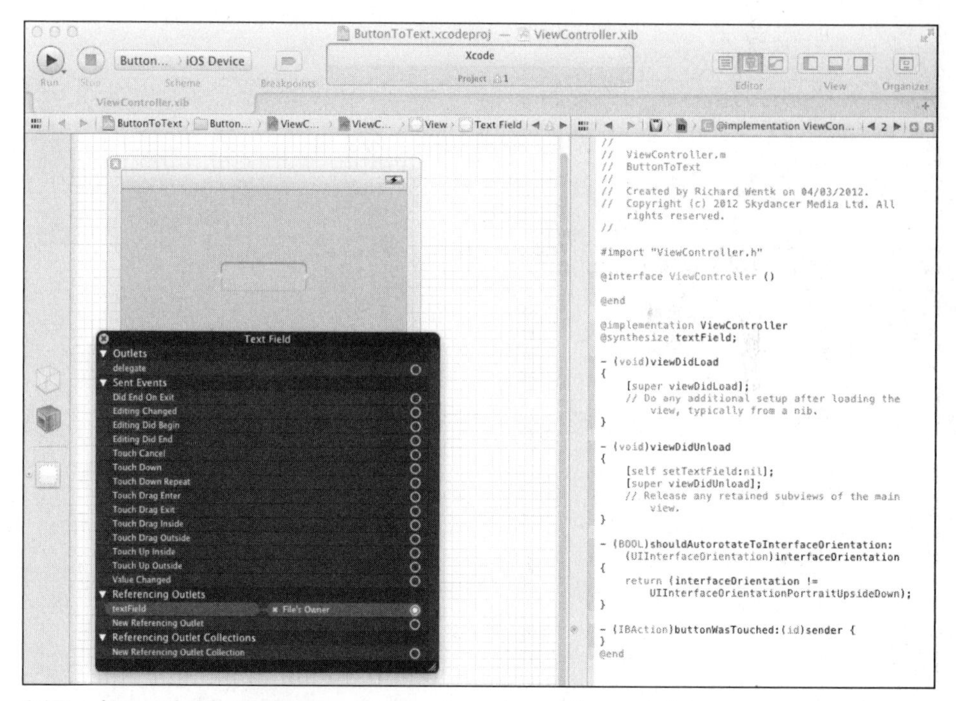

8.17 Looking at the changed code and connections after creating an outlet.

Using an outlet

To use the outlet in your code, access the connected object's properties in the usual way. Let's create a very simple example that replaces the blank text in the text field with the word "Tapped" when the button in the view is tapped.

Replace the code in the buttonWasTouched: method with the following:

```
textField.text = @"Tapped";
```

Figure 8.18 shows the result. The text field is updated with text when the user taps the button.

Note

As an exercise, see if you can use the Attributes inspector for the text field to center the text. And add another button that clears the text field.

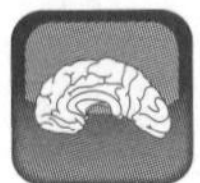

Genius

As a slightly more advanced project, use a single button to toggle the text between two different messages. You'll need to create a variable that flips between one of two values every time the button is tapped and is tested to select the text for each message.

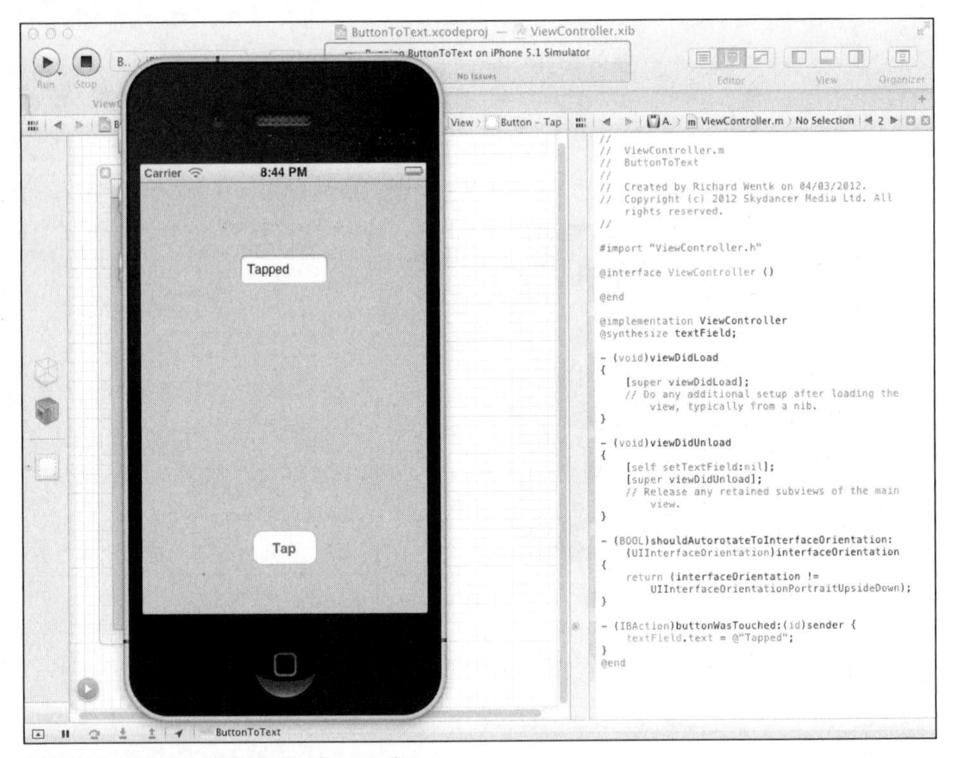

8.18 Updating a text field through an outlet.

Using the Responder System

As mentioned earlier, the responder system is a generic user event manager. It doesn't send messages to a specific object; it sends them to the *responder chain*, which is a list of related objects that may decide to handle an event or may decide to ignore it.

The responder chain is dynamic, and the objects in it can be updated at any time. You don't usually need to manage the updates yourself—with one exception. The first object in the list is called the *first responder*, which is synonymous with the object currently "live" for your user.

Some objects don't work properly if you don't control their responder status. So your app may need to nominate an object as first responder, specify whether or not an object can become first responder, or tell an object to stop being first responder—which is called *resigning* first responder.

Note

The first responder is similar to the idea of *focus* in some other operating systems.

As elsewhere in iOS, the theory of the responder chain is only loosely related to the practice. In practice, you need to know the following:

- **As explained earlier, some features don't work unless you include a method that tells iOS that an object *can be* first responder.** There's no consistency to this; it's a requirement for some objects, but not for many others.
- **Some features are manipulated through the responder chain.** For example, to hide the keyboard after editing a text field, you don't send your text field a "hide the keyboard" message, as you might expect; you send it a message to resignFirstResponder. When it stops being first responder, iOS automatically hides the keyboard for you.
- **The responder chain also manages touch events, shake events, and gesture recognition.** The simplest way to work with these features is to use standard boilerplate code. A key point is that you can add code for these features to many objects in your project. It's up to you to decide where it works most conveniently.

The responder chain system has a few quirks and gotchas, and it isn't possible to list them all in a short book. If you're having trouble getting some UI feature to work, it's a good idea to check online to see if someone else has solved your problem. You may find your issue is related to the responder chain.

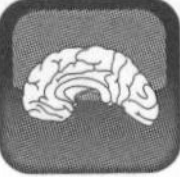

Genius

Advanced developers sometimes duplicate responder messages and pass them through multiple objects for special effects. A common technique is to create an invisible transparent view that captures and processes touch events and passes them to objects under it. This is a workaround for some of the greedier objects in iOS, such as the Google map view and the web browser view, which grab and destroy touch messages before your application can do anything else with them.

Working with a text field

Let's explore some simple examples of using the responder system. For this example, keep the code from the previous example. We'll extend it so your user can type text into the text field and your app can read it after the user presses Return. Your app will also use the first responder system to hide the keyboard.

Follow these steps:

1. **Using any of the techniques introduced earlier in this chapter, create a method to your project called "exitTextField."** Connect it to the Did End on Exit action message sent by the text field.
2. **Add code to the new method, as follows:**

```
UITextField *thisTextField = (UITextField *) sender; //Cast sender to a textfield
[thisTextField resignFirstResponder];
NSLog (@"The user typed: %@", thisTextField.text);
```

3. **Build and run the project.**

Figure 8.19 shows the result. When the user taps the text field, it's automatically promoted to first responder and the keyboard appears. As the user types, the text in the field changes.

When the user presses Return, the "Did End on Exit" message is sent. The new method is triggered. It does three things:

1. **It converts the (id) sender pointer to a UITextField pointer with a cast and duplicates it to a new pointer called thisTextField.** This step makes it possible to access the properties of the text field.
2. **The resignFirstResponder message hides the keyboard.**

3. **The code accesses the text property of the text field and logs it to the debug window so you can see it.**

Note

If your button is still connected, it will still update the text field to "Tapped." Note that this *doesn't* trigger an exit message. The Did End On Exit method is triggered only when the user taps the Return button on the keyboard. Writing new text doesn't trigger it.

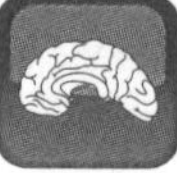

Genius

Some of the other text field messages make it possible to do clever tricks. For example, Editing Change is sent every time the user types a character. You can use this to make it impossible for a user to type certain characters—for example, punctuation and numbers. You can check each character as it's typed and update the contents of the text field only if it's acceptable.

8.19 Responding to edited text after an exit message.

Working with touch events

The four touch messages—touchesBegan, touchesMoved, touchesEnded, and touchesCancelled—were introduced in Chapter 7. Let's look at them in more detail now. The signature of all the messages is similar. We'll use touchesBegan as an example:

-(void) touchesBegan: (NSSet *)touches withEvent(UIEvent *) event;

All messages in this collection arrive with two parameters. The first is a collection of touch objects, each of which holds information about the position of a single touch. Technically, the collection is held in a set using the NSSet class. (A set is like a bag full of objects that are grouped together but aren't arranged in any order. There's more about sets in Chapter 7.)

The second is an instance of a class called UIEvent. This includes optional information about the timing of the touch events. In simple code, you can ignore this data.

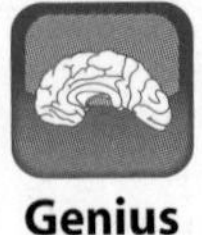
Genius

In an advanced project, you can use information about the time and location of multiple touch events to estimate the speed at which the user is dragging a finger. You don't need to know this for simple touch tracking.

Working with single touch events

By default, multi-touch tracking is turned off for your app. This means your code will receive only single touch events, which simplifies the code you need to write.

Typically, you want to find the location of the one possible touch event in its view. You can use this code:

```
-(void) touchesBegan: (NSSet *)touches withEvent(UIEvent *) event
{
     UITouch *thisTouch = [touches anyObject];
     CGPoint touchPoint = [thisTouch locationInView: self];
}
```

This code is only two lines long, but a lot is happening.

The first line asks the touches set for any object. You can't ask a set for a specific object, so the set makes a semi-random choice about which object to give you. Without multi-touch, only a single object is in the set, so this line always gives you the latest touch object.

The second line uses a method called locationInView:+ to find the position of the touch event relative to the surrounding view.

Caution

If you add this code to a view, you can use it as-is. If you add it to a view controller, replace "self" with "self.view" to make sure the code doesn't try to find a location in a view controller—which is impossible, by definition.

The location is copied to a structure called a CGPoint, which is part of the Core Graphics library in iOS 5. It includes the data structures used to define points, rectangles, and other useful geometrical elements. The functions and data types that are available are listed in a document called the CGGeometry reference. Take the time to search for it now.

Note

There are some very useful functions in CGGeometry, so you should look through it carefully. If you work with graphics, you'll spend lots of time defining points and rectangles. Use CGPointMake() to convert a couple of float values into a CGPoint and CGRectMake to convert an origin point, a size, and a width into a structure called a CGRect, which is used in iOS to define rectangles.

To access the x and y coordinates of a touch event, you can use touchPoint.x and touchPoint.y. For logging, you can also use a handy function called NSStringFromCGPoint() that converts the point coordinates into a log-able string, like this:

```
NSLog (@"Location: %@", NSStringFromCGPoint(touchPoint));
```

Figure 8.20 shows an example project that uses this code to log the location of touch events to the debug window.

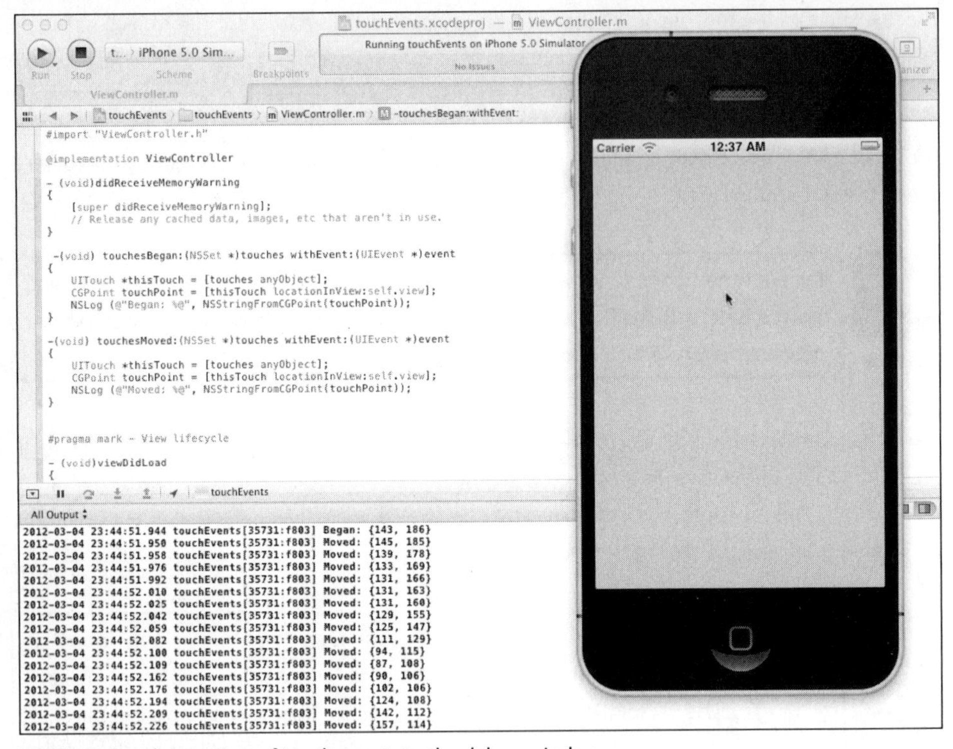

8.20 Logging the position of touch events to the debug window.

Working with multi-touch

You can enable multi-touch in a view in two ways:

- **Select the view in IB, open the Attributes inspector, find the Interaction field, and make sure to check the Multiple Touch box.**
- **In code, like this:**

```
aView.multipleTouchEnabled = YES;
```

When multi-touch is enabled, the touches set can hold more than one item. There are various ways to access them. One option is to copy the set to an array and then step through each item in the array using a "for" loop.

Another—simpler—option is to use *fast enumeration,* introduced in Chapter 7. You don't need to count the items, because fast enumeration does that for you automatically.

Here's some example code:

```
-(void) touchesBegan: (NSSet *) touches withEvent: (UIEvent *) event
{
      for (UITouch *aTouch in touches)
      {
            CGPoint touchPoint = [thisTouch locationInView: self];
            NSLog (@"Touch object %p at location %@", aTouch, NSStringFromCGPoint(
   touchPoint));
      }
}
```

The line with "for" is the fast enumerator. It's equivalent to saying "for every object in the set, apply the code between the curly brackets."

The code between the curly brackets displays the location of the touch point for each touch, as before. This version also displays the memory address of each touch event, so you can tell them apart in the debug window.

Figure 8.21 shows what happens when you enable multi-touch and add touchesBegan and TouchesMoved messages based on this code. The debug window shows multiple touch events and locations as your fingers move over the screen.

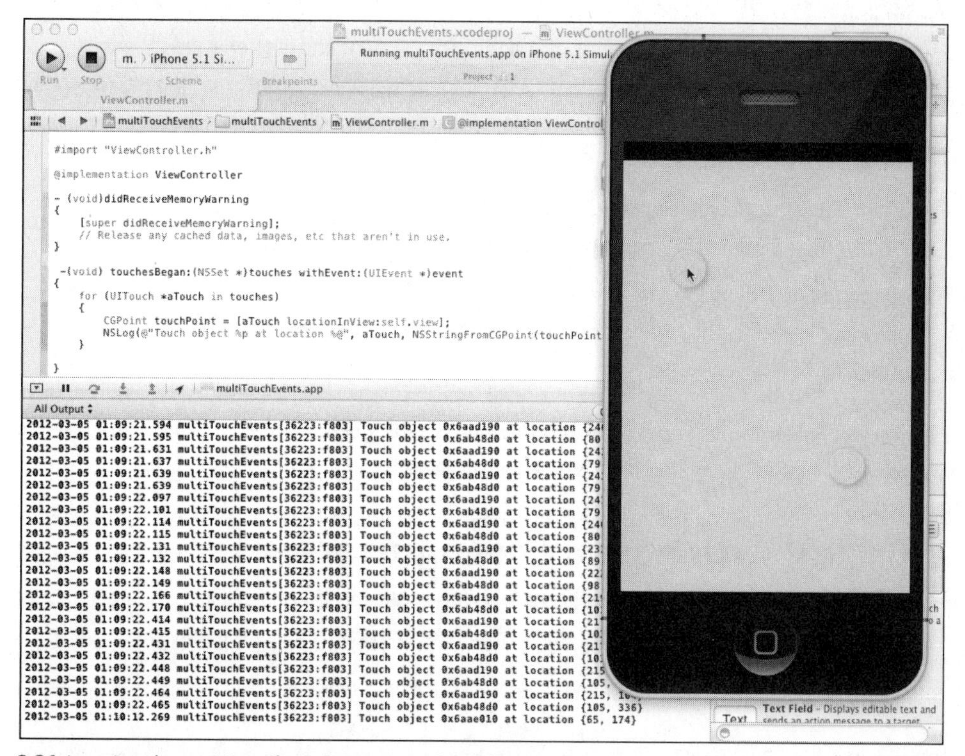

8.21 Logging the position of touch events to the debug window.

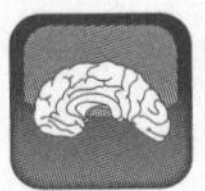
Genius

You can simulate two touches in the Simulator by holding down the Option key as you move the mouse.

Introducing gestures

It's not always obvious what multiple touch events should mean to the user. In a music synthesizer app, multi-touch may make perfect sense—each note corresponds to a touch. But it's less obvious what multi-touch should mean in a spreadsheet app or in a doodle app. So it's up to you to decide how your app responds to multi-touch events.

However, over time some single and multi-touch movements have become standards. You can add them to your app with a *gesture recognize,* which sends your app a message when the user moves his fingers in a recognized way.

In iOS 5, the recognized gestures include the following:

- **Tap.** Single, double, and multiple taps can all be recognized.
- **Pinch.** This gesture uses two fingers to zoom or expand screen content.
- **Swipe.** This is a single or multi-touch dragging movement and is often used to switch content screens. The gesture looks for a direction and a preset number of fingers. You can set up different recognizers for the same direction with different numbers of fingers, and they'll operate independently.
- **Pan.** This gesture typically moves content within a single screen. You can set the maximum and minimum finger count for each recognizer.
- **Long Press.** This gesture is used to reveal a feature after a short delay. You can set the delay time and the number of touches and taps required, so you can create tap/touch combination gestures.

Gesture recognizers arrive with useful information about finger movements. You can use them to create sophisticated interaction effects with very little effort.

Working with gesture recognizers

A class called UIGestureRecognizer provides a template for the recognizers for each gesture. Typically, you'll use a subclass; for example, UIRotationGestureRecognizer recognizes rotation events.

Note

You can see more details in the UIGestureRecognizer Class Reference in the documentation.

In outline, you use a gesture recognizer as follows:

1. **Create a new gesture recognizer object.** Select one of the subclasses to pick the gesture you want your app to respond to.
2. **Set up basic properties such as the number of touches, direction, and so on.** These properties are different for each subclass.
3. **Create a gesture recognizer method to handle messages generated by the recognizer.**
4. **Plug the method into the recognizer.** Fill the method with code, as needed, to implement the app feature triggered by a gesture.
5. **Add the recognizer to the view in which you want it to work.**

Let's look at some code that can be added to the viewDidLoad method of the view controller of a SingleView Application template:

```
- (void) viewDidLoad
{
     [super viewDidLoad];
     self.view.multipleTouchEnabled = YES;

     UIPinchGestureRecognizer *pinchRecognizer =
                  [[UIPinchGestureRecognizer alloc] init];

     [pinchRecognizer addTarget: self
                  Action: @selector(handlePinchGesture)];

     [self.view addGestureRecognizer: pinchRecognizer];
}

- (void) handlePinchGesture: (UIGestureRecognizer *) theGesture
{
     UIPinchGestureRecognizer *thisPinch =
                  (UIPinchGestureRecognizer *)theGesture;
     NSLog(@"Pinched - scale: %f"), thisPinch.scale);
}
```

Figure 8.22 shows the code being tested on a real device. The scale value is relative to the initial distance between the two touches that define the pinch; it's less than one as the pinch narrows from the initial distance and more than one if it expands beyond it.

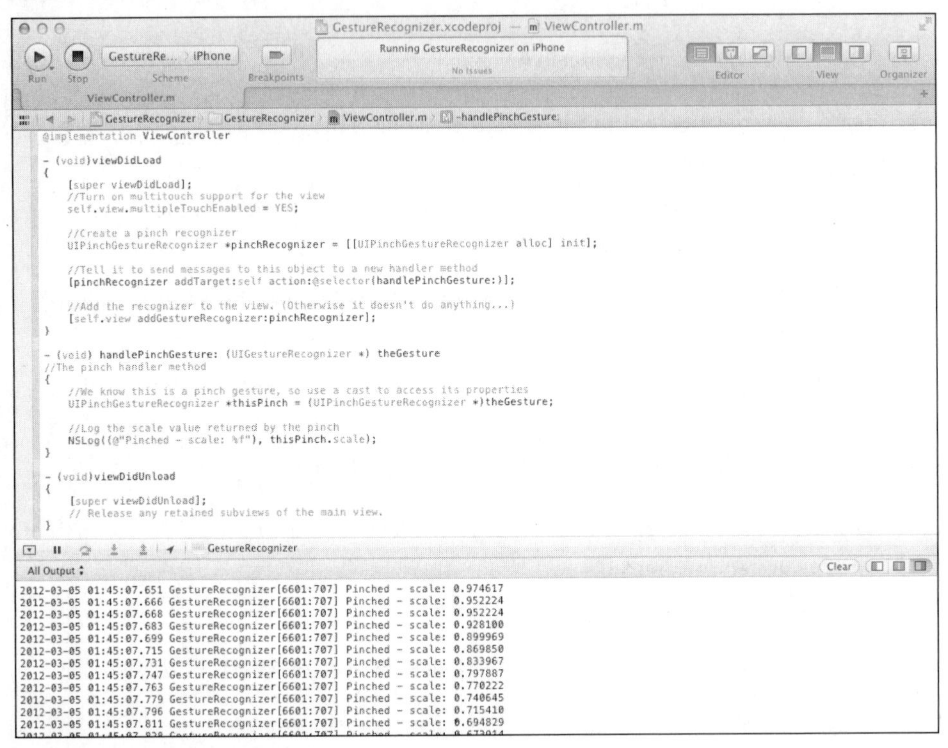

8.22 Using a pinch recognizer.

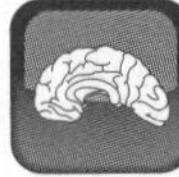

Genius

Sometimes, it's useful to access the touches that make up the gesture. You can get the number of touches by reading the numberOfTouches property. You can then count through this number and pass it as an index to the locationOfTouch: inView: method to get a CGPoint with a location for each touch.

Subclassing in IB

This section includes critical information about linking objects in your app to objects on the screen. Whenever you subclass an onscreen object, you *must* tell IB to use the subclass. You must do this manually.

Caution Until you get into the habit of subclassing in IB, it's easy to forget this step and then wonder why your new code does nothing. It's useful to create a sanity list of basic checks for development, and it's a very good idea to include subclassing in IB on the list.

Let's see what this means in practice. We'll create another sample project using the SingleView Application template, subclass the view that's included, and add some code to it. We'll see that IB ignores the code—a very bad thing—until we tell it to display our subclass instead of the default UIView class.

Follow these steps:

1. **Create a new sample project using the SingleView Application template, following the steps in Chapter 3.** Save it as IBSubclassing, although the name isn't critical.
2. **Follow the instructions in Chapter 6 to add a new subclass of UIView to the project.** Save it as MyView, although again, the name isn't critical.

Caution Make sure you select UIView from the class list in the New File dialog box, and not UIViewController.

3. **Add a touchesBegan: method that logs touches to the implementation file for MyView, as shown in Figure 8.23.**
4. **Build and run the project.** You'll see the code does nothing. You can click/tap on the screen, and touch events are ignored.

Why does the project ignore your code? To fix the problem, follow these steps:

1. **Click the project nib file to select it in the editor and open IB.**
2. **Click the view object in the Objects list at the left.**
3. **Open the Utilities pane at the right, if it isn't already open.**
4. **Click the Identity inspector icon in the row at the top.** It's the third from the left and looks like a small pane of information.
5. **Make sure the Custom Class sub-pane is visible.** If it isn't, click the reveal triangle to open it.

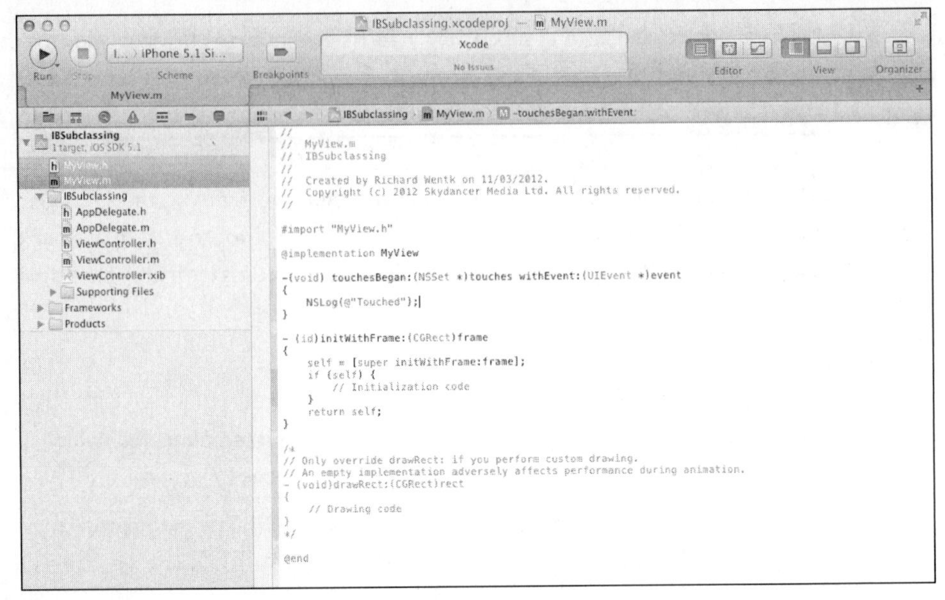

8.23 Creating a subclass of UIView, which does nothing…yet.

Figure 8.24 shows that the Custom Class menu is still showing UIView. *IB doesn't know it's supposed to use your custom class.*

The solution is easy. It's shown in Figure 8.25. Select your custom MyView class from the menu, and build the project. You'll see that IB replaces the default version of UIView with your customized version. Features included in the subclass are now included in the app—and in this example, you'll see touch messages when you tap/click the screen.

Caution

You must set the Custom Class field for *every* object you subclass. You also can set it for the File's Owner placeholder, which is often used when you subclass a view controller. Generally, if your code doesn't seem to run at all, check that you've set the Custom Class fields correctly for every object in a nib.

Caution

The class selection menu is smart, and it displays all possible subclasses of a relevant class. Usually, this is a distraction, and you can ignore it. Typically, you're only interested in two classes in the menu—the original class and your subclass. Note also that when you subclass an object in a nib, your subclass is added to the menu automatically.

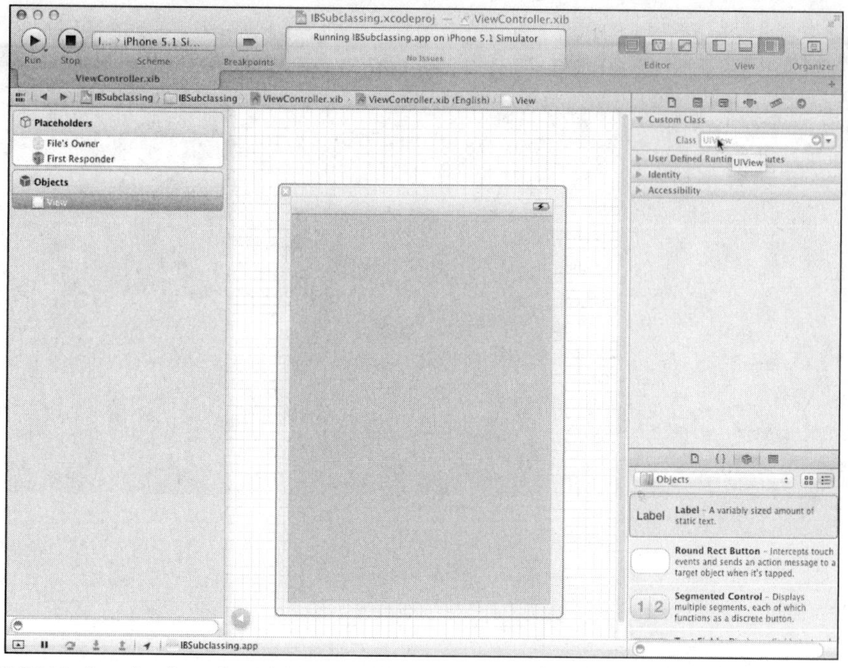

8.24 Finding the class of an object in IB using the Identity inspector.

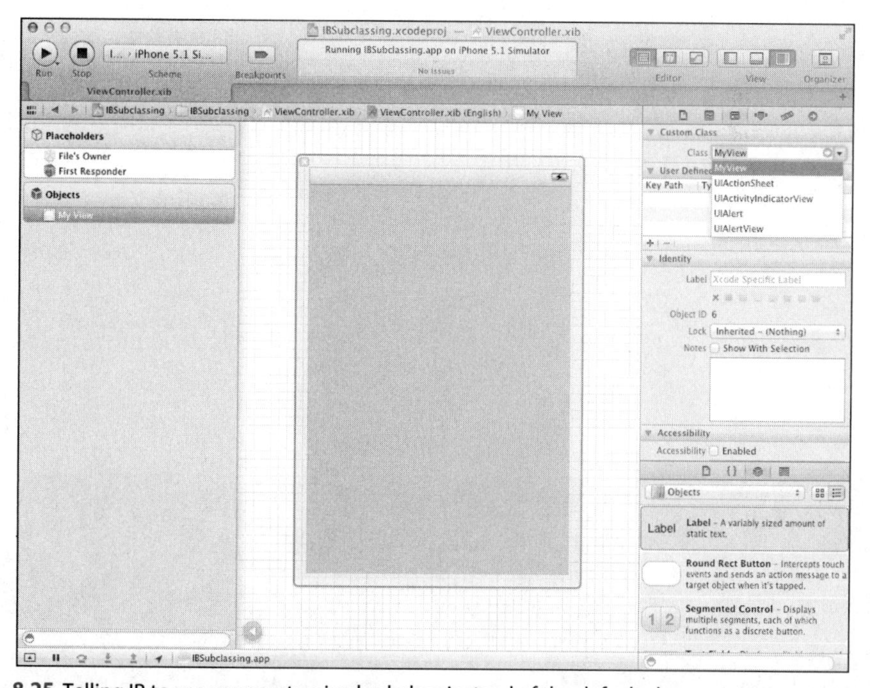

8.25 Telling IB to use your customized subclass instead of the default class.

What Are Frameworks and How Do I Use Them?

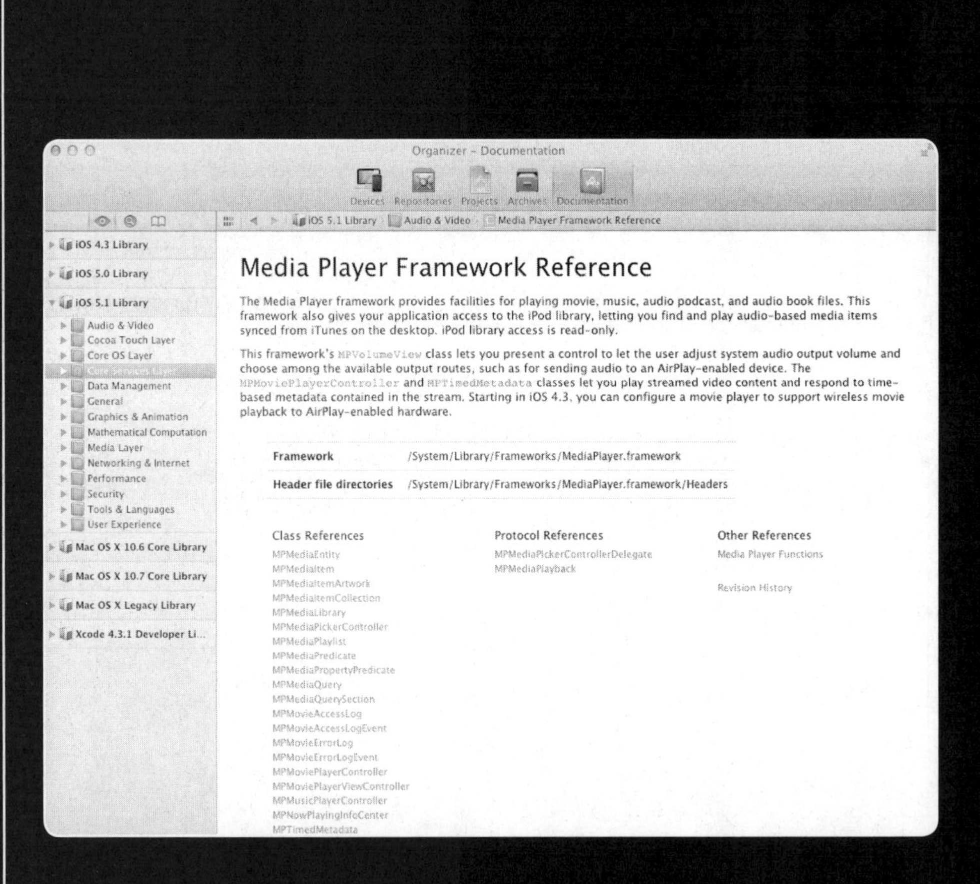

You can use frameworks to add related objects from the iOS kit of parts to your app, such as video and audio features, map support, enhanced graphics, and so on. You can also use frameworks to include objects and other features created by other developers. iOS frameworks are easy to find and easy to add, but they aren't always easy to use. Third-party frameworks are harder to find, but they often include a sample project that you can customize and copy into your own apps.

Understanding Frameworks

In outline, a framework is a collection of objects, functions, and other code that adds optional features to your app.

There are two kinds of frameworks:

- **iOS frameworks.** These are created and updated by Apple. They're included in the iOS "kit of parts."
- **Third-party frameworks.** These are created and updated by other developers or groups of developers. They're available online, but you have to search for them.

Understanding iOS frameworks

Although iOS is a kit of parts, you don't necessarily want to include every possible part in your app. If you did, your app would be huge and full of unused code, and it would take a very long time to build.

To keep your app lean and trim, related features are grouped into code libraries called frameworks. When you want to add a feature—video, audio, map tracking, web display, and so on—to your app, you select the relevant framework from the documentation and add it manually to your project. When you build your app, the finished file includes only the features you use in the frameworks you add.

Note

Small size isn't quite as valued today as it was in earlier versions of iOS. The current version of Garageband arrives as an 800MB download, and a few games are larger than 1GB. But most of this is essential data. Including unused code is still wasteful and a good thing to avoid.

iOS frameworks have some special features compared to third-party frameworks.

- **They're listed and described in the documentation.** The documentation isn't entirely comprehensive, but it usually includes enough information to give you a basic orientation.
- **They're built into Xcode.** You don't need to download them or install them separately. You also don't need to search for them online.
- **They don't include source code.** You're given a header file with the usual list of class features and a blob of pre-compiled binary. But you can't see what's inside the framework, and you can't modify the original code.
- **They (mostly) just work as advertised.** Bugs do appear sometimes, but they're not very common.

- **Some applications offer more than one framework.** For example, there are three independent graphics frameworks and another couple of frameworks you can use for image-related effects. Graphics, audio, and video all offer a simple framework (with limited features) that's easy to use and a more complex framework (with more features) that's more challenging to work with. (For graphics, you can use a further super-complex framework that's very fast but very difficult to work with.)

Caution

Although all iOS frameworks are documented, this doesn't guarantee they're easy to use. I've emphasized sample code throughout this book because it's often the only way to find examples that work. Some frameworks are almost impossible to master without help—either because they have quirks and special requirements that aren't mentioned in the official documentation, or they're so complex and difficult to understand that they're very hard to work with without a practical guide.

You can explore the list of frameworks included in iOS by loading the documentation and opening the Frameworks item in the list at the left, as shown in Figure 9.1.

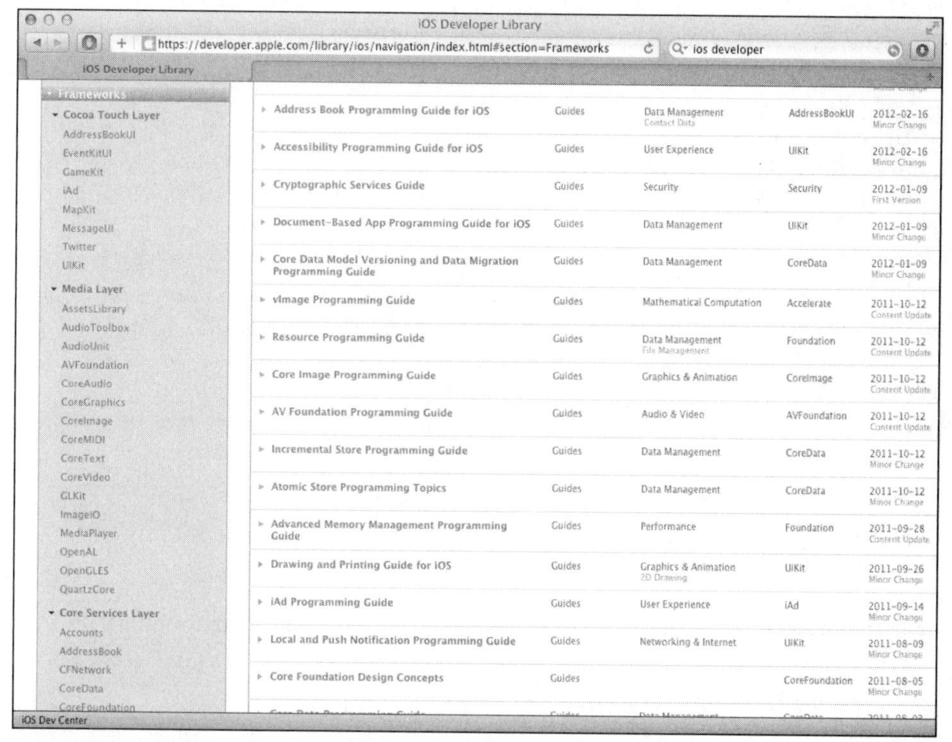

9.1 Looking at the frameworks in iOS.

Exploring the list in detail, you'll discover the following:

- **Frameworks are named in the list, but there's no description.** It's easy to work out what most frameworks do from the name, but a few, such as OpenAL and QuartzCore, are more obscure. To find out what they do, you have to click through to list the documents that are relevant to them.
- **Frameworks are grouped into "layers."** But the groupings are artificial and not entirely helpful. For example, graphics features are spread across multiple frameworks and layers.
- **Most frameworks have their own reference documents.** But you have to find them. And a few frameworks—again, OpenAL—don't have a reference. Other items in the Frameworks list, such as Core Audio, shown in Figure 9.2, are really groups of other frameworks.

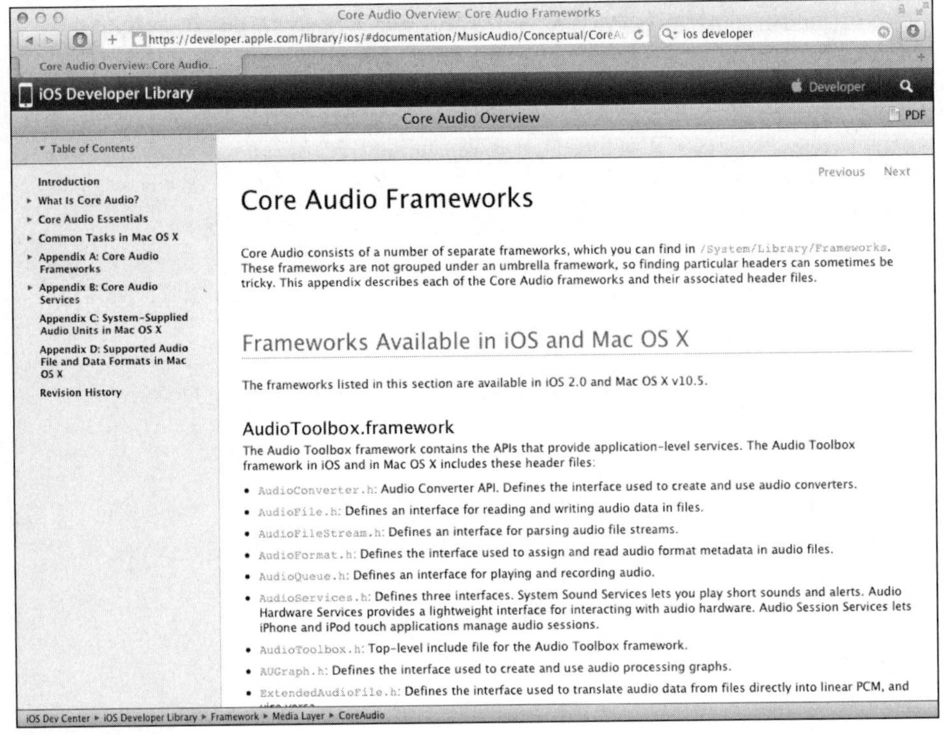

9.2 Is Core Audio a framework or a group of frameworks?

Generally, many of the frameworks in iOS aren't the simple drop-in solutions they could be. You'll need to do some research and experimentation to move from a problem to a specific solution. You may even need to ask for help online.

This is a normal part of development, so don't be surprised to find it's necessary. All developers work through this process.

Introducing third-party frameworks

Third-party frameworks aren't built into Xcode. They're available online only, and there's no single central list of frameworks you can refer to. They're usually supplied as source code or as an Xcode project, so you can modify them if you choose to.

These are other common features:

- **The quality varies.** Some frameworks are professionally coded while others are slapped together casually in hobby time.
- **The programming style varies.** iOS frameworks are designed to a relatively consistent standard. Third-party frameworks can take many forms and can be organized in many different ways.
- **The programming language varies.** It's not unusual to see frameworks written in C++. Some projects provide solutions in multiple languages for multiple environments—for example, for Android, Windows, iOS, and so on. These multi-frameworks may have slightly different features in each platform.
- **Documentation is patchy.** Sometimes, it's good, with detailed information and sample code. Sometimes, it's less good. Occasionally, it's non-existent.
- **The code may be outdated or incomplete.** Some frameworks are *abandonware*—started in a rush of enthusiasm, but abandoned when a developer decides other projects are more interesting.
- **There may be more than one framework solving the same problem.** It's up to you to choose which framework to use. You can search online for user comments to help you make this choice.
- **Some frameworks are built on underlying iOS frameworks.** This might seem like redundant effort, but a framework that simplifies access to an existing iOS framework can save you lots of time.

Caution

You'll also see third-party projects described as libraries, toolkits, components, and suites. Technically, these words all have different meanings. But this doesn't usually matter in practice, because they all provide the same thing—code you can drop into your projects to solve a problem.

In iOS, the frameworks you can use are listed in the documentation. There's no equivalent complete list of third-party frameworks, so you can't see what developers have done already. This matters for two reasons:

- **You don't know which problems have already been solved.**
- **You don't know what's possible.** This affects the design of your app. Some frameworks are so powerful that they can push you toward imagining completely new kinds of apps.

Figure 9.3 shows one example—a framework called OpenCV that can be used for computer vision and live video processing applications. If you don't know that OpenCV exists, it's impossible to imagine applications for it. After you do, you can begin to design apps around its features.

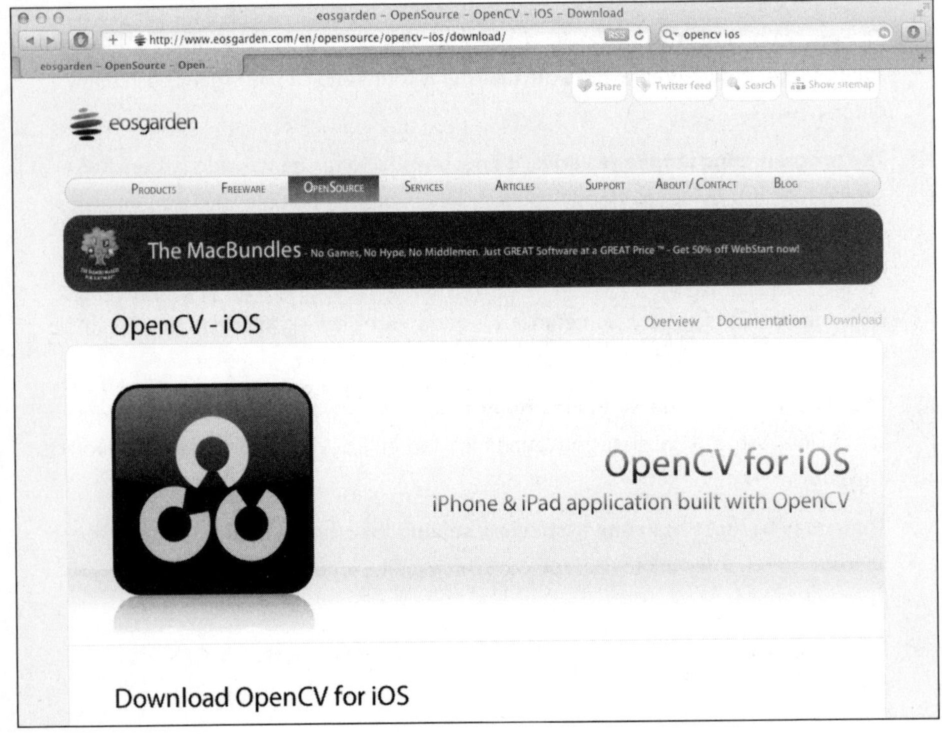

9.3 OpenCV—a useful framework for computer video applications.

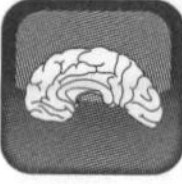
Genius

Frameworks save you time. Some problems are so common that it makes no sense for developers to solve them again and again. With a framework, you can drop an existing solution into your code, add the code you need to use it, and get on with the rest of your app. Even when frameworks are poorly documented and difficult to understand, they'll still take you less time than working up your own solution from a blank project. So you should *always* look for an existing solution before attempting to create one yourself.

Adding an iOS Framework to a Project

Adding an iOS framework requires four steps:

1. **Look through the documentation to try to find a framework that helps you solve a problem for your app or add a feature.**
2. **Add the framework to your project manually.** This option is somewhat hidden in Xcode. It isn't difficult to use after you find it.
3. **Include any headers in the framework in your project files.** Don't forget this step! If you do, your project won't build.
4. **Use the objects, functions, data structures, constants, and other features of the framework in your code.** You'll probably need to do further research and experimentation to get them to work as advertised.

Let's look at each step in more detail. We'll try to create an app that draws a map on the screen.

Finding the framework you need

There are many ways to approach this. You can:

- **Look through the frameworks list to see if any names look relevant.**
- **Look through the topic guides in the documentation to see which frameworks are mentioned.**
- **Check online to see which frameworks are being used by other developers.**

In this example, there's no mapping topic, so we can't immediately see a guide, how-to, or introduction. But we can see that the frameworks list includes a framework called MapKit, which looks promising.

The Framework Reference is shown in Figure 9.4. We can see that it is indeed used for map drawing.

The figure also shows the list of objects and other elements in the framework. Looking down the list, we can see a class called MKMapView, which looks like it might be the main map drawing class.

Checking the Class Reference, shown in Figure 9.5, shows that—as the name suggests—it's a view that draws a map. We can use this class to solve the original problem and draw a map in an app.

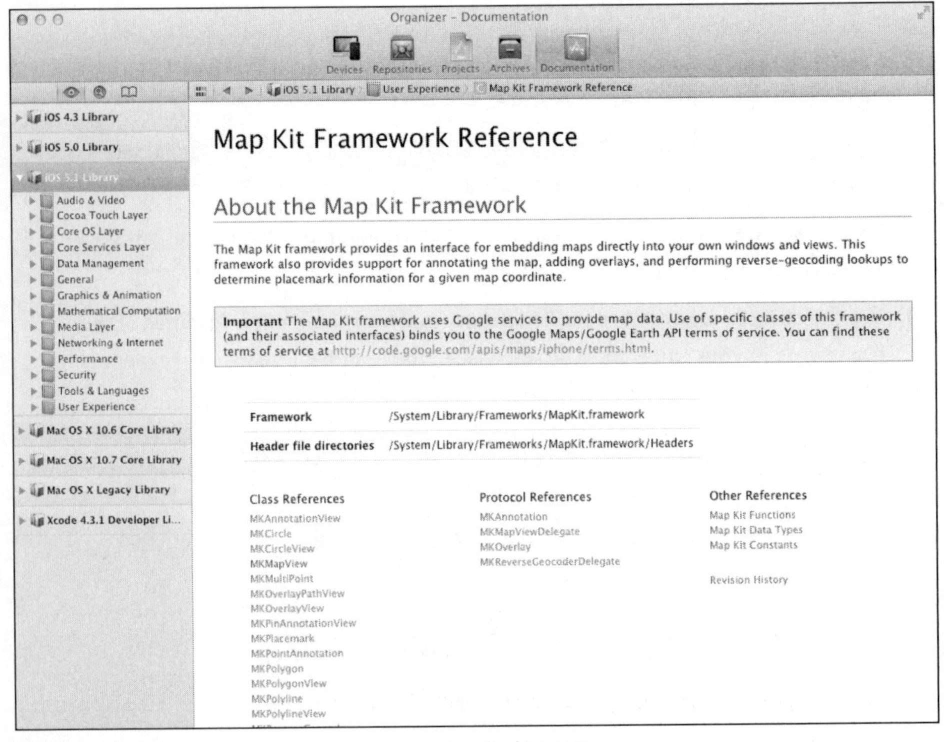

9.4 We've found the map drawing framework. It's called MapKit.

Adding a framework to a project

Before we can use MKMapView, we must add the framework to a project. Follow these steps:

1. **Create a new Single View Application from the template.** Save it as "MapView."
2. **Click the project name at the top of the Project navigator.** *Don't* select any of the files.
3. **Click the Build Phases tab at the top of the window.**
4. **Click the Link Binary With Libraries item to open it, as shown in Figure 9.6.**
5. **Click the "+" icon at the lower left of the pane**. You'll see a dialog box with a long list of frameworks.

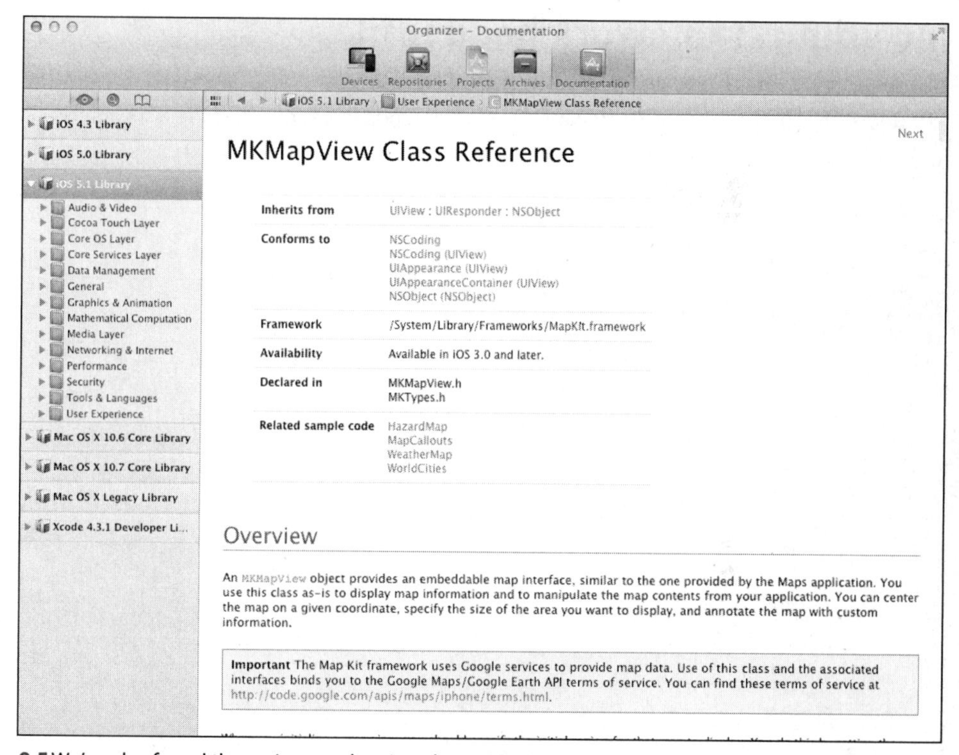

9.5 We've also found the main map drawing class—MKMapView.

6. **Scroll down the list to find the MapKit.framework entry.**
7. **Select it as shown in Figure 9.7, and click the Add button at the bottom left.** You'll see two things happen: The MapKit.framework is added to the list in the Link item, and a new MapKit.framework icon appears at the top left of the Project navigator, under the project name.

8. **Optionally, you can open the Frameworks group in the Project navigator and drag the framework into the group.** This doesn't change the build process, but it makes the contents of the navigator look tidier, as shown in Figure 9.8.

You can build and run the project now. Including a framework makes no difference to the app, because you haven't yet added any objects from it. But after the steps in this section, you *can* add objects from the framework. And if you add them correctly, they will work.

Including framework header files

You must perform this next step on every file that uses objects from the framework. It tells Xcode to include the headers from the framework. This makes it possible for Xcode to find the references to those objects when it tries to build the project.

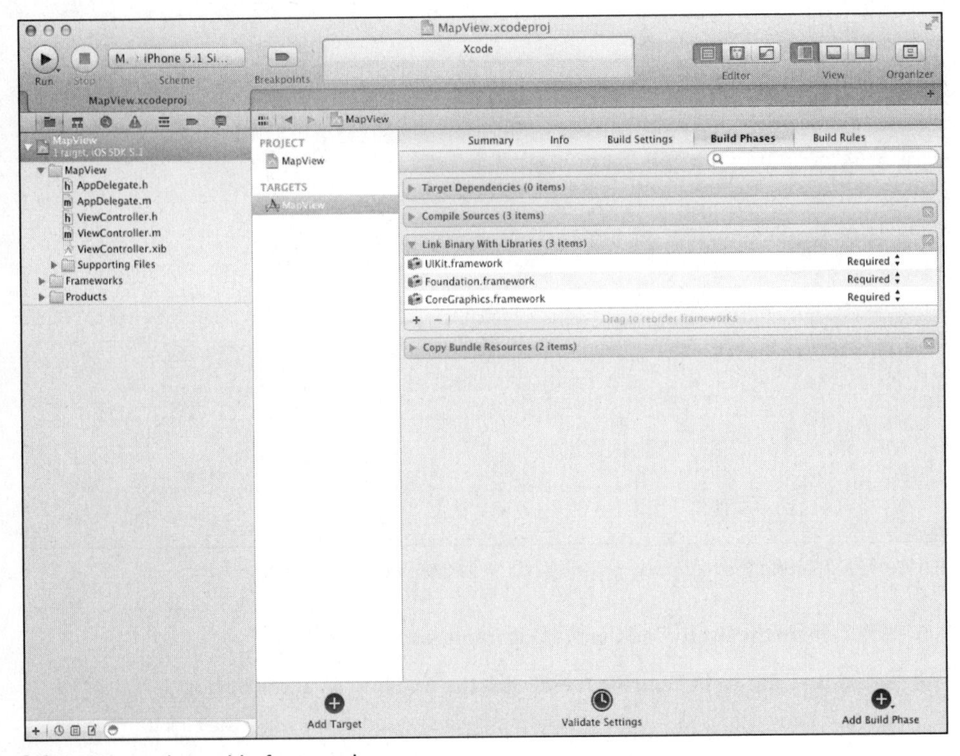

9.6 Getting ready to add a framework.

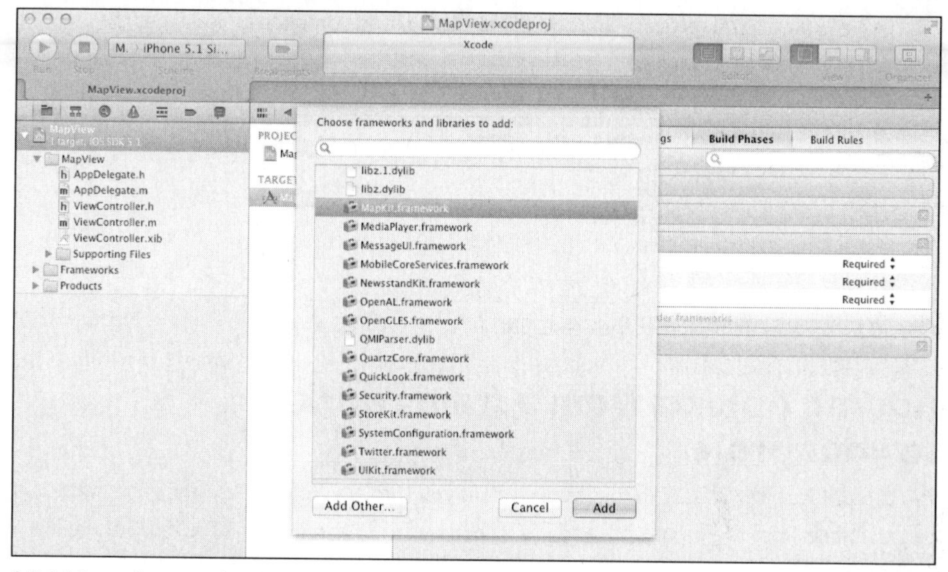

9.7 Adding a framework makes two changes to a project.

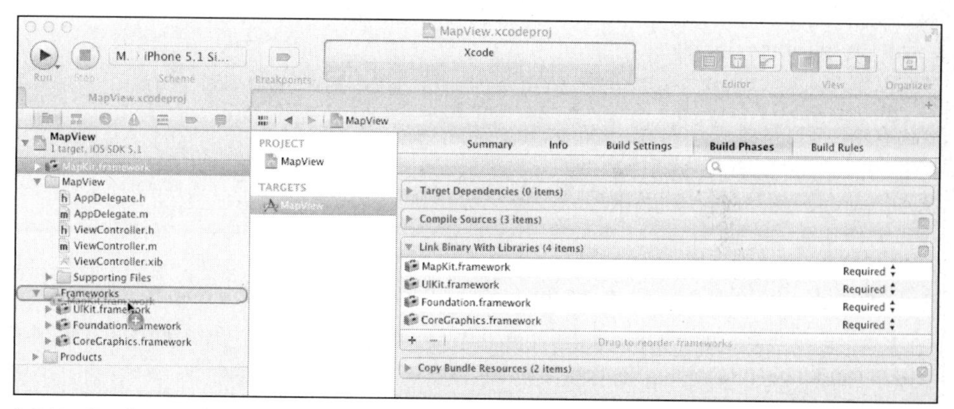

9.8 Moving the new framework into the old Frameworks group.

Follow these steps:

1. **Click the header file of the class to which you want to add the new objects.** In this example, we'll add them to the view controller.
2. **Copy or retype the "#import" compiler directive under the first #import directive for UIKit.**

3. **Type "<MapKit/MapKit.h>".** Xcode doesn't try to auto-complete as you type. The result is shown in Figure 9.9.

```
//
//  ViewController.h
//  MapView
//
//  Created by Richard Wentk on 12/03/2012.
//  Copyright (c) 2012 Skydancer Media Ltd. All rights reserved.
//

#import <UIKit/UIKit.h>
#import <MapKit/MapKit.h>

@interface ViewController : UIViewController

@end
```

9.9 Adding the new framework to the header list.

Adding objects from a framework to your project

You can now use the classes in the framework in your project. You can use the alloc method to create objects from the framework and use Add New File to create your subclasses of objects in the framework.

We'll create a simple example that adds an MKMapView to the view controller. Adding the view also displays it automatically.

Add the following code to the viewDidLoad method in the view controller:

```
MKMapView *myMapView = [[MKMapView alloc] initWithFrame: self.view.frame];
self.view = myMapView;
```

Figure 9.10 shows that when you build the project, it automatically loads a map centered on the U.S. You can scroll the map in any direction and use pinch gestures to zoom in and out. The map object includes gesture recognizer code that adds these features automatically.

Note

Adding the new map view to the view controller deletes the view that was included in the nib file. iOS does this automatically. This is a *memory management* feature. For details, see Chapter 11.

Caution

Map data is downloaded live as it's needed. It isn't stored inside MapKit. If you are running the project in the Simulator, your Mac must be connected to the Internet to display the map correctly. On a device, the device must have WiFi or cellular data access.

This is an impressive result for two lines of code, and it illustrates how you can use a framework to drop in complete features.

9.10 Displaying a map.

However, it's not a complete mapping solution. In a commercial app, you might want to add the following:

- **A blue dot showing the current GPS location.** Ideally, there should be an option to center the map on the GPS location and to update the map position when the GPS location changes.
- **UI options to change the map style so it displays satellite or hybrid views as well as the map view.**

Optionally, you may want to add more advanced features, such as annotation pins, highlighted circles and polygons, paths, and forward and reverse geocoding. These features are built into the Map Kit framework, and you can find out more about them in the Framework Reference.

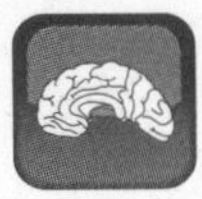

Genius

As an exercise, try to build a simple GPS tracker app with a blue indicator dot in the center of the view and automatic position updates that scroll the map as you move. You can find the method you need in the documentation for MKMapView.

Understanding Delegates and Protocols

Earlier chapters introduced two ideas:

- **Protocols.** A protocol is a bundle of optional methods that can be "adopted"—or used in—any object.
- **Delegates.** A delegate is an object that handles optional messages. In practice, delegates typically include code that makes protocol methods do something useful.

Many frameworks use protocols and delegates, because they're a convenient way to implement certain kinds of features.

Understanding delegates

Officially, a delegate is an object that handles a message on behalf of some other object. But this definition is misleading in practice. Objects often delegate messages to themselves. If you don't know how delegates are used in iOS, it's difficult to understand why.

In practice, delegate messages are usually used to add extra code that runs when something significant is about to happen, something has already happened, or iOS is asking for data and/or an object. This extra code is usually optional, and you can build a useful app without it. But it provides some extra "hooks" you can use to make your app behave in a more sophisticated and useful way.

Note

"Something just happened" can mean "the user did something" or "a process finished." It's common for delegate methods to be triggered when a process completes—for example, when an animation ends, some data arrives over a network connection, a web page finishes loading, and so on.

Let's look at an example. In the documentation for the MapKit framework (refer to Figure 9.4), you can see that MKMapView is associated with a protocol called MKMapViewDelegate.

Figure 9.11 shows the introduction to the MKMapViewDelegate Protocol Reference document. This document tells us that any object can receive a set of optional messages that are generated as the user works with the map. By default, these messages do nothing. But if we "adopt" the protocol, we can use them in our code.

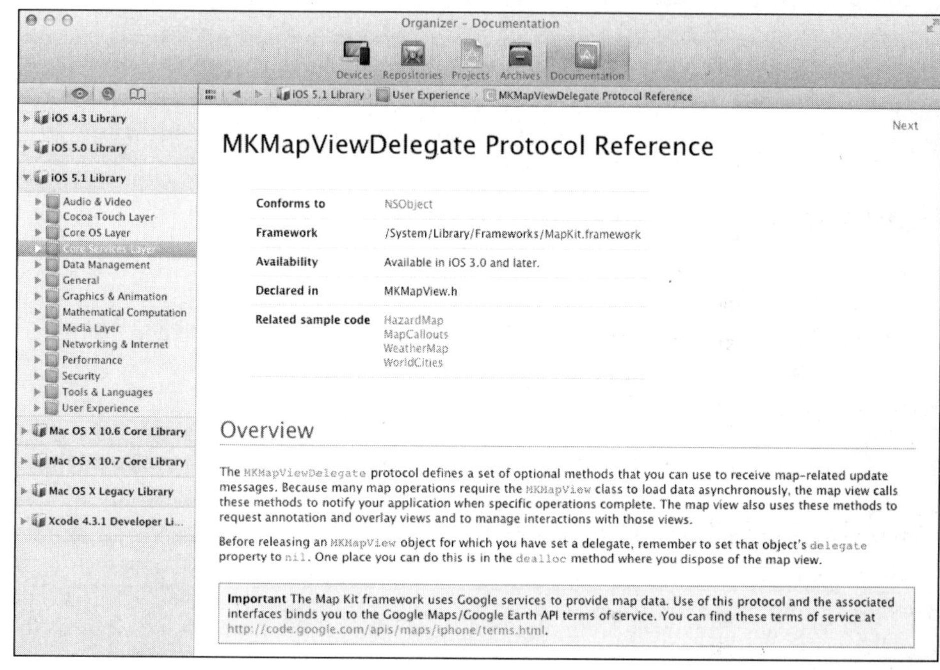

9.11 A first look at the MKMapViewDelegate Protocol Reference

To see what this means in practice, look at Figure 9.12, which lists the optional methods. You can see that methods are generated when the center point of the map changes, as the map loads data, as the user position changes, and so on. Further methods manage annotation and overlay views; in simple English, these are typically map pins and highlighted areas.

You can see that a method such as mapViewWillStartLoadingMap: may be needed occasionally. For example, you could use it to start a timer and display an error alert if it takes too long to display the map. But this won't be an essential feature in many apps.

Other methods, such as mapView:regionDidChange:Animated:, are more likely to be useful. You can use this method to "watch" the map and run extra code whenever the center point changes, either because of an automatic location update or because the user dragged the map with his finger.

The mapView: viewForAnnotation method illustrates a different delegate technique. This method is triggered when the map asks for a view object associated with a pinned point on the map. By default, the MKMapView draws a standard pin. But this method interrupts the drawing operation and asks your app if it wants to supply a custom view. If you add this method to your app and include code that draws a custom annotation, your custom view appears instead of a pin.

This is an example of a delegate method being used to ask for data. It runs automatically for every annotated point visible on the map. You don't need to cycle through every visible point because iOS does that for you. Your app simply needs to supply a custom view when it's asked to.

Using delegates and protocols

To use a delegate and a protocol in your app, follow these outline steps:

1. **Add the name of the protocol in angle brackets to the header of the object that will act as a delegate.** This step "adopts" the protocol.

Note

The protocol goes after the parent class name, because the subclass includes the features of the parent class *and* the protocol.

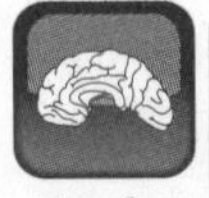

Genius

You can add as many protocols as you need between the angle brackets, separated by commas.

2. **Every object that supports a delegate has a property called "delegate."** Load this property with a pointer to the object that will be the delegate.
3. **In the delegate, add code for some or all of the methods defined in the protocol.** If you don't need to use a method, you can ignore it. (Xcode may sometimes generate a warning when you do this, but you can ignore the warning too.)

If you follow these steps, your delegate object should run one or more of the methods defined in the protocol. iOS defines *when* these methods run; for many objects, the "when" is decided behind the scenes. But your app can now include code for these extra methods, and they will be triggered as needed.

As a practical example, we'll trigger a log message when the map position changes, using the mapView: regionDidChangeAnimated: message. We'll continue with the same project we created earlier in this chapter.

Follow these steps:

1. **In Xcode, select the ViewController.h file in the Project navigator.**

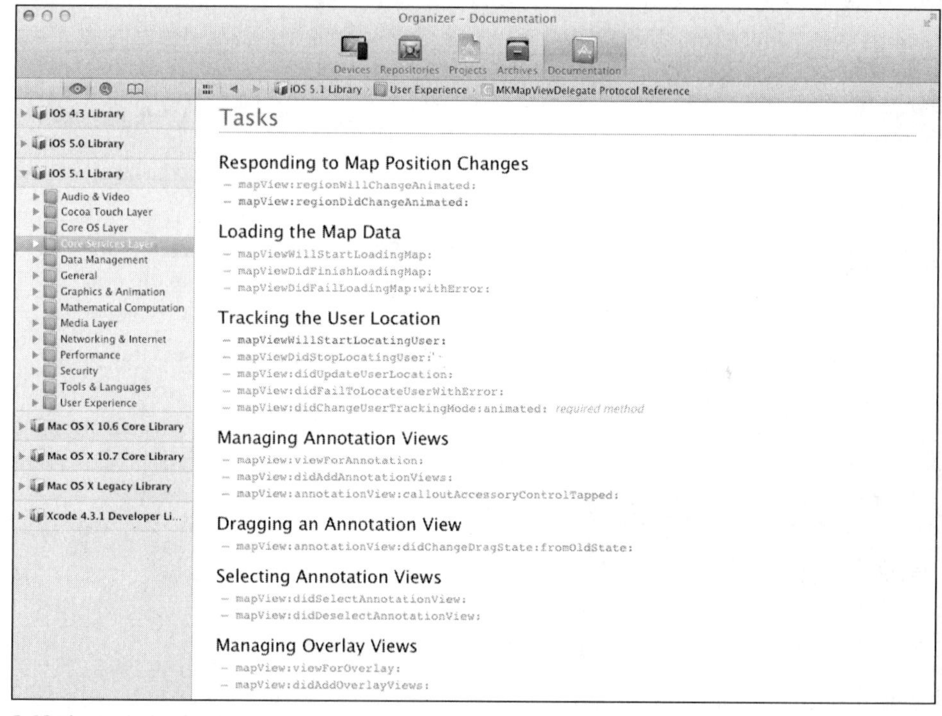

9.12 The Tasks list for the MKMapViewProtocol reference.

```
//
//  ViewController.h
//  MapView
//
//  Created by Richard Wentk on 12/03/2012.
//  Copyright (c) 2012 Skydancer Media Ltd. All rights reserved.
//

#import <UIKit/UIKit.h>
#import <MapKit/MapKit.h>

@interface ViewController : UIViewController <MKMapViewDelegate>

@end
```

9.13 Adopting a protocol.

2. **Add "<MKMapViewDelegate>" after "UIViewController," as shown in Figure 9.13.** The ViewController subclass now includes support for the delegate methods in the protocol. It doesn't include any code yet, but we'll add that in the next steps.

3. **In the viewDidLoad method, add a line of code as follows, after you create the map view:**

```
myMapView.delegate = self;
```

Note

This step tells iOS to route the protocol messages to the view controller instead of some other object. For the messages to arrive, you must nominate a delegate object *and* make sure it adopts the protocol.

4. **Add code to implement the regionDidChangeAnimated method.** The easy way to do this is to copy the message signature from the documentation, paste it into the view controller, and add the usual curly brackets after it, as shown in Figure 9.14. (You can also type the signature by hand, but copy and paste are simpler, quicker, and less error-prone.)

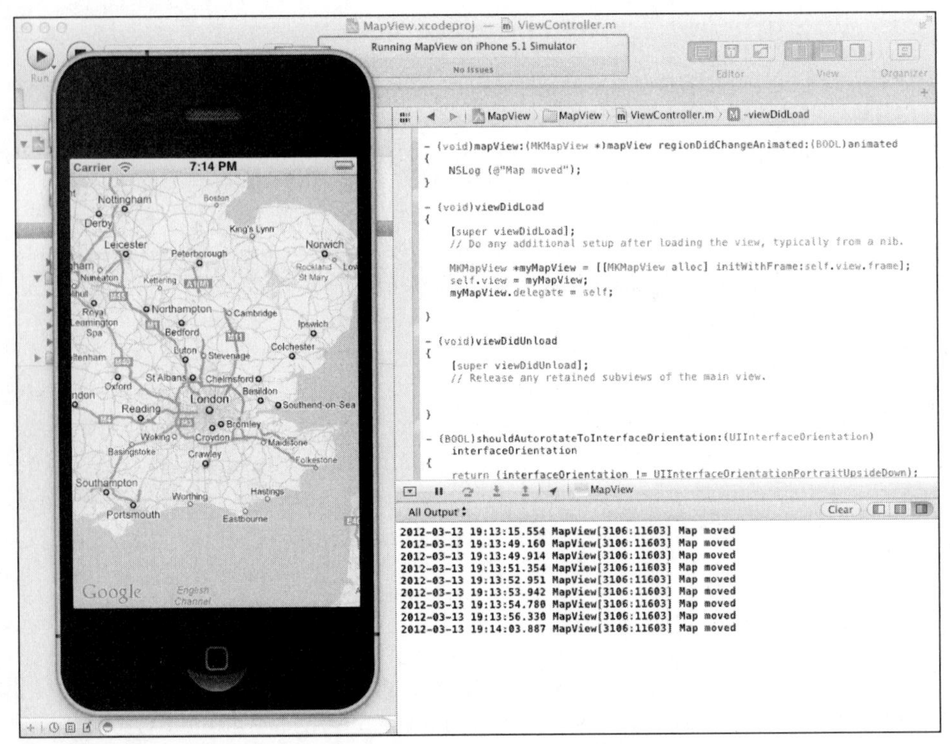

9.14 Adding and testing the code that routes delegate messages to the view controller and processes one particular message.

5. **Add some code that does something when the method is triggered.** In this example, we'll add a simple log message, using the code below.

```
NSLog (@"Map moved");
```

6. **Build the project, and open the Debug window.** You will see the "Map moved" message whenever you drag or resize the map.

You've now created a simple app with a map and added an optional map delegate feature. You can now continue to experiment with the delegate methods to create more complex effects.

Clearly, every delegate protocol includes different methods and features. But as long as you remember to adopt the protocol *and* set the delegate object *and* copy one or more method signatures from the protocol documentation, delegation will work for you.

Adding a Third-Party Framework to a Project

Because there are so many different third-party frameworks, there's no one way to do this. However, you'll often find the framework packaged into an Xcode project, so you can download the project, open it in Xcode and use it, expand it, or modify it as needed.

Figure 9.15 shows the web page of a sample project called PGMidi. iOS and OS X include a framework called CoreMidi, which is used to trigger synthesizers. CoreMidi manages MIDI connections, and you can use it to send messages from an iPhone or iPad to a software synthesizer.

Unfortunately, CoreMidi is poorly documented and difficult to use. PGMidi is a popular sample project created by developer Pete Goodliffe. It packages some of the features of CoreMidi into a more accessible framework. It's also an example of a project that uses a *repository* to store and share the project code. The sample code not only includes a simplified version of CoreMidi, it also includes a working MIDI monitor app that displays currently active MIDI connections and displays MIDI events.

Caution

Although the creator of PGMidi has provided the code as open source, always check the terms of use and licensing terms yourself before using anyone's code.

9.15 A first look at PGMidi.

Note

github has many features and options, and it can be integrated closely with Xcode. Integration is optional, and you don't need to use github's features to develop successful apps. A full description of github is outside the scope of this book. For all the details, see *Xcode* in Wiley's Developer Reference series.

To view the code, visit https://github.com/petegoodliffe/PGMidi, as shown in Figure 9.16. The code is kept on a site called *github*, which is a web-based repository that simplifies code sharing.

You can see the group structure of the project on github, and you can click through the groups to see the code files inside them. Although you can download the project files one by one, there's a simpler and quicker alternative.

The two key options are near the top of the page. Make sure that "HTTP" is selected, and then click the ZIP button to its left. github automatically creates a zip file with the current project code and downloads it. After it's downloaded, you can unzip it in Finder and then double-click the .xcodeproj file to open it in Xcode.

Figure 9.17 shows the project as it appears when you open it. There are two main class groups. The UI group holds the usual app delegate and a view controller. The view controller also includes the sample code that uses PGMidi to create a MIDI monitor app.

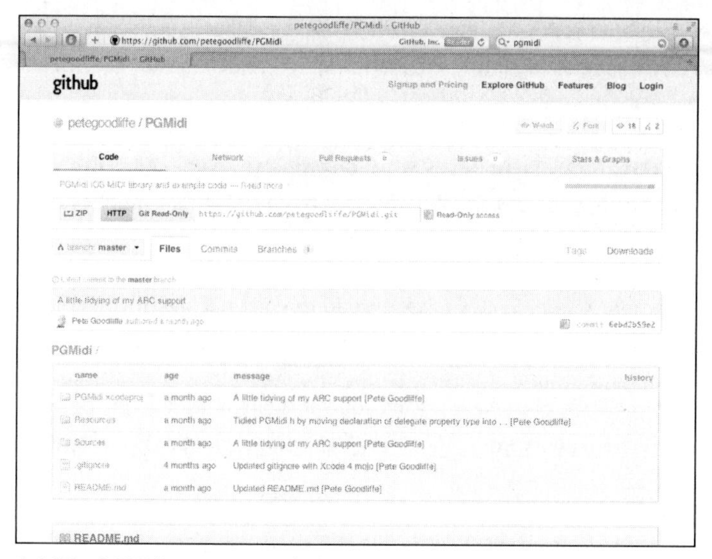

9.16 The PGMidi project on github.

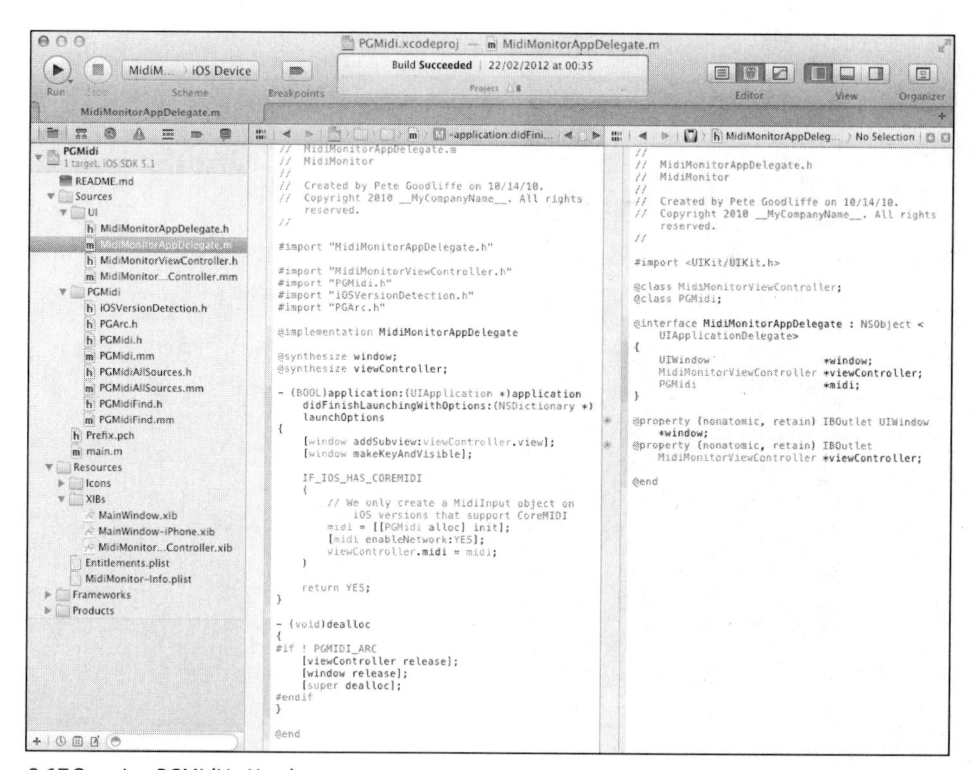

9.17 Opening PGMidi in Xcode.

The PGMidi folder includes the framework code. If you want to use these files in your project, you can copy them in manually by right-clicking in the Project navigator, selecting Add Files…, and navigating to the files.

Note that if you check the option to "Copy items into destination group's folder" in Add Files, you'll create a physical copy of the files in your project. You can edit the files without modifying the originals.

If you leave this option unchecked, Xcode creates a *reference* to the original files. If you edit the original files, the changes will appear in every other project that imports the files by reference.

This is a useful option for a framework, because it means you can share a single copy between multiple apps. If you change the framework, your changes will appear automatically in every app that references it.

Figure 9.18 shows the app running. You typically have two options with a sample project like this:

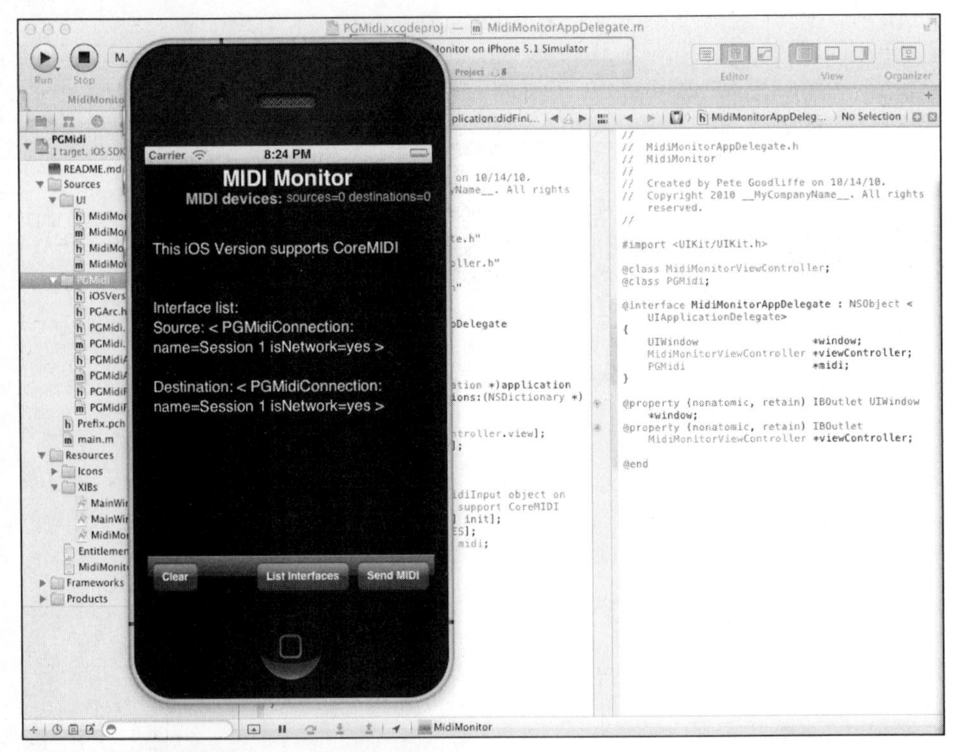

9.18 Running the MIDI Monitor app in the Simulator.

- **Use it as-is.** You can reverse-engineer the code in app delegate and the view controller to access the features of the framework. But you use it as a "black box" without worrying about how it works.
- **Customization.** More advanced developers may want to break open the framework, look at the source code, and perhaps make changes to it.

Either option is valid. The first choice is simpler for beginners, but the second option is more educational.

A Note about Licensing

It's important to understand that third-party code is supplied under many different licenses. Some code is supplied for free with no obligations. But most code isn't. These obligations apply even if the code is freely available and doesn't cost anything.

GPL is one common license. GPL code is free, but if you use it, *you're obliged to make the source code for the rest of your project freely available on your website.* This obligation works well for certain projects, but isn't ideal for many applications.

Common alternative licenses include BSD, Apache, MIT, and other UNIX licenses. These vary in specifics and may come in different variants. You'll need to check the details online. Wikipedia includes useful descriptions of the most popular licenses.

A Creative Commons license usually has a tag that describes your obligations. For example, with an "attribution" tag, you're expected to name the original creator in your app's credits. You also may be limited to non-commercial use.

Finally, some developers expect you to license their framework for cash if you use it in a commercial project. If this is a requirement, it's always clearly stated.

How Do I Add Custom Graphics to My App?

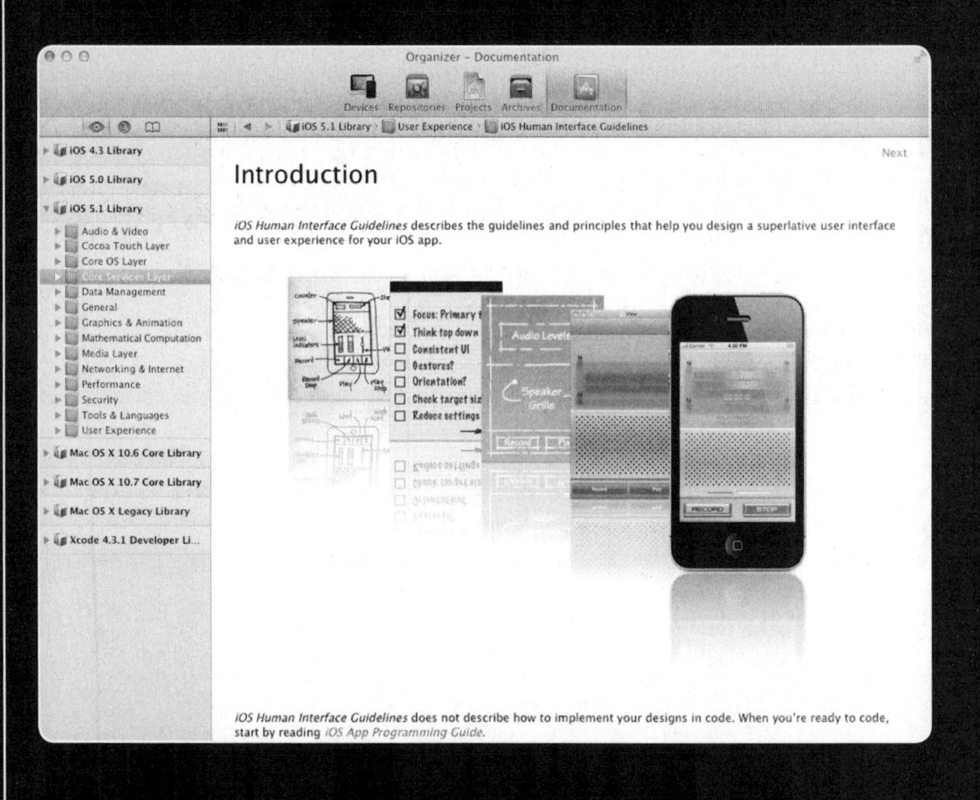

Successful apps have a strong visual impact. Basic color choices can change the feel of an app, but the best UI designs create a consistent, integrated, and coherent feel that reassures users while also highlighting the main user benefits of an app. Adding graphics is partly a mechanical process and partly a creative one. When both work well together, the user experience is satisfying and positive.

Understanding UI Design

iOS includes a very basic selection of objects that you can use in your UI designs. You can add standard buttons and sliders, and you can embed buttons in toolbars and tab bars. Many apps use these standard objects without changing them.

But these objects aren't visually exciting. You can make your app stand out by customizing the appearance of onscreen objects. Customization can be as simple as using an original icon in a toolbar button or as complex as creating an entire customized UI with your own original collection of onscreen objects.

Creating an excellent UI

Good design is critically important in iOS apps. Attractive apps with limited features can be at least as successful as sophisticated apps with mediocre graphics.

A good UI isn't just about graphic design and layout. It's important to give the user the information they need to use and understand your app with the minimum of learning and effort. The ideal iOS app doesn't need a manual, because all features are clearly labeled graphically or with text. Although it isn't always possible to create designs that live up to this ideal, it's a good goal to aim for.

Apple's design guidelines are worth reading. They're listed in a document called the iOS Human Interface Guidelines. Figure 10.1 shows the User Experience section from the guidelines.

Here are some other suggestions:

- **Use graphics and icons instead of text.** If you use English text, you'll either have to translate the text if you sell your app in foreign markets or limit your sales to English-speaking countries. Translation takes time and/or money, and adding support for multiple languages adds complexity to your app.
- **If you use graphics with text labels, don't "hard code" the text into the artwork.** You can float a textfield over an image, which makes it easier to include translated text later.
- **Keep the design as simple and sleek as possible.** Features should be accessible with a minimum of taps, slides, and other actions.
- **Simplify repetitive tasks.** If a user can access an important feature only by repeating a sequence of actions, streamline your design.

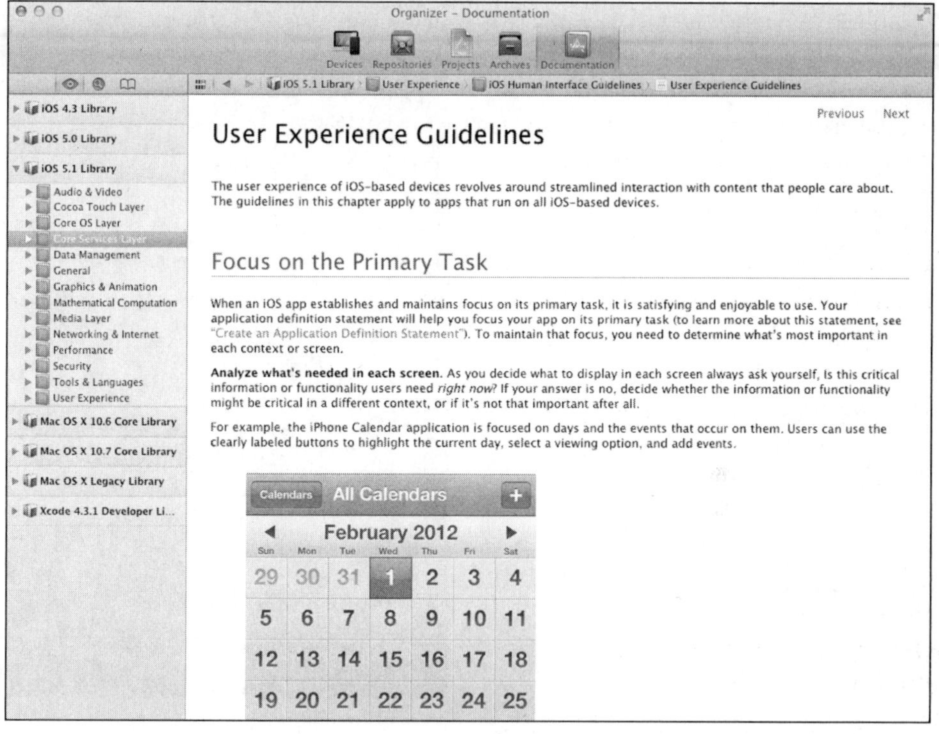

10.1 Discovering Apple's suggestions for the app User Experience.

- **Keep user options as simple and as useful as possible.** It's tempting to make apps almost infinitely customizable, but it's better to keep an app as simple as possible.
- **Remember that your UI can change dynamically.** iOS makes it easy to create a UI that reconfigures itself as the user works with it. You're not limited to swappable pages of static content. Icons, buttons, and labels can all be updated "live." You can even make elements move.

Designing a UI step by step

Although there's no set formula for a successful UI, you may find the following steps useful:

1. **Define the main goals.** How does the app benefit the user?
2. **Design a logical flow to reach those goals.** Put key information on the main screen of the app, but clearly label supporting screens.

3. **Make a rough sketch of the UI.** You can use paper and pencil, or you can rough out the layout in Interface Builder.
4. **Build a test app with a basic version of the UI.** If you can, give it to some users for testing of the logical flow.
5. **When the flow is correct, enhance the design with custom graphics.** Include an eye-catching splash screen. Remember that your App Store submission must include screen shots, so making the app look as good as possible improves its sales prospects.

10.2 The iPhone Weather app is a good illustration of focused app design.

Figure 10.2 shows the iPhone weather app—a design classic that shows useful information at a glance with a clean and intuitive combination of text and graphics. Note that the app doesn't display much information. But it does display the *right* information, with the details that a user is most likely to want.

Paid and Free Apps

You can support your apps with ad revenue using Apple's iAD framework. Traditionally, developers include ads in free or "lite" apps with limited features and remove them in paid apps. Including ads in paid apps is likely to annoy users. Some developers do it anyway, but it isn't a popular design choice.

Many free apps also include Apple's "in-app purchase" option, which gives buyers a chance to unlock or add features in return for extra payment. In-app is a good sales strategy, because users are more likely to accumulate multiple in-apps than they are to pay for an app with a large initial price. But don't push in-app upgrades too aggressively in your app.

Similarly, you can promote your app in the app store by asking users to give it a star rating. The easiest way to do this is by downloading a useful framework/library called iRate, currently at http://cocoacontrols.com/platforms/ios/controls/irate. Don't be too aggressive about demanding ratings.

As a rule, *don't distract the user.* Leave users undisturbed when they're using the main features of your app. But it's acceptable to distract them occasionally when they're using low-priority features, such as a preferences page. You can create occasional features by comparing a random number with a threshold value and displaying an alert or reminder only when the number is greater than the value.

Sourcing Custom Graphics

It certainly helps if you have solid design skills, but there are many ways to source custom graphics:

- **Use clip art or other web sources.** Common design elements such as glassy buttons are freely available online, as are free icon collections.
- **Create art manually.** If you have access to image-editing software such as Adobe Photoshop, you can use its features to create custom button graphics, icons, and other art.
- **Pay a graphic designer.** This is an expensive choice!

Let's look at each option in detail.

Finding clip art and icons

The web offers an almost endless supply of wallpapers, icons, and button designs. Many are free, although you should always check the copyright status of wallpapers before using them in an app.

To find icon files that you can embed in toolbar buttons, search the web for "free icons." Figure 10.3 shows one of many possible hits—a set of free icons called gcons. Other possible sources include iconspedia, freeiconsweb, findicons—all with the usual .com web address—and many, many others. Free icon sets may not be specifically designed for iOS, but you'll be able to use them anyway.

Creating art manually

If you have image-editing experience and plenty of time, you can create almost any artwork from scratch. It's easy to find online tutorials for standard graphics such as glassy buttons. But various automated solutions that require minimal artistic skill are available as well.

For example, http://glassybuttons.com/glassy.php, shown in Figure 10.4, features a free online graphic generator that can create files to order if you specify the dimensions, color, text, and so on.

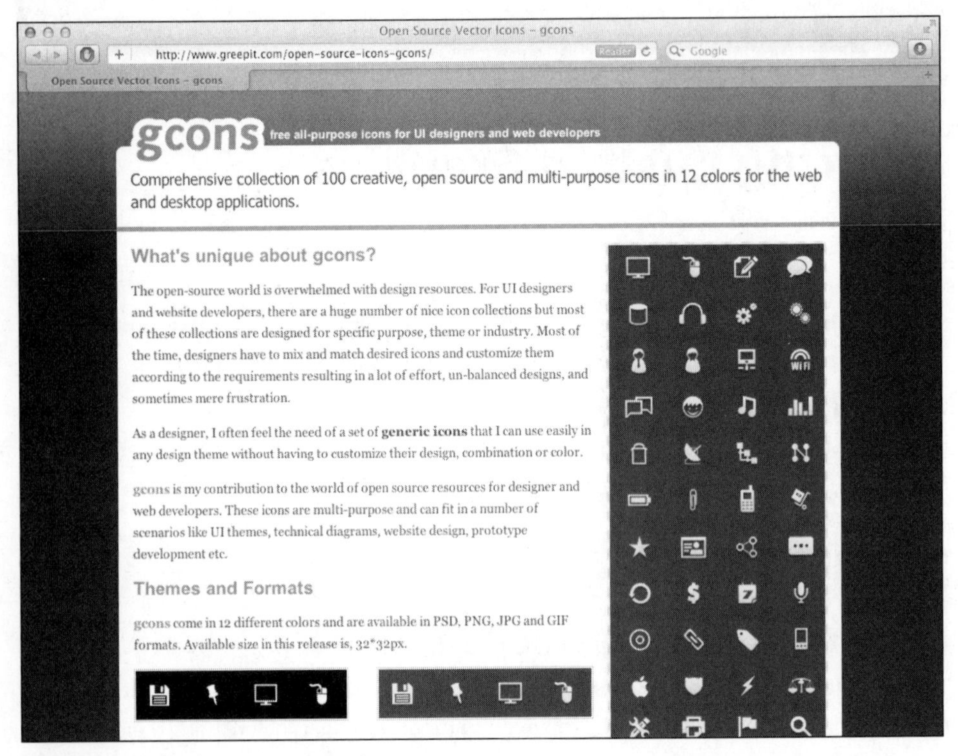

10.3 gcons are free icons you can use in your app.

Caution

It turns out that iOS includes a glassy button object. Unfortunately, Apple hasn't made this object public, and it's reserved for Apple's own use. This is called an *undocumented feature*. Apps that use undocumented features can't be accepted into the App Store. However, you can experiment with undocumented features in the Simulator.

Note

To create custom button graphics or floating icons, save your image file in the PNG format and use a mask to remove any colored background. This makes the background transparent and can make the button appear to float against the background without a visible border. You *must* use the PNG format for transparency effects. For practical examples and tutorials, search online for "transparent PNG."

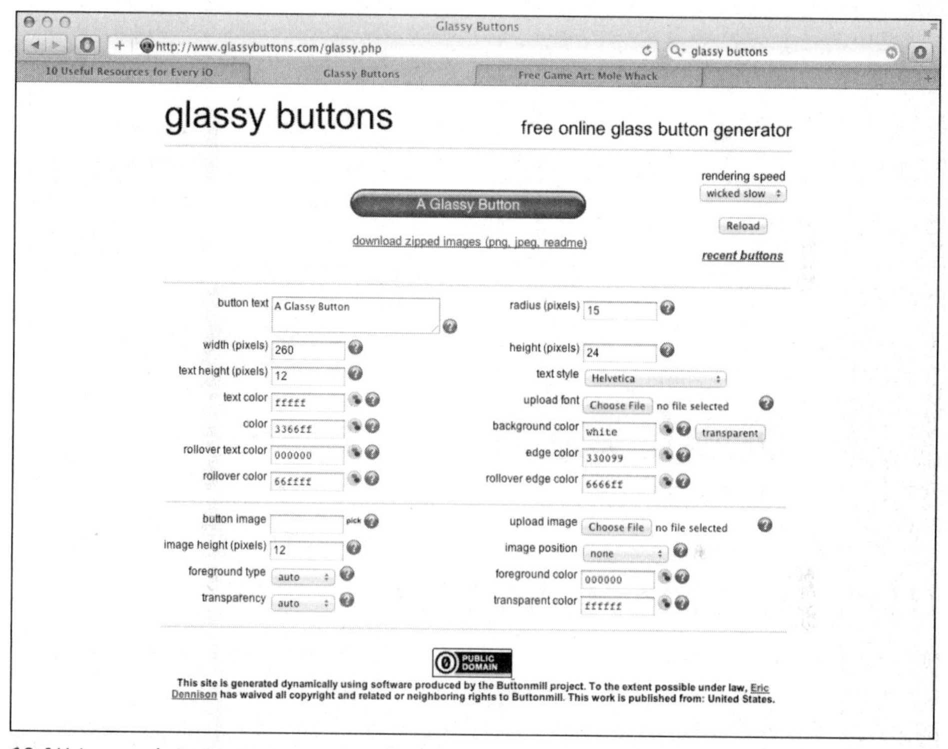

10.4 Using a website to create a custom glassy button.

Note that even if you don't have the skill or the time to create art from scratch, you can still use an image editor to customize art you find online. Figure 10.5 shows Zettaboom's Car Finder app, which uses a free button set. The set was customized in Adobe Photoshop by modifying the button colors using a simple hue shift.

Don't forget that iOS supports two different resolutions for the iPad and the iPhone. You can use the lower resolution as a view background, and it will automatically be stretched to fit the larger resolution. But your app also requires icons and splash screens, and these must be supplied in at least two resolutions. There's more about this requirement later in this chapter.

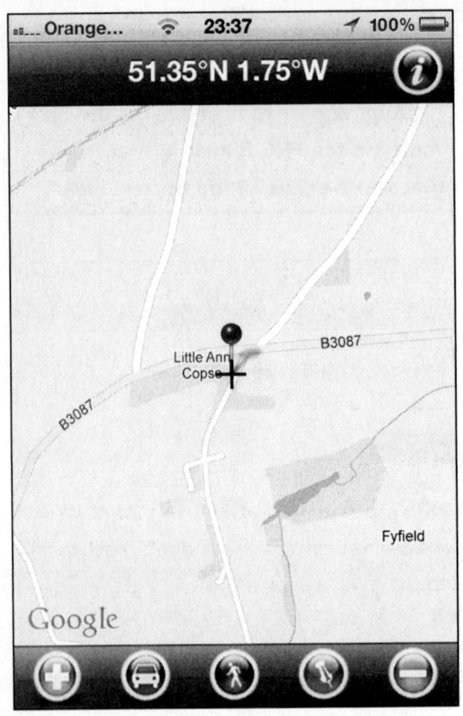

10.5 Customizing graphics with simple color shifts.

Paying a graphic designer

Given that it's so easy to find free art online, you should consider paying a designer only for complex projects. You can use a site like www.elance.com to find designers and view their portfolios. You can also post a job with a budget and see who applies.

Don't forget that design is now an international business. As long as you like the look of a portfolio and the price suits your budget, you can work with designers who are based anywhere in the world.

Using Custom Graphics

However you source your custom graphics, you have to add them to your app. Typically, you do this in Interface Builder. Views and controls include customization options that can load and display files you build with the app. The details vary, but the rest of this section includes some common techniques.

Adding a media file to your project

To use a file in a project, you must add it to the project manually. It's efficient to keep graphics and other media in a single folder on disk and reference them as needed. It's less efficient to copy media files into a project folder—although if you then make a backup copy of your project, media files will be included automatically and you won't have to worry about restoring them separately.

The steps for adding media files to a project don't depend on the media type. They're identical for all media, including graphic images, video clips, sounds, and custom data.

For this example, start by creating a new project using the Single View Application template. Save it as UIExamples. (This is just a convenient name. There is no class called UIExamples.) Either create or source an image file with the basic iPhone resolution of 320 x 480. The contents of the file don't matter.

After you have your file and a project to add it to, follow these steps:

1. **Right-click the Supporting Files group in the Project navigator.**
2. **Select Add Files to... item from the menu.**
3. **Navigate to the file you're about to import in the file sheet.**
4. **If you want to copy the file into the project folder, check the Copy items into destination group's folder (if needed) box, as shown in Figure 10.6.** If you don't check this option, Xcode creates a reference to the file at its original location on disk.
5. **Click the Add button at the lower right.**

Xcode adds the file to the project. You can preview image files in the editor by clicking them.

Creating a customized app background

You can customize the background of a view by adding an object called an image view. As the name suggests, an image view loads and displays an image file, with optional automatic resizing.

Image views are easy to use, but you need to set the size carefully. The standard iOS screen layout includes a *status bar* at the top of the screen. If you use a toolbar, tab bar or navigation bar, these features take up extra space at the top or bottom of the screen, and you must allow for this when you lay out the view. If you don't, the view contents may appear stretched or squashed.

You can also hide these elements so they don't appear. The easy way to hide the status bar in an app is to add the following line of code near the start of the application: didFinishLaunchingWithOptions: method in the app delegate:

```
[[UIApplication sharedApplication] setStatusBarHidden: YES];
```

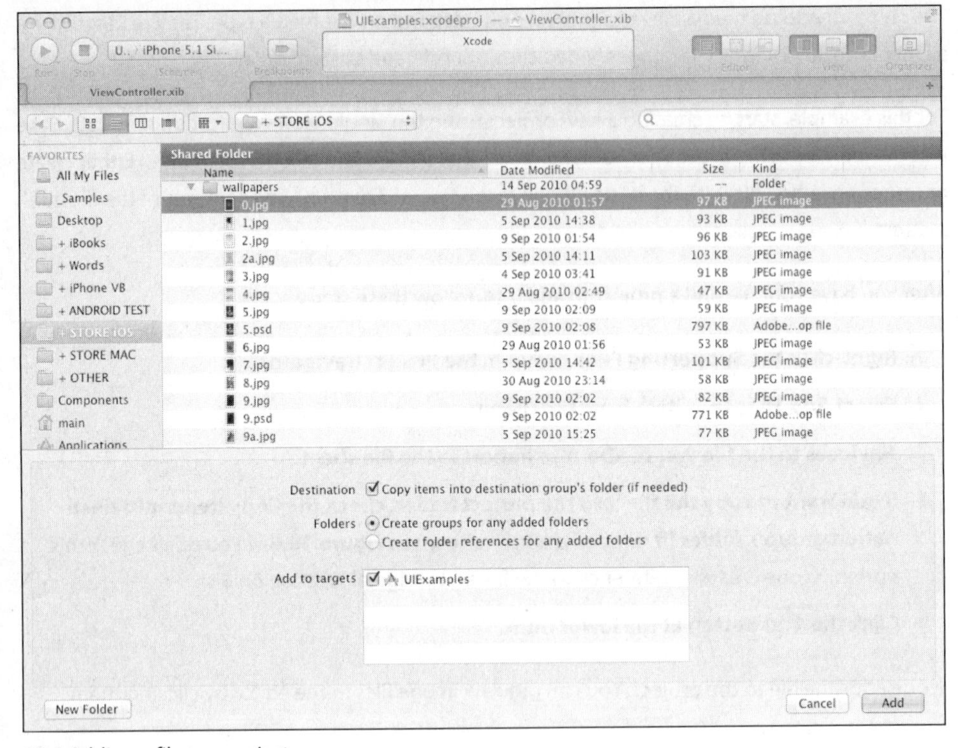

10.6 Adding a file to a project.

Caution

In fact, this is the *only* way to hide the status bar. You can find options that pretend to hide the status bar in Xcode and in IB. But . . . they don't work.

This example assumes you want to hide the status bar in your app when you add an image view. In addition to adding the code above, you must also make the following changes in IB:

1. **Click the ViewController.xib file to load it into IB.**
2. **Open the Utilities pane if it isn't already open.**
3. **Click the view included in the file to select it.**
4. **Select the Attributes icon.** It's the third from the right.
5. **Use the Status Bar menu to change the status bar option from Gray to None, as shown in Figure 10.7.**

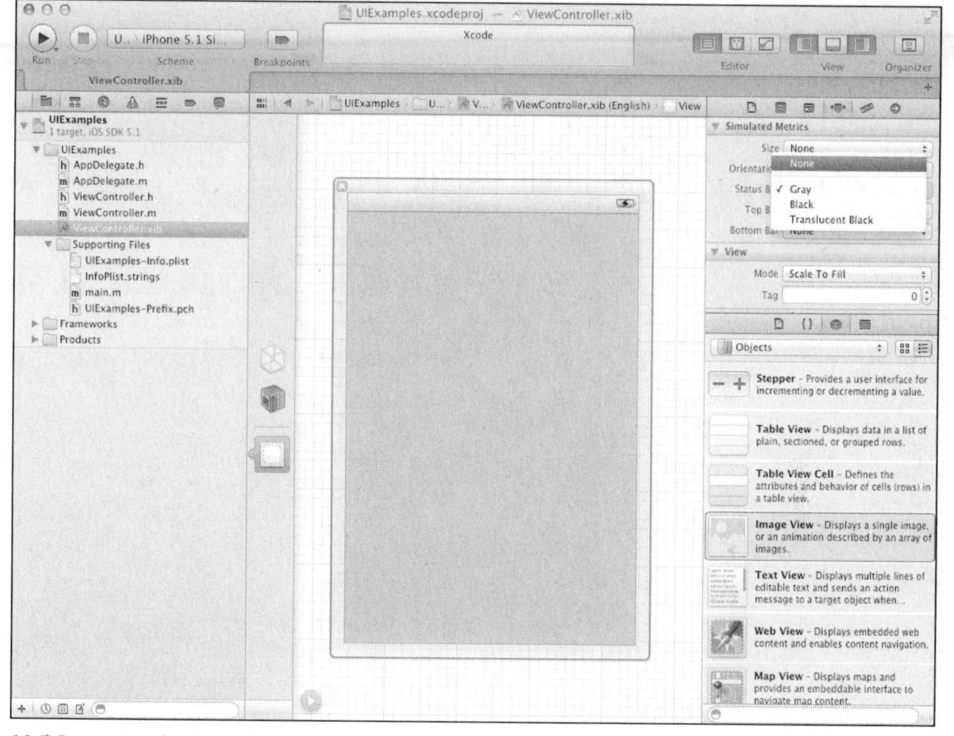

10.7 Removing the status bar.

6. **Click the Size inspector icon to the right of the Attributes inspector icon.**
7. **Change the Height field to 480.** If you skip this step, the image view will be an incorrect size. If you *don't* want to remove the status bar, you can ignore this step.
8. **Click the Object library icon in the bottom half of the Utilities pane.** It looks like a cube.
9. **Scroll down to find the Image View object.**
10. **Drag it from the Library, and drop it on the main view.** Take care to center it. It should fill the area of the view automatically.
11. **Click the Attributes inspector icon in the top half of the utilities pane.**
12. **Select the image you want to assign to the view using the Image menu, as shown in Figure 10.8.** Whenever you import an image into your project, it's added to this list. Xcode automatically previews the image, as shown in the figure.

When you build the project, you'll see that the default gray background has been replaced with the image you imported. You can add further views and controls to the nib file, and they'll appear on top of this image.

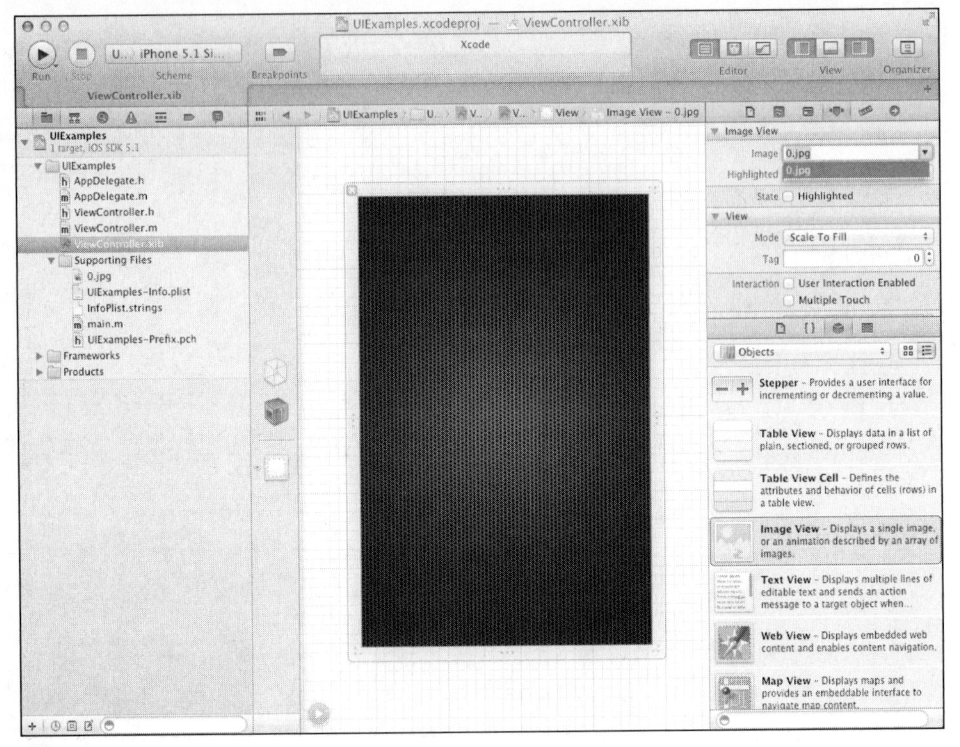

10.8 Selecting and previewing an image view.

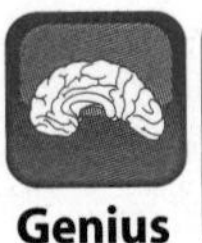

Genius

You may want to try to import multiple images, to see which looks best in your app.

Customizing controls

Controls such as buttons, sliders, and switches don't use a separate image view, because one or more image views are built in. Controls that can be customized give you access to these image views in IB or through custom code.

Figure 10.9 shows an example. To create a custom button, add a Round Rect button from the library to your project and change the Type in its Attributes to Custom. Add an image PNG file—with transparency—to your project, and select the new image in the menu for the Image attribute. (When this list gets long, you'll need to scroll down.) The graphic replaces the default gray rounded button. The image darkens automatically when a user taps it.

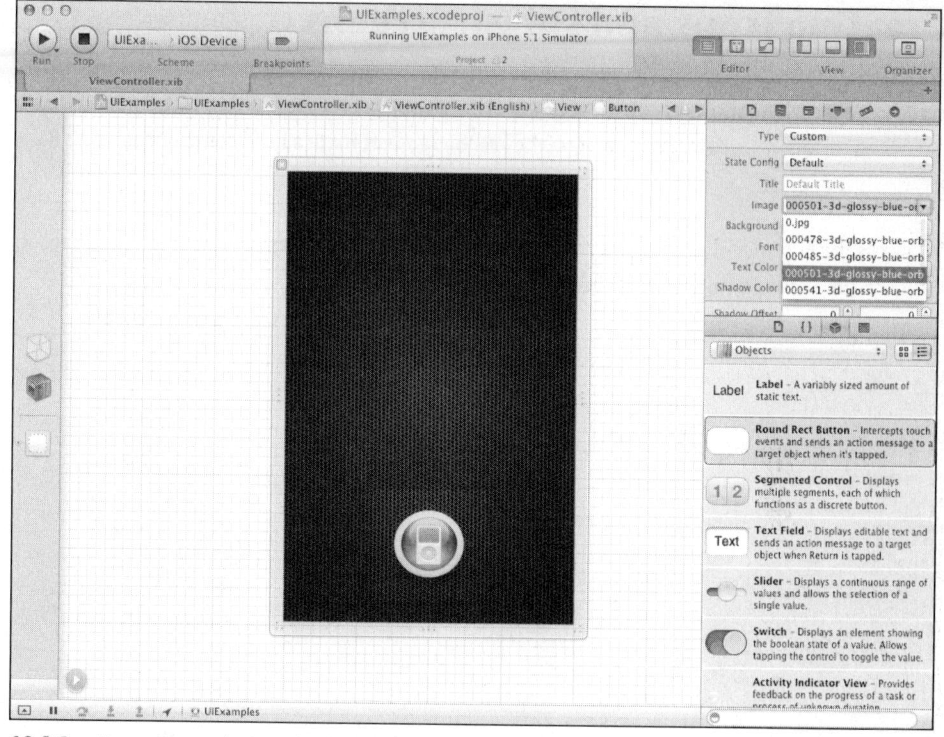

10.9 Creating a custom button from a graphic file.

To show a different graphic when the button is being tapped, select the Highlighted state from the State Config menu and set a different Image property. You can also set a further image for the Selected state. To display it, add code to your button message handler to set the "selected" property of UIControl—which is the parent class of UIButton—to YES. Typically, you'll want to toggle this state so the button switches between selected and unselected states at each tap.

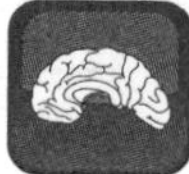

Genius

Glow effects are popular for selected objects. You can use the blur tool in an image editor to create a halo around an image and use this version of a button for the selected state.

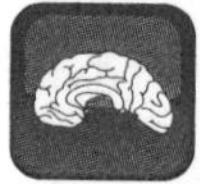

Genius

Your app doesn't have to use the controls that are built in to iOS. You can find a huge library of third-party controls for your app at www.cocoacontrols.com. Some are more useful than others, but at the time of writing, there are more than 40 pages of controls listed on the site.

Creating icons and splash screens

So far your apps have appeared in Springboard with a blank placeholder icon and no splash screen. Figure 10.10 shows the Summary tab where you can set icon and splash screen files for your project. When you define them here, they're loaded automatically on startup. You don't need to add further code.

To access the Summary tab, click the project name at the top of the Project navigator. Click Targets in the column toward the left, and click Summary.

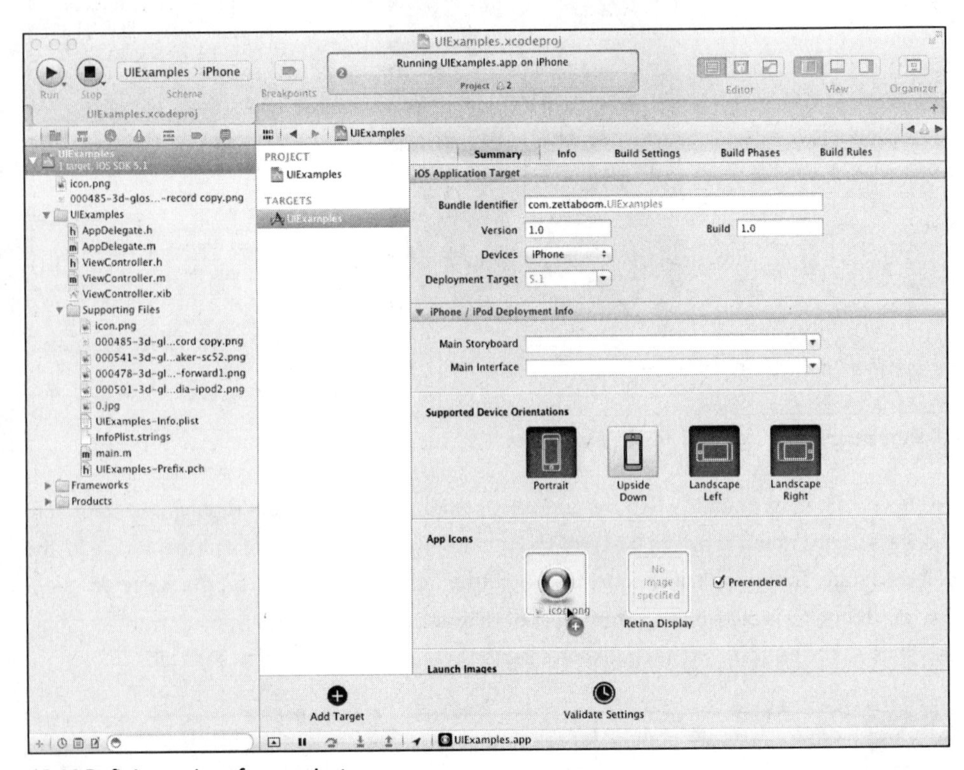

10.10 Defining an icon for a project.

To set your apps icons and launch images, add them to the project in the usual way, drag them from the Project navigator, and drop them on the empty boxes. If you check the "Prerendered" box, iOS displays the icon without applying the standard glass effect. Otherwise, it adds the effect automatically.

The files must have specific dimensions and filenames. For example, iPhone icons are 57 x 57 pixels, and the file must be called "icon.png." You can find a list of the dimensions and filenames in the "Custom Icon and Image Creation Guidelines" in the documentation. The table listing the dimensions is shown in Figure 10.11. The names are listed in the associated Guidelines.

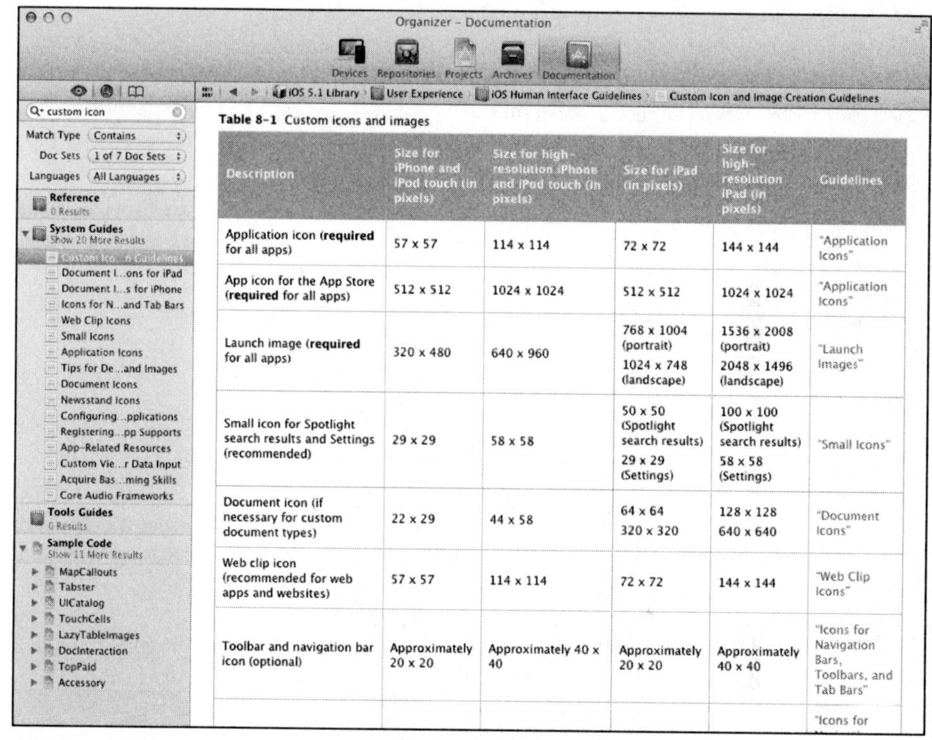

Table 8-1 Custom icons and images

Description	Size for iPhone and iPod touch (in pixels)	Size for high-resolution iPhone and iPod touch (in pixels)	Size for iPad (in pixels)	Size for high-resolution iPad (in pixels)	Guidelines
Application icon (**required** for all apps)	57 x 57	114 x 114	72 x 72	144 x 144	"Application Icons"
App icon for the App Store (**required** for all apps)	512 x 512	1024 x 1024	512 x 512	1024 x 1024	"Application Icons"
Launch image (**required** for all apps)	320 x 480	640 x 960	768 x 1004 (portrait) 1024 x 748 (landscape)	1536 x 2008 (portrait) 2048 x 1496 (landscape)	"Launch Images"
Small icon for Spotlight search results and Settings (recommended)	29 x 29	58 x 58	50 x 50 (Spotlight search results) 29 x 29 (Settings)	100 x 100 (Spotlight search results) 58 x 58 (Settings)	"Small Icons"
Document icon (if necessary for custom document types)	22 x 29	44 x 58	64 x 64 320 x 320	128 x 128 640 x 640	"Document Icons"
Web clip icon (recommended for web apps and websites)	57 x 57	114 x 114	72 x 72	144 x 144	"Web Clip Icons"
Toolbar and navigation bar icon (optional)	Approximately 20 x 20	Approximately 40 x 40	Approximately 20 x 20	Approximately 40 x 40	"Icons for Navigation Bars, Toolbars, and Tab Bars"
					"Icons for

10.11 Checking the size requirements for different icon and launch page files.

Caution

All apps for the App Store must include both standard and high-resolution icons and launch images.

Note

There's no way to create an animated launch screen. You can create an animation that loads after the app launches, but the image that appears while the app loads initially must be static. Note also that launch images don't appear for long after the app loads for the first time. The initial launch takes a while because iOS loads the app into memory. But subsequent launches happen more quickly—so quickly that users may not see the launch image at all.

Working with fonts

Fonts can add lots of character to an app, and buttons, labels, text fields, and text boxes can use a range of fonts. Unfortunately, you *can't* use just any font you have installed on your Mac—only a selection. The list of supported fonts isn't small, but it is limited. You can see a listing with examples on websites such as iOS Fonts (www.iosfonts.com).

To select a font, click a control that supports text to select it, open the Attributes inspector pane in IB, and click the Font box. Choose Custom for the Font menu, and select a family name and style from the list, as shown in Figure 10.12. The list is pre-filtered so you can select only fonts that work on a device. Other fonts on your Mac are ignored.

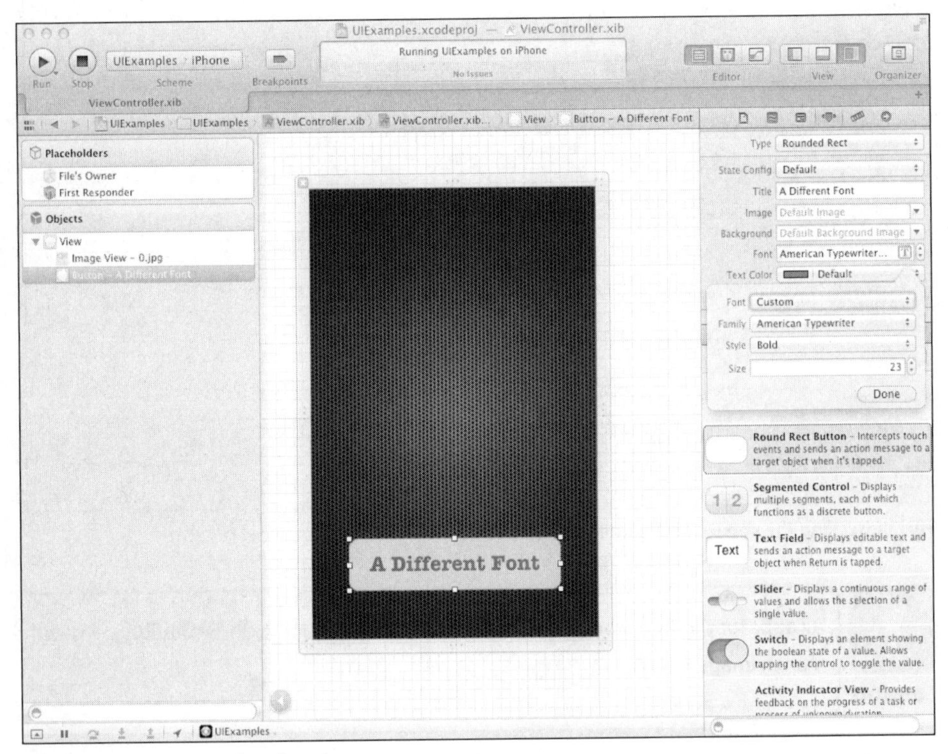

10.12 Setting a custom font for a button.

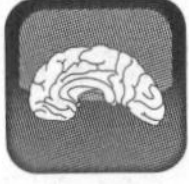

Genius

You can also assign fonts in code. Use the UIFont object, initializing it with the name of the font you want to use. To set the font, set the "font" property of any compatible object.

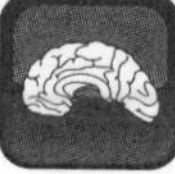
Genius

As an advanced technique, it's possible to use almost any font in an iOS project. But you must add the font file to the project and make a change to the list of properties in the project's Info table, which is next to the Summary page listed earlier in this chapter. This is a slightly tricky process, and not all font files are compatible. You can find many tutorials describing the process online.

Drawing Graphics with Code

You can draw graphics with code in two ways. You can use a set of drawing commands that are built into iOS views to create custom graphics. And you can create objects in your code and add them to the current view. This is similar to adding them to a view in IB, but you can control the position and appearance of objects from your code, and you're not limited to a static layout.

Using paths, strokes, and fills

The UIView class includes a method called drawRect: that is a ready-made space for graphics commands. Shapes are defined using a class called UIBezierPath, which can be used to draw lines, boxes, circles, and ovals. You can also draw curved lines with "handles" that control the shape of an arc. And you can join paths indefinitely, so almost any shape is possible.

Paths remain invisible until you either *stroke* them or *fill* them. Stroking a path draws an outline. Filling a path fills the area inside the path. (A path should be closed before you try to fill it.)

To make drawRect: work for you, you must subclass UIView. You can follow the steps in Chapter 5 to add a new subclass of UIView to your project. You must also tell IB to use the subclass, as described in Chapter 9.

To work through this example, create a new SingleView project called ViewDrawing. Use the New File option to create a subclass of UIView called MyView. Tell IB about the subclass. Now we'll add some code to draw some shapes.

Uncommenting drawRect:

Click your MyView.m file in the Project navigator to load it into the editor. You'll see that the drawRect: method is surrounded by comment marks, which begin with "//." Remove the comments from the top and bottom of the method leaving the lines with the method name and the curly brackets.

Note

Before going further, look again the CGGeometry Reference in the documentation. It defines the data types and functions you'll be using when you work with graphics.

Understanding screen coordinates

The iPhone and iPad support more than one screen resolution. Although you can use absolute screen coordinates in your code, it's better to draw relative to the screen dimensions.

Views in iOS are defined as CGRects, with an *x,y* origin and a size that includes a width and a height.

The *bounds* system works inside the view. The origin is always 0,0, because it defines the top left of the view.

The *frame* system locates the view in its superview, if there is one. The origin holds the *x* and *y* offset from the top-left corner of the parent view, if there is one.

The size is the same in both systems.

You can set a view's frame to change its position in its parent view. Use its bounds to find its size and to set the coordinates for path drawing.

You can find the dimensions of the area you can draw in like this:

```
CGFloat viewWidth = self.bounds.size.width;
CGFloat viewHeight = self.bounds.size.height;
```

Caution

If an app includes a status bar, the view won't use the full screen. This isn't a problem: You don't want your graphics to trip over the status bar. Similarly, if you add a navigation bar, toolbar, or tab bar, you should decrease the size of the view in IB by dragging the size of the view so it doesn't overlap these elements. The height and width of the bounds will change accordingly.

Creating a CGRect for a path

Let's draw a square box with sides of 100 pixels at the center of the view.

It would be useful if we could tell iOS to draw the center of the box at the center of the view. Unfortunately, we can't do this, so we have to do some slightly tricky basic math. (Coordinate, size, and position calculations are often tricky and complex.)

A box is defined as a CGRect, and we need to set the origin to the top-left corner. This means the origin must be half the width and height of the box, and it should be up and to the left of the center of the view. So to find the origin, subtract half the box width from half the view width—likewise for the height.

```
CGRect boxRect = CGRectMake (0.5*(viewWidth - boxWidth),
                             0.5*(viewHeight - boxHeight),
                             boxWidth,
                             boxHeight);
```

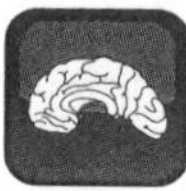

Genius

We've simplified the math so it does as few multiplications as possible. Graphics can be time critical, so it's always a good idea to use any speed tricks you can. Similarly, we've multiplied by 0.5 instead of dividing by 2, because multiplication is quicker than division. The difference in this example is trivial. But a commercial app may do hundreds or thousands of calculations 30 times a second to create animations, and speed tricks can make an obvious difference to the frame rate.

Note

A file called CGGeometry includes a list of *very* useful functions for working with CGRects. The functions CGRectMidX and CGRectMidY return the center coordinates of a CGRect. But you still need to do some extra work to offset the origin from the center, so we won't use them here.

Creating the path

After you have a CGRect, you can create a Bezier path object from it like this:

```
UIBezierPath *myPath = [UIBezierPath bezierPathWithRect: boxRect];
```

Figure 10.13 shows the methods that can be used with UIBezierPath. Creating a box with a rect is one of many options. For example, you could use the bezierPathOvalInRect: method to draw a circle.

Note also that you can use moveToPoint: to move the "draw" point to any location before using addLineToPoint: and the other construction methods to continue adding elements to a path. So a path doesn't have to be continuous. It can be made of many separate disconnected elements. This can save time when drawing multiple repeating objects; you can create many copies within a single UIBezierPath, even if they're not connected.

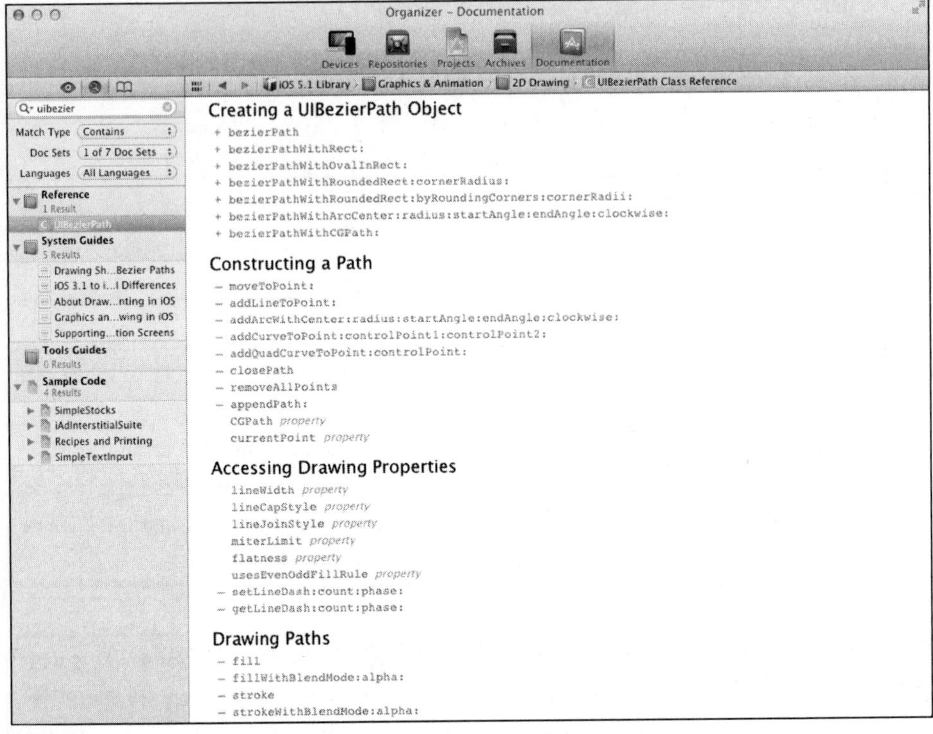

10.13 Looking at UIBezierPaths addition and creation methods.

Caution

Paths *do* have to be continuous if you want to fill the shape inside them. Otherwise, the fill color leaks out and fills the view.

Stroking and filling a path

Before you can make a path visible, you must select a color. Colors are defined as UIColor objects. A small selection of preset color objects can be created like this:

```
UIColor *aColor = [UIColor whiteColor];
```

Likewise for black, green, blue, and the other standard colors listed in the UIColor Class Reference.

To create a custom color, you can specify it as a blend of RGB (Red, Green, Blue) components or as HSB (Hue, Saturation, Brightness) components. Both include an additional component called alpha, which sets transparency. A value of 1 is opaque, and 0 is transparent.

For example, to specify the brightest possible yellow—which is equivalent to the standard yellowColor preset—you can do either of the following:

```
UIColor *aColor = [UIColor colorWithRed: 1 green: 1 blue: 0 alpha: 1];
UIColor *aColor = [UIColor colorWithHue: 0.167 saturation: 1 brightness: 1
   alpha: 1];
```

Note

Wikipedia has an exhaustively detailed article about the relationship between RGB and HSB color at en.wikipedia.org/wiki/HSL_and_HSV.

For this example, we'll use a preset blue shade. Add the following code:

```
UIColor *aColor = [UIColor blueColor];
[aColor setStroke];
[myPath stroke];
```

The setStroke method sets the stroke color—for example, the color that will outline the path. To set a fill color and fill a path, do this:

```
[aColor setFill];
[myPath fill];
```

Figure 10.14 shows the stroked path in the Simulator.

Note

Paths, strokes, and fills are based on underlying C-based code, which is part of a framework called Quartz 2D, which is part of the Core Graphics framework. UIKit offers most of the options you need, with a simple code interface. Core Graphics is useful for more advanced effects, such as gradient fills. It's more difficult to work with, and—confusingly—it also uses different screen coordinates, with 0,0 at the bottom left. If you're new to iOS, it's best to master the basic graphics options in UIKit first before trying to use Core Graphics.

Note

Whenever you update a view, call the setNeedsDisplay method on it to refresh it. This method runs drawRect: indirectly. Don't run drawRect: directly. setNeedsDisplay uses a built-in screen update timer to coordinate all screen refreshes. You can call setNeedsDisplay from multiple locations, and it will run drawRect: only once, when it's needed.

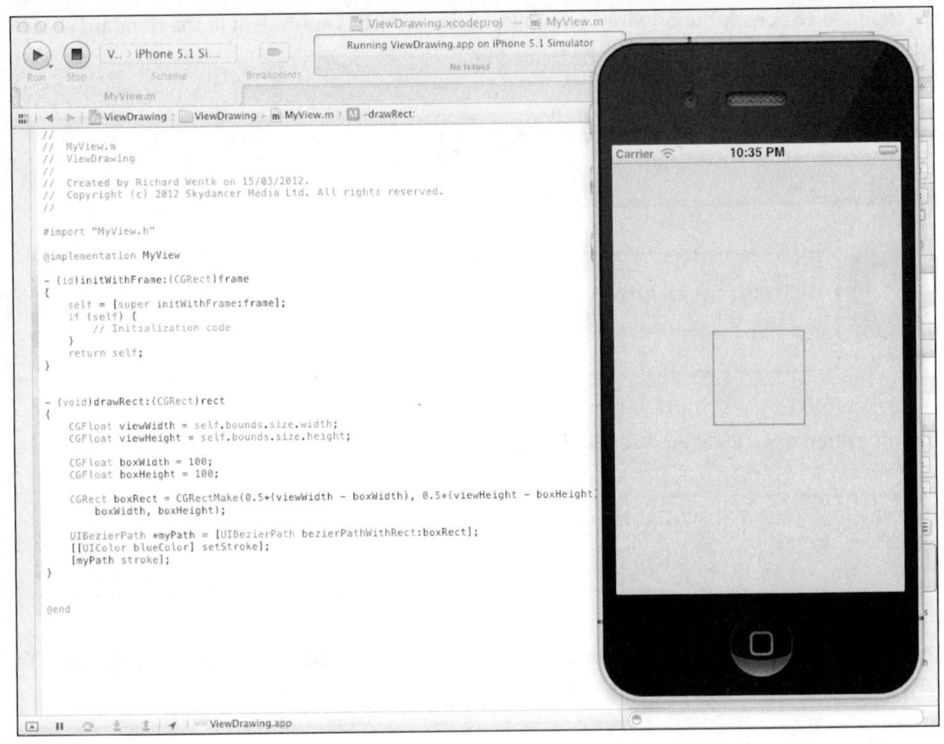

10.14 The finished box in the Simulator.

Creating views and controls with code

You don't have to lay out your UI with IB. You can add objects to a UI with code, and then set their action methods to define the messages they send. Or you can create a hybrid UI where some elements are loaded from a nib file and others are created at run time.

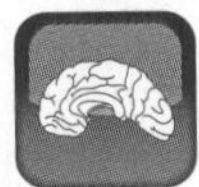

Genius

> For very advanced 3D effects, you can use the OpenGLES framework. OpenGLES is difficult to work with. A framework called GLKit hides some of the complexity of OpenGLES, but it still requires advanced techniques and knowledge that are outside the scope of this book.

Figure 10.15 shows the code for a simple example—a project that adds six buttons to a view when the app launches. Creating views with code can be moderately complex. This example uses a new method called initUI that is called once from the viewController and adds the buttons to the view.

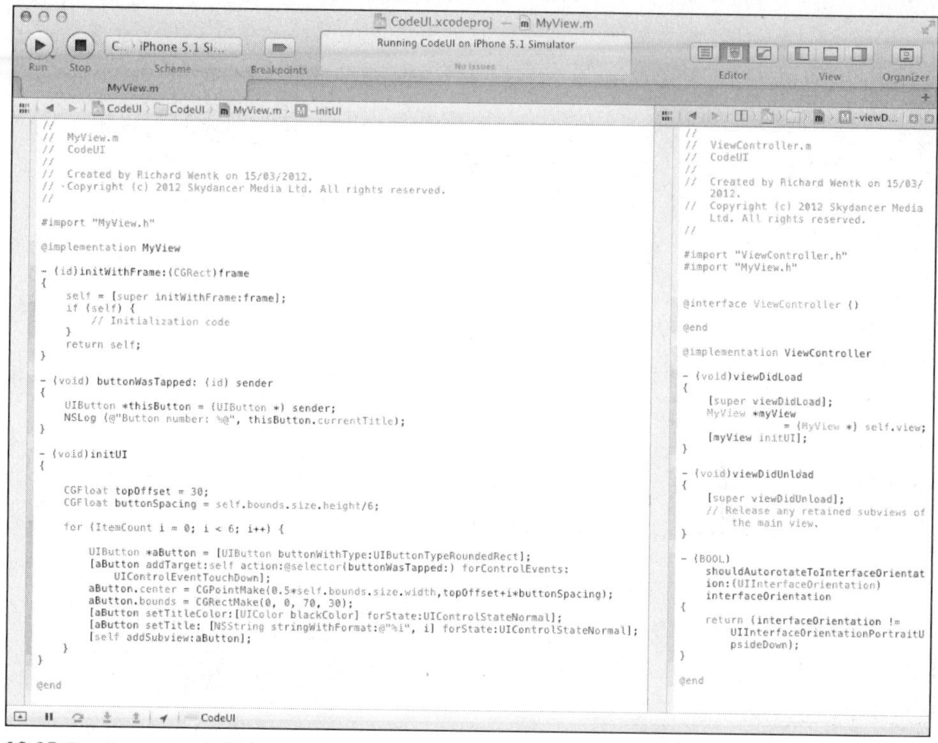

10.15 Creating a simple UI with code.

Caution

Don't draw a UI in drawRect:. drawRect: is called more than once on startup, and you'll get multiple copies of your UI objects.

initUI is listed here.

```
- (void)initUI
{


    CGFloat topOffset = 30;
    CGFloat buttonSpacing = self.bounds.size.height/6;

    for (ItemCount i = 0; i < 6; i++) {

        UIButton *aButton = [UIButton buttonWithType:UIButtonTypeRoundedRect];

        [aButton addTarget:self action:@selector(buttonWasTapped:)
   forControlEvents:UIControlEventTouchDown];
```

```
        aButton.center = CGPointMake(0.5*self.bounds.size.width,topOffset+i*
    buttonSpacing);

        aButton.bounds = CGRectMake(0, 0, 70, 30);

        [aButton setTitleColor:[UIColor blackColor]
    forState:UIControlStateNormal];

    [aButton setTitle: [NSString stringWithFormat:@"%i", i]
    forState:UIControlStateNormal];

        [self addSubview:aButton];
    }
}
```

The code does the following:

1. **It sets up some initial spacing estimates for the buttons.**
2. **It loops six times through a button creation routine.**
3. **Each repeat creates a round rect button.**
4. **The button is set up to send Touch Down messages to a method called buttonWasTapped.**
5. **The button is centered horizontally, but spaced vertically at equal offsets.** View objects *do* include a center property, which makes them easier to position.
6. **The title color is set to black.**
7. **The title is set to the number of the loop repeat.** This counts up from 0. Note how stringWithFormat: is used to convert the loop count into a string object.
8. **The button is added to the view as a subview.**

Figure 10.16 shows the result. The buttons appear in a vertical row, and they send messages to a single method called buttonWasTapped:. Code in the method reads the label from the button object that arrives. In this example, it simply logs the label. In a more complex app, each button could be made to respond in a unique way.

Note

The best place to draw a UI is in viewDidLoad in the View Controller. Because you've subclassed your view, you must use a cast to tell Xcode to use your class definition for it. Otherwise, Xcode won't be able to find your UI initialization method.

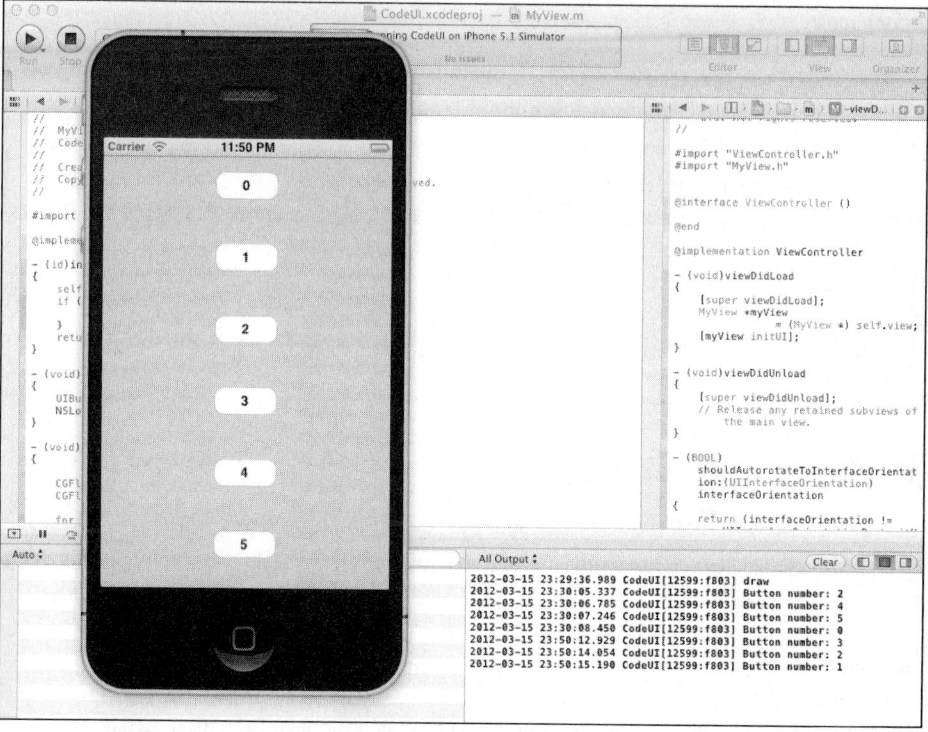

10.16 Checking the UI. It draws the buttons automatically and logs the button taps.

View-based UIs versus Graphics-based UIs

You can design a UI in two ways. You can draw objects manually and use the location of touch events to manage the drawing and the screen updates. Or you can build a UI out of multiple views and coordinate event management between them.

The first option may seem simpler to code. But in fact it's often easier to create a UI from multiple views. View objects and controls include smart features that can simplify hit testing and animation. You can also use messaging to coordinate view updates. Because subviews are stored in an array, you can use the data collection methods to run a single method on all views in your UI.

The initial design of a view-based UI is more complex—getting the layout looking good can be a challenge—but you'll often find it makes the code simpler while giving you many more creative options. And view-based hit testing is fast enough for basic games.

continued

continued

Target-action makes it possible to do a lot with barely any code. And don't forget that you can modify targets and actions in your code at any time. For example, you might use code to create a set of game tiles, and then modify targets, actions and drawRect: methods to change how each tile appears and responds as the game progresses.

Caution

When you subclass a view to add a UI initialization method, don't forget to tell IB about the subclass. And don't forget to include its header file in any class that references it, including the main View Controller.

Swapping Screens

To create an app with multiple screens, begin by creating multiple view controllers. Each should have its own nib file. If your app needs more than two screens, the main controller object is designated the parent controller.

There are three schemes for swapping screens:

- **Modal screens.** These appear temporarily to display optional information such as preferences. When the user has finished with this screen, it disappears and reveals the original view.
- **Manual screen swaps.** You can create as many screens as you need, using whatever logical flow works best for your app. Non-modal screens suggest a permanent change in the state of the app or in the information it displays.
- **Storyboards.** You can use these to sketch out a logical flow, with optional transition animations.

Adding a modal screen

Follow these steps:

1. **Create a new Single View Application project.** Save it as ModalScreenSwapping.
2. **Add some distinctive content to the main nib file.** The exact content doesn't matter.
3. **Use the Add File... option to add a new subclass of UIViewController to your project.** Check the option that creates a nib file. Save the file as SecondViewController.

4. **Add some different distinctive content to the SecondViewController.xib file.** Again, the details don't matter as long as the content is recognizably different from the original view controller.

5. **Add a touchesBegan: method to the first view controller, as follows:**

```
-(void) touchesBegan:(NSSet *)touches withEvent:(UIEvent *)event
{
    SecondViewController *secondViewController = [[SecondViewController alloc]
  init];

    [self presentViewController:secondViewController animated:YES
  completion:^{}];
}
```

Note

This code creates an instance of the second view controller and then uses a method called presentViewController: to display it. The completion parameter defines code that runs after the second view has appeared. In this example, there's nothing between the curly brackets, so this feature does nothing.

Build the project, and you'll see that when you tap the screen, the second view slides up from the bottom and covers the original screen.

Caution

If you can't get the code to build, make sure you've included the header file of SecondViewController at the top of the original ViewController.

In this version, you're stuck with the new screen, because you haven't yet added the code that restores the original screen. To fix this, add another touchesBegan: method to SecondView Controller, as follows:

```
-(void) touchesBegan:(NSSet *)touches withEvent:(UIEvent *)event
{
    [self dismissModalViewControllerAnimated: YES];
}
```

Build the project again. You'll see that when you tap the screen of the second controller, it slides back down again.

Note

In a commercial app, you'd be more likely to trigger a view swap from a button than a touch method. The code is similar, but you'd place it inside a button message handler instead of touchesBegan:.

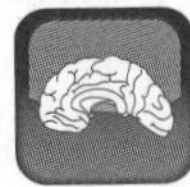

Genius

You can select three different animation styles by setting the second view controller's modalTransitionStyle property. The options are a horizontal flip/spin, a vertical slide, and a cross dissolved. (There's a fourth partial page curl option, but this isn't often useful.) The constants to use to select these styles are listed in the UIViewController Class Reference.

Creating more complex screen swaps

You can swap screens in an app in an almost infinite number of ways. The method in UIView Controller called presentViewController:animated:completion is very similar to its modal equivalent and offers the same transition animations.

For more complex effects, you typically nominate the main view controller object as a parent or container. It stays in memory permanently, while other controllers are swapped in and out as needed. You can then swap screens in two ways:

- **Use the transitionFromViewController: toViewController: duration: options: animations: completion method to switch between controllers.** This automatically switches the visible views, applying standard UIViewAnimationOptions options that are defined at the end of the UIView class reference.
- **Switch views manually.** Load two view controllers, access their view properties, and run the removeFromSuperview method on the old view and the insertSubview: atIndex: method on the new view. The index should be 0.

Neither option is completely straightforward, so app developers often use Xcode's new storyboard feature now.

Using a storyboard

A storyboard assembles a collection of view controllers and defines the order in which they appear to the user. The move from one screen to another is called a *segue*. Each segue includes details of the before and after controllers and the animation used to move between them. The view controller that appears when the app loads is called the *entry point* or *initial view controller.*

Storyboards give you less control over animations than code does. But it's much easier to see the logical flow through an app, so using a storyboard can save you time. They also include some of the support for actions and outlets that IB does, so you can continue to add controls to your screens and connect them to your code in the traditional way.

Note

Storyboards are a new feature, and they're a work in progress. They have the potential to eliminate screen swapping code. But currently, they're more limited than manual screen swaps, and some features still require supporting code. They're also bug-prone. Currently, storyboard-driven UIs often cause problems in the Simulator.

In this example, we'll create an app with three views: an initial view and two parallel subviews called A and B. We'll use a navigation controller with buttons to select the views.

Follow these steps:

1. **Create a new Single View Application project called Storyboards.** Make sure the "Use storyboards" option is checked before you save the project.
2. **Click the Mainstoryboard.storyboard file to view the storyboard in its editor, as shown in Figure 10.17.** When you use storyboards, this alternative editor replaces IB. It includes many familiar features—and some new ones.
3. **Drag a Label object from the Object library, and drop it on the view controller.** Double-click it, and change the text to "Main View." (This step is for display only, so you can see which view controller is loaded.)
4. **Click the view controller to highlight it.** A blue border appears when it's selected correctly.
5. **Select Editor ⇨ Embed In ⇨ Navigation Controller from the main Xcode menu.** This step adds a master navigation controller to the project, with a navigation bar that supports buttons.
6. **Drag a bar button item from the object library, and drop it at the top left of the navigation bar.** Double-click it to label it "Show A."

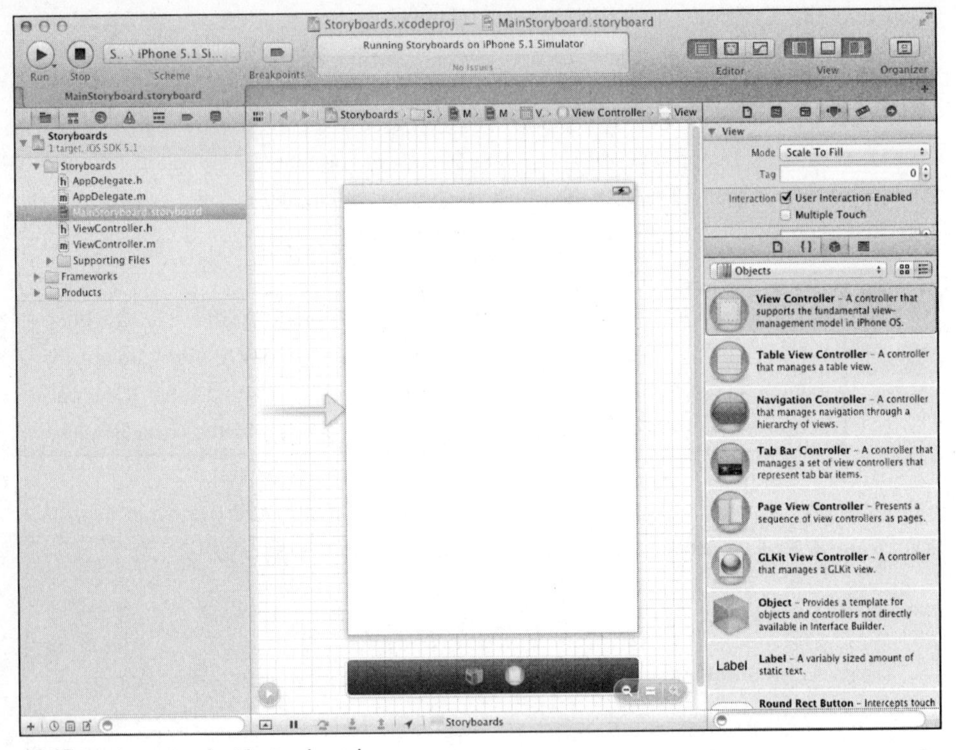

10.17 Getting started with storyboards.

7. **Repeat for another bar button item, dropping it at the top right.** Double-click it to label it "Show B," as shown in Figure 10.18.
8. **Drag a View Controller from the object library onto the editor grid.**
9. **Add a label object, and label it "View A."**
10. **Repeat with another View Controller; add a label called "View B."**

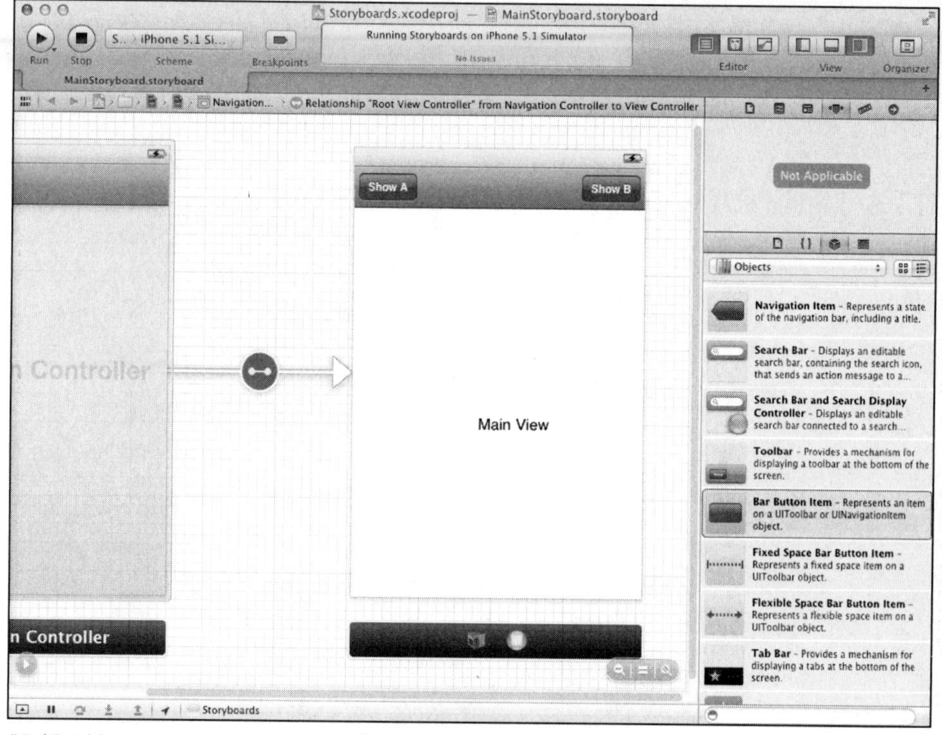

10.18 Adding a navigation controller (shown at the left edge) and two buttons.

11. **Arrange the view controllers vertically to the left of the main view controller, as shown in Figure 10.19.** This step makes the storyboard easier to follow, but doesn't affect its operation.
12. **Hold down the Ctrl key, and drag a link from the Show A button to View A.**
13. **Release the mouse, and select Push from the Storyboard Segues floating menu.**
14. **Ctrl-drag another link from the Show B button to View B.** Select Push again. Figure 10.20 shows how the view controllers are now connected.

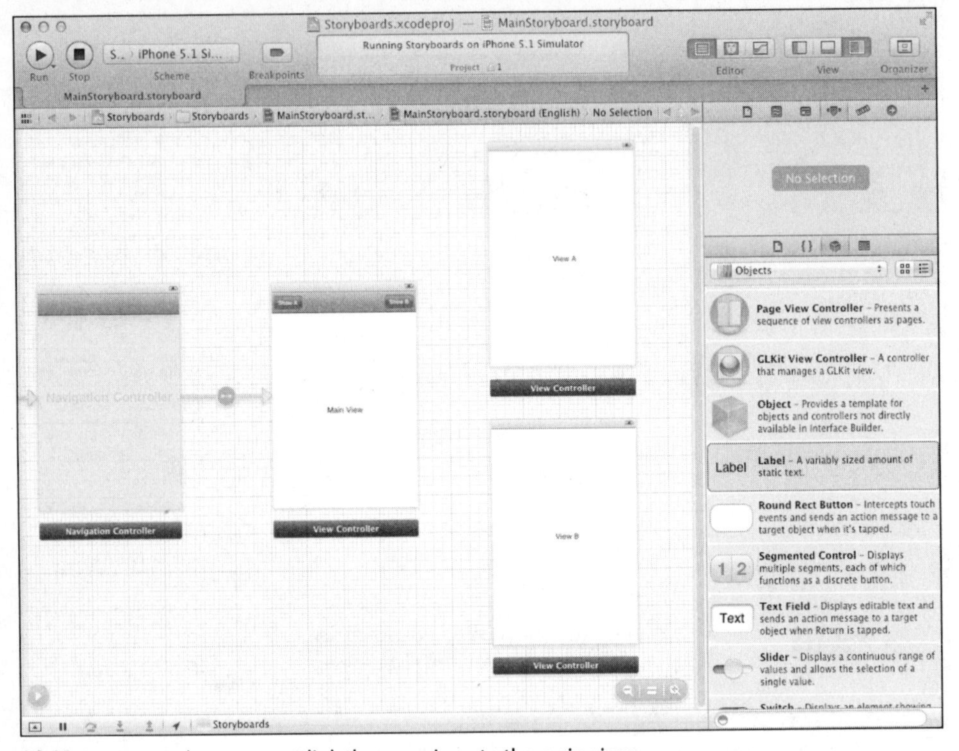

10.19 Getting ready to connect link the new views to the main view.

Build the project. It loads with the main view. You can use the Show A and Show B buttons to select the alternative views. A sliding push animation is added automatically, as is a "Back" button that's visible when View A and View B appear.

You've just created a three-screen app with no code at all. You can now subclass the views and view controllers to add further features.

Caution

The push segue works only with the navigation bar. It does nothing if you simply add a button to a view and try to set up a segue by linking. The modal segues are identical to the modal methods introduced earlier in this chapter. They don't add a back button or feature, so you'll have to add one manually and link to a dismiss ModalViewController in your code.

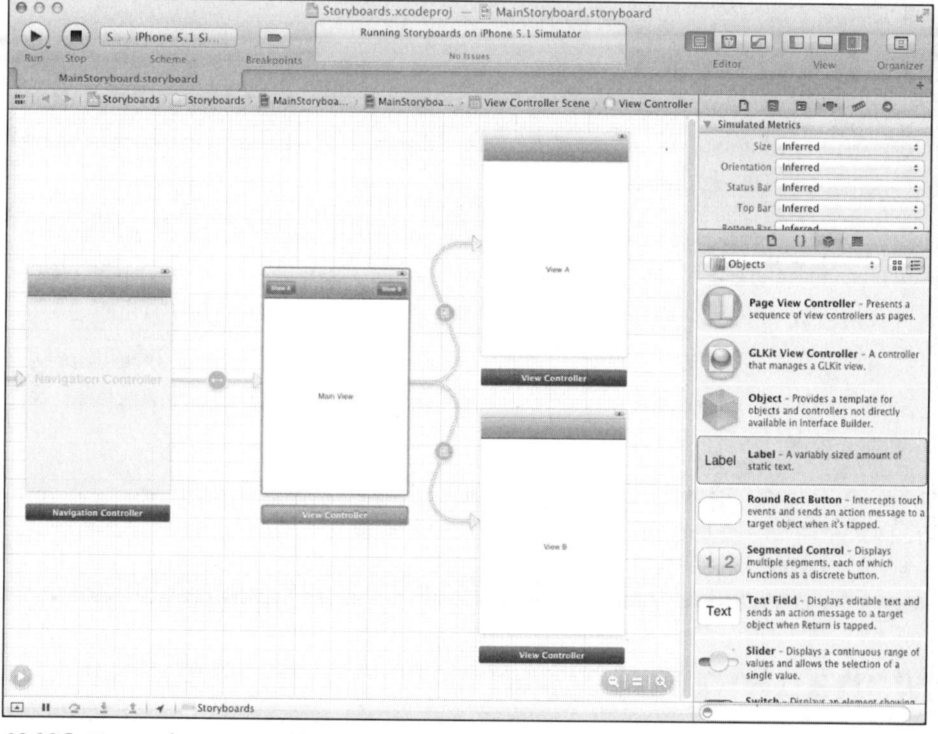

10.20 Getting ready to connect the new views to the main view.

Using UITableView

UITableView is the class that creates the famous iOS table effect. It's used by many apps to create tables and item lists with optional screen swapping. Typically each item can be tapped to show a further table, or more information about that item.

UITableView is a complex class. If you start your app using the Master-Detail Application Template you'll get a very basic skeleton with some equally basic code.

The key point to remember is that items are specified by *index paths* that include both a row count and a column count. The column count indicates how many times a user has tapped a cell. The row indicates the number of a table cell. Rows can be split further, into sections.

continued

continued

iOS asks your app to return a UITableViewCell object for each item in the table using a method called cellForRowAtIndexPath:. Cell objects can include text and graphics arranged in various ways, selected using the UITableViewCellStyle constants defined at the end of the UIViewTableCell reference.

Screens are swapped using a *navigation controller,* which keeps track of the user's position in multiple tables. Screens are "pushed" when the user taps a table cell, and "popped" when the user taps the back arrow at the top left of the navigation bar.

Creating a complete UITableView solution with navigation can take a while. Luckily, table views are so common you can find many examples online, and in Apple's own sample code.

It's worth taking a couple of days to pull apart some examples to see how they work. Once you have working code, you'll find you can reuse it in your own projects with relatively minor modifications.

Managing rotation

Some apps support auto-rotation, while others don't. View controllers support auto-rotation by default. But you may need to do extra work to make sure onscreen elements remain aligned correctly after a rotation.

Controlling rotation

You can control the rotations supported by your app by modifying the shouldAutoRotateToInterfaceOrientation: method in any view controller. This method works in a slightly lateral way. When a user rotates a device, iOS runs this method to ask your app if an orientation is supported. If your app returns YES, it auto-rotates the screen. If not, it doesn't.

You can define the supported rotations like this:

```
return ((interfaceOrientation == <orientation constant>)
|| (interfaceOrientation ==  <another orientation constant>)
|| <etc…>);
```

Note

The "||" character means "or."

For example, to support upright portrait mode and left landscape only, do this:

```
return ((interfaceOrientation == (UIInterfaceOrientationPortrait)
|| (interfaceOrientation == UIInterfaceOrientationLandscapeLeft));
```

If you specify a single orientation, such as UIInterfaceOrientationPortrait, the display will be locked to that orientation. If you return (YES) without any conditionals, all rotations are supported.

You don't need further code. The auto-rotation just works.

Controlling object layout

If you add some objects to a nib in portrait mode and enable auto-rotation, you'll see the object positions are scrambled in landscape mode. By default, positions are locked at their top and left coordinates. This lock remains in place when the view rotates, and the result is usually a jumble.

To fix this, select an object in the nib, and open the Size inspector in the utilities pane. In the Autosizing box, shown in Figure 10.21, click the two red bars at the top and left of the object. These lines are *anchors*. They lock the object's position relative to the top, left, bottom, and right edges. Clicking them unlocks the object position.

When the view rotates, it's moved automatically to a new position proportional to its old position. When the view rotates back, it automatically moves back where it started.

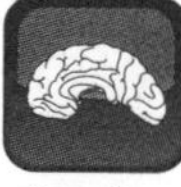
Genius

Note that sometimes you'll want to lock an object to one edge, even when it's auto-rotated, because that's the only way to make the layout work.

Sometimes, it's impossible to create a layout that works for all rotations. For more control, use the willRotateToInterfaceOrientation: method to swap the current view with a customized rotated version.

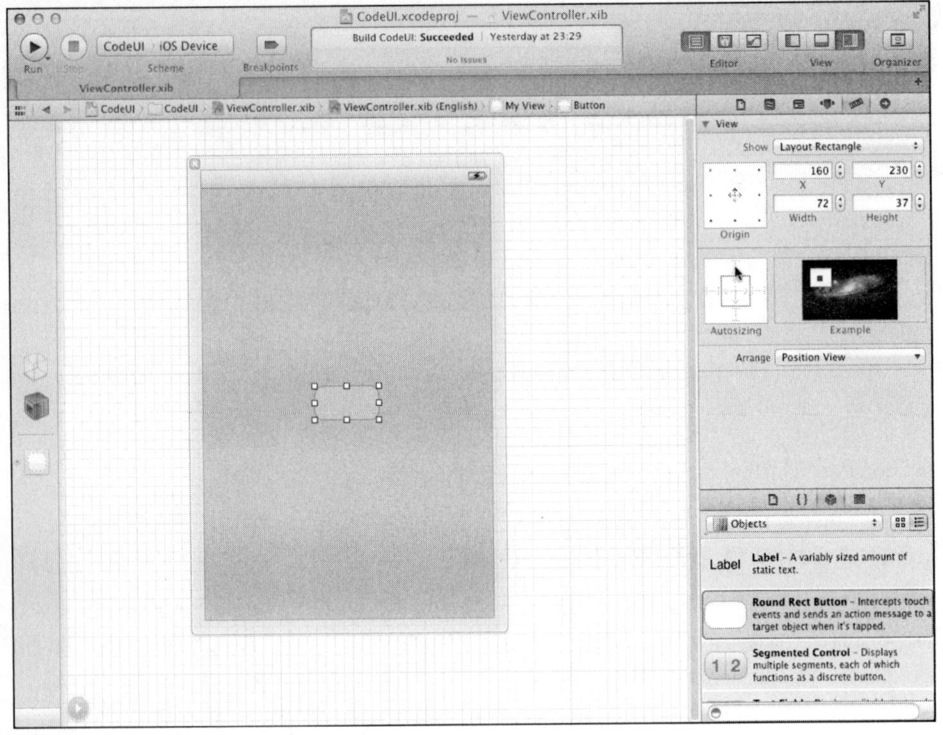

10.21 Unlocking objects so they're free to move as the view rotates.

Adding Animations

You've already seen how to add basic preset animations when swapping screens. Animation is widely used in apps to make UIs appear more dynamic and interesting. You can animate almost any property of almost any visible object, so the possibilities are almost limitless.

Understanding animation technologies in iOS

You can choose from the following:

- **Direct timer control.** You can set up a timer in a view or view controller, update some element in a view, and call setNeedsDisplay to refresh the screen. This option works well for repeating animations and for game designs where, for example, you need to bounce objects off each other.
- **UIView animations.** UIView includes a selection of built-in animation effects. You can animate the initial and final values of any property in an animation block, and you can control the animation curve to create smooth transition effects.

- **CALayer animations.** The low-level Quartz Core framework supports various complex animation objects. It's powerful, but it isn't particularly easy to work with and a full tutorial would be complex. For more details, see the Core Animation Programming Guide in the documentation.
- **OpenGLES.** Use this for games. It's a very challenging framework, with excellent 3D performance and many non-standard features.

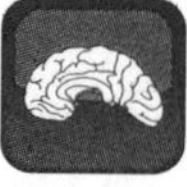
Genius

These basic animations can move and resize objects, and change basic properties such as color. For even more advanced techniques, you can use a framework called Core Image, which can apply animated filters—ripple effects, blurs, tiles, and so on—to any image. For details, see the Core Image Programming Guide in the documentation.

Creating a UIView animation

Let's use UIView animations to create a simple effect—a button that gets bigger for a short period when it's tapped.

Here are some key points about UIView animations:

- **UIView animations are run on the UIView class, not on individual objects.**
- **You can animate the size, position, color, and transparency of any object in the view.**
- **Apple suggests animation code is defined in a *block*.** Blocks are discussed in Chapter 11. For now, think of a block as a method you embed in the code that runs it. A block starts with a "^" (caret) character and is placed between curly brackets.
- **Animation methods include a completion parameter, which is defined as a second block.** This block is nested inside the first block. (This can make the code difficult to read, especially on a small monitor!)

Let's add an animation using these features of UIView. Follow these steps:

1. **Create a new Single View Application project called ButtonAnimation.** Don't use storyboards.
2. **Add a single button to the view from the object library.**
3. **Use IB to create an IBAction method for the button, called by the touchDown event.**
4. **Add the following code to the method:**

```
UIButton *thisButton = (UIButton *) sender;

[UIView animateWithDuration: 5
                animations: ^{
                thisButton.bounds =
                CGRectMake(0,0,thisbutton.bounds.size.width*2,
                          thisButton.bounds.size.height*2);
                }
                completion: ^(BOOL finished) {
                     [UIView animateWithDuration: 5
                          animations: ^{
                          thisButton.bounds =
                          CGRectMake(0,0,thisbutton.bounds.size.width/2,
                             thisButton.bounds.size.height/2);
                          }
                          completion: ^(BOOL finished) {}
                     ];
                 }
];
```

Build the app, and test it. You should see the button blipping in size to twice its usual dimensions when it's tapped. (The effect here is exaggerated. In a real app you'd be likely to use a much shorter animation duration, such as 0.1 second.)

Figure 10.22 shows one way to lay out the code. Layout standards for code that uses blocks haven't been finalized yet, but if you keep the delimiters of each section—the curly and square brackets—aligned and on separate lines, it's easier to follow the code.

```
- (IBAction)buttonWasTapped:(id)sender {

    UIButton *thisButton = (UIButton *) sender;

    [UIView animateWithDuration: 0.1
                    animations: ^{
                        thisButton.bounds = CGRectMake(0, 0, thisButton.bounds.size.width*2, thisButton.bounds.size.height*2);
                    }
                    completion: ^(BOOL finished) {
                        [UIView animateWithDuration: 0.1
                                        animations: ^{
                                            thisButton.bounds = CGRectMake(0, 0, thisButton.bounds.size.width/2, thisButton.bounds.size.
                                                height/2);
                                        }
                                        completion: ^(BOOL finished){}
                         ];
                    }
     ];
}
@end
```

10.22 Laying out the block code for the animations.

In outline, this code creates an animation that doubles the size of the button by setting its bounds. The code is placed in between curly brackets in the "animations" field.

If the view had more than one object, each could be animated separately with its own line of code. When the code is in a single statement like this, all the animations start and end at the same time and run with the same duration. But you can easily create independent animations by giving each object its own animation code and using a more sophisticated method called animateWith Duration: delay: options: animations: completion, which includes an optional delay.

Note

> When you set a view's bounds, the center is fixed so the object doesn't move. If you try to achieve the same effect by changing an object's frame property, you'll find you have to work much harder to keep it from moving.

The animateWithDuration: method includes a space for another block of code that is run automatically when the animation ends. The code in this example creates a *second* animation that halves the size of the button, restoring it to its starting size. The completion option for the second method is left empty.

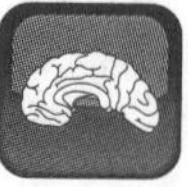

Genius

> If you use the sophisticated method that allows options, you can select various preset animation curves that control how the effect varies over the time. The curves are defined as UIViewAnimationCurve constants. You'll find them in the UIView documentation. The default linear curve is unsophisticated. You can start your animation slowly and stop it suddenly, or vice versa. Or you can start and stop slowly, with a burst of speed in the middle—the EaseInEaseOut. These curves add polish and impact to animations, and they can have a dramatic effect on the feel of an animation. So they're well worth experimenting with.

How Do I Add Other Standard App Features?

1 2 3 4 5 6 7 8 9 10 11 12 13

Although app UIs can be very different, many apps have similar internal features. Most apps need to save data, manage memory, and support preferences and settings. Many apps need to access the Internet and play sounds. And some apps need to support multiple languages. This chapter includes a grab bag of useful features that you're likely to want in your app. It also explains some of the key secrets you need to know to make your app look professional and successful in international markets.

Multitasking

Usually, only one app can run at a time. When the user quits an app, it can be reloaded by tapping its icon in the App Switcher. Apple calls this *Fast App Switching*. The iPad version of the Multitasking bar, which implements Fast App Switching, is shown in Figure 11.1.

A user can remove an app from the Multitasking bar by touching and holding its icon and tapping the "-" (minus) icon that appears. This forces the app to restart from cold the next time the user runs it.

11.1 You can access the App Switcher on any iOS device by quickly clicking the home button twice.

Note

Removing an app from the Multitasking bar deletes it from memory. But you usually don't need to do this manually. If you launch an app that needs more memory than is available, iOS automatically removes as many non-running apps as it needs to create enough free memory. In practice, the Multitasking bar is a recently used app list—and no more than that. Apps in the list aren't necessarily using resources. They may not even be in memory.

Apps with selected features can keep running *in the background:* They keep working behind the scenes while the user works with some other app. In iOS 4 and 5, the features include the following:

- **Music playback.** The app can play iPod files and stream music from online sources.
- **Location.** The app can use the GPS feature to find the current location coordinates.
- **AirPlay.** The app can stream audio and video to compatible TVs and other media devices.
- **Newsstand.** Apps can download new content.
- **VoIP (Voice over IP).** The app can respond to incoming phone calls over the Internet.
- **Apps designed to work with a hardware accessory.** These apps can receive updates from the accessory.

A separate but related feature allows apps to respond in a very limited way to *push notifications*—messages generated by a web server and sent to the device over cellular data or WiFi. Push notifications can play an alert sound, display an alert message, and add a red badge with a couple of letters or numbers to the app's icon. The app *doesn't* run automatically when it receives a push notification. But it displays an alert, and the user sees an option to launch the app manually.

Note

The App Store app uses this feature to tell you how many app updates are available.

In addition to the formal multitasking options, you can also use other features of iOS to make your app appear to do more than one thing at a time. *Local Notifications* can set up a timer that continues to run after the user quits your app. *Threads* can split your code and make sections of it run in parallel. You can use threads to start a slow operation, such as a large file download or some intensive processing, without freezing the rest of your app.

Setting up task switching

You don't need to do anything to set up task switching. It just works. But you may need to add extra code to make sure your app can be switched reliably. The methods that control task switching are included in the App Delegate file in all the default iOS templates.

Figure 11.2 shows the methods and comments that explain how you can use them. These are the methods:

- **applicationWillResignActive:** This tells your app that it's about to become inactive, either because of a temporary interruption or because the user has quit it.
- **applicationDidEnterBackground:** This tells your app that it's been moved to the background. You can use this method to save the state of the app.
- **applicationWillEnterForeground:** Your app is about to start running again, either because the interruption ended or because the user restarted it.
- **applicationDidBecomeActive:** Your app is running again. You can use this method to restore its state, update the UI, restart timers, and so on.
- **applicationWillTerminate:** In spite of the name and the comment text, this is called only if your app is set up so it doesn't support task switching. It *isn't* called when the user quits your app or kills it in the Multitasking bar. It *is* called if your app is running in the background and iOS decides to kill it, or if your app is set up without multitasking support.

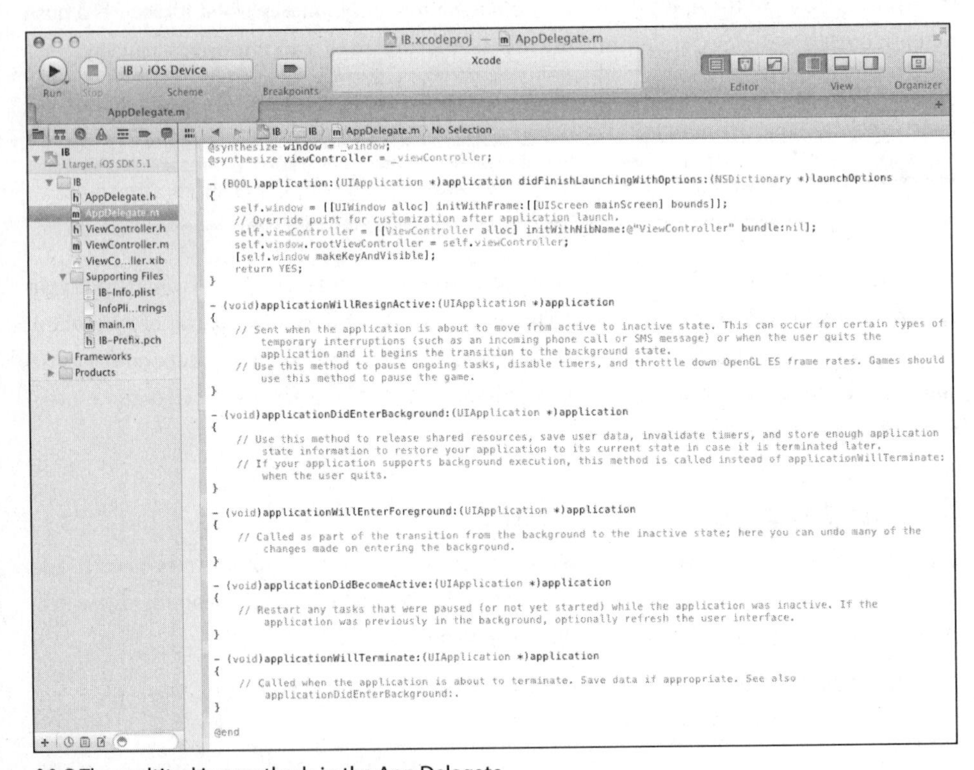

11.2 The multitasking methods in the App Delegate.

To understand more about these methods, it's important to understand that an app can be in one of five possible states:

- **Not Running.** The app is doing nothing. It isn't loaded into memory, it isn't receiving messages, and it isn't running code.
- **Active.** The app has control of the screen, and the user can work with it.
- **Inactive.** The app is loaded in memory, but it isn't receiving messages. When the user locks his or her device or it's interrupted by an incoming call, the app becomes inactive.
- **Suspended.** The app is in memory, but isn't running.
- **Background.** This is the only state in which the app is truly multitasking in the technical sense. It's running code, in a limited way, but it doesn't have control of the screen. More than one app can be in background mode at a time.

Entering background mode

You can enter background mode in two ways:

- **Your app can request extra time before it's suspended.** The best way to do this is to spin off a separate thread. Threads are introduced in more detail later in this chapter. Your app won't get much extra time, so the code must complete within a few seconds. The absolute maximum amount of time is 30 seconds.
- **Your app can tell iOS it uses one of the available background options to play audio, find the current location, and so on.** iOS usually allows it to continue running.

For the first solution, the App States and Multitasking Document shown in Figure 11.3 includes sample code that you can copy and use as-is. The code uses a method called beginBackground-TaskWithExpirationHandler: and includes an optional *expiration handler* that handles any final cleanup that may be needed.

Note

The code uses blocks, which are explained in more detail later in this chapter.

Introducing the info.plist file

Before looking at the other background options, we'll make a brief detour into a topic you need to understand first—the info.plist file.

Your app comes packaged with many settings that define how it loads and runs. The settings are kept in a file called info.plist. By default, the file includes a bare minimum of essential settings. But many optional settings can be added, including multitasking settings.

You can work with the file in two ways:

- **Open the Supporting Files group in the Project navigator, and select the <project name>-info.plist file.** The file loads it into a special editor.
- **Click the blue application tab at the top of the Project Navigator window, and select the Info tab.** This loads the same file into the same editor, as shown in Figure 11.4.

Note

The second approach displays extra options, so it's more useful.

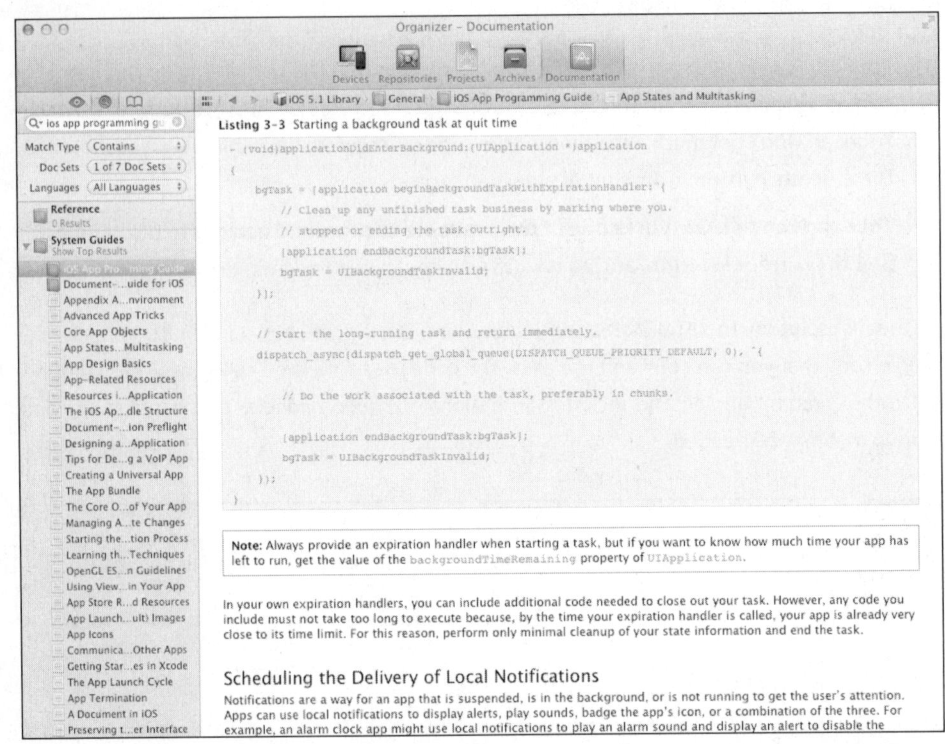

11.3 Locating Apple's sample code for running a short cleanup task in background mode after an app quits.

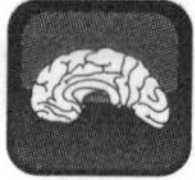

Genius

You can create your own plist files if your app needs a simple way to package a collection of settings. A plist file is really just an NSDictionary packaged into a specific text format, called XML. You can edit plist files by hand with any text editor, but the format is very structured and it's easy to make a mistake and make the file useless. It's better to use the built-in editor.

Adding multitasking options to info.plist

To tell iOS that your app needs to run in the background, follow these steps:

1. **Right-click any item in the key column.**
2. **Select the Show Raw Keys/Values menu item.** This changes the key display so it shows the real name of each key, not its description.
3. **Click any of the items that don't have a reveal triangle**. Most of them don't. When you select an item, it's highlighted in blue and "+" and "-" icons appear.

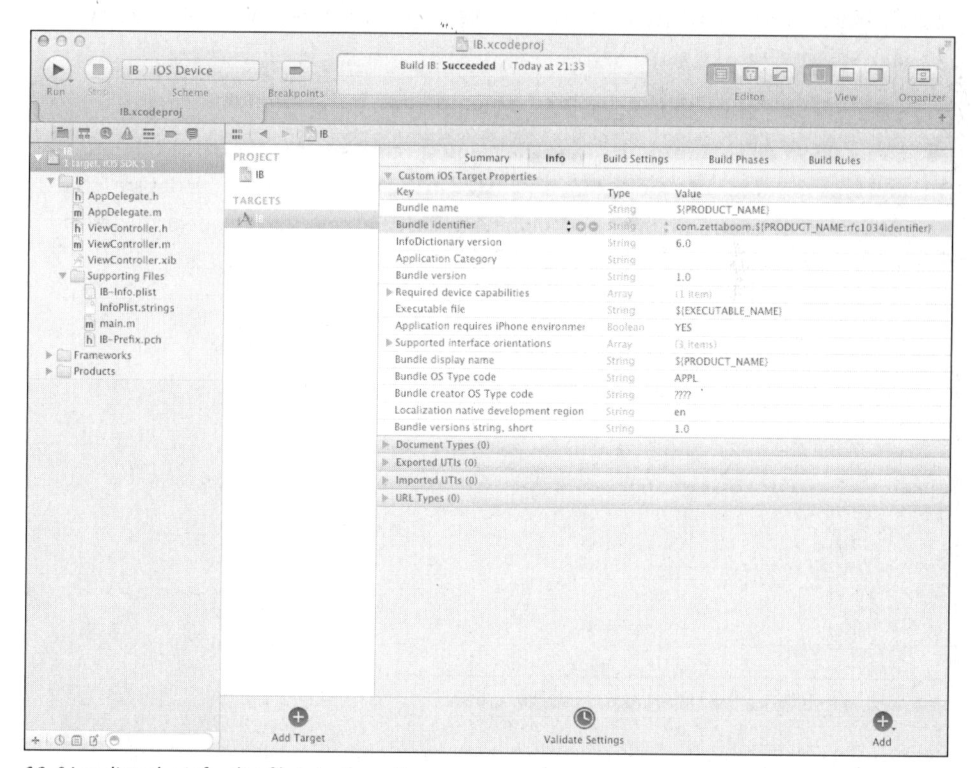

11.4 Loading the info.plist file into the editor.

4. **Click the "+" icon.**
5. **Scroll down the list in the pop-up menu, and select UIBackgroundModes, as shown in Figure 11.5.**

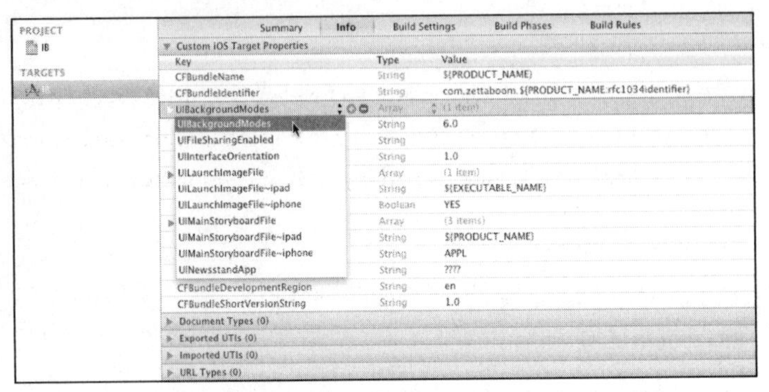

11.5 Adding the UIBackgroundModes key.

6. **Click the reveal triangle to the left of the UIBackgroundModes key.** A single empty item appears.
7. **Click in the value column to display the menu shown in Figure 11.6.**
8. **Either select one of the modes from the menu OR click again in the value column and type the name of a mode that isn't listed in the menu.** The other modes are listed in a document called App States and Multitasking. They are "newsstand-content," "external-accessory," or "bluetooth-central."

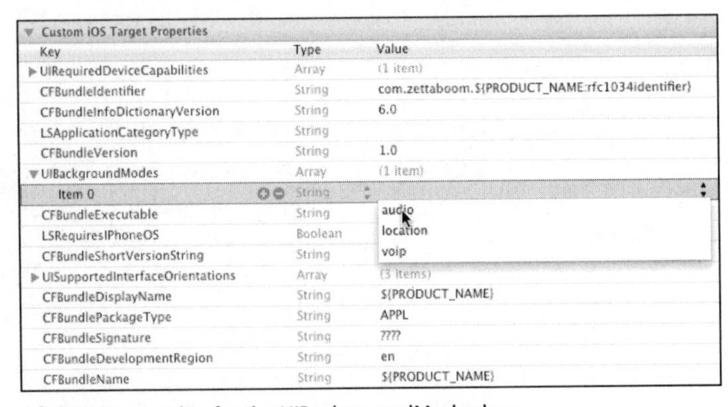

11.6 Adding a value for the UIBackgroundModes key.

Note

You can add more than one value. For VoIP apps, you should also add the audio key.

Working in the background

Your app is now ready to continue working in the background. Some features, such as audio playback, will now just work. You don't need to add any extra code. If your app is playing audio when the user quits it, it will continue playing audio until the user stops playback, either by relaunching the app, or by using the standard iOS transport controls.

Other features are slightly more complex. To make VoIP work, you must use a method called the setKeepAliveTimeout: handler to add code that is called regularly to keep the VoIP connection active. You can find more information in the App States and Multitasking document.

Note

You can keep your app from multitasking by adding a key called UIApplication ExitsOnSuspend and setting the value to YES. If you add this key, the applicationWill Terminate: method is called just before the app quits.

Working with event notifications

It's often useful to create apps with a countdown or event timer that does something at a certain time or date. If iOS supported full multitasking, you could simply create a timer object and allow it to run to completion. Unfortunately, it doesn't, so you have to create a more complex solution. A class called UILocalNotification is designed to solve this problem. It's somewhat like a timer object, but it runs inside iOS rather than inside your app.

Unlike a full timer, the features of a notification object are very limited. You can set a fire date with an option to repeat at a set interval. Because your app may not be running when the notification fires, the "payload" is limited to a couple of message strings that are displayed in an alert box, an optional sound file, and an optional image file.

Creating notifications

You create a notification like this:

```
UILocalNotification *notification = [[UILocalNotification alloc] init];
notification.fireDate = <code to define a date object with your chosen fire
   date>
notification.alertBody = @"The alert message you want the user to see";
[[UIApplication sharedApplication] scheduleLocalNotification: notification];
```

Add extra code to set the soundName or alertLaunchImage properties, as needed. You also can set a property called "alertAction," which appears as a button in the alert—or as the name of the main unlock slider when a device is locked—and gives the user the option to launch the application. Optionally, you can include a dictionary property with a collection of objects that can be passed back to your app when it receives the notification.

Responding to notifications

Notifications are delivered in two ways. When an app isn't running, notifications appear as alert boxes. When an app is running, no alerts appear, but a method called application:DidReceiveLocal Notification: is triggered in the App Delegate. The original notification object is passed to this method, and you can read its properties to decide how to handle the notification. If you included a dictionary when you created the notification, you can pack extra objects into it and retrieve them when the notification arrives.

To create a virtual countdown timer that appears to continue running whenever an app is reloaded, save the initial fire date outside the app and reload it whenever the user restarts the app. You can use the difference between the initial date and the current time to update the displayed countdown time. Optionally, you may want to add a timer object that continues to update the countdown as long as the app is running.

Typically, you want the countdown visible only on specific pages, so it's usual to create the timer *for that view controller only*. Invalidate the timer when the user moves to a different page. The notifications will still fire, and the user sees a countdown timer that appears to run in the background even when the app is stopped.

If the current time is after the fire date of a notification or if you want to stop the countdown, you can use this to remove the notification:

```
[UIApplication sharedApplication] cancelLocalNotification: aNotification];
```

Using threads

Even though only specialized apps can multitask, your app can still do more than one thing at a time. You can use *threads* to split your code and make some features run in parallel with others.

For example, you might want your app to download a large file data, work on a complex operation, or generate sound or video without glitching.

Without threading, some features would pause, judder, or stop working while the app does something else.

With threading, you can split your app into two or more units. One thread, known as the main thread, keeps running and updating the interface. The other thread, or threads, work independently. Threads can be created or destroyed as needed.

Threading is an intermediate and advanced technique, and there's more than one way to make it happen in iOS—for example, you can create a thread using a class called NSOperation. The simplest and most useful threading option is called *Grand Central Dispatch.* A full introduction to GCD is outside the scope of this book. But you can use the following code as-is. It uses blocks, which are described in the next section.

```
dispatch_async (dispatch_get_global_queue (
                                    DISPATCH_QUEUE_PRIORITY_DEFAULT, 0), ^{

//Code for the background thread goes here

     dispatch_async(dispatch_get_main_queue(), ^{

//Code to notify the main thread when the background thread finishes goes here

          });
});
```

Note

If an iOS device has more than one processor, iOS may decide to run a separate thread on it—so your app will literally be able to do more than one thing at a time.

Using blocks

Blocks are a relatively new feature in iOS, and they're often used to replace delegate and protocol methods with inline code; in other words, you can see the code at the point at which it runs. It isn't in some other object or method. It's often embedded directly in a method call, like this:

```
[anArray enumerateObjectsUsingBlock: ^(id object, NSUInteger index, BOOL *stop)
     {
     [object doSomethingToEachObject];
     //Set stop to YES to stop the enumeration
     }
];
```

Blocks are defined by a ^ (caret) character, followed by the code between curly brackets. The code looks unusual if you haven't seen it before, but blocks aren't difficult or mysterious. The example code above shows how you can pick parameters passed into the block. In this example, "object" is set to each object in an array and passed to the block code, and then the block code runs. There's often a BOOL value you can set to stop the block early.

Blocks are often used in code that creates an independent sub-task, such as an animation effect. Where previously you would specify a method that runs when an effect finishes, now you can create the same result with inline code. This makes it easier to see what your code is doing, but there are some drawbacks.

The biggest problem is making sure you've matched brackets correctly. Block code mixes square, curly, and round brackets in variable proportions, with occasional semicolons. Xcode warns you when the brackets don't match, but current versions aren't smart enough to fix mismatches for you.

Note

You can create blocks anywhere in your code and use them rather like methods. For examples, search for "ios blocks example" online. The one gotcha is that if you use a variable inside a block, its value stays fixed, even if you try to set it. To make a true variable, prefix it with "__block." This tells Xcode to make the variable, well, variable.

Managing Memory

Memory is a finite resource. Your app has to tell iOS when it wants to keep objects in memory and when they can be deleted to free the memory for other uses.

Before Xcode 4.3, developers managed memory manually. Many sample projects on the web still use manual memory management code, so this chapter explains how to recognize this code and how to update it.

From Xcode 4.3 onward, memory management is automated and uses a technology called Automated Reference Counting (ARC). As long as you tell Xcode to enable ARC when you create a new project, you can leave it to work behind the scenes. In some specialized situations, some manual adjustment is still needed, but they're mostly reserved for code that uses older C-based libraries. Simpler object-based code works as-is.

Note

Internally, the old and new schemes for memory management work the same way. The difference is that in the older scheme, you were responsible for adding explicit memory management instructions to your code. In the new scheme, Xcode adds the instructions for you when it builds your app. Mostly they just work, so you don't have to worry about them.

Understanding manual memory management

The original memory management code is easy to understand, but very difficult to work with. Unfortunately, if you get it wrong, your app is likely to crash. In fact, memory management issues were—and sometimes still are—one of the biggest causes of app crashes.

There are five main methods:

- **retain.** This tells iOS to keep an object in memory.
- **assign.** This copies a pointer to create another reference. It doesn't retain the object.
- **release.** This tells iOS that it's safe to delete an object and free its memory.
- **copy.** Duplicate an object in memory.
- **autorelease.** This is used when an object is created. It tells iOS to make a best guess about when to free the object.

The key point is that *every retain, copy or alloc must be balanced with a release.* Figure 11.7 shows some legacy code that creates local notifications. You can see how each notification object is created and then released immediately—telling iOS that this code will make no more references to that object.

Keeping track of retains and releases looks easy. But it isn't, for the following reasons:

- **The retain statement may appear where a property is declared.**
- **The object may be retained by other objects.** If you add an object to an array, it's retained automatically. But there's no explicit retain statement, so it's not obvious that you need to include a balancing release.
- **Delegates and a few exceptional classes can cause problems.** When you declare a delegate object, you should use assign instead of retain—in theory. In practice, if the delegate is also being used by some other object or class you *have* to use retain, because otherwise the delegate object can be released without notice. Generally, some situations require *lots* of thought, and are unlikely to "just work."
- **release doesn't actually mean "release."** It actually means that code will make no more references to the object, and iOS is free to remove it from memory. Internally, each object includes a retain counter that totals the release/retains. Objects are released only when the counter reaches zero.

Using ARC with Objective-C code

Because it's difficult to manage memory manually in practice, ARC was invented to replace it. To use ARC, you do very little. Mostly, memory is managed without further effort. But the system adds some new keywords that are used in header files, and it's important to understand how they work. Figure 11.8 shows Apple's own introduction to ARC. Very detailed and extended practical tutorials are plentiful online.

Properties are now *strong* and *weak*. A strong property owns the object and is similar to the old retain method. iOS takes all strong references into account as it manages memory. A weak property is similar to the old assign method, but weak references are now zeroed automatically when iOS removes an object from memory.

Properties are strong by default. Use weak references in special circumstances. It's also a good idea to manually zero strong properties when your code no longer needs an object.

Typically, you only want to use a weak reference to a delegate object, because it's created and released elsewhere. You also should use it for outlets. You still can use the assign keyword for basic C types such as float, int, and so on.

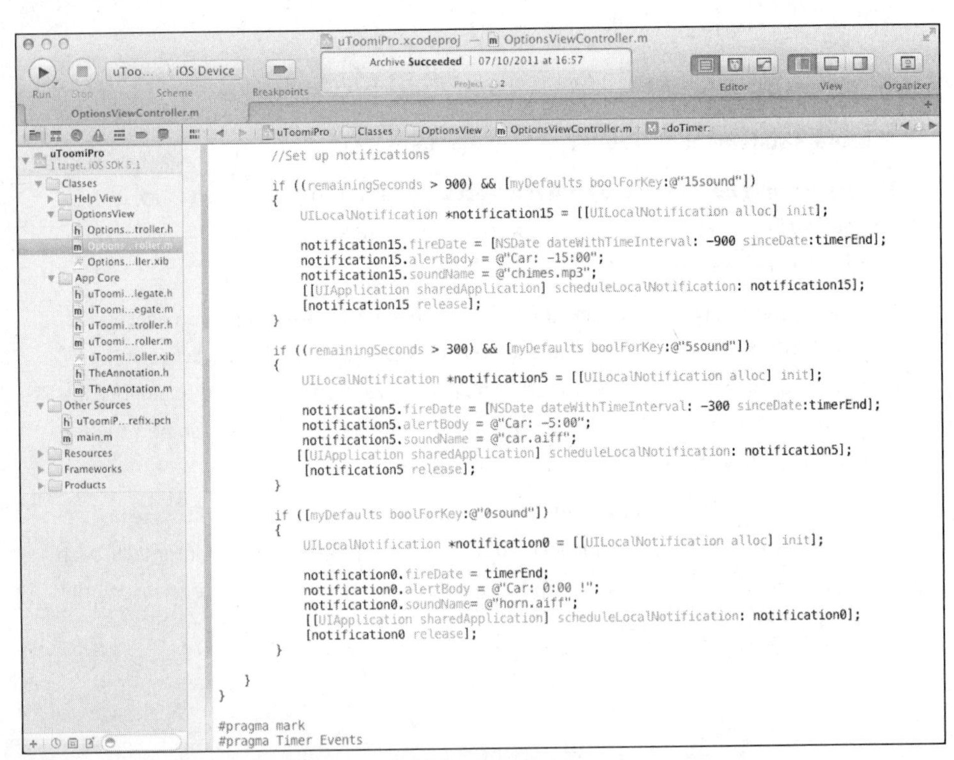

11.7 Creating and releasing objects the old-fashioned way.

Caution

ARC needs extra help when you use the lower-level C frameworks in iOS—especially Core Foundation. Sometimes these frameworks are described as "toll-free bridged" with Objective-C objects. The details are somewhat complex. You can find an explanation in the Managing Toll-Free Bridging Section of the Transitioning to ARC Release document.

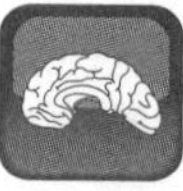

Genius

You'll often find code in online projects that still uses manual memory management. You can convert this code to support ARC manually by taking out all the memory management keywords. But Xcode includes a one-click tool that can do the conversion for you. To use it, open a file in the Xcode editor, select Edit Refactor Convert to Objective-C ARC. The process works well with Objective-C code. If there's any C code, you may need to make some manual adjustments before Xcode can complete the conversion.

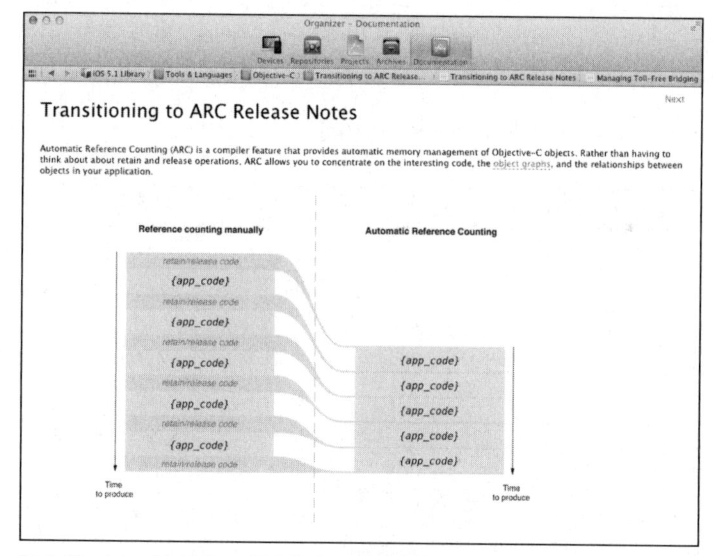

11.8 The introduction to ARC in the official documentation.

Working with Files

The easiest way to save and load data is to use the methods built into the data collection objects—NSArray, NSDictionary, NSSet, NSString, and so on. The easy way to save other objects is to add them to an array and save the array.

Note

Plain C types must be wrapped inside an NSValue object first. For details, see Chapter 7.

Caution

This option works for objects that support NSCoder—the system iOS uses to convert objects into save-able and load-able binary. If an object doesn't support NSCoder, you have to add appropriate encoding and decoding methods yourself. (In this context "encoding" and "decoding" mean "converting to and from binary.") You can find detailed tutorials online, and also in *Cocoa* in Wiley's Developer Reference series.

To save an array, use the writeToFile:atomically: method, like this:

```
[anArray writeToFile: pathString atomically: YES];
```

Saving atomically guarantees the file is saved correctly. If there isn't enough disk space, the method returns a BOOL as anerror code.

To read an array, use the arrayWithContentsOfFile: method, like this:

```
NSArray *arrayReloaded = [NSArray arrayWithContentsOfFile: pathString];
```

How do you create the pathString? iOS uses a limited "sandboxed" filing system, so apps can save files only in very limited locations in a protected user space. To create a suitable path string, use the following boiler plate code:

```
NSArray *paths = NSSearchPathForDirectoriesInDomains
   (NSDocumentDirectory, NSUserDomainMask, YES);
NSString *documentsDirectory = [paths objectAtIndex: 0];
NSString *pathString = [documentsDirectory stringByAppendingPathComponent:@"file
  name.ext"];
```

This slightly convoluted code—there is no easy way to simplify it—reads the path for /Documents directory, which is the main user file space. The stringByAppendingPathComponent: method adds a specific filename. This method automatically produces strings that can be used as a file path.

Figure 11.9 shows the list of standard directories available to each app. Note how you can use /Documents/Inbox to share files with iTunes.

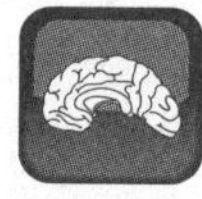

Genius

For more advanced file operations, including directory management and file deletion, use a class called NSFileManager. There are methods for listing directories, checking whether files exist, removing files, comparing files, and so on. After you know how to create a path, the class is very easy to use.

Caution

Sandboxing means iOS doesn't have the open filing system you may be used to in Windows or OS X. Apps can't easily access each others' directories, which makes it very difficult to share files between apps and with other computers. You can make /Documents shareable in iTunes by adding the UIFileSharingEnabled key in the Info page of Build Settings and making sure it's set to YES. More complex sharing—with DropBox, iCloud, or other technologies—is outside the scope of this book.

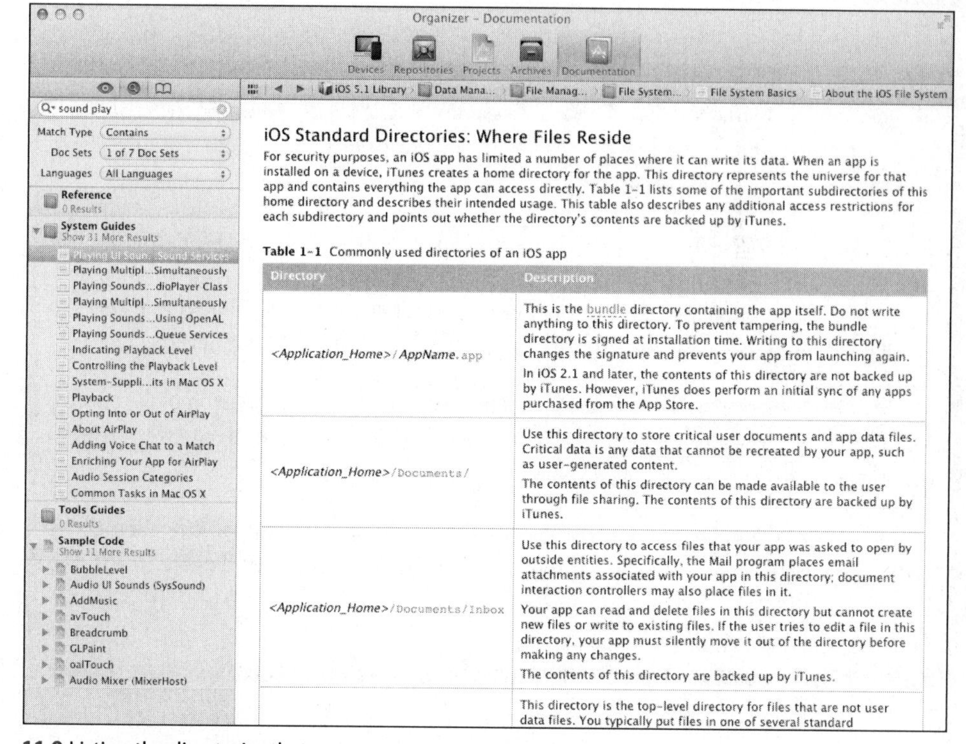

11.9 Listing the directories that your app can access.

Playing Sounds and Videos

iOS is capable of complex real-time sound synthesis. But a full introduction to all the features in Core Audio, Media Player, and the other media frameworks would need a much bigger book.

Fortunately, you don't need to be an expert on synthesis to play a simple sound. You can use a class called AVAudioPlayer to load a sound and play it with just a few lines of code.

Playing a sound with AVAudioPlayer

The AVAudioPlayer class provides simple playback of sampled audio files. The class can do much, and it's easy to work with. But you must add extra setup code to load a file you package with your app and optionally to handle errors.

Caution

AVAudioPlayer is part of the AVFoundation framework. Don't forget to add this framework to your build and include its headers in your project before you work with it.

Files and URLs in iOS

You're almost certainly used to the idea that files are collections of data stored on disk and URLs are online addresses.

iOS (and OS X) blurs this distinction. In iOS, you can load any file—local or remote—by specifying a URL instead of a file path. The NSURL object can hold a representation of a local file path or an online URL. Both are stored in a special format. Objects that can use NSURL for file access don't care whether the URL points to local or online storage.

This makes it very easy to download content from the Internet. For example, you can simply specify a remote URL and load data from it into an NSString. If the URL is a standard web address, NSString will load the page source.

You also can download online content straight into a data collection object, such as an array. This works only if the data is formatted correctly. Web pages usually aren't, but you can use this option to pre-package data for your app and place it on a web site. Your app can download it when it's needed.

Creating an NSURL for a file in the app bundle

When you add a file to your project using the Add Files… option, it's automatically included in the final bundle. You can use the code below to load it into an object as needed. This scheme is used for many media file types, including audio, video, and image files. The "ext" extension specifies the file type—.wav, .aiff, .mp3, .jpg, and so on.

```
NSString *filePath =
              [[NSBundle mainBundle] pathForResources:@"filename" ofType:
   "ext"];
NSURL *theURL = [NSURL fileURLWithPath:filePath];
```

Introducing NSError

Before going further, let's look at NSError—an object that holds an error report. It's often embedded into file operations to check that they work correctly.

To create an error object, do this:

```
NSError *error = nil;
```

You can also create a single error object at the start of your class and set it to nil before you want to use it.

Because NSError is unusual, you use it in an unusual way. Only a small number of objects use NSerror. In those that do, you prefix it with an ampersand to pass the address of the pointer. Typically you embed the error in a more complicated statement that checks for a YES/NO result after an operation:

```
if ([<some method that returns an error> error: &error])…
     //code that runs if there was no error
else
     //code that runs if there was an error…
```

This code is standard, but slightly tricky. The error condition is flagged by checking for a YES or NO result from the main operation. (YES means the operation succeeded. NO means there was a problem.)

It *isn't* flagged by checking the error object directly.

After you have an error, you can use a method called localizedDescription to log a description like this:

```
NSLog (@"Something went wrong: %@", [error localizedDescription]);
```

Working with AVAudioPlayer

After you have the code to find a file URL and set up an error object, the rest of the process is straightforward. In outline, you create an AVAudioPlayer object, load the audio data, and initialize it with a method called prepareToPlay that loads the file into the device's audio hardware ready for an instant start. After the file is initialized, you can use the play method to trigger playback.

The code looks like this:

```
AVAudioPlayer *aPlayer
    = [[AVAudioPlayer alloc] initWithContentsOfURL: theURL error: &error];
[aPlayer prepareToPlay];
[aPlayer play];
```

Optionally, you can use delegate methods to trigger an event when the file completes. For more advanced effects, you can use the properties of AVAudioPlayer, which are shown in Figure 11.10, to create loops, set the volume, and so on.

Caution

Different audio file formats have different levels of hardware support. You can play multiple .wav/.aiff files at the same time, and they'll be mixed automatically. But the hardware can't play more than one MP3 file at a time.

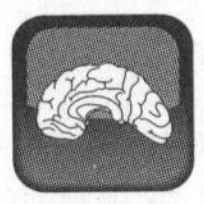

Genius

To improve the look of your app, you can use a timer to trigger the averagePowerForChannel: and peakPowerForChannel: methods to read the current level of the audio and drive an animated bar graph display, created with simple graphics code. (Even a basic filled box can look good.)

Working with MPMoviePlayerController

The video equivalent of AVAudioPlayer is MPMoviePlayerController. You can initialize it from a file URL and use the play method to display a movie player object. To display a full set of controls, do this:

```
theMoviePlayer.movieControlMode = MPMovieControlModeDefault;
```

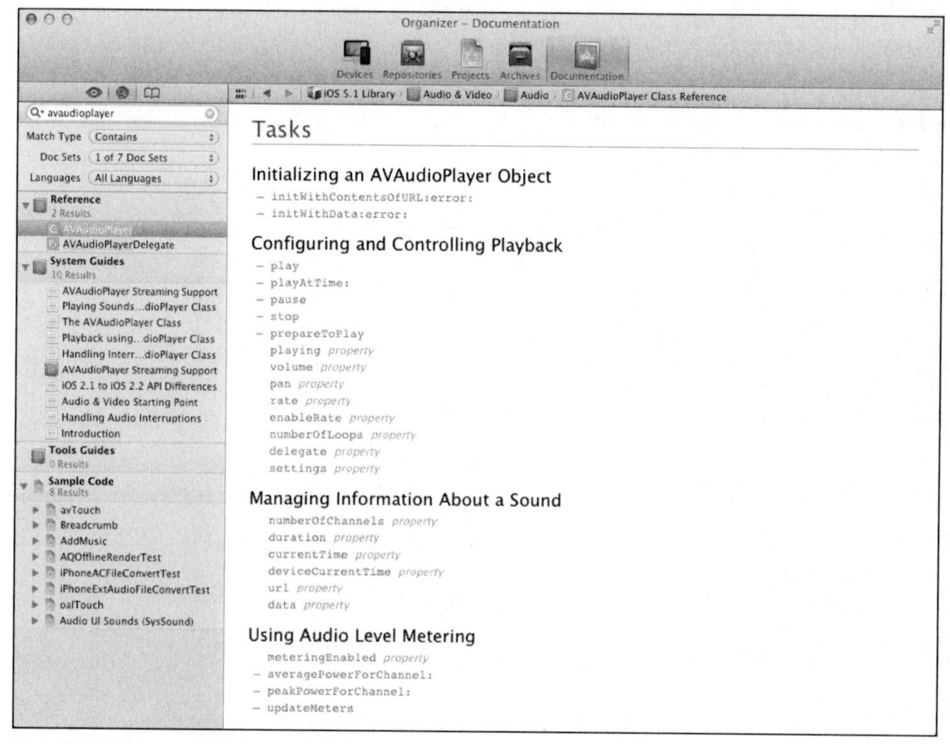

11.10 Tasks supported by AVAudioPlayer.

Connecting to the Internet

Although iOS includes more complex options, the simple way to download data from the Internet is to use data collection objects, including NSString. As long as the device has an active connection, you can supply these classes with an online URL and downloads of web content just work.

Checking for a connection

If a connection doesn't exist, the download methods will fail. You can handle this in two ways:

- **Include a simple check on return.** If the data collection is nil, the download failed.
- **Use code from a sample application called Reachability, shown in Figure 11.11.** Reachability tests whether a device is online and tells you if it's connected via WiFi or a cellular/mobile connection.

Reachability is a fairly complex project, but you're allowed—even encouraged—to copy and modify the code to your own requirements.

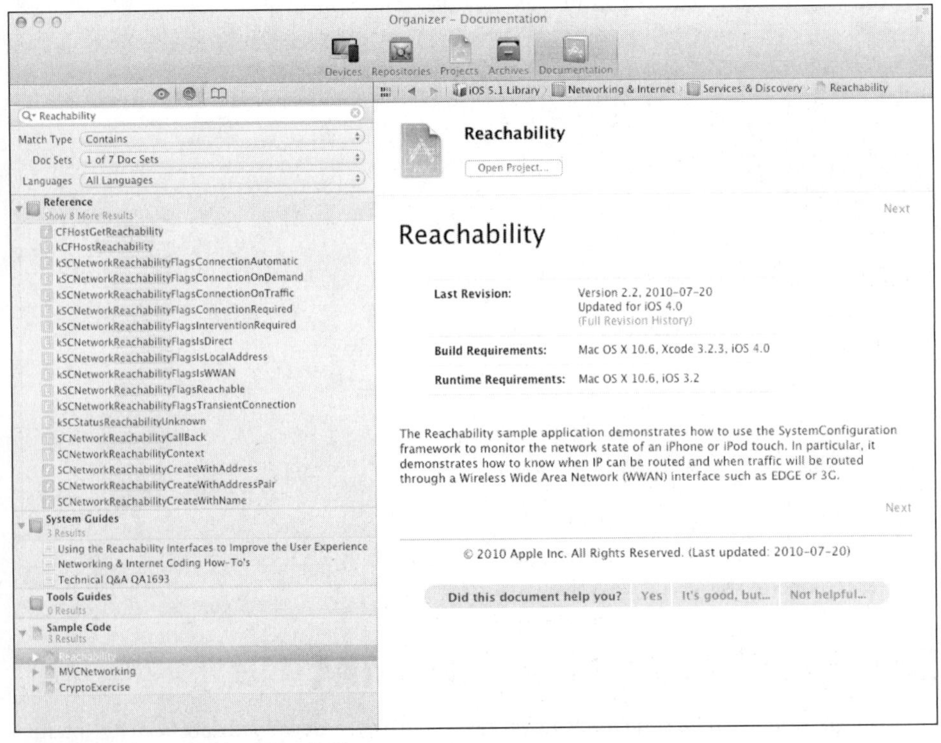

11.11 Tasks supported by AVAudioPlayer.

Using APIs

On the Internet, an Application Programming Interface (API) is a "door" you can use to access third-party services. All the household names in computing—Google, Yahoo!, Facebook, Twitter, and so on—have their own APIs. Many smaller and less well-known companies and organizations, such as the bit.ly URL shortening service, offer similar public access.

Figure 11.12 shows the API page for the Google Chart Tools service. You can use this service to convert data into a graphic image. As long as your app is connected to the Internet, it can access this API and create attractive graphic files on demand.

You access many APIs by sending a request to a web server. Instead of web pages, the server returns raw data. For example, Yahoo!'s weather API provides weather forecasts for almost any location on Earth. Table 11.1 lists some of the common APIs used in apps.

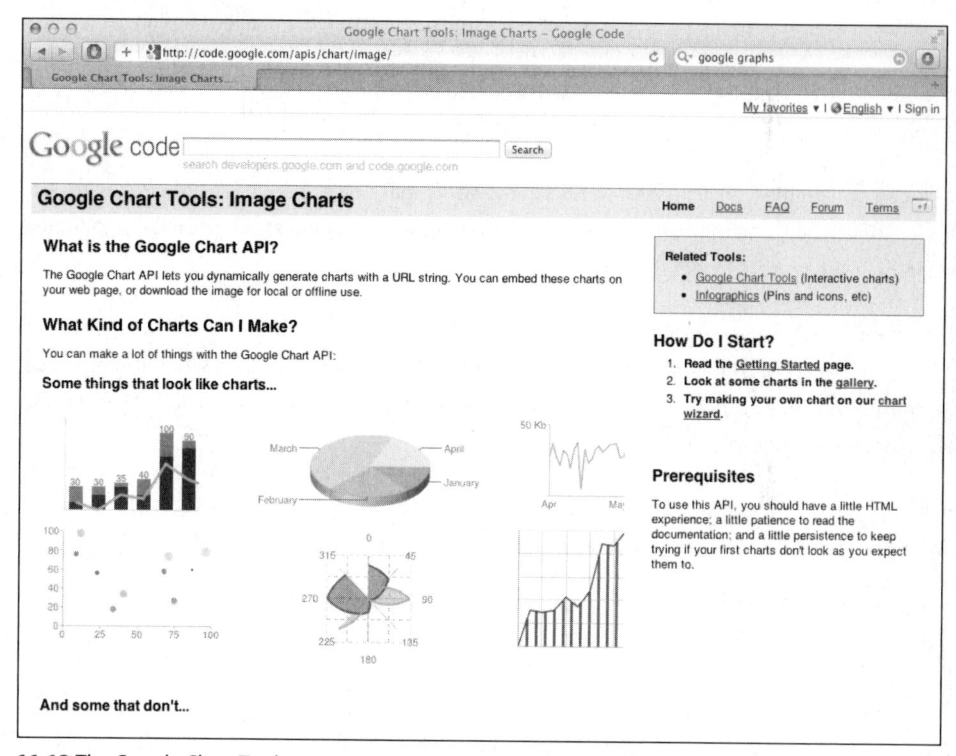

11.12 The Google Chart Tools page is a typical introduction to a public API.

Table 11.1 A Very Short List of Public APIs

API	Used for...
Google Maps	Map display, directions, forward and reverse geocoding (in other words, converting place names and addresses into geographical coordinates, and vice versa)
Google Charts/Visualization	Drawing charts and diagrams from data
Facebook	Accessing most features of Facebook—timelines, photos, wall posts, and so on—from apps and other web pages
Twitter	Accessing most features of Twitter from apps and web pages
Yahoo! Weather	Getting a weather forecast for a geographical location
JanRain	Authenticating users by allowing them to log in using many popular social web services
Amazon S3	A commercial—paid for—web storage API that can handle almost unlimited volumes of data and traffic

APIs can be complex, so it's useful to find frameworks that make them easier to work with. The frameworks hide some of the complexity involved in requesting data and receiving—and understanding—the response from the server.

Frameworks help you use APIs in two ways. Data is usually sent and returned in various special text formats. The two most common formats are called JSON (JavaScript Object Notation) and XML (eXtensible Markup Language). iOS includes options that can convert familiar NSArray and NSDictionary objects to and from JSON and XML.

In theory, you can use a class like NSJSONSerialization to simplify API access. In practice, the JSON and XML classes are complex and difficult to work with.

But you can usually find sample code that does the job for you. If you search for "<API Name> iOS," you can often find a complete solution that you can drop into a project and modify as needed.

Figure 11.13 shows one example—a widely-used API component called OAuth, which is used by Twitter, Facebook, and many other services to confirm user identity before allowing access to secure features. As the figure shows, various solutions are written in Objective-C, and one in particular is designed for iOS.

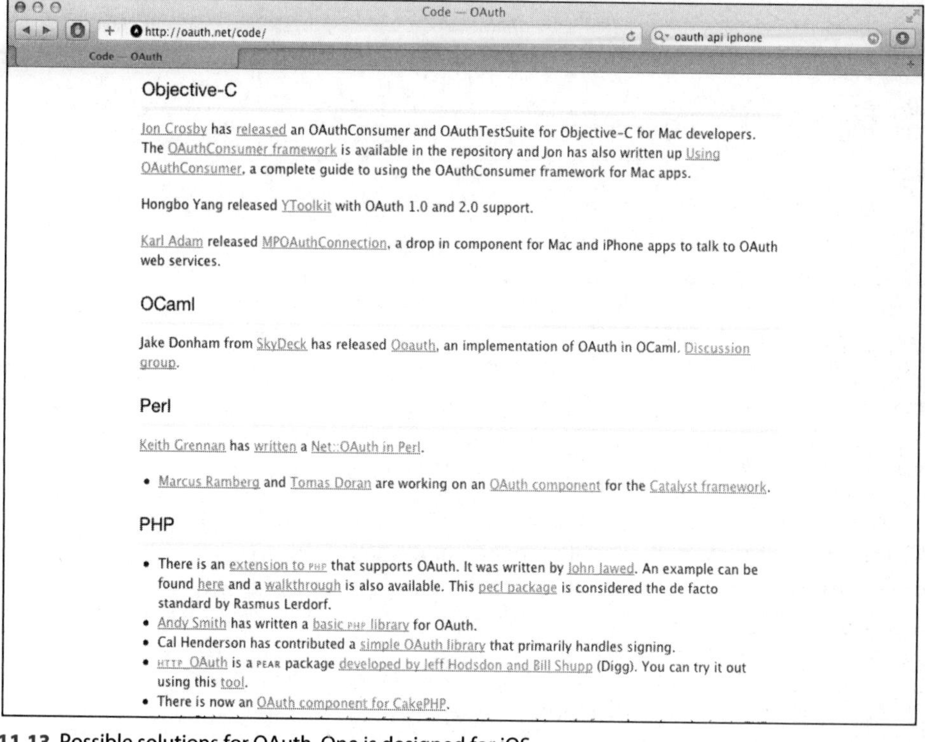

Code — OAuth
http://oauth.net/code/
oauth api iphone
Code — OAuth
Objective-C
Jon Crosby has released an OAuthConsumer and OAuthTestSuite for Objective-C for Mac developers. The OAuthConsumer framework is available in the repository and Jon has also written up Using OAuthConsumer, a complete guide to using the OAuthConsumer framework for Mac apps.
Hongbo Yang released YToolkit with OAuth 1.0 and 2.0 support.
Karl Adam released MPOAuthConnection, a drop in component for Mac and iPhone apps to talk to OAuth web services.
OCaml
Jake Donham from SkyDeck has released Ooauth, an implementation of OAuth in OCaml. Discussion group.
Perl
Keith Grennan has written a Net::OAuth in Perl.
• Marcus Ramberg and Tomas Doran are working on an OAuth component for the Catalyst framework.
PHP
• There is an extension to PHP that supports OAuth. It was written by John Jawed. An example can be found here and a walkthrough is also available. This pecl package is considered the de facto standard by Rasmus Lerdorf.
• Andy Smith has written a basic PHP library for OAuth.
• Cal Henderson has contributed a simple OAuth library that primarily handles signing.
• HTTP_OAuth is a PEAR package developed by Jeff Hodsdon and Bill Shupp (Digg). You can try it out using this tool.
• There is now an OAuth component for CakePHP.

11.13 Possible solutions for OAuth. One is designed for iOS.

Creating Preferences

Many apps include a Preferences pane that appears in the Settings app, as shown in Figure 11.14. Users can access this pane to change basic settings in the app.

Internally, your app can access these preferences by loading a defaults object, like this:

```
NSUserDefaults *myDefaults = [NSUserDefaults standardUserDefaults];
```

Although NSUserDefaults isn't a subclass of NSDictionary, it holds key-value pairs in the same way. Figure 11.15 shows some of the critical tasks that can be used to get and set values.

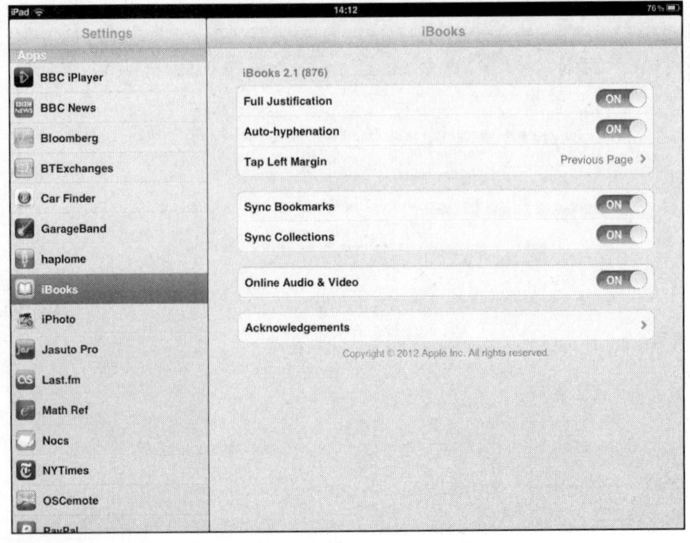

11.14 A preferences pane on the iPad. iPhone panes have identical settings but are smaller.

You work with preferences in four steps:

1. **Add a file called a Settings Bundle to your app.**
2. **Edit the file to define the settings you want to include.** The file is a plist, and you can use the standard Xcode plist editor.
3. **When your app starts, you must *register* defaults for the preferences.** You can then load them into your app wherever they're needed.
4. **You can now read and set keys in your app.** If you set a key in your app, its value is saved to the Settings Bundle. The updated value appears in the preferences the next time the user views them.

Adding and editing a Settings Bundle

To add a Settings Bundle, follow these steps:

1. **Right-click the Supporting Files group in the Project Navigator.**
2. **Select New File....**
3. **Select iOS ⇨ Resource and Settings Bundle, as shown in Figure 11.16.**
4. **Click Next, and then click Create.** The Settings Bundle is added to the project.

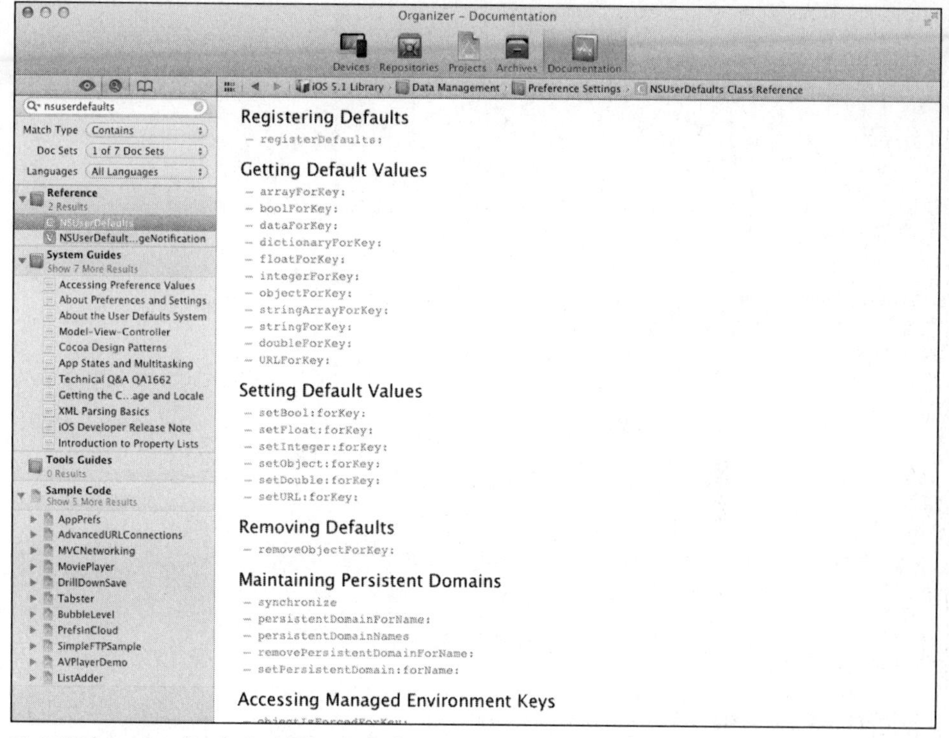

11.15 Value-related tasks for NSUserDefaults.

To add or remove items from the Settings Bundle, click the reveal triangle and the en.lproj folder, and then click the Root.plist file. This file holds the items that appear in the preferences. The following item types are available:

- **Group.** This creates a group of preferences—in other words, the preferences appear inside a rounded rectangle headed by the name of the group.
- **Multi Value.** This creates a list of values, stored in an array. The user can select one item from the list.
- **Slider, text field, toggle switch.** This creates the corresponding object.
- **Title.** This displays a text string. It can't be edited.

The organization is nested, but the default file—which you'll want to edit—includes useful examples of some of the basic types. You can use these examples to work out how to add other types you may want to include. To add and remove rows, click the "+" and "-" icons that appear when you select a row.

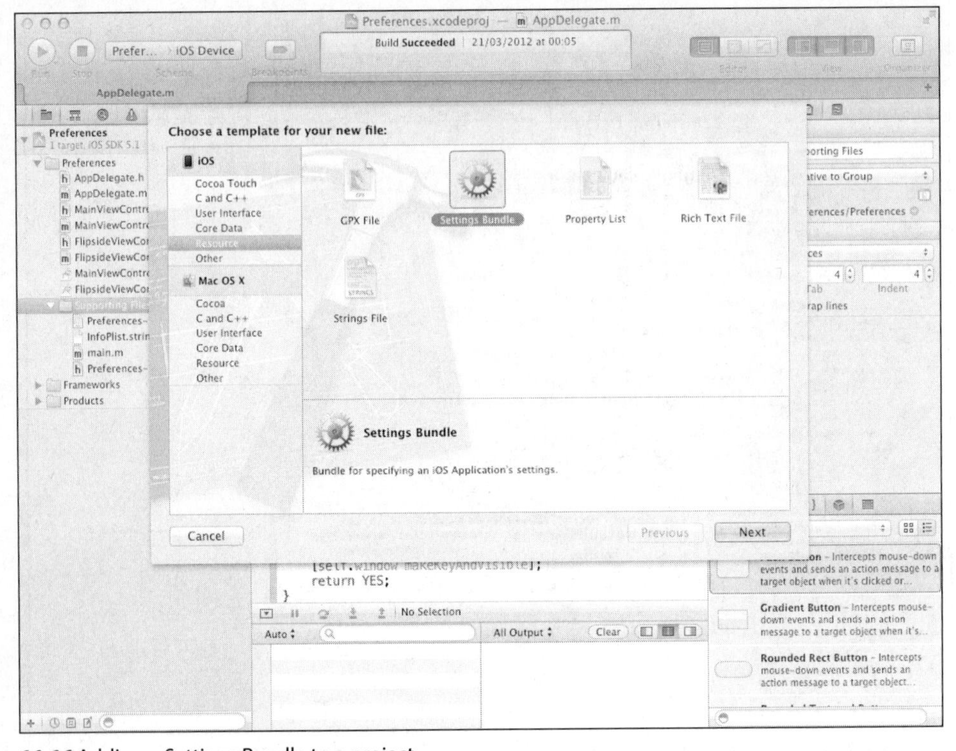

11.16 Adding a Settings Bundle to a project.

Registering preferences

Before you can use defaults in your app, you must *register* them. This makes the values accessible and makes it possible for your app to update the values if it needs to. Bizarrely, it doesn't load values into your app; you must do this in a separate operation.

Note

Registering defaults doesn't set the values back to their defaults; it tells iOS what the defaults are, so it can keep track of further changes and load the settings correctly.

To register defaults, use the following code:

```
NSUserDefaults *myDefaults = [NSUserDefaults standardUserDefaults];
NSDictionary *initDefaults = [NSDictionary dictionaryWithObjectsAndKeys: <list
   of objects and keys>];
[myDefaults registerDefaults: initDefaults];
```

The list of objects and keys matches the names and value types you added to the Root.plist file. Figure 11.17 shows some sample code. The list of values and keys in your app will be different.

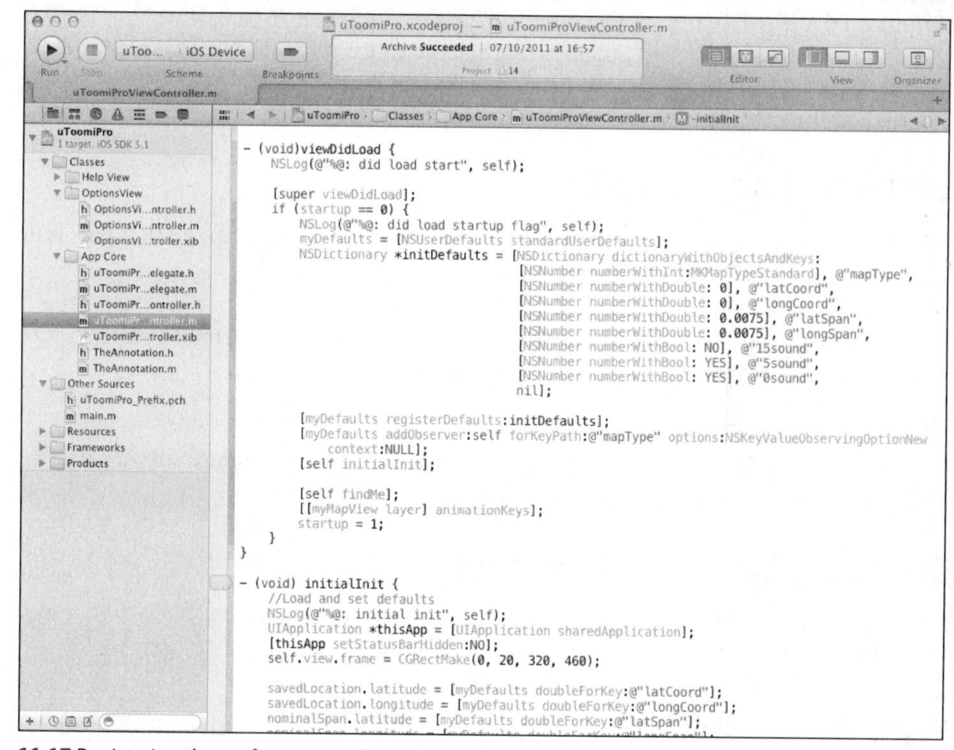

11.17 Registering the preferences and setting defaults.

Accessing and setting values

After registration, you can read and set values in myDefaults just as you would access keys in a dictionary. For example:

```
someValue = [myDefaults: aValueForKey: @"SomeKey"];
[myDefaults setValue: aValueForKey forKey: @"SomeKey"];
```

Unlike a dictionary, values are written to the Settings Bundle as soon as you set them. You don't need to save the defaults again as your app quits.

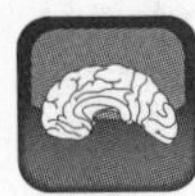

Genius

Although it's not recommended practice, you're not limited to storing preferences in myDefaults. You can write and then read any key-value pair you want. It doesn't have to have a corresponding entry in the preferences pane. This makes myDefaults useful as a temporary data store that you can access without having to specify a full file path and name.

Localizing Apps

You can improve app sales by providing local translations of the text and labeled UI elements in your app. This process is called *localization*. There are two elements:

- **A file called Localized.strings provides support for general text, including alert messages.** Optionally, it also can manage labeled UI elements.
- **You can create localized versions of nib files.** The localized nib can include text labels and other text elements that are pre-translated. It also may need to include size adjustments to allow for the different width of text in each language.

Creating Localized.strings

If you want to support multiple languages, you must add a file called Localized.strings to your app. Follow these steps:

1. **Right-click the Supporting Files group in the Project navigator.**
2. **Select New File....**
3. **Select iOS ⇨ Resource and Strings File, as shown in Figure 11.18.**
4. **Save the file as "Localizable.strings".** No other name will work.
5. **Select the file, and open the Utilities pane at the right if it isn't already open.**
6. **Select the File inspector in the Utilities pane, if it isn't already visible.**
7. **Open the Localization sub-pane.**
8. **Click the "+" icon, and select English.**
9. **Click the "+" icon again, and add as many further languages as you want your app to support.**

Using Localized.strings

The contents of each Localized.strings file pairs keys with strings, like this:

```
"TopLabel" = "This is the top label text";
```

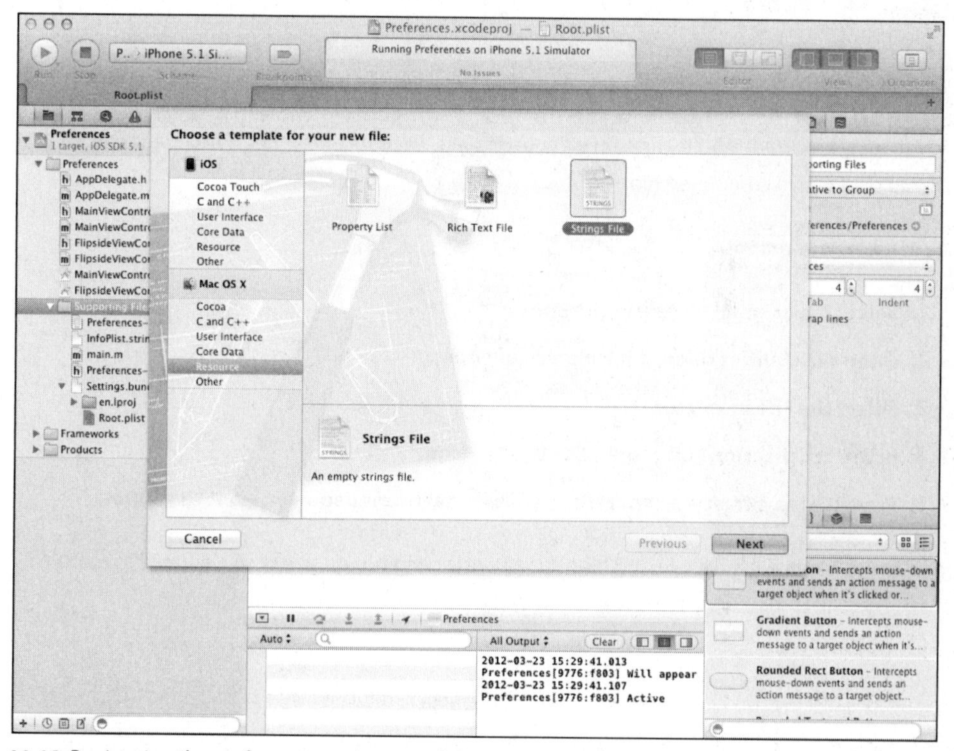

11.18 Registering the preferences and setting defaults.

Each language has its own file. The TopLabel key remains the same, but you replace "This is the top label text" with the corresponding translation.

To display the localized text, use NSLocalizedString, which is a macro (a piece of pre-packaged code) and not an object.

```
NSString *topLabelString = NSLocalizedString(@"TopLabel", nil);
```

Adding this macro automatically pulls the required string for each key out of the Localized.strings file that matches the language setting of the device.

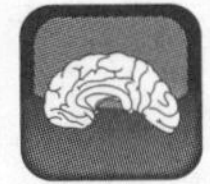

Genius

Extracting every text string from your project can take a while. The iOS SDK includes an optional helper application called Genstrings that automates the process. Look for Genstrings online.

Creating localized nib files

To create a localized nib file, first finish your project. Each localized file is independent, so you should start with a completed nib.

Next, follow these steps:

1. **Select the original nib file in the Editor.**
2. **Open the Utilities pane, if it isn't already open.**
3. **Select the File inspector.**
4. **In the Localization sub-pane, click the "+" icon.**
5. **Repeat Step 4 to add a separate nib file for each language you want to support.**

You can now edit each file by hand, translating and changing the size of UI elements as required.

How Do I Test and Fix My App?

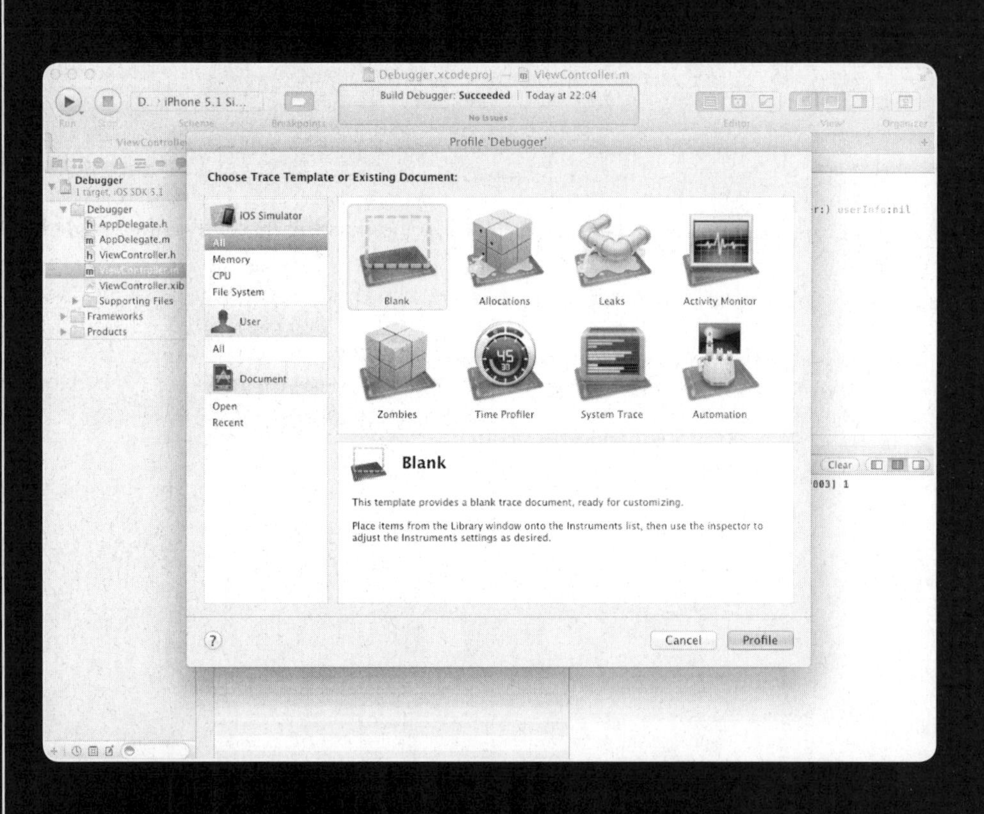

Testing an app means two things. Users have to be comfortable with it, and they have to find it easy to work with—or play with. But as a developer, it's also your responsibility to make sure your apps work reliably. If an app loses data or crashes, it inconveniences users and creates a bad impression. Xcode includes testing and profiling tools that can help you track down and fix basic errors in your code. You can use these tools to make your app as reliable as possible before you upload it to the App Store.

Testing Apps

It's impossible to develop a non-trivial app without making any mistakes. Broadly, there are three common problems in code:

- **The code works, but the app doesn't do what a typical user expects it to.** This is a design problem.
- **The code doesn't work.** You expect your code to do something, but it does something else. A feature may not work as expected, or it may not allow the user to do what they want to.
- **The app crashes.** Technically, this is an example of code not working. But the results are more obvious and damaging.

User-testing your app

A UI isn't just an interface to your app; it also guides the user's expectations of your app. When the features of an app match a user's expectations, the design is called "intuitive." The user makes little or no conscious effort to find critical features, understand them, and benefit from them.

Avoiding unintuitive design

Hidden features, features that are difficult to access, and features that work in an unexpected way are all "unintuitive." If the UI is overly complex and has too many unrelated options, users won't enjoy working or playing with your app. They'll also be less likely to recommend it to others.

Note that intuitive design doesn't mean the app has to be trivial to use. The features of the famously successful Angry Birds game, shown in Figure 12.1, are very easy to understand, but that doesn't mean the game is trivially easy to play.

Note

Note also how the cartoon graphics and the music help create a strong look and feel for Angry Birds. Although the design features aren't difficult to code, a game with the same basic code features—but cruder graphics—would be less appealing.

Unfortunately for users, developers literally don't think in the same way as non-technical users. Their expectations of intuitive behavior are different. If your background includes years of technical experience, it can be very difficult to imagine the needs of a less-skilled and experienced user.

But it's critically important to design your app so that it appeals to as many people as possible—not just to you. Features that seem self-evident to you may baffle other users. Also keep in mind that users come from many different backgrounds, and their needs may not be the same as yours.

12.1 Angry Birds—an intuitive design for a difficult game.

Getting user feedback

The best way to check whether your app is intuitive is to hand it out to as many testers as possible and listen honestly to their feedback. You'll certainly be surprised by some of their comments. But this kind of open testing is critical to successful development.

Don't try to do all the testing yourself. Even if your code works correctly, your design may still confuse or frustrate users. If you're attempting to create a commercial app, it's better to discover and fix possible user satisfaction issues well before the app goes on sale.

If you can find a good mix of testers, concentrate on common issues, not outliers. If one user is very unhappy about a design feature but a majority of users aren't, it's more likely your design is good. Pay more attention when the numbers are reversed.

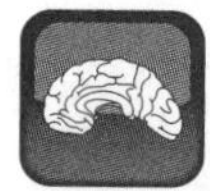

Genius

Apps that do well in the App Store often sell well to teenagers—a huge market. If you make a clever app that's too complex for average users, you're eliminating a large number of possible sales. Depending on the target audience, this may not be a bad thing—but it's a factor to consider.

Introducing test builds

You can't distribute a test build through the App Store. Because iOS is a secure environment, you must use a somewhat complex distribution system based on a technology called *ad hoc provisioning*. Ad hoc distribution bundles a version of your app with a "key" that locks it to a list of devices. Testers can run your test build only if their device is on the list.

You must create the list and the key manually. In outline, the process works like this:

1. **Collect the UDIDs (unique device identifiers) of the devices owned by your testers.** Users can find their UDIDs in iTunes.
2. **Use the list of UDIDs to create a special provisioning profile ("key") for your app on the Provisioning Portal.** You can access the Provisioning Portal by logging in to the iOS Developer Portal.

Note

You must sign up for the iOS Developer Program to use this feature.

3. **Download the profile file, and install it in Xcode.**
4. **Create a special build of your app, using the profile.**
5. **Upload your app to a web page.** Embed it in the web page with some special code.
6. **Email the URL of the page to your testers.** They can then download and install the app "over the air" by loading the URL in Safari.

For more details, see Chapter 13, which explains how to build apps for testing and for final distribution through the App Store.

Getting started with debugging

Testers can give you useful feedback about design problems. They may also discover more basic problems with crashes and features that don't work as they should.

Getting useful feedback about code issues can be difficult. Some bugs are easy to reproduce and will always appear after a set sequence of operations. Others are harder to track down and will appear only sporadically. Testers may not always be able to reproduce bugs, but you should still listen if they report a problem.

It's up to you to find and fix these basic problems in your code.

Note

On the App Store, the bar for app reliability is surprisingly low. Many commercial apps crash regularly. Apple tests apps for basic functionality, and if an app crashes immediately, it's rejected. But some apps crash only after they've been running for some time or in very specific and limited circumstances. Apple's cursory testing doesn't usually find these problems. But this doesn't mean you can ignore these issues. Users will give your app poor feedback if it crashes too often, and it's better to make a good initial impression.

Caution

Testing is difficult and time-consuming. Expect to spend between a third and a half of the total development time fixing problems!

Xcode includes two tools for testing:

- **The Debugger.** This tools "freezes" your app as it's running. You can check variable values and object properties, step through code line by line, and then restart the app so it continues to run normally.
- **Instruments.** You can use this tool, which is shown in Figure 12.2, to literally "x-ray" your app as it's running. You can list the objects in memory, check when objects are created and destroyed, and monitor the performance of your app.

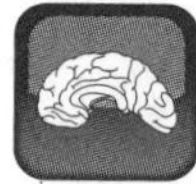

Genius

Xcode includes further options for more advanced developers. *Unit Tests* compare the values produced by code with expected values. *Scripting and automation* can feed events into an app to simulate user interaction. These powerful features come into their own in more complex projects. For details, see the *Xcode* in Wiley's Developer Reference series.

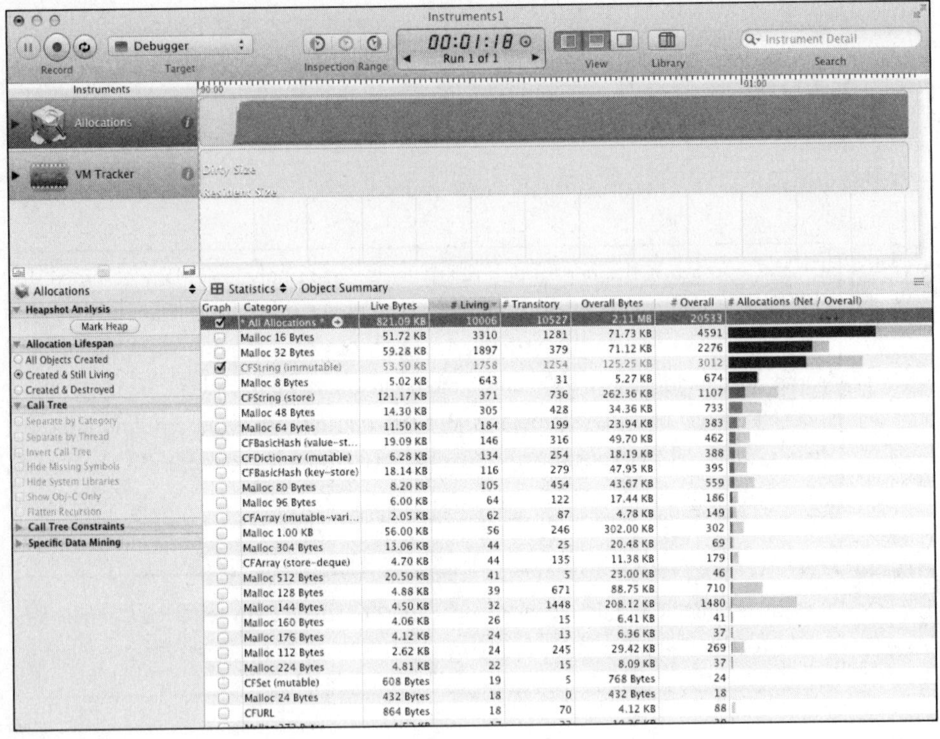

12.2 A first look at Instruments in Xcode.

Using the Xcode Debugger

You can use the debugger to do the following:

- **Pause your app at any line of code.**
- **Pause your app if a condition is true.**
- **Step through code line by line.**
- **Skip over methods and functions.**
- **While the app is paused, view variables, objects, and memory.**

The debugger is built into Xcode. You don't need to modify your code to use it. But you do need to set one or more *breakpoints*, or pause locations.

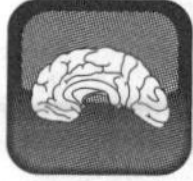

Genius

Breakpoints have many powerful options. You can set them to play a sound, run an external script, or generate a log message—among other options. Most of these options are specialized, and you don't need them for basic debugging. But it's useful to know that they're available.

Breakpoints can be unconditional or conditional. Xcode always pauses at an unconditional breakpoint, but pauses at a conditional breakpoint only if a condition you specify is true. For example, you may want to pause your app on the last repeat of a loop.

Adding a breakpoint

We'll create a basic test app to explore breakpoints and debugging. Create a new Single View Application, and save it as "Debugger." Modify the ViewController.m file as follows:

```
@implementation ViewController
int itemCount;
NSTimer *theTimer;
NSMutableArray *anArray;

-(void) viewDidLoad {
     [super viewDidLoad];
     anArray = [[NSMutableArray alloc] init];
     theTimer = [NSTimer scheduledTimerWithTimeInterval: 1.0
                                                 target: self
                                               selector: @selector(doTimer:)
                                               userInfo: nil
                                                repeats: YES];
}

-(void) doTimer: (NSTimer *) theTimer {
     itemCount++;
     NSLog (@"%i", itemCount);
     [anArray insertObject[NSString stringWithFormat:
                        @"%i", itemCount] atIndex: 0];
}
```

The finished code is shown in Figure 12.3. It creates a mutable array and a timer, and it adds a new string to the array on every timer tick.

The string is created using NSString's stringWithFormat: method. It converts the integer counter into an ASCII digit string. There's no stop condition for the timer, so the app will run indefinitely—at least until it runs out of memory.

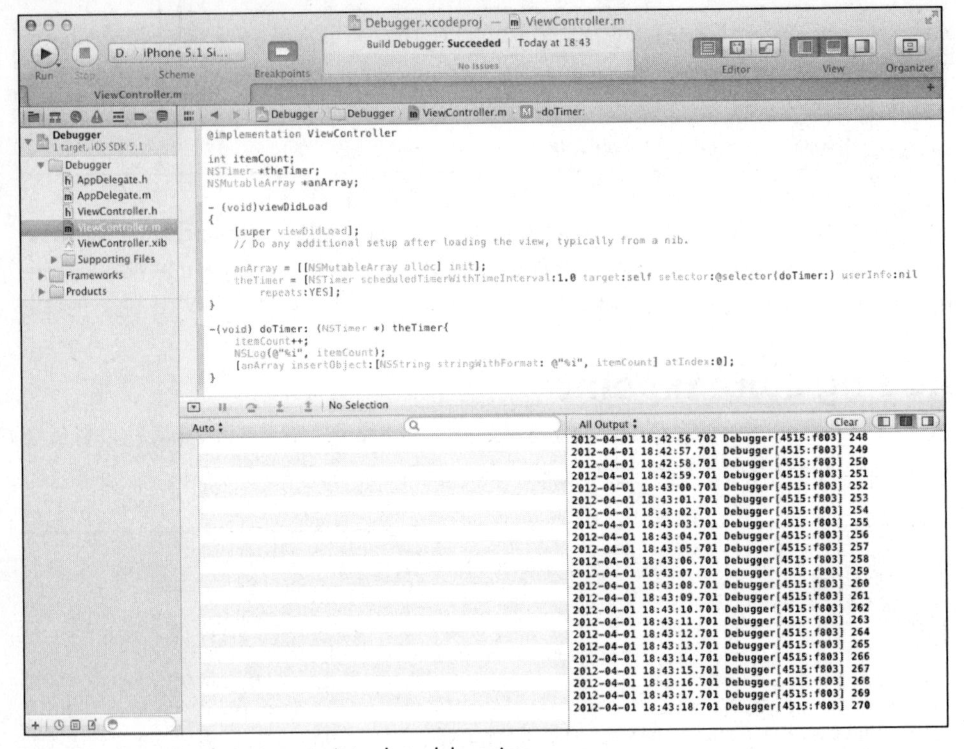

12.3 Creating a simple test app to introduce debugging.

To add a breakpoint, click in the gutter to the left of the code, as shown in Figure 12.4. In this example, we'll add a breakpoint at the start of the timer handler.

You'll see that two things happen:

- **A blue arrow icon appears in the gutter.** This tells you that a breakpoint exists at that line, and Xcode will pause your code when it reaches it.
- **The Breakpoints icon in the main Xcode toolbar is inverted.** This is a master switch that turns breakpoints on and off. When the switch is off, breakpoints are ignored. When it's on—or inverted—Xcode pauses whenever it reaches a breakpoint.

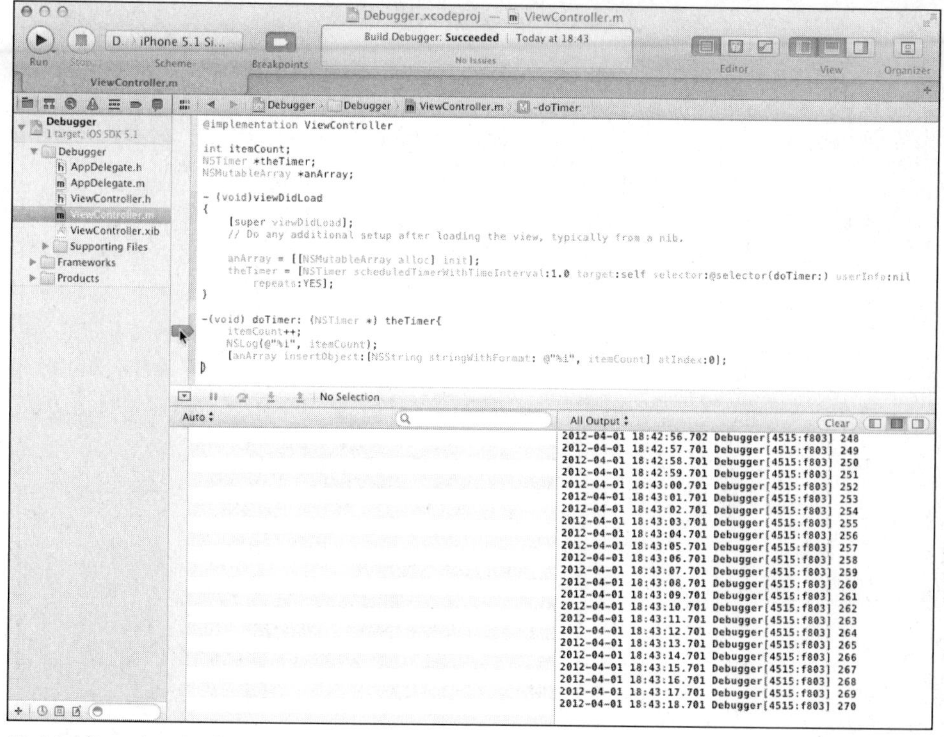

12.4 Adding a breakpoint.

Make sure that Breakpoints are enabled, and build the app. You'll see that it loads into the Simulator or a device in the usual way; debugging works equally well with either option. The app launches, the usual gray window appears, and then Xcode pauses as shown in Figure 12.5.

The breakpoint line is highlighted in light green, and a slightly darker arrowhead appears in the gutter to further emphasize the line at which Xcode has paused.

A debug window appears automatically at the bottom of the screen. It's split into two parts. On the right is the usual log area, which we've been using throughout this book. When the app generates a log message, it appears here in the usual way.

On the left is a new window, which shows a list of current objects. In this example, you can see the view controller object, the timer, and the itemCount int variable.

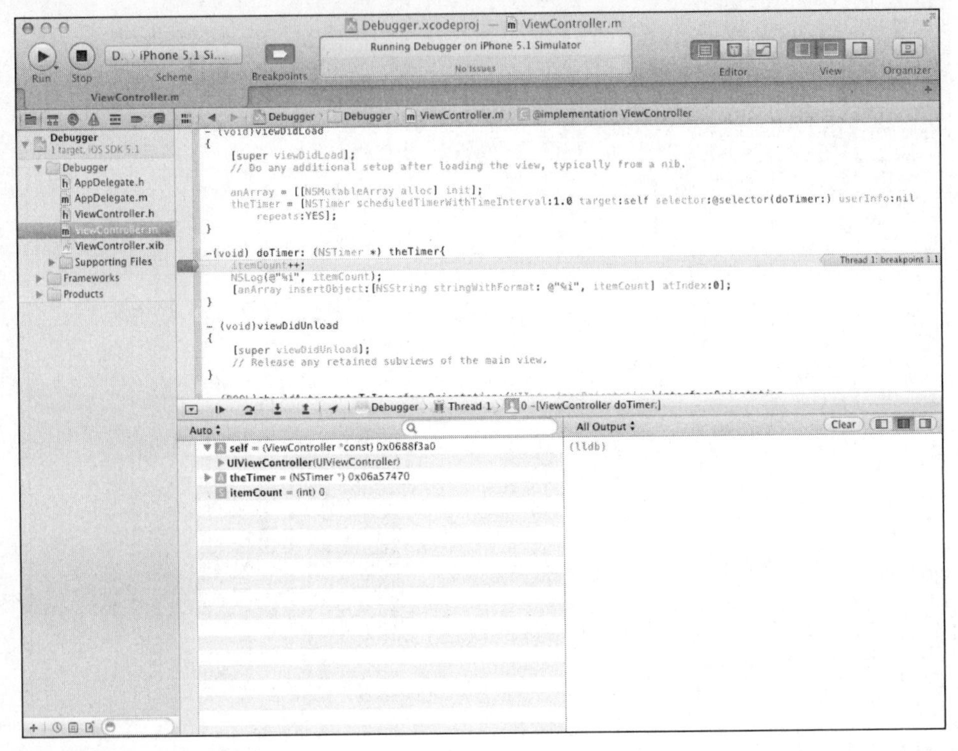

12.5 Pausing at a breakpoint.

Stepping through code

Halfway up the window, you'll see a list of icons. From left to right, you can use these to do the following:

- **Hide the debug area.** Clicking this icon hides the two lower areas and moves the debug icon bar to the bottom of the window.
- **Continue.** Click this icon to end the pause and continue the run. Your app will continue running until you quit it or it hits another breakpoint (or until it hits the same breakpoint again).
- **Step over a line of code.** This doesn't mean the code is ignored; it means the line runs in its entirety. If the code includes a function, Xcode runs the function and pauses after it returns.

Genius

You can use this feature to get to the result of a function like CGMakePoint without having to step through it line by line. You can also use it to skip over the code generated by the @synthesize directive.

- **Step into a line of code.** Click this to run the current line of code. You can also use it to step into a function and start running it line by line, if you want to see what it's doing internally.
- **Step out of a function.** Click this to run to the end of the current function, if there is one.

Caution

If you click Step Out when you're not inside a function, the debugger takes you into the internals of iOS. You'll see lines and lines of hexadecimal addresses and terse instructions in *assembler*—the simplest readable computer language. You can't do much after you're in iOS, so click the Continue icon to restart the app.

- **Set a location.** This is a special "bonus" feature of the debugger. If your app uses the GPS, you can click the GPS arrow icon to send it a location message. (This is particularly useful in the Simulator.)

Viewing objects, variables, and memory

When an app is paused, you can view objects and variables in two ways. The obvious way is to use the listing in the lower-left window. You can click the reveal triangles to the left of each object to "open" it and view its properties. Because C-type variables don't have properties, they don't have a reveal triangle. They show a single value preceded by a type specifier.

Using the variables and objects view

Figure 12.6 shows a typical display. In this example, the log messages at the right show how many times the timer has fired and the timer handler method has run. At the left, there's a jumble of objects and properties. You can see that the itemCount int now has a value of 10. But the rest of the information is less useful; it's mostly just a list of pointers and unfamiliar object internals.

You'll find that this view either shows too much detail or too little. If you click the reveal triangle to the left of the UIViewController object, you'll see a huge list of properties, each of which has a further list of sub-properties. It can be useful to view these properties after you have more experience working with iOS. But lots of the information is unnecessary; it's used exclusively by iOS for its own housekeeping.

At the other extreme, you'll see that even if you click every reveal triangle of the NSArray object, you still won't be able to see a list of the strings your code has stored inside it.

Data collection objects don't display their contents in this window. This is unhelpful, but there is a workaround, as shown in Figure 12.7. Right-click an object, and select the Print Description of... menu item. This calls the "description" method on the object. For data collection objects, this logs their contents to the debug window. (For other objects, the results vary.)

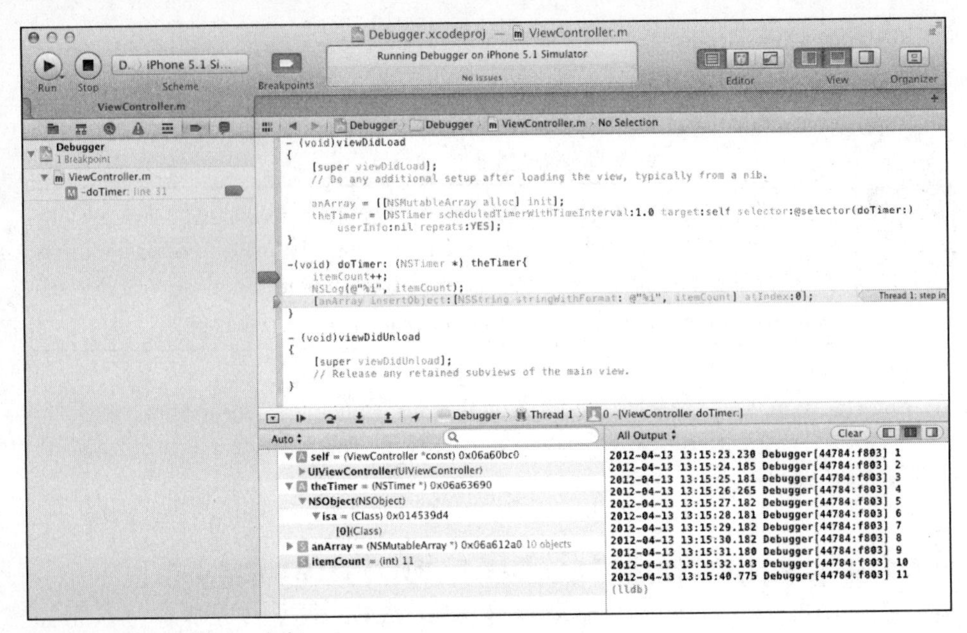

12.6 Viewing variables and objects.

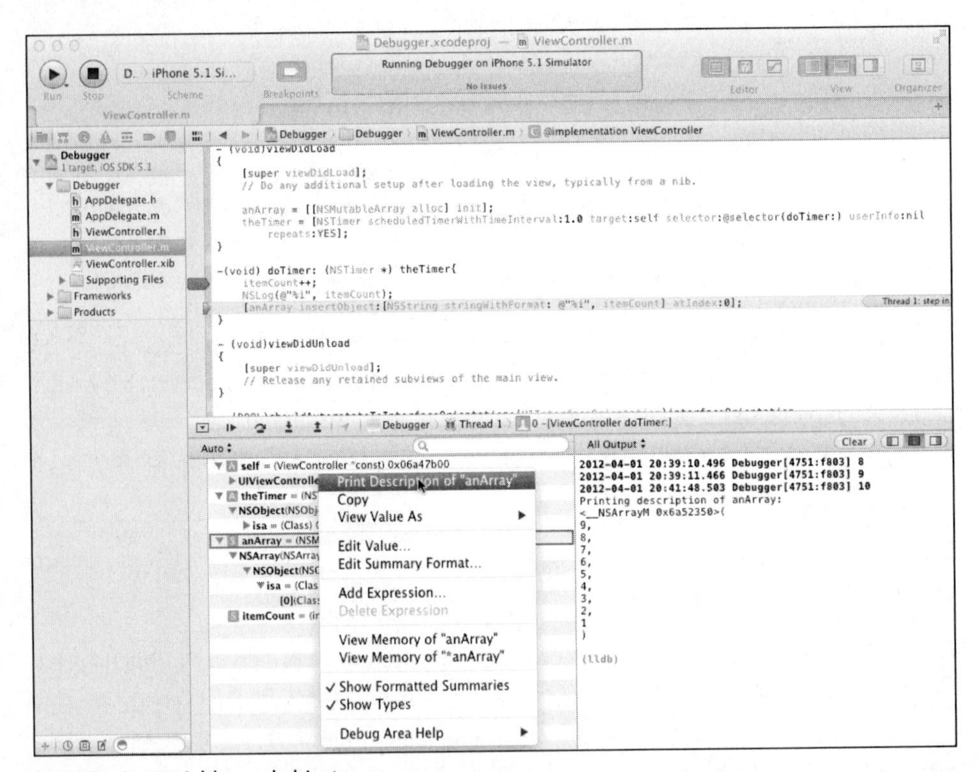

12.7 Viewing variables and objects.

Hovering over objects and variables

The other way to check values and properties is to hover the mouse over an object or variable in the code. Xcode displays the contents, as shown in Figure 12.8.

The same restrictions apply. C-type variables are displayed in a useful way, but objects either show very little useful information or a complete list of properties with too much detail.

This can be a quick way to view values in a complex project where the complete list of objects and values doesn't fit into the lower-left display.

Caution

Getting an object to reveal its properties can be tricky. In theory, you should just be able to hover over it. In practice, the selection and display process doesn't work very consistently. You may need to hover over the object and display its contents by clicking a gray triangle that appears to its right.

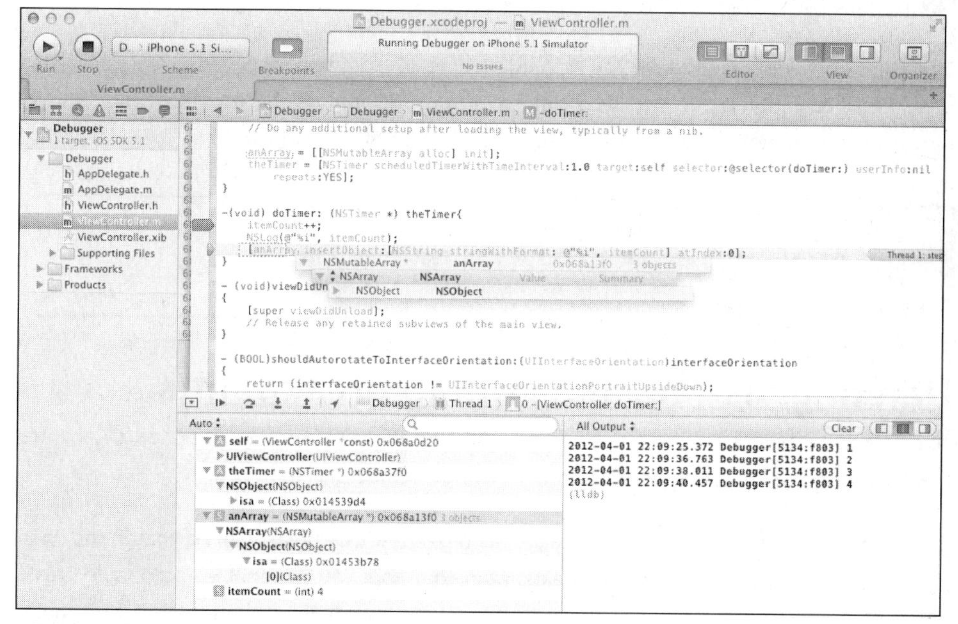

12.8 Using the hover method to display values.

Creating conditional breakpoints

To set a conditional breakpoint, right-click it and select Edit from the floating menu. You'll see the pop-up shown in Figure 12.9. To set a condition, type it using the usual syntax, but don't add a semicolon to the end. For loops, you can also set an ignore counter. The breakpoint becomes active only after the ignore count is exceeded.

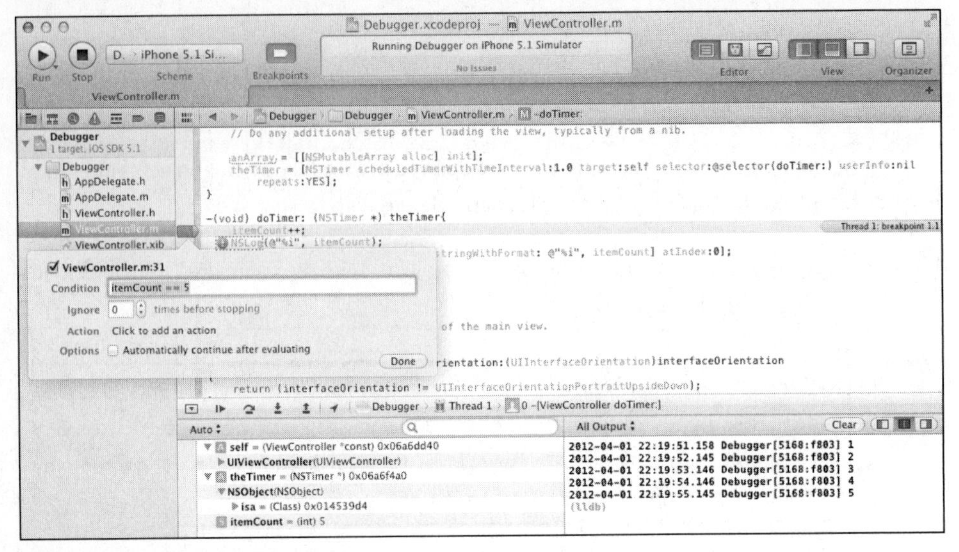

12.9 Creating a conditional breakpoint.

Conditional breakpoints can save you debugging time. It's common for code to create problems only when a condition is true. With a conditional breakpoint, you can check for that condition and bypass the breakpoint on the tens, hundreds, or thousands of other repeats.

Caution

Don't forget to use "==" instead of "=" to test for equality.

Deleting, listing, and editing breakpoints

To delete or disable a breakpoint, right-click it and select the Delete or Disable option. Disabling a breakpoint turns it off but keeps its settings. Deleting it removes all trace of it.

In a complex app, it's useful to keep breakpoints organized. The Breakpoint navigator, shown in Figure 12.10, displays a list of every breakpoint in your app. You can enable and disable breakpoints by clicking the blue arrows in the list, and you can change the settings of each breakpoint by right-clicking it.

You also can bulk-disable or bulk-delete all breakpoints by right-clicking the blue app name at the top of the list and selecting the Disable or Delete options.

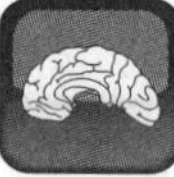

Genius

Click the word "action" to add an action label to add extra behaviors to a breakpoint. Click the Debugger Command item to select a behavior from a menu. Although it's not obvious, the debugger accepts text commands. (See lldb.llvm.org/tutorial.html for an introduction.) Advanced developers can combine AppleScript with text commands and optional further features to create very sophisticated behaviors. For example, you might use a script to send yourself an email when a certain breakpoint is triggered.

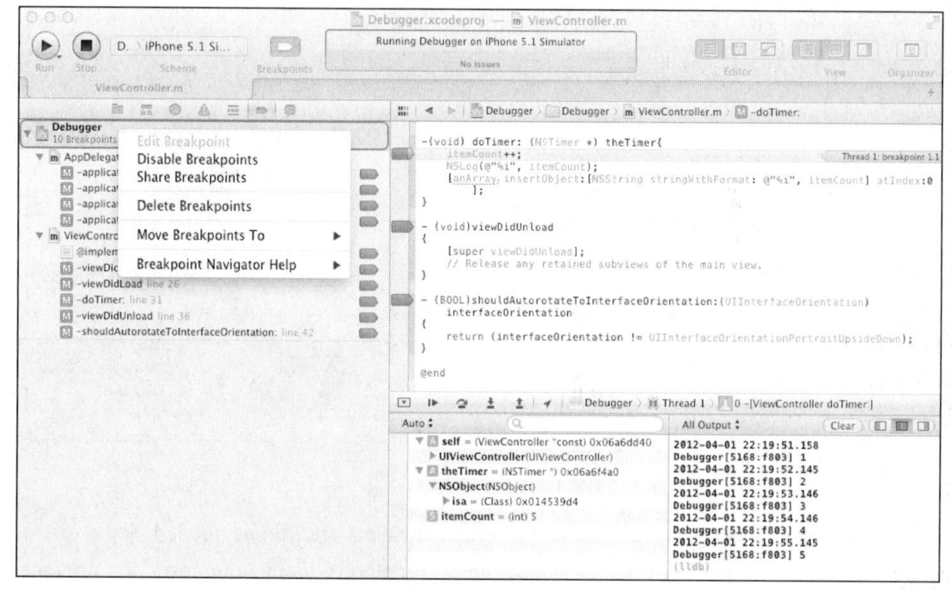

12.10 Reviewing all breakpoints in the Breakpoint navigator.

Getting Started with Instruments

Instruments is a real-time profiling tool that gives you useful information about your app as it's running. Instruments is a complex application with many features. You can use it for iOS and OS X development, and you can even use it to "look inside" existing Mac applications. Figure 12.11 shows Instruments monitoring CPU and memory performance of a Mac.

Caution

"Profiling" in this sense isn't related to "provisioning profiles." The profiles created by Instruments give you a statistical snapshot of your app's performance. A provisioning profile is completely different; it's a digital key that makes it possible to run your app on a real device. There is no connection between the two.

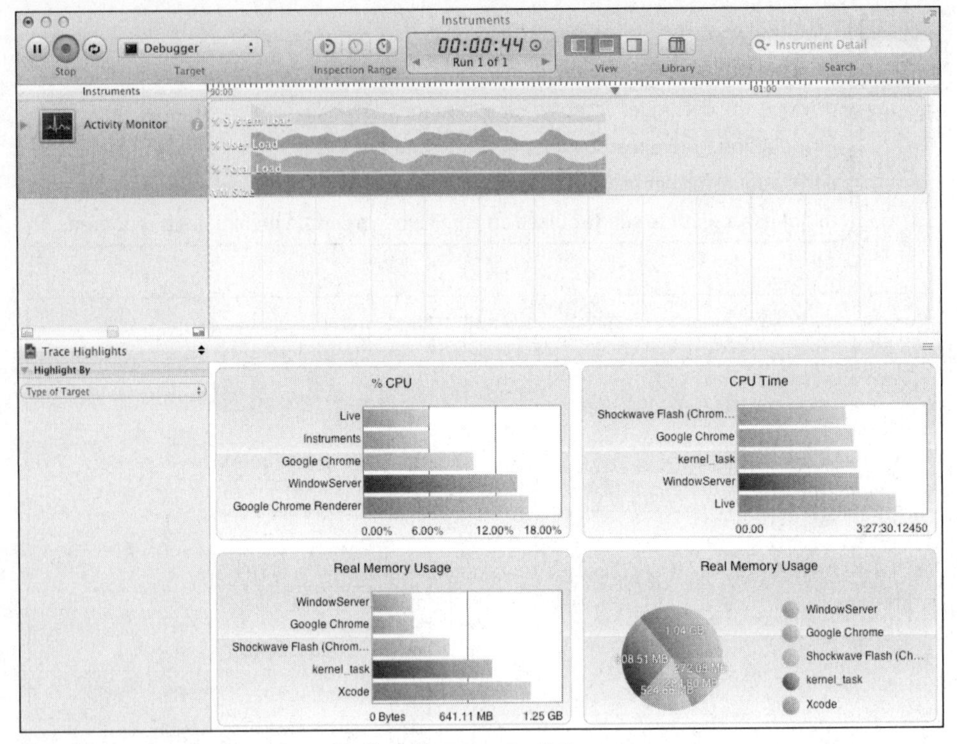

12.11 Using Instruments to view a Mac's performance statistics.

Instruments is a bag of tools—"Instruments"—you can select and run as needed. Some instruments use a live timeline that updates as your app is running to graph your app's performance. You can record the data on the timeline and review it later.

Although you can use Instruments to check CPU and file system performance, Instruments is most often used to diagnose memory issues—or at least, it used to be. Now that memory management (mostly…) just works with ARC, as described in Chapter 11, Instruments can still be useful to check object allocations. But it isn't quite as essential as it was when memory was managed manually. In the rest of this section, we'll use Instruments to view the objects and memory used in an app, and we'll discover how to make sense of the information.

Running Instruments

There are two ways to run Instruments. One way is used for more general development and for profiling Mac applications. The other is specific to iOS projects. Although you won't usually use the first method for app development, it's useful to know that it exists.

Launching Instruments manually

Select Xcode ⇨ Open Developer Tool ⇨ Instruments, as shown in Figure 12.12. You'll see a list of options for iOS, the Simulator, and OS X. Feel free to experiment with these options. You can't break your app, but most of these options are tangential to app development, so we won't say more about them here.

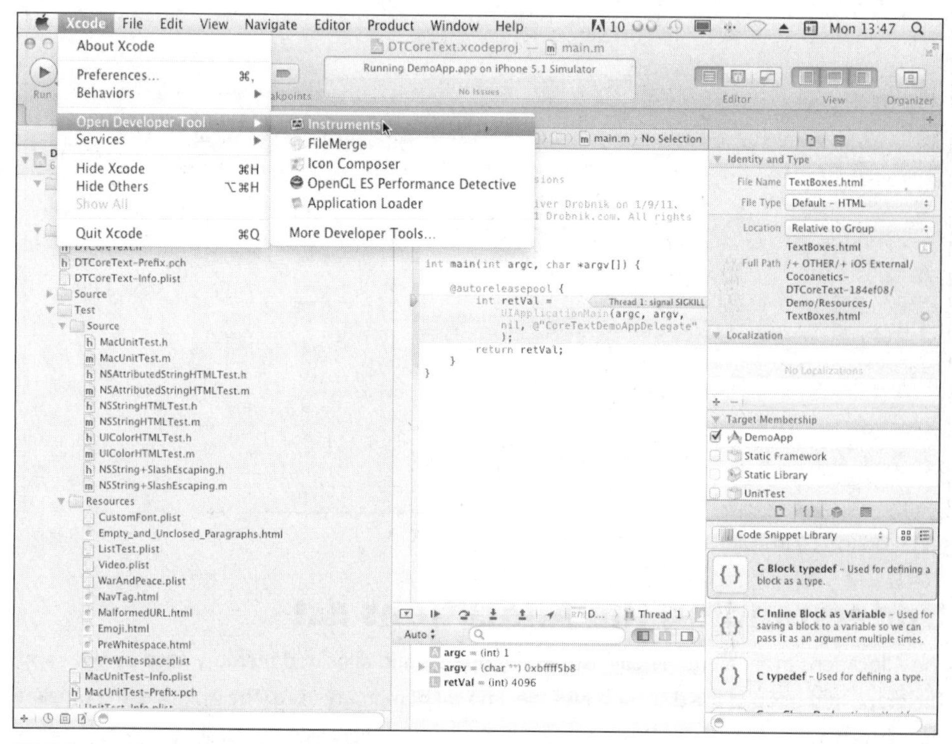

12.12 Launching Instruments manually.

Launching Instruments for app profiling

Let's profile the test app we created to demonstrate debugging. Don't change any of the code. Select Product ⇨ Profile in the main Xcode menu. This builds your app (if it hasn't already been built), launches Instruments, and creates a link between the two so Instruments can collect statistics from your app as it's running.

To view object and memory allocations, select the Allocations icon and click Profile in the lower-right corner. After a while, you'll see the graph and list shown in Figure 12.13.

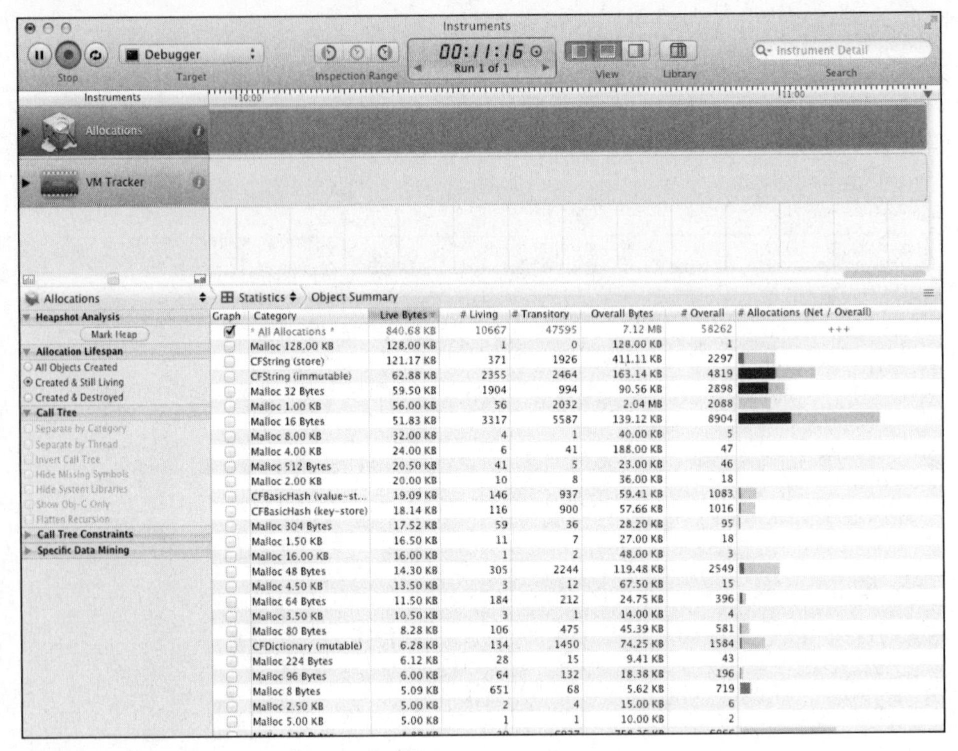

12.13 Launching Instruments for app profiling.

Understanding the Allocations list

The Allocations Instrument literally lists all the objects and allocated memory used by your app. The graph at the top of the display shows the amount of memory used. The list under the timeline shows every type of object or data type used in the app. Each entry in the list shows the number of objects or data types that are in memory, with a total memory count.

You can rearrange the list by clicking each column header. For example, Figure 12.14 shows the list sorted by object/data type name.

Before you can make sense of the list, you need to know some critical facts:

- **The list shows every object, not just the objects defined in your app.** iOS creates lots of extra objects as overhead. Your app doesn't control these objects, but they still appear in the allocations list.
- **Many "objects" are displayed as their Core Foundation (C-type) equivalents.** You may think your app is using an NSArray, but under the hood, iOS is really using the

lower-level Core Foundation CFArray data type. Because many of these types are "toll-free bridged," they're practically interchangeable. To a very good approximation, you can assume that a CFArray is the same as an NSArray.

- **Some memory is allocated using C-style "malloc" instructions.** Unless you've used these instructions in your code, these allocations are internal to iOS and your app can't control them.
- **You can select the object lifespan using a radio button group at the left.** You can select all objects, objects that are still in memory, or objects that were in memory but have now been destroyed.
- **The "#Living" total tells you whether objects are being created but not released.** If this number is increasing steadily, your app isn't releasing memory correctly. (In this example, you'll see that the number increases steadily because a string is being added to the array on every timer repeat. So this is expected behavior. Most apps wouldn't—or shouldn't—work like this.)

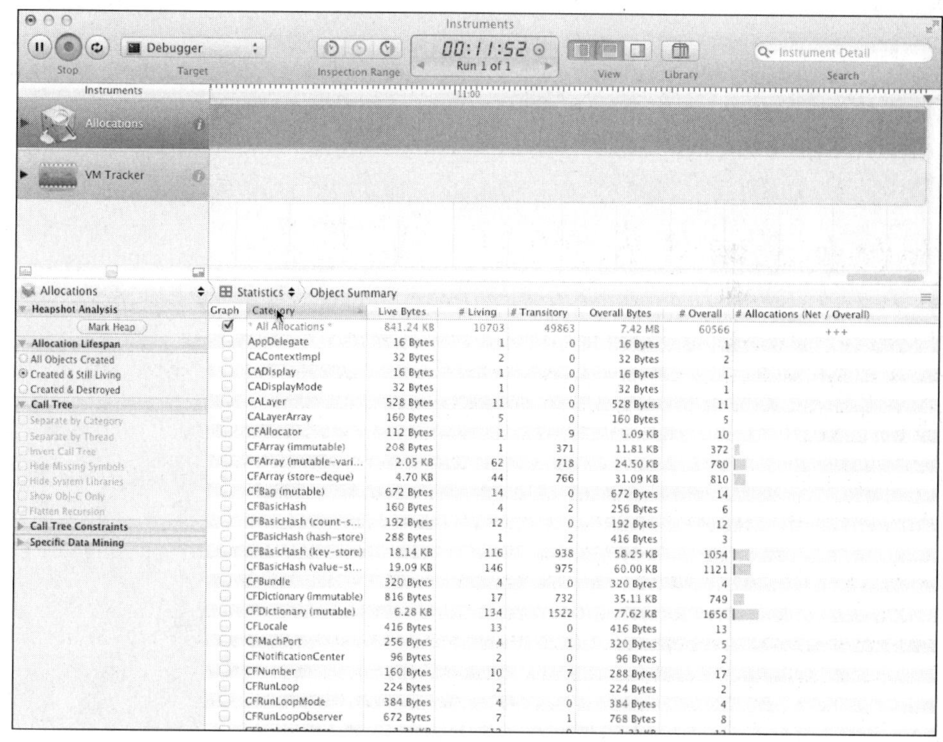

12.14 Listing the objects, data types, and memory in a running app.

After you've mastered the display, this somewhat intimidating list of objects should hold no mysteries. It's an excellent diagnostic snapshot of the operation in your app. You can work with your app in the Simulator, flip screens, touch buttons, and use features, and you'll see the allocations changing in real time.

Caution

Note that iOS isn't bulletproof, and it sometimes leaks memory internally. You can't fix this in your app; you just have to live with it. For confirmation that it's really a problem with iOS and not your code, search the Stack Overflow site (stackoverflow.com) to see if other developers have had the same problem.

Caution

One further debugging feature to be aware of is the Analyze tool. To run it, select Product ➪ Analyze. The tool highlights various possible issues in your code—if there are any. It's not an infallible bug fixer, but it can suggest where code might be improved.

How Do I Distribute Apps for Sale and Testing?

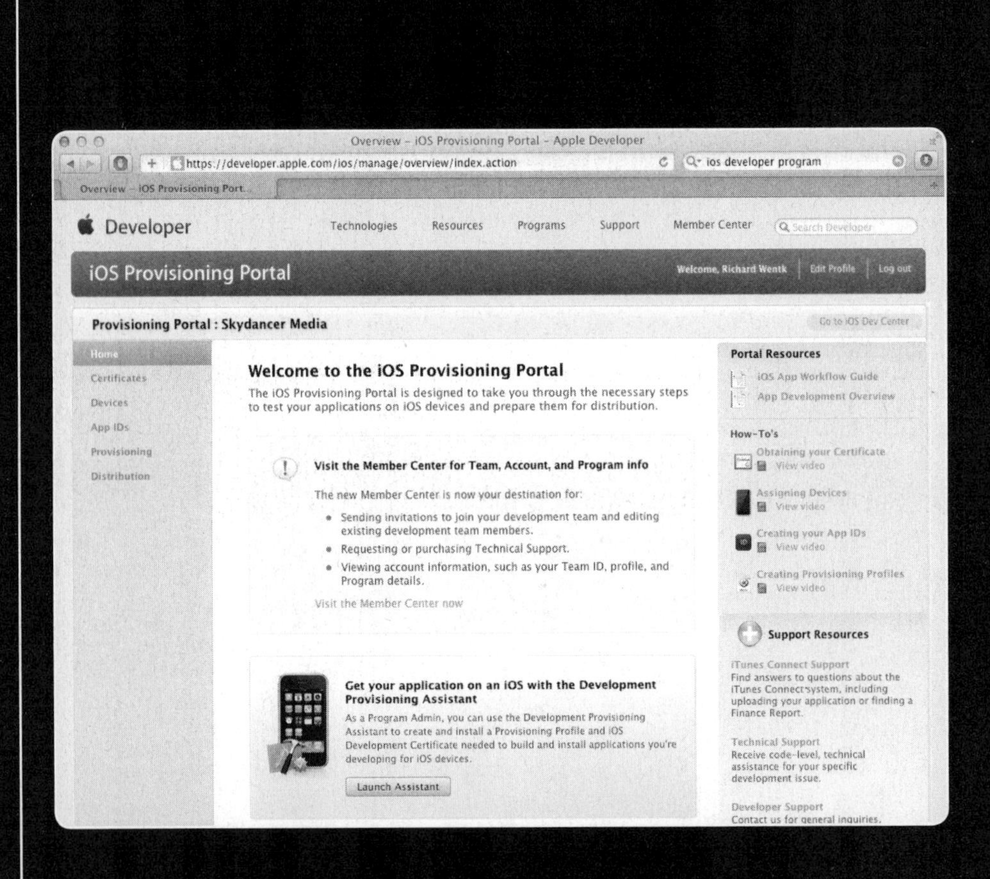

When you finish an app—or finish it enough for testing—you can distribute it to testers. After testing, you can distribute it to end-users through the App Store. Neither kind of distribution is completely straightforward, so allow plenty of time to set it up and get it working. This chapter takes you step-by-step through both types of distribution—testing, and final sale.

Understanding App Distribution

When you have completed an app, you'll want to distribute it to other users, either for testing or for sale. App distribution remains one of the more complex parts of app development. The process is neither simple nor intuitive. But you need to set it up only once.

Caution

You can distribute apps only if you're a paid-up iOS App Developer. To use the information in this chapter, you must enroll in the iOS Developer Program, as described in Chapter 1.

Caution

Your app must include both standard and HD icons and launch images before Xcode allows you to distribute it. For more details, see Chapter 10.

In outline, you can:

- **Upload your app to the App Store.** To do this, you need to create supporting "paperwork," which includes screen grabs for the store, as shown in Figure 13.1, supporting icon images, supporting marketing text, and—ideally—an external website for both marketing and support.
- **Distribute your app for testing, using Apple's "Ad Hoc" distribution system.** You can either email testers a copy of your app for installation through iTunes, or you can upload it to a website, email them the URL, and allow them to install the app from Safari—an "Over the Air" (OTA) installation.

Caution

If your app file is larger than around 10MB, it's better to distribute test copies by email. If a user tries to download the app over a cellular link instead of WiFi, it can eat into their data allowance. Apple's own limit for cellular app downloads is 20MB. You can, of course, warn users to use WiFi instead of a cellular data for the download.

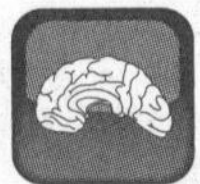

Genius

If your testers live locally and can be persuaded to lend you their devices, the easy way to give them test copies of your app is to register their devices for development in Xcode. You can then plug in their device and build your app, and Xcode will install it automatically. This is only practical for small numbers of testers, but it's much simpler and quicker than setting up full ad hoc distribution.

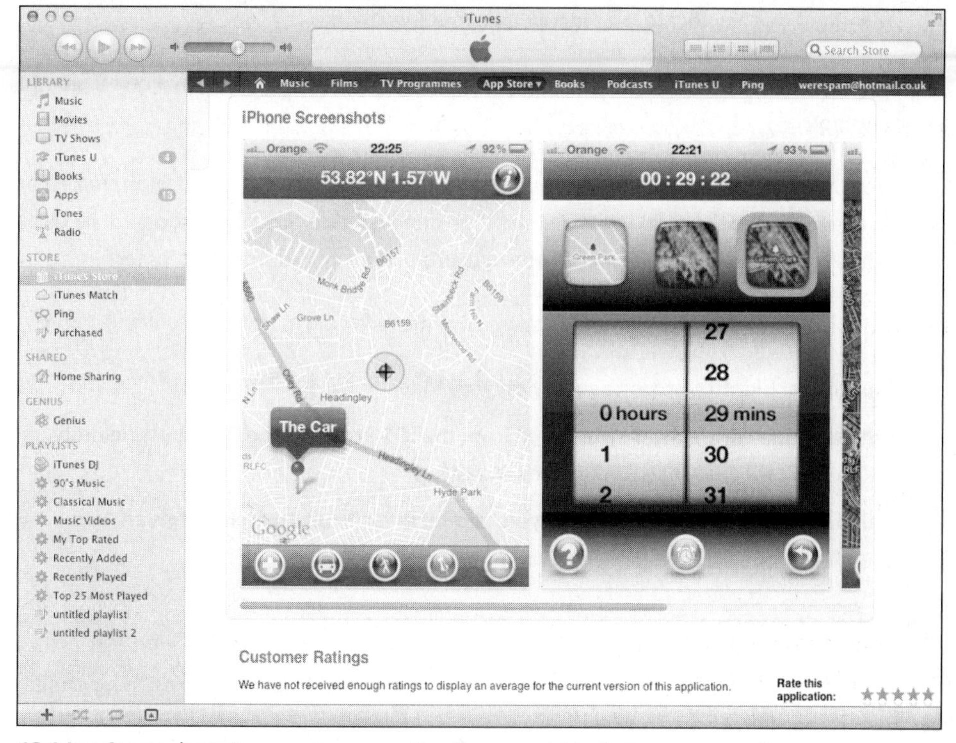

13.1 App Store submissions require supporting "paperwork", including screen grabs.

Introducing digital identities

As Chapter 3 explained, Xcode uses digital key files to control app development. When you test an app on a device, Xcode automatically generates and installs these key files for you.

Distribution permissions are more complex, because you must create and install key files manually. In this section, we'll outline the steps, and look at them in more detail later in this chapter.

In outline, the steps are as follows:

1. **Create a digital identity file.** This is a unique personal key, used as an identity check throughout the rest of the process. The key is stored in your Mac's *keychain*—a collection of security files accessed using the *Keychain Access Utility* application.
2. **Upload the digital identity file to the iOS Provisioning Portal.** Technically, this is called *creating a certificate signing request (CSR).*
3. **The portal reads your file and creates a *distribution certificate*—a file that tells Xcode you have permission to distribute apps.**

4. **Download this certificate, and install it in your keychain.**

Xcode now has the information it needs to identify you and check that you have permission to distribute apps.

But there's more work to do! For each app you distribute, you must create a *distribution profile* that includes an *app identifier*—a unique text string that identifies each app. The associated file gives you permission to upload that *one specific app* to the App Store or to distribute it for testing.

The provisioning process is complicated because all of the following must be present and correct:

- **Your digital identity, stored as a key on your Mac.**
- **A distribution certificate downloaded from the iOS Provisioning Portal.** The identity in the certificate must match your Mac's stored key.
- **A distribution profile that matches your digital identity *and* matches a given App ID with a build setting called the *bundle identifier.***

If any element is missing or incorrect, Xcode won't build your app.

If all the elements are correct, the Provisioning Portal creates a "distribution provisioning profile" that supports one type of distribution.

Note

For simplicity, we'll call these profiles "distribution profiles" in the rest of this chapter. The iOS Provisioning Portal tends to use the full "distribution provisioning profile" name for these files. But the short version means the same thing.

Getting started with distribution profiles

It would be useful if you could use a single distribution profile for testing and for App Store uploads. Unfortunately, you can't; you must create a separate profile for each. The steps for both options are similar.

1. **Create an Application ID on the iOS Provisioning Portal for the app you want to distribute.** This is a unique identifier for each app. You need to do this only once for each app. You can reuse the same ID for testing and for the App Store.
2. **For Ad Hoc distribution, collect the UDID (Unique Device Identifier) of each device used for testing and upload the UDIDs to the iOS Provisioning Portal.** You can skip this step for App Store distribution.
3. **Create the distribution profile file.** Select whether you want an App Store or Ad Hoc file.

4. **Download the file, and install it in Xcode.**
5. **Modify the build settings for your app so it uses your new distribution profile.** The app's *Bundle Identifier* must match the App ID you created earlier.
6. **Archive the App instead of building and running it.**

Caution

In this context, "archive" is another word that probably doesn't mean what you expect. An archive isn't a backup copy of the app; it's a finished app file that can be uploaded to the App Store or distributed for testing.

Creating a Digital Identity

The distribution provisioning and App Store preparation process can seem intimidating the first time you work through it. There's much to remember, and there are no shortcuts. Expect it to take between half a day and two days.

The easy way to approach the process is to work through it methodically. You can't complete later stages until you complete the earlier steps. The first step is to create a digital identity on your Mac.

Generating a certificate signing request

Although this part of the process is buried in jargon, it's simple in practice. You need to:

1. **Create a file using the Keychain Access Utility on your Mac.**
2. **Upload the file to the iOS Provisioning Portal.**

The Provisioning Portal uses the file—or more specifically, a digital key in the file—when it creates a distribution profile. When Xcode builds the app, it checks your Mac's keychain to make sure the key in the profile and the key in the keychain match. If they don't, the build process fails.

Creating a CSR file

Follow these steps:

1. **On your Mac, launch the Keychain Access Utility.** You can find it in /Applications/Utilities.
2. **Select Keychain Access ⇨ Certificate Assistant ⇨ Request a Certificate from a Certificate Authority.**
3. **Fill in the details, as shown in Figure 13.2.** Use your iOS Developer Program email address. Leave the "CA Email Address" blank. Select the "Saved to disk" option.
4. **Click Continue, and save the file to a convenient location.**

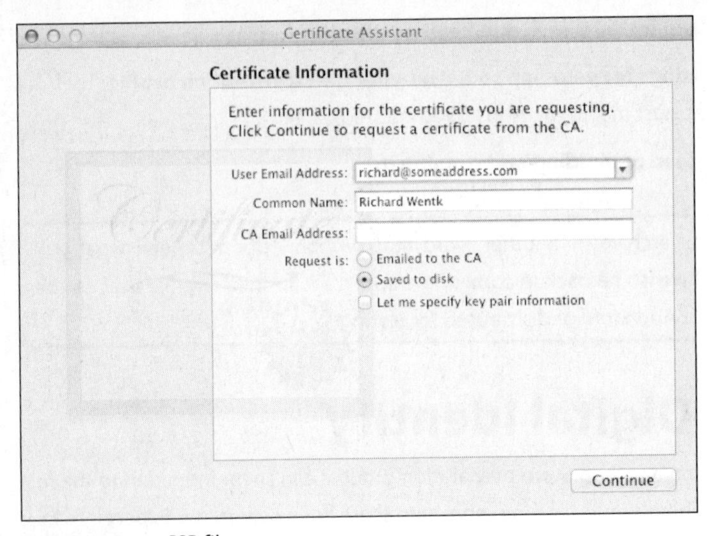

13.2 Creating a CSR file.

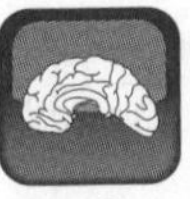

Genius

It's useful to create a folder called "Provisioning" somewhere on your Mac and use it as a single location for all your certificates and provisioning profiles.

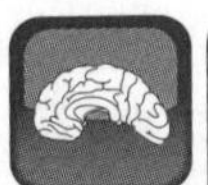

Genius

Technically, the key is linked to a specific Mac. If you move Macs or need to develop on more than one Mac, you can use the File⇨Export feature of the Keychain Assistant to export the key file to a different Mac. Xcode also includes an export/import feature for provisioning profiles in the Organizer. You can use it to duplicate your distribution privileges on more than one Mac. You can either export provisioning profiles individually or, if you have a team set up—even if you're the only person in it—you can select the TEAMS item under Devices in the Organizer and use the import/export options there.

Creating a distribution certificate

Remember that the distribution certificate is a digital key file that tells Xcode you're allowed to distribute your apps to testers and to upload them to the App Store. It isn't the only digital key you need, but it's an essential one, so you must create it before you do anything else.

Follow these steps:

1. **Log in to the iOS Provisioning Profile.** You can find a link to it near the top right of the main iOS Dev Center page.

2. **Select Certificates from the list at the left, and then click Distribution.**
3. **Click the Request Certificate button.**
4. **When you see the page shown in Figure 13.3, scroll down and click the Choose File button.**
5. **Navigate to the CSR file you created in the previous section, and upload it.** Click the Submit button at the lower right.

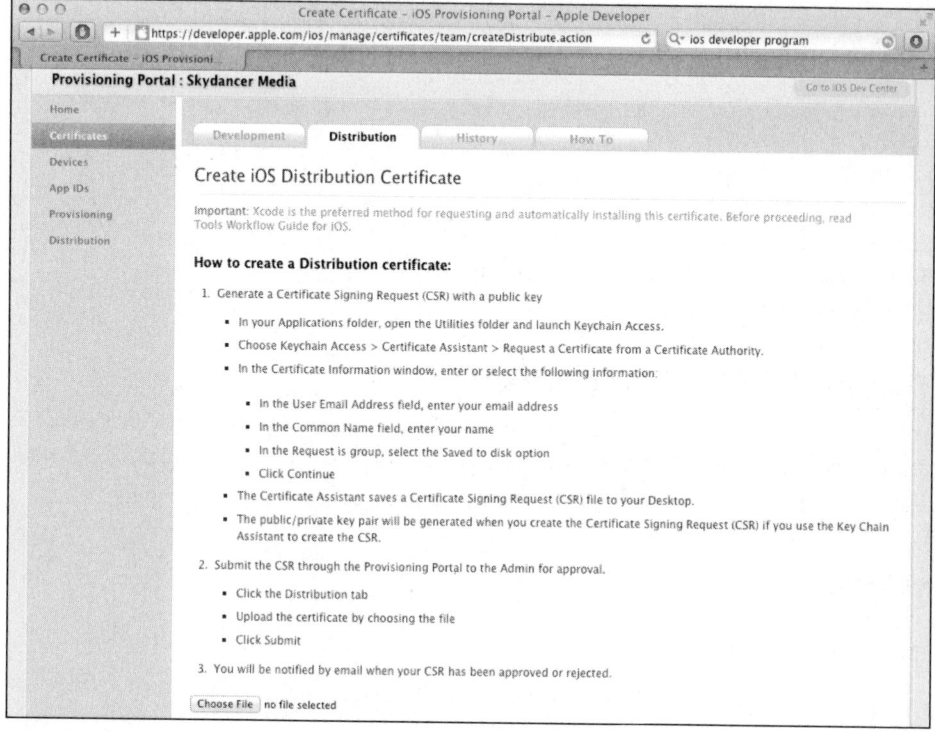

13.3 Creating a distribution certificate from the CSR.

The page refreshes, and you'll see a certificate file with an Issued status. To download it, reload the page. You'll see a button marked "Download." Click it to download the file, preferably to your "/Provisioning" folder.

You'll also see a link under the file telling you to download a "WWDR intermediate certificate," as shown in Figure 13.4. This is a further key that double-checks that your distribution certificate is legitimate. Click the link to download it to your "/Provisioning" folder.

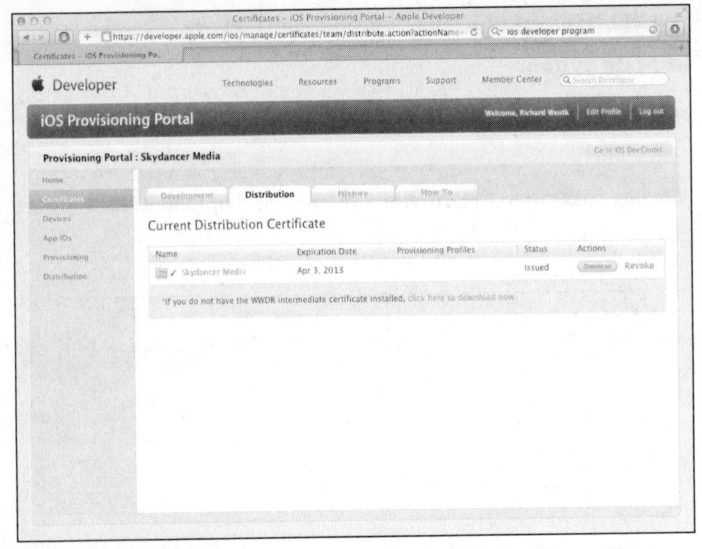

13.4 Downloading the distribution certificate and the WWDR certificate that authenticates it.

Installing the certificates

To install the certificates, open the Keychain Access Utility, select the login keychain and Certificates category in the left column, and drag the two certificates from a Finder window into the list of certificates at the left. They're installed automatically when you drop them, as shown in Figure 13.5.

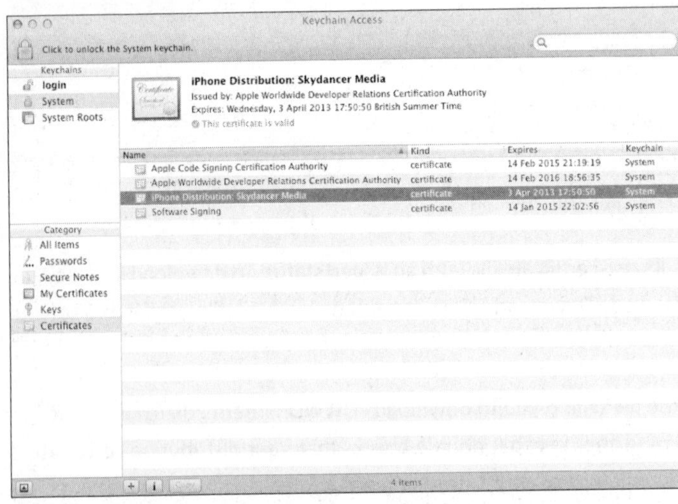

13.5 Installing the certificates in the Keychain Access Utility.

Creating an App ID

Xcode can now authenticate you as a developer with distribution privileges. But because distribution is controlled on a per-app basis, you must create a unique ID for your app.

An app ID has two elements:

- **A bundle seed ID.** This is a ten-character string. It's generated automatically by the iOS Provisioning Portal. You don't need to type it into Xcode.
- **A bundle ID.** This is a separate string you enter manually into the Provisioning Portal and—sometimes—into Xcode.

Caution

In this context, "bundle" means "all the files in your app collected into a distributable package."

Understanding app IDs

When you set up Xcode for device testing, a bundle seed ID is created automatically. You can use this seed ID for all your apps. It's valid for both development (on-device testing, for example) and distribution.

There's no good reason to create further seed IDs. If your apps share the same seed ID, they can automatically share passwords and other "secret" details stored in a device's keychain—a special secure folder on "disk" that holds sensitive information in an encrypted form.

The simple way to create a bundle ID is to name it with a single asterisk. This creates a *wildcard ID.* You can reuse a wildcard ID for multiple apps. This saves you the effort of creating a new ID for each app. But apps with a wildcard ID can't use Apple's Game Center, In-App Purchase, or Push Notification technology.

If you're sure this won't be a problem for your apps, save time by creating a wildcard and reusing it. But it's often better to create separate app IDs anyway, in case you want to add these specialized features later.

Using reverse domain names

iOS and OS X use an unusual naming system for apps and system processes. It's recommended that bundle IDs follow this naming scheme.

Where the Internet uses standard domain names, such as "something.com," Apple's naming system reverses this. So your bundle ID will look something like this:

```
com.domainname.appname
```

"domainname" will be the name of your website's domain.

Note

If you don't have a website with a custom domain name, now is a good time to get one. You need to specify support and sales web addresses when you describe your app in the App Store.

Note

Technically, your web domain name doesn't have to match the domain name in the app ID. But there are a few—very rare—instances where using a different name can cause problems. For consistency, it's better to keep them identical.

This system is built into Xcode, as shown in Figure 13.6, which shows the main build settings for an app. The bundle name is set to be the app name; the '${PRODUCT_NAME} entry is a *macro*. It takes the name of the app and writes it automatically into the Bundle Name entry. The other entries in this list also use macros to fill in their values automatically.

The Bundle identifier field uses the reverse domain system to create the complete bundle ID from a reverse domain name and the product name. If the product name were "thisApp," the macro would automatically write "com.zettaboom.thisApp" into the bundle identifier field.

How do you set the product name? It's copied from the name under the TARGETS icon at the left. This is set to match your project name when you create the app. You can change it manually by clicking it and setting a new name. When you restart Xcode, the new name will be copied into the build settings.

▼ Custom iOS Target Properties

Key	Type	Value
Bundle name	String	${PRODUCT_NAME}
Bundle identifier	String	com.zettaboom.${PRODUCT_NAME:rfc1034identifier}
InfoDictionary version	String	6.0
▶ Required device capabilities	Array	(1 item)
Bundle version	String	1.0
Executable file	String	${EXECUTABLE_NAME}
Application requires iPhone environme	Boolean	YES
▶ Supported interface orientations	Array	(3 items)
Bundle display name	String	${PRODUCT_NAME}
Bundle creator OS Type code	String	????
Bundle OS Type code	String	APPL
Localization native development region	String	en
▶ Supported interface orientations (iPad)	Array	(4 items)
Bundle versions string, short	String	1.0

13.6 Finding the bundle identifier in the Info pane of the Build Settings.

Note

Remember that you can view the build settings by clicking the blue app name at the top of the Project navigator.

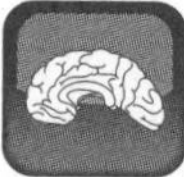

Genius

You can override the macro by replacing it with any string. Edit the field, and replace the macro with the name you want. Similarly, you can change the "Bundle display name"—the name that appears under the app icon in Springboard—to a different string. This can be useful if the original project is too long to fit under an icon. The Bundle display name *doesn't* need to match the app ID, so you can set it to whatever you want.

Creating a matching bundle ID

To create a new app ID, log into the Provisioning Portal and select App IDs. The Manage tab appears by default. Click the New App ID button to define a new app ID.

Figure 13.7 shows the page that appears. There are three fields.

- **Description.** You can use any text here. It's for reference only.
- **Seed ID.** The simplest option here is to select Use Team ID from the menu. (This option will appear automatically when you set up Xcode to allow on-device testing.)
- **Bundle Identifier.** This must match the bundle ID in the Build Settings. The default is the app name with a reverse domain prefix. If you've overridden the settings, use the name you entered instead of the defaults.

However you define the bundle ID, *it's critically important that it matches the ID you use for your app in Xcode.* If the fields don't match, Xcode won't let you build your app.

As an example, if the bundle ID you set in Xcode is com.mydomain.myappname, type the same ID with the full prefix into the Bundle Identifier box on the Provisioning Portal.

Click the Submit button at the lower right when done. The Provisioning Portal adds your new ID to a list. You'll be able to select it later when you create a distribution profile.

Caution

There's no way to delete an app ID after you create it. It's a good idea not to create too many experimental IDs because they can clutter up the ID list, and you'll never be able to get rid of them.

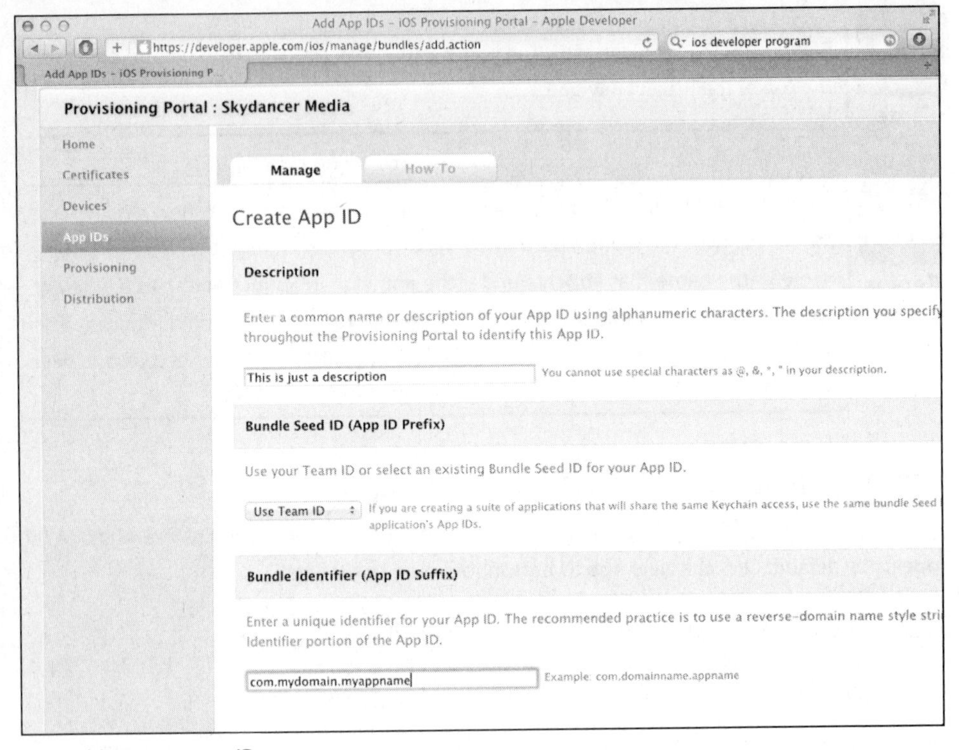

13.7 Adding a new app ID.

Adding Test Devices

When you set up Xcode to support on-device testing, Xcode automatically registered your device with the Provisioning Portal. If you want to support Ad Hoc testing, you must add further devices manually. When you create an Ad Hoc Distribution Profile, your test app is "locked" to the devices you select. Your app can still be installed on other devices, but it won't run on them.

Note

You don't need to add further devices to create an App Store Distribution Profile. This step is necessary only for an Ad Hoc Distribution Profile.

Finding a device UDID

To register a device with the Provisioning Portal, you need a unique identifier known as the UDID. Your tester can find the UDID in iTunes, as shown in Figure 13.8, by following these steps:

1. **Connect the device over USB, and launch iTunes.**
2. **Select the device in the DEVICES list at the left.**
3. **Click the Summary tab.**
4. **Click the Serial Number field in the list near the top.** iTunes shows the UDID instead of the serial number.
5. **Select Edit ⇨ Copy Identifier (UDID).**

Your tester can then paste the ID into an email and send it to you.

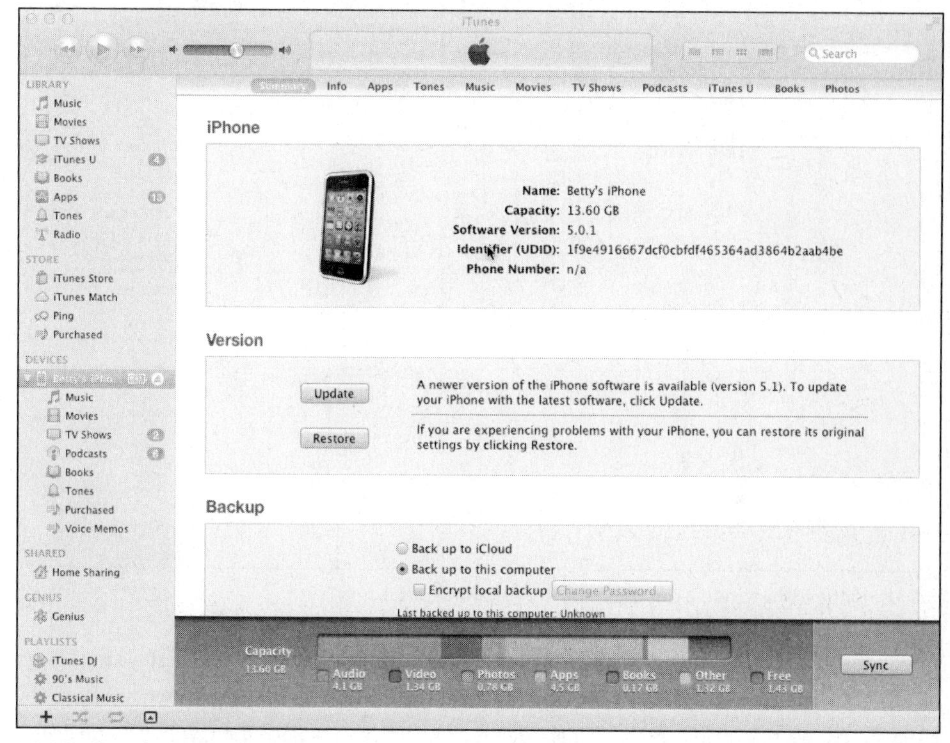

13.8 Finding the UDID of a device.

Adding a device UDID

To add a device to the Provisioning Portal, follow these steps:

1. **Log in to the Provisioning Portal.**
2. **Select Devices from the list of items at the left.**

3. **Click the Add Devices button near the top right.**
4. **Enter a device name, and paste the UDID into the Device ID field, as shown in Figure 13.9.**
5. **Click Submit at the lower right.**

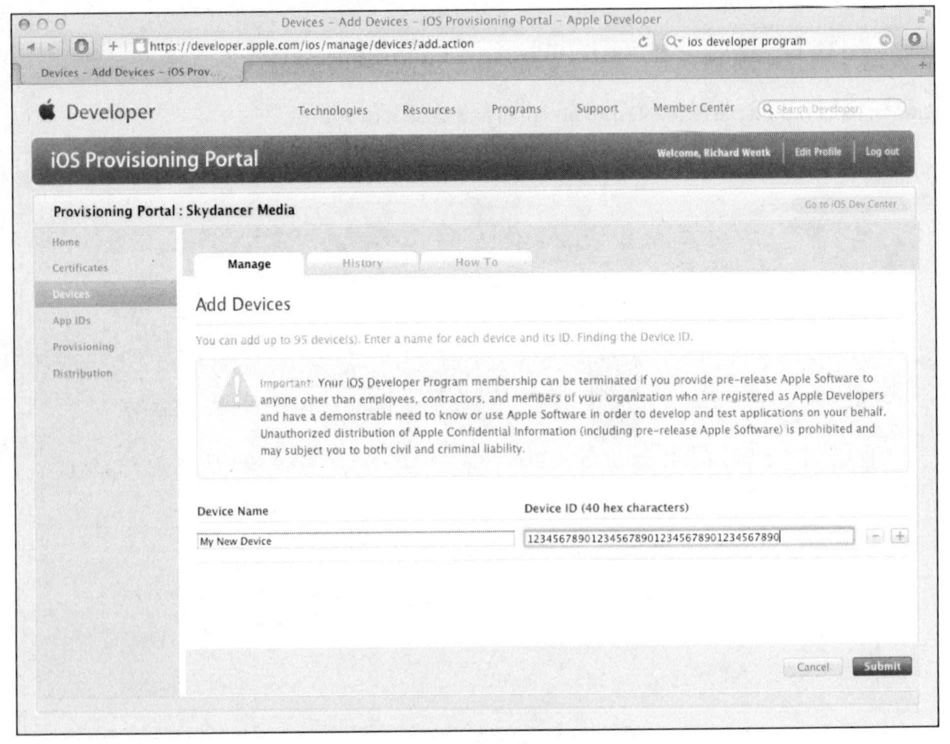

13.9 Using the UDID to add a device to the Provisioning Portal.

Note that you can add only 100 devices. You can't delete devices, so each device stays registered for the duration of your annual developer subscription. When your subscription renews, any devices you have removed from the list are deleted and you can replace them with new devices.

Creating and Installing Distribution Profiles

At this point, you've given the Provisioning Portal the information it needs to give you a distribution profile you can install in Xcode. Ad Hoc and App Store Distribution Profiles are created in a similar way. The only difference is that an Ad Hoc profile includes a list of devices, but an App Store Distribution Profile doesn't need one.

Note

Ad Hoc and App Store distribution profiles are officially both called "provisioning profiles." Provisioning simply means the profile includes a key that enables one kind.

Creating a distribution profile

To create a profile, follow these steps:

1. **Log in to the Provisioning Portal.**
2. **Select Provisioning from the list of items at the left.**
3. **Click the Distribution tab.**
4. **Click the New Profile button near the top right.**
5. **Select App Store or Ad Hoc distribution.**
6. **Type a Profile Name.** (This is for display only. This name will appear as one of the profiles you can select in Xcode.)
7. **Select an app ID.**
8. **For Ad Hoc profiles only, select one or more test devices from the list at the bottom of the page, as shown in Figure 13.10.**
9. **Click Submit at the lower right.**
10. **Reload the page to change the profile status from Pending and to show a download link.**

Installing distribution profiles

After you complete the process, you'll see a download button for each profile you create, as shown in Figure 13.11. Profiles are simple binary files with a ".mobileprovision" extension. You can click the Download button to download them to any convenient location—your "/Provisioning" folder would be a good choice.

Next, you must install them in Xcode. Follow these steps:

1. **Launch Xcode, and click the Organizer button at the top right.**
2. **Select the Provisioning Profiles item at the top left.**

3. **Open a Finder window, and navigate to the downloaded profile file (or files).**
4. **Drag each file from Finder into the main Organizer pane, as shown in Figure 13.12.**

When you drop each file, Xcode installs it and checks it. If you've completed the process correctly, Xcode marks the Status column with a green check mark and a "Valid profile" description.

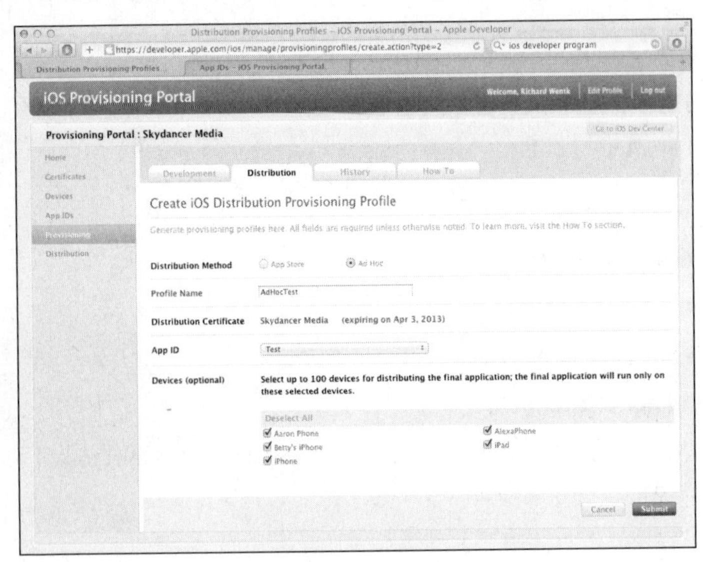

13.10 Creating an Ad Hoc distribution profile.

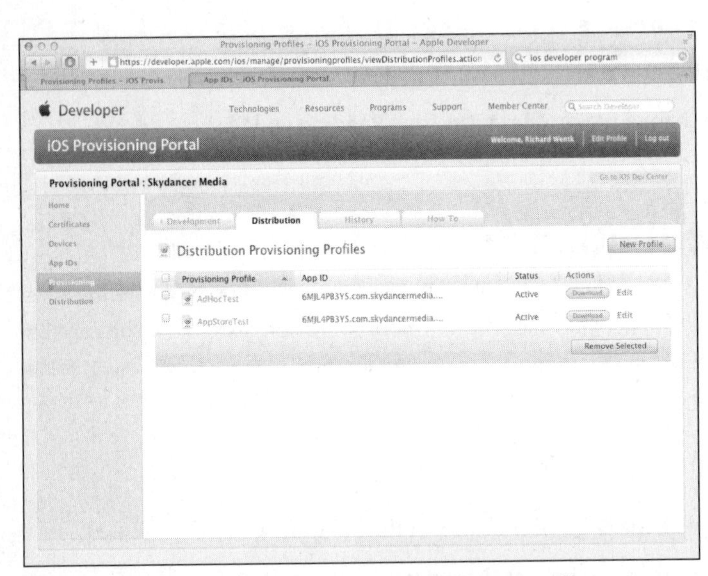

13.11 Viewing the Download links for each distribution profile.

You can now use the profiles to build apps for distribution, as described in the next section.

Note

If you've set up Xcode to support on-device testing, you'll see that an "iOS Team Provisioning Profile" is already installed. Xcode works with the Provisioning Portal to create, download, and install this profile automatically when you set up on-device testing.

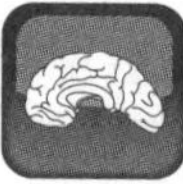

Genius

Note that you can select Edit and then Modify on the Provisioning Portal to update a profile—for example, to add more devices. After it's updated, you must download the new file, delete the old profile from Xcode, and install the new profile. Xcode probably won't register the change immediately, so you usually need to select a different distribution profile before archiving—as described in a later section—before reselecting the changed profile. You also may need to restart Xcode. (This should just work, but unfortunately it doesn't.)

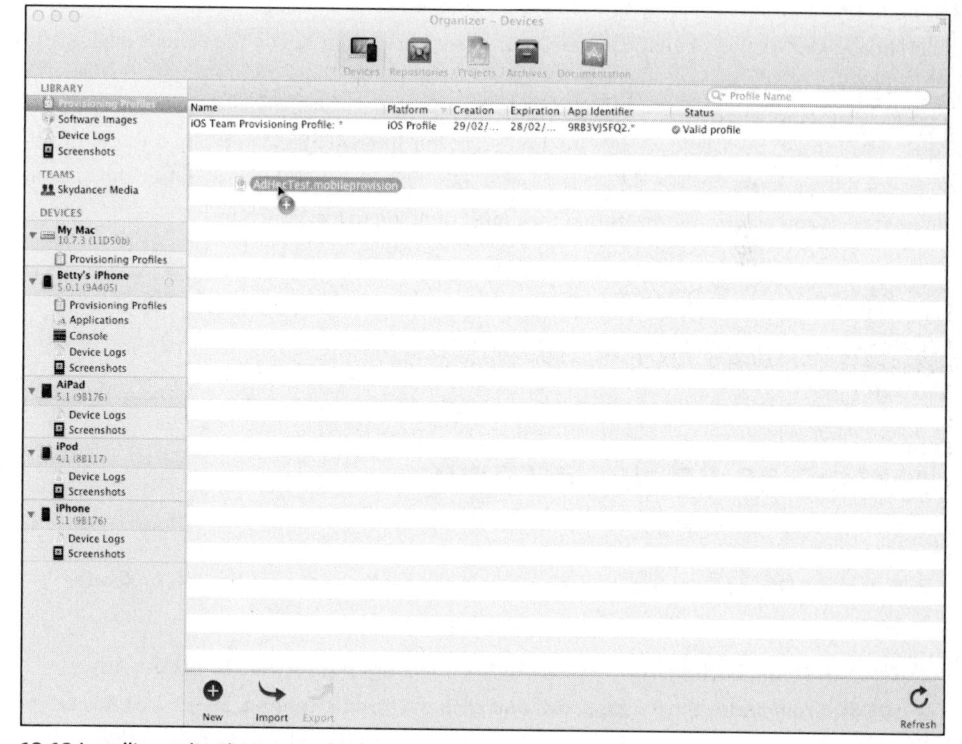

13.12 Installing a distribution profile file in Xcode.

Creating an Ad Hoc Build

You can distribute Ad Hoc builds as email attachments or web downloads. You can also use Over the Air distribution to give your testers the option to install your test build directly from a web download. The build process for both options is slightly different.

Caution

OTA distribution isn't officially supported. It works in Xcode 4.3.1, but it's really intended for corporate and enterprise developers. Don't be surprised if this feature is withdrawn without notice.

Setting the Deployment Target

Whichever distribution option you choose, make sure you set a build setting called the *Deployment Target* before continuing.

Developers often have access to beta versions of iOS, and it's likely you'll build your app for the latest beta. Your testers are likely to have older public versions of iOS. So you must tell Xcode to build for an older version of an iOS. (Otherwise, your app won't install on the tester's device, and iOS will show a terse error message with no details about the problem.)

Figure 13.13 shows the Deployment Target menu in the Summary Build Settings. If you're developing for a beta version of iOS, select the last public iOS version. Otherwise, select the current public version and warn your testers that they must upgrade to test your app.

Caution

Older devices don't support the latest release of iOS. For example, an iPhone 3G can't run iOS 4.0 and later. If your tester has an older device, he won't be able to test your app.

Creating an Ad Hoc archive

There are two steps to building your app for Ad Hoc distribution.

1. **Select iOS Device from the Scheme menu in the toolbar near the top left of Xcode.** Do this even if you don't have a device connected.
2. **Open the Build Settings, scroll down to the Code Signing section, select the Any iOS SDK row under the Release row, and click the middle column.** Select your Ad Hoc Distribution Profile, as shown in Figure 13.14. (Make sure you don't select your other distribution profile by mistake. And don't select the Automatic option.)

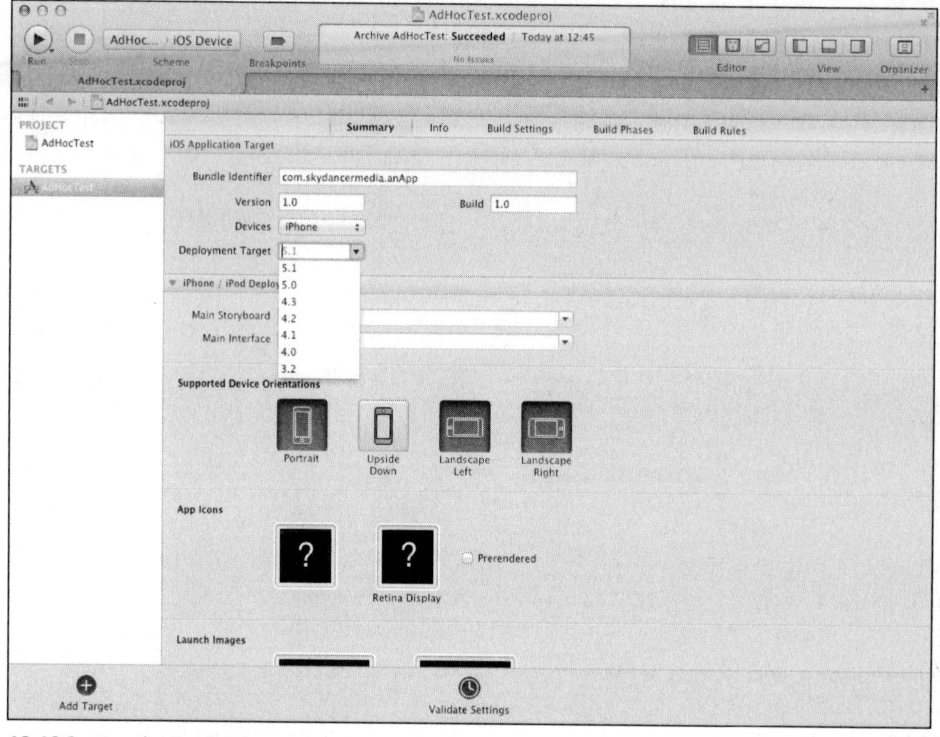

13.13 Setting the Deployment Target.

The profile selector option in the Build Settings "signs" your app with your distribution profile. Xcode uses this feature to check your identity and confirm that you have distribution permissions when you build the app.

It also automatically generates a provisioning—"key"—file that is installed on your tester's device when she installs the app. This file allows your tester to run that one app on that device. The provisioning file includes the list of devices that you selected for testing when you created the distribution profile.

Note

Luckily, this happens behind the scenes. If you can get the process working correctly, you don't need to worry about the details. But testers do sometimes wonder why a new Profiles entry has appeared in their device settings after they install your app.

Caution

Provisioning is time-limited. Your app will stop working after a couple of months when the provisioning profile expires.

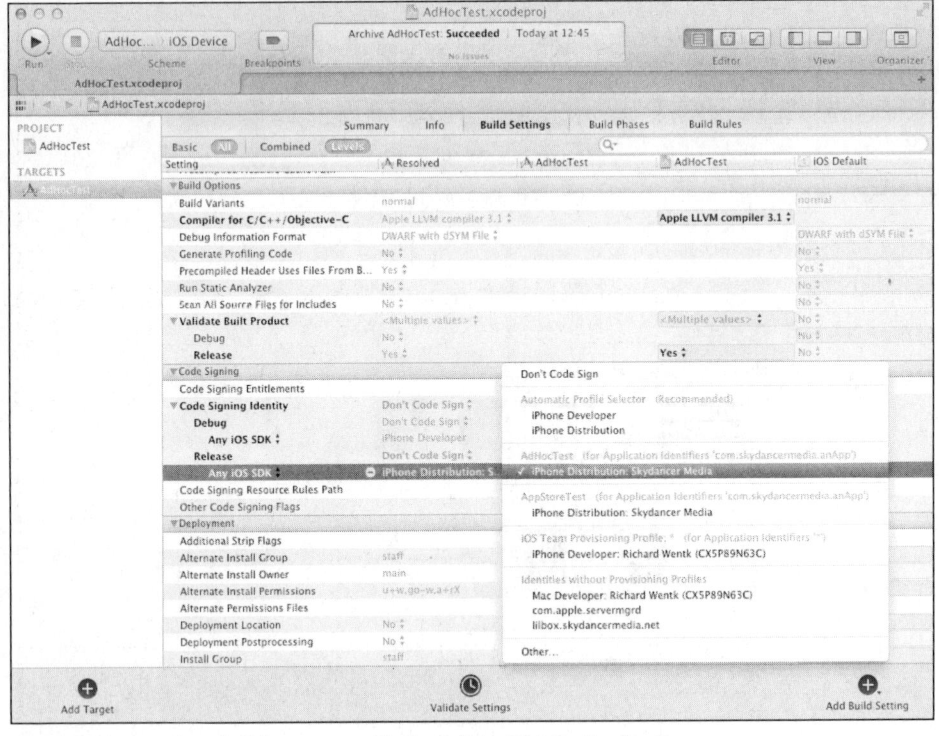

13.14 Getting ready to build your app with the Ad Hoc Distribution Profile.

After you've selected the correct profile, select Product ➪ Archive from the main Xcode menu. This builds your app, but doesn't try to run it. Instead, it creates an archive that appears in the Archives window in the Organizer, as shown in Figure 13.15.

Distributing an Ad Hoc app for testing

To prepare your app for distribution, click the Distribute button near the top right. To distribute an Ad Hoc build, click the "Save for Enterprise or Ad Hoc Deployment" option and click Next.

On the next page, shown in Figure 13.16, use the menu to select your Ad Hoc Distribution Profile again.

Caution

You *must* select the correct profile on this page. Even though the menu is likely to say "(iOS Distribution)," the default selection won't work for Ad Hoc testing.

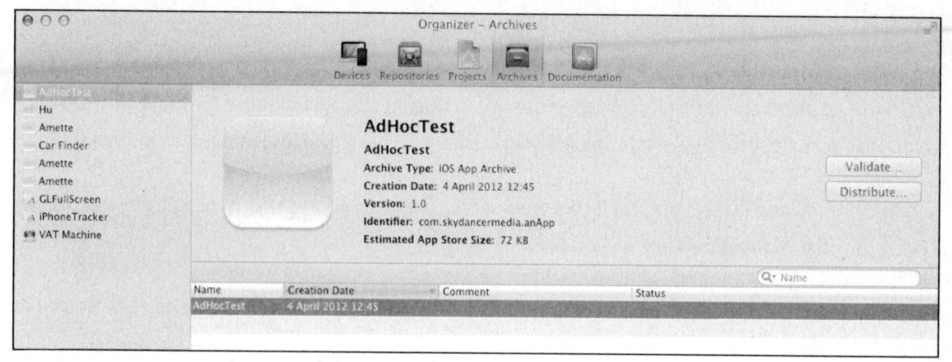

13.15 Looking at the archive after a successful build.

Distributing via iTunes

To save for standard iTunes distribution, leave the "Save for Enterprise Distribution" box unchecked. Select a destination directory and click Save at the lower right, and Xcode will create a *.ipa file* that contains your app. If the file is small enough, you can email it to your testers as an attachment. You can also upload it to a web page for download.

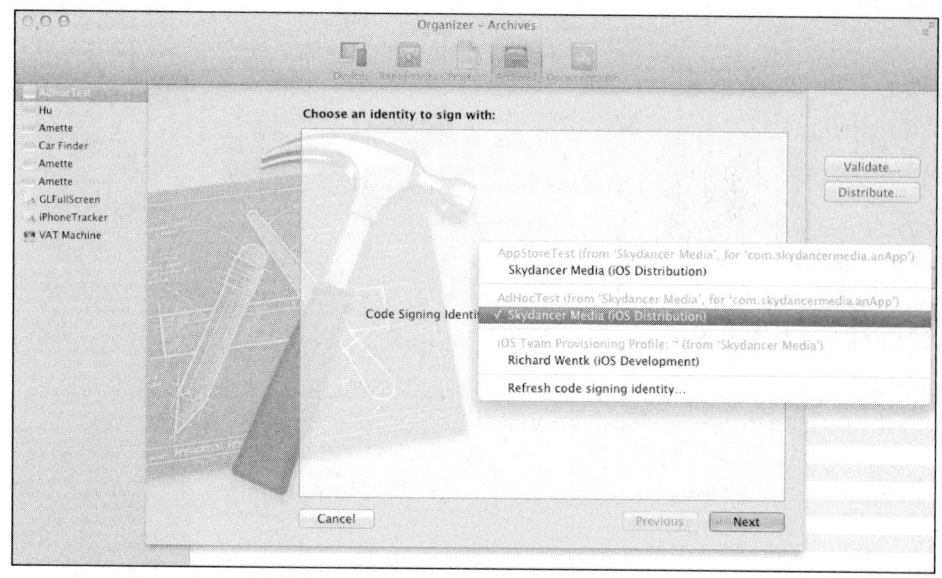

13.16 Selecting the correct distribution profile to sign the app.

Testers can install the app on their devices by dragging the .ipa file to the Library section at the top left of iTunes and syncing the app to their device. (Depending on their iTunes settings, they also may need to select the app for manual syncing in their device's Apps list in iTunes.)

OTA distribution

To save for OTA distribution, check the "Save for Enterprise Distribution" box. Enter the download URL in the Application URL field, and give the app a title, as shown in Figure 13.17. When you click Save, Xcode creates *two* files—the .ipa file and a .plist file that includes installation information.

To make the file installable, upload it to a web server. You can add as much, or as little, decorative HTML around the download link as you like.

The following is a bare minimum. Save it as "index.html," and upload it into the same directory as the two app files.

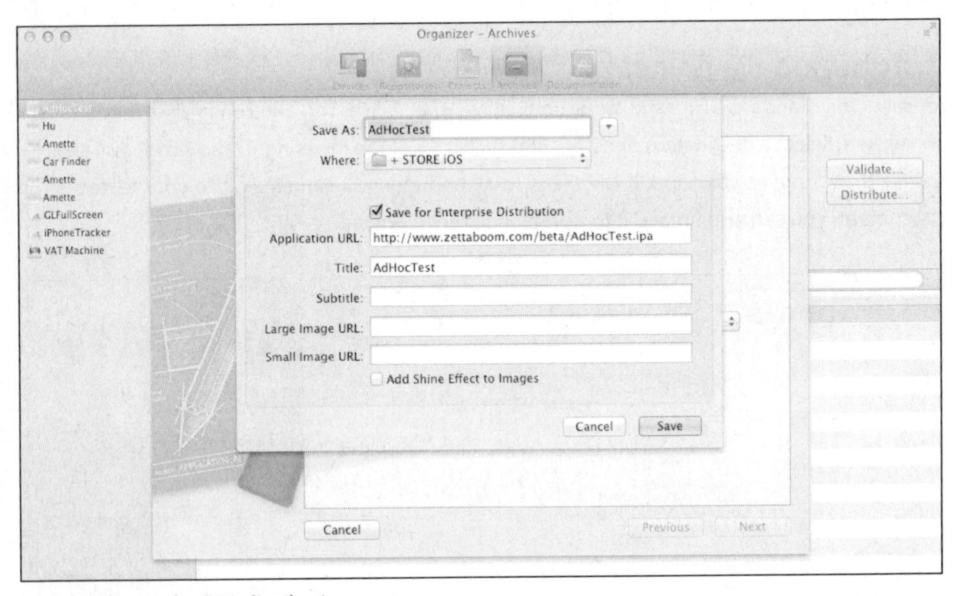

13.17 Preparing for OTA distribution.

```
<!DOCTYPE HTML PUBLIC "-//W3C//DTD HTML 4.01 Transitional//EN" "http://www.
  w3.org/TR/html4/loose.dtd">
<html>
<head>
     <title>Ad Hoc Test App Beta Download</title>
</head>
<body>
     <h1>
     <a href="itms-services://?action=download-
  manifest&url=http://<yourURLhere>/AdHocTest.plist">Tap here to install</a>
     </h1>
</body>
</html>
```

When the user taps the link in Mobile Safari, they'll see a dialog box asking them if they want to install the app, as shown in Figure 13.18. If they confirm, the app is downloaded and installed automatically.

Caution

Use <h1> tags or some other text scaling option to make your link big enough to read. If you use the default HTML text size, Safari will make the link tiny.

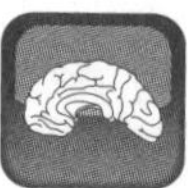

Genius

Mobile Safari—and only Mobile Safari—supports a URL scheme called "ITMS Services." The sample HTML tells Safari to download a plist, read its contents, find the app it contains, and attempt to install it. For consistency, the URL in the HTML must match the Application URL you specified when you created the two files—with the difference that it points to the plist instead of the .ipa file.

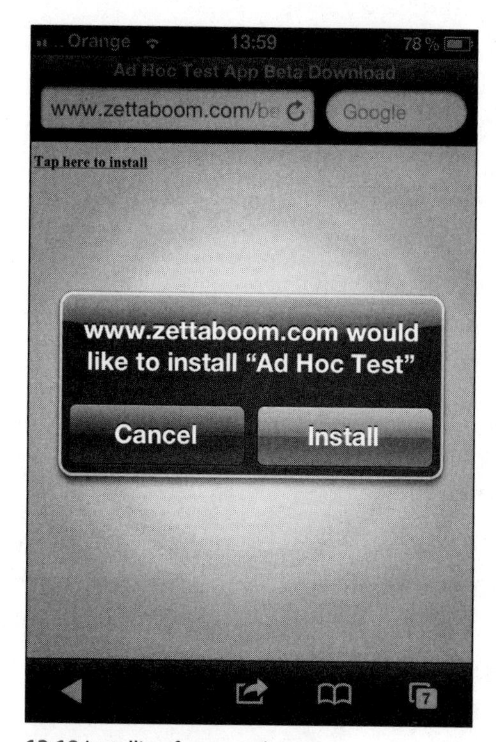

13.18 Installing from a web page.

Uploading to the App Store

Uploading to the App Store is a two-stage process:

1. **Log in to iTunes Connect, and fill in the "paperwork" to support your app.** This includes a mix of administrative data—price, availability date, and so on—and marketing information, including a text description and screen shots.
2. **When the paperwork is complete, build your app as an archive and upload it to the App Store.** As you may have guessed, to build for the App Store, you must select your App Store Distribution Profile before building.

As the app is uploaded, it's checked for basic errors such as missing icons or an incorrect app ID. If it passes the checks, it enters Apple's review queue. Most apps are reviewed within a few days. Occasionally, the process can take longer. (Very occasionally, it can take much longer. A handful of apps have stayed in the review queue for months. This happens very rarely.)

Note

Apps are primarily rejected for four reasons: obvious crashes, unacceptable content, misuse of Apple code, and third-party complaints. Apple is arguably strictest about the third reason. If your app uses unofficial and/or undocumented features in iOS, it *will* be rejected.

Creating support materials

You need the following:

- **An app name.** This is the name that the app is listed under in the App Store. It may or may not match your app's bundle ID.
- **A SKU (Stock Keeping Unit) Number.** This is an arbitrary combination of numbers and letters you can use for internal accounting. Each app must have a unique SKU number. (If you're not sure what to use, use a short three-letter code and the upload date reversed.)
- **A bundle ID.** Use the ID you created earlier, when you created your App Store Distribution Profile.
- **An availability date.** You may want to delay the date to allow time for a marketing campaign. More usually, apps go on sale as soon as they can.
- **A price.** On the App Store, prices are set in *tiers.* Tier 1 is the cheapest. International prices are recalculated and displayed automatically.
- **Discount options.** You can choose to offer a bulk discount for educational institutions. (This isn't a good choice, unless you're marketing your app directly for education.)
- **A version number and copyright details.**
- **Primary and secondary categories.** These options set which App Store categories the app appears in.
- **App Rating details.** Each app is self-graded for mature content and given an overall age rating, as shown in Figure 13.19. The lower the rating, the wider your audience.

- **Marketing materials.** These include a sales description that appears on the App Store, supporting and marketing URLs, keywords, and screen grabs.
- **A large 512 x 512 icon image.** This should be a larger version of your app icon.
- **Sundry other details.** For example, you'll be asked if your app includes any encryption technology that might prevent its sale in certain countries.

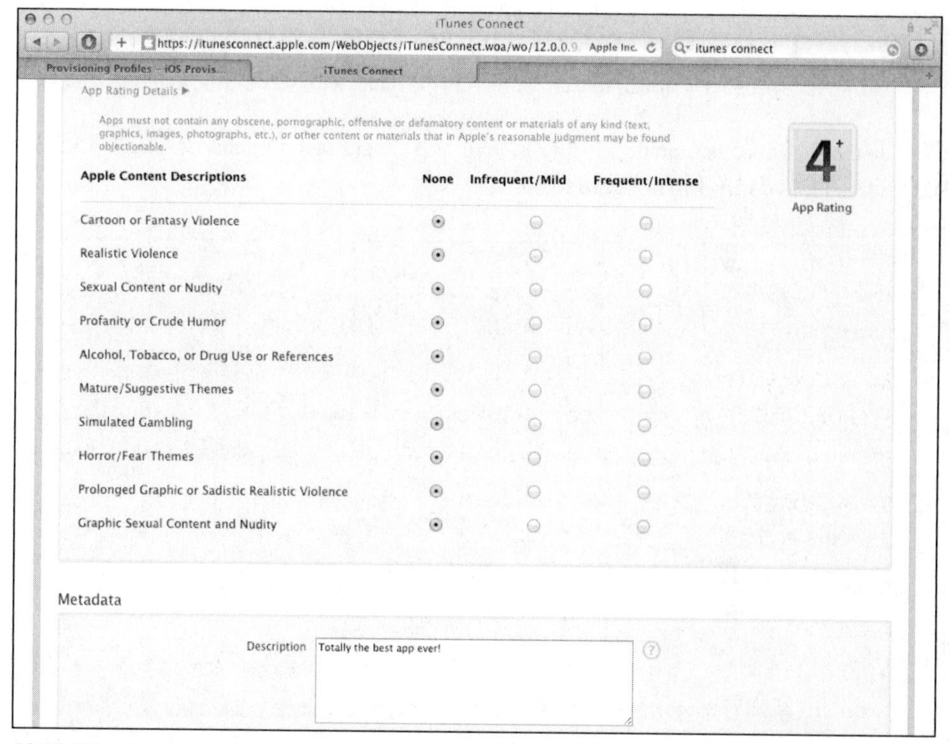

13.19 Filling in your app's ratings and description—part of the iTunes Connect "paperwork."

Note

In theory, developers should use unadorned screen grabs. In practice, some developers decorate their grabs with extra text or highlights. Similarly, instead of creating a large version of their main app icon, some developers use the 512 x 512 image as an eye-catching splash image. This isn't quite playing by the rules, but as long as it's not too blatant, it's usually accepted.

Preparing the marketing materials can take a while. Don't rush the process. Your app's listing is its shop window, and a good first impression can lead to immediate sales.

At the end of the process, you'll be told you can "upload a binary." You don't need to do this immediately. In fact, you can create an iTunes Connect record well before your app is ready for prime time. But you do need to create a record before iTunes Connect accepts your app.

Building and distributing to the App Store

The build/archive process is similar to that for an Ad Hoc build, with some critical differences.

When you select a Code Signing Identity in your app's build settings, choose your App Store Distribution Profile, as shown in Figure 13.20.

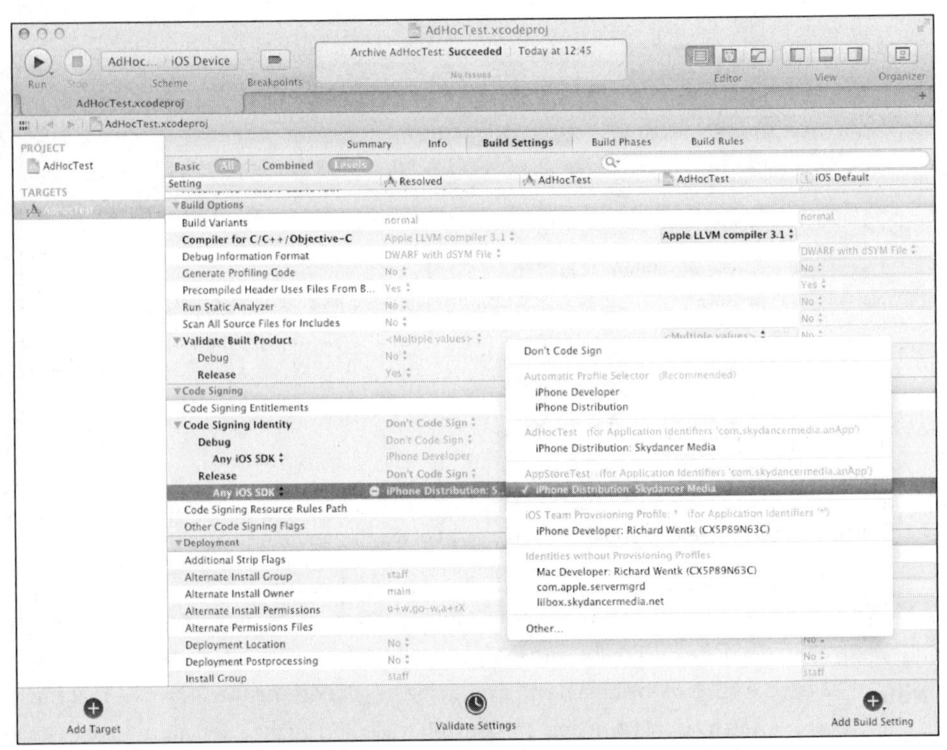

13.20 Selecting the App Store Distribution Profile ready for an App Store build.

Select the iOS Device scheme, and build your project as an Archive. It appears in the Archives page of the Organizer as before. Click the Validate button to check it for consistency. If it passes the tests, click the Distribute button and select "Submit to the iOS App Store," as shown in Figure 13.21.

Select an application record (you'll see the record you created earlier) and your App Store Distribution Profile as the Code Signing Identity.

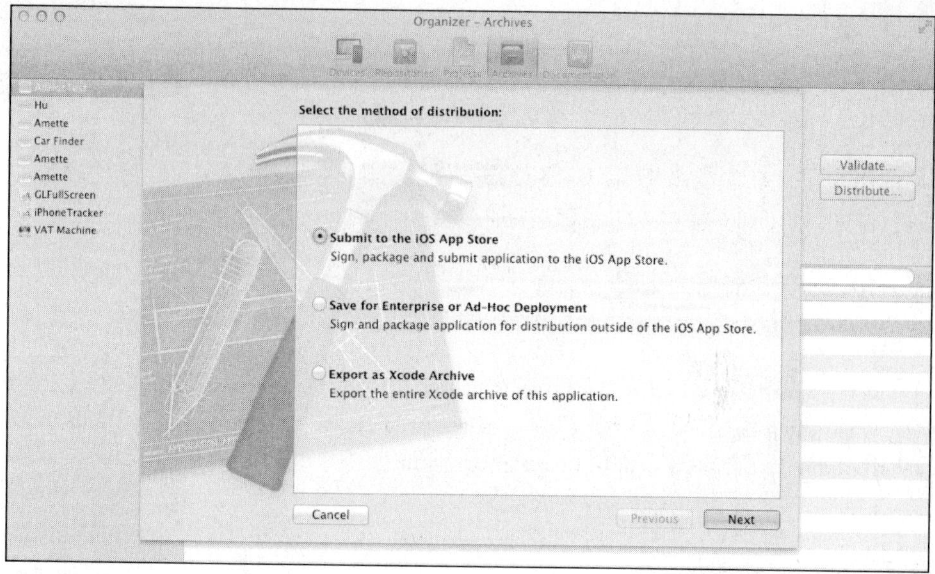

13.21 Submitting to the App Store.

The app is then validated one last time before upload. If there are no issues, it's uploaded to the App Store and enters the review queue. After review, you'll receive an email telling you if your app was accepted or rejected. Accepted apps go on sale within an hour or so.

Appendix A

C Cheat Sheet

If you're not already an expert in C, it's easy to overlook its key features. Use the following cheat sheet while you're learning. It's not a comprehensive language reference. You can find those online, but this is a useful collection of basic information.

C Data Types

Table A.1 shows the fundamental C language data types. You can use them in Objective-C code, but you must convert them into objects if you want to use them inside Objective-C data collections.

Note that the double type is much slower for floating-point calculations, but far more accurate than the float type.

Caution

The names of C data types are standardized, but the sizes are *implementation dependent.* The sizes in the table are correct for iOS. Other computer systems use different sizes. This doesn't matter if your code runs only on iOS devices. It can matter if you use code written for other computers, or share your code with developers who work on other computers. Note also you may come across further types such as short, long double, long long, and so on. The table includes the types you're most likely to use in your code. The other types are much less common, and only used for specialized tasks.

Table A.1 Fundamental C Data Types

Type	Size	Range
void	n/a	No value. Often used to define functions and methods that end without returning a value.
bool	1 bit	Takes one of two values: 0 = FALSE 1 = TRUE (Technically this isn't an original C data type, but it's valid and widely used.)
unsigned char	8 bits	0 to 255. Also used for ASCII characters.
char	8 bits	-128 to 127
unsigned int	32 bits	0 to 4294967295
int	32 bits	-2147483648 to 2147483647
unsigned long	32 bits	0 to 4294967295
long	32 bits	-2147483648 to 2147483647
float	32 bits	1.17549435 * (10^{-38}) to 3.40282347 * (10^{+38})
double	64 bits	2.2250738585072014 * (10^{-308}) to 1.7976931348623157 * (10^{+308})
size_t sizeof	16 bits	A special type that calculates the size of the following data type or expression and returns an unsigned int.

C Storage Classes

Table A.2 shows the fundamental C language storage classes. Unlike Objective-C classes, these are simple modifiers that you can use to control where and how variables are defined and how they can be accessed.

Table A.2 C Storage Classes and Modifiers

Class	Description
`const`	Defines data that doesn't change. Must be followed by an assignment.
`extern`	Indicates that a variable is defined outside the current file.
`static`	Keeps a variable in memory between calls to a function.
`typedef`	Creates a new custom data type. Must be followed by a name for the data type.

Composite C Data Types

C supports simple arrays. The initial values in an array are undefined, and the number of elements is a constant set at compile time.

```
int arrayOne[10];
//Creates an array of ten ints, arrayOne[0] to arrayOne[9]
//The initial values are undefined, and the number of elements is a constant
```

Use the struct keyword to create a composite data type made of fundamental data types. structs are rather like the ancestors of Objective-C's objects. They're simpler, they don't support methods, and they don't use Objective-C's automatic memory management.

```
struct playerOne{
   char name[20];
   int xpos;
   int ypos;
}
```

A union is like a struct and is defined in a similar way, but it can hold only a single value. In the following example, the union can hold a character array, an int called xpos, or an int called ypos. If you set one element in a union, the other elements become undefined. (This exotic behavior saves memory, but it's largely unnecessary now.)

```
union playerOne{
   char name[20];
   int xpos;
   int ypos;
}
```

C Statements and Functions

Table A.3 lists useful C statements. Use these statements to repeat code, or to test values in your app and select code accordingly.

Table A.3 C Statements

<table>
<tr><th>Statement</th><th>Name and description</th><th>Notes</th></tr>
<tr><td><pre>
if (condition_test)
{
  doSomething;
}
else
{
  doSomethingElse;
}
</pre></td><td>if statement:
Tests for a condition.
doSomething if true.
Otherwise,
doSomethingElse.</td><td>The condition test must be in round brackets.
Don't forget to use "==" to test for equality.
Else is optional.
The curly brackets are optional if the code between them fits on a single line.</td></tr>
<tr><td><pre>
a_variable =
   (condition_test) ?
   value_if_true :
   value_if_false;
</pre></td><td>inline if/conditional (ternary) operator:
Returns or assigns one value if the conditional test is true, another if false.</td><td>This is a terse alternative to the if statement.
It can make code hard to read.</td></tr>
<tr><td><pre>
switch
   (variable_to_test)
{
   case
   first_possible_
   value:
         do_stuff;
         break;

   case
   second_possible_
   value:
         do_other_
   stuff;
         break;

   (...)

   default:
   do_this_if_no_
   match;
   break;
}
</pre></td><td>switch statement:
Tests a variable for various possible values, selects code accordingly.</td><td>The default option is chosen if none of the case statements matches the value of the variable.
If you don't include a break statement in the code for each case, switch executes all the following code, including the code for other cases. (This isn't usually what you want.)
Switch works only with integer C data types or return values. You can't use it to test Objective-C strings or other objects.
default: doesn't have to go at the end of the switch statement, but it usually does.</td></tr>
<tr><td><pre>
while (condition_test)
{
  do_stuff;
}
</pre></td><td>while statement
Tests first, then keeps doing something for as long as the condition is true.</td><td>The test is always performed at least once. The code after the test is run only if the result is true.</td></tr>
</table>

continued

Table A.3 continued

Statement	Name and description	Notes

`do {`
`  do_stuff;`
`} while`
`  (condition_test)`
	do…while statement
	Does something first, tests afterward, keeps doing it until the test is false.
		The code after do is always run at least once. The test is performed after the code completes. Sometimes you want to test a condition before a loop, sometimes after it. Use this statement or the previous one, as needed.

`for (do_once_only,`
`  condition_test,`
`  do_on_every_repeat`
`{`
`  do_stuff;`
`}`
	for loop:
	Sets up an initial condition and repeats the loop while the condition is true. Uses a separate control statement to manage the repeats.
		This is often used to repeat code a set number of times; the initial statement sets the initial counter variable, the control statement increments it on every repeat, and the conditional test checks its value.

`break`	break statement: Breaks out of a loop or switch statement.	This is a quick way to break out of a switch statement or looping test. Typically, you embed break in an if statement to create a test that ends the loop or conditional.
`continue`	continue statement:	This skips the rest of the code inside a loop. Unlike break, which ends the loop, continue ends a single repeat of a loop.

`goto a_label`
`(...)`
`a_label: doStuff;`
	goto statement:
	Skips straight to a named label.
		Don't use goto if you can avoid it. It makes code hard to read, maintain, and debug. Professional developers really don't like it.

`return`	return statement: Ends a function or method and returns a value	Any code after a return statement is ignored. You can use return with Objective-C methods as well as C functions.

Comparing C and Objective-C

The key difference between C and Objective-C is that Objective-C deals only with objects. You can include C data types in Objective-C code, but if you want to integrate them with Objective-C objects—for example, if you want to store numbers in an NSArray object—you must "objectify" them first by wrapping them inside an object. Full details are moderately complex and outside the scope of this book. For more information, see *Cocoa* in Wiley's Developer Reference series.

Note also that Objective-C includes denser and more abstract options than C. For example, you can use *automatic enumeration* to loop through every object in an array and run code on each object repeatedly. The enumeration works even when the array contains objects of different types. For details and example code, see the NSArray class reference.

NSLog and printf Format Specifiers

Table A.4 lists the most useful format specifiers that can be used for debugging with printf and NSLog statements.

Table A.4 NSLog and printf Format Specifiers

Specifier	Description
`%c`	char
`%i or %d`	signed int. %d assumes the number is a decimal.
`%u`	unsigned int
`%x or %X`	int as hexadecimal
`%f`	float or double. Use "%0.xf" to round the output to x decimal places.
`%s`	C-format string, defined without Objective-C "@" prefix.
`%@`	Object displays the output of an object's description method. Also used for Objective-C strings, defined with the "@" prefix.
`%p`	Memory address. (Similar to %x, but adds a "0x" prefix.)
`%zu`	size_t
`\r or \n`	Inserts a new line in the output.

Glossary

accelerometer A hardware feature that measures the acceleration of an iOS device. Often used for estimating physical orientation. See also *gyroscope*.

accessors See *setters and getters*.

action Another name for a method. See also *target-action*.

alert A small pop-up window with text and optional graphics that warns the user of an alert condition. Defined by the UIAlertView *class*.

animation Moving screen content. iOS includes various *class*es that can simplify animation programming.

app Short for "application," software that runs on an *iDevice*.

archive A packaged version of an app that can be uploaded to the app store. Not an archive in the sense of a backup.

array A collection of data accessed through a sequential *index*.

Assistant A feature in the *Xcode* editor that automatically displays two related files at the same time.

Automatic Reference Counting (ARC) A simplified system of memory management introduced with iOS 5.

beta Unfinished software typically used for testing and development.

beta tester A user who tests beta software and reports its strengths and weaknesses.

Bluetooth A technology for sharing data between devices in close physical proximity without a physical connection. Used to share information across devices in game design, among other applications.

breakpoint A temporary deliberate pause added to aid *debugging* while an app is being tested.

build process The sequence of events and operations that converts the text files and other elements of a *project* into a finished *app*.

C language A programming language used in app development.

category An advanced customization option that modifies an iOS class "in-place" without creating a new subclass.

char One of the *fundamental data types* in **C** used to store a single text character.

class A template for an object. The class specific lists the properties and methods available to other objects and includes the code that implements them.

@class A *directive* that imports the features of a class into another so they can be accessed.

Class Reference A document in the official iOS documentation that lists all the methods and properties of a class, with possible extra detail and discussion.

command line A text-based interface that offers powerful and direct control of a server, but relies on typed commands instead of windows and menus.

conditional Code that tests values and responds differently if the test is true or false.

control An object that can appear onscreen and offers the user a virtual control device, such as a switch, slider, or stepper.

Core Data A complex data storage system that can be included in an app to manage large collections of data.

data collection object An object that provides a store for other objects and supports operations on those objects.

debugging The process of removing errors from code.

Debug window A special pane in Xcode used to view debug messages from Xcode and from an app as it's being tested.

delegate An object that processes messages on behalf of some other object. Often used with a **protocol.**

developer profile A digital "key" file that allows a developer to test apps on iDevices.

distribution profile A digital "key" file that allows a developer to upload completed apps to the App Store.

dictionary A *data collection object* that uses *key-value coding* to organize the objects it holds.

directive A fragment of code that contains instructions for the *compiler* and controls part of the *build process.*

enumerator A feature of *data collection objects* that steps through the objects in the collection in order, even when no sequential index is defined.

if statement Code that is selected if a given conditional is true (or optionally, if it's false).

file manager An iOS object that manages the opening, closing, renaming, and deletion of files.

File's Owner A placeholder in *Interface Builder* used to send messages to the object that owns and manages a *nib file.*

First Responder The object given the first opportunity to handle user events. See also *Responder Chain.*

float One of the *fundamental data types* in C, used to store low-precision floating point numbers.

for loop A simple counting loop.

framework A collection of classes, protocols, functions, and data types that implements a broad but related group of features in *iOS.*

function A block of code in *C* that takes zero or more input values and returns zero or one values after working through a series of instructions.

fundamental data type A set of predefined data types in C used to store numbers and text.

GPS (Global Positioning System) A hardware device that reports the latitude, longitude, and elevation (height above sea level) of an iDevice.

gyroscope A hardware device that measures the movement of an iDevice. Together with the *accelerometer* and the *magnetometer,* these devices report orientation and motion measurements through a framework called Core Motion.

header file In C, a file that includes function prototypes. In Objective-C, a file usually associated with a framework that lists the methods and properties in the framework for easy *import* into other classes.

Hypertext Markup Language (HTML) The data format used on the World Wide Web to define web pages.

icon file A small file included in an *app* that defines the icon that appears in *Springboard.*

id A "catch-all" data type that makes it possible for Objective-C to work with objects without an explicit type.

iDevice A device that runs the *iOS* operating system—currently, iPhone, iPod touch, or iPad.

implementation The file that includes the code for the methods available in a class. See also *interface.*

#import A *directive* that imports one or more *header files* into a class so that their contents are included in the build.

index A value that selects one of the elements in an *array.*

instance An object in memory with properties and methods defined by its *class.*

Instruments A set of testing tools that can look inside an app as it runs to report memory use, performance, and other information useful for testing and *debugging.*

int One of the *fundamental data types* in C, used to store whole number values.

interface The file that defines the method signatures and properties available in a class.

Interface Builder A tool built into *Xcode.* Usually used for screen content, it can also be used to predefine objects that load when an app launches.

iOS Formerly "iPhone OS," the simplified and modified version of the OS X operating system used on Mac computers.

JSON (JavaScript Object Notation) A data format used to download information from the Internet into an *app.*

key-value coding (KVC) A system that organizes data that matches text or object keys with text or object values. Used throughout *iOS.*

key-value observing (KVO) A system that allows objects to monitor the properties of objects and to respond automatically when they change.

magnetometer A hardware device that measures the local magnetic field around an iDevice and can estimate magnetic North.

method A piece of code inside an object that receives trigger messages and performs some action or behavior.

MVC (Model-View-Controller) A system of app design that aims to display data using as few resources as possible by splitting the visible representation of the data from its underlying organization.

multitouch The optional ability to handle multiple *touch events* in an *app*. See also *single touch*.

mutable *Data collection objects* that support the addition and deletion of objects.

nib file A file that contains objects created and prefilled with data by *Interface Builder*.

Objective-C An app development language that uses *objects* to manage the internal features of an app and its screen content.

Organizer A feature in Xcode that displays and manages device information, documentation, and project archives.

orientation The four possible rotations in which a device can be held: two portrait for maximum screen height and two landscape for maximum screen width.

parent class Identical to a *super-class*.

plist Short for "property list," a list of essential settings organized as *XML* that iOS can load when an app launches.

preferences A list of persistent settings that give a user some control over the appearance, features, or performance of an *app*.

private A variable or method that is internal to a class and can't be accessed by other classes.

project The set of files used to create an app.

property A data storage area in an object. Properties can be simple *C* data types, complex *C* structures, or objects.

protocol A bundle of optional methods that doesn't belong to any object, but can be added to many objects to add common extra features.

profile A file in Xcode and on an iDevice that includes provisioning information.

provisioning The security system used by Apple that limits development to authorized and paid-up developers.

public A property or method in a class that can be accessed from other classes.

OpenGLES A version of the OpenGL graphics programming language optimized for mobile devices with relatively slow processors and small screens.

open source Software supplied with the original source code—the instructions created by a programmer—that can be modified and extended by anyone who understands how to program.

password A hidden word or sequence of characters used to identity a user and gain access to one or more network features.

property A data storage area in an object. Properties can be simple C data types, complex C structures, or objects.

QuickTime Apple's movie playback and editing technology. Used in the creation of podcasts.

repository A collection of projects, usually online, that supports version control and can be accessed by multiple users.

Responder Chain The list of objects in an app that can respond to user events. Events that aren't processed are passed up the chain until an object responds to them.

Retina Display Apple's marketing term for a display with a physical resolution so high that the human eye can't see individual pixels. Used on recent versions of the iPhone and the new iPad.

sequential Any collection of data or objects organized with a clearly defined numerical order.

set A collection of data. Objects in a set can be counted, tested to see if some other objects are in the set, and sorted by some arbitrary specification.

setters and getters Methods that must be defined to allow access to object properties. See *@synthesize.*

single touch By default, apps can receive only a single *touch event* at a time.

Springboard The main user interface in iOS, which displays app icons and launches apps when they're tapped.

storyboard A system for creating multiple screens of content, selecting between them, and animating transitions between them.

sub-class A customized version of an existing class, with extended or modified features.

super-class The unmodified class used to create a sub-class.

@synthesize A *directive* that automatically creates setter and getter methods for selected properties.

target-action A feature in Objective-C that makes it possible for objects to select the message an object sends and redirect it to various target objects while an app is running.

Tasks list A definitive summary list of the properties and methods in a class that appears in the *Class Reference.*

templates Prewritten file collections in Xcode that provide a basic starting point for app development.

timer An object that triggers an event after a certain time and that may repeat regularly.

touch event One of a collection of *messages* that are sent by *iOS* to an app when the user touches the screen, drags one or more fingers over the screen, or lifts a finger from the screen.

transition An animated change, often from one screen full of content to another.

Unit Tests Optional code added throughout an app to check automatically if code produces wrong or unexpected results.

User Interface (UI) Onscreen graphics that respond to user actions, designed to give the user an intuitive mental model of the app.

User Experience (UX) The experience of using an app, including the clarity and simplicity of its **UI** and its overall performance and usefulness.

version control A feature in the Xcode editor that manages file versions automatically and makes it possible to restore earlier versions.

view An object that draws the onscreen content of an app and can respond to *touch events.*

view controller An object that manages the onscreen content of an app.

WiFi A technology for connecting devices to a local network and from there to the Internet. (Originally short for Wireless Fidelity, but this meaning is now rare.)

Xcode The iOS development toolset.

XML (eXtensible Markup Language) A system of formatted text used to store settings and other data.

Index

Symbols and Numerics

A

E

F

G

H

I

N

O

P

Q

R

T

U

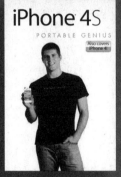

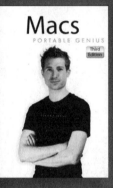